MY YESHIVA COLLEGE

75 YEARS OF MEMORIES

Edited by Menachem Butler and Zev Nagel

Introduction by Richard M. Joel
With Afterword by Jonathan D. Sarna

Yashar Books, 2006

MY YESHIVA COLLEGE: 75 YEARS OF MEMORIES

Edited by Menachem Butler and Zev Nagel
Introduction by Richard M. Joel
With Afterword by Jonathan D. Sarna

Yeshiva University, now in its 120th year, is the country's oldest and most comprehensive institution combining Jewish scholarship with academic excellence and achievement in the liberal arts, sciences, medicine, law, business, social work, Jewish studies and education, and psychology. Its three undergraduate colleges—Yeshiva College, Stern College for Women, and Sy Syms School of Business—form the backbone of the university's ethos, *Torah u-Madda*, the dual pursuit of traditional Jewish learning and secular wisdom. Consistently ranked among the top 50 universities by *U.S. News and World Report*, Yeshiva University is comprised of a network of graduate schools and affiliates, including the Albert Einstein College of Medicine, Benjamin N. Cardozo School of Law, Bernard Revel Graduate School of Jewish Studies, Ferkauf Graduate School of Psychology, Wurzweiler School of Social Work, Rabbi Isaac Elchanan Theological Seminary, Philip and Sarah Belz School of Jewish Music, and Yeshiva University High Schools.

MENACHEM BUTLER, YC '06 and president of the Student Organization of Yeshiva, served as "YUdaica" editor of *The Commentator* in 2004-2005.

ZEV NAGEL, YC '05, served as editor-in-chief of *The Commentator* Vol. LXIX, from 2004-2005, during which Yeshiva College's 75th anniversary was celebrated.

Copyright © 2006 Board of Directors of Yeshiva College

A complete CIP record is available from the Library of Congress
Printed in the United States of America

ISBN 1-933143-12-6

ABOUT THE BACK COVER: The passage is excerpted from an early draft of Herman Wouk's *This Is My God*, found in the Rare Books and Manuscripts Collection of the Yeshiva University Archives (MS. 1325) and reprinted here for the first time with Mr. Wouk's permission.

Photographs in this volume are courtesy of the Yeshiva University Archives and used with permission.

BOOK SPONSORS

Rabbi Julius and Dorothy Berman
In honor of Zev S. Berman YC '82
Eliott M. Berman YC '87

Henry Kressel

Harriet and Joshua Muss
In memory of Hyman (YC '32) & Ruth Muss
and Morris & Charlotte Grossman

Sheri and Stanley Raskas

BOOK SUPPORTERS

Chemia J. Kleinman

Mark A. Koslowe

Meryl and Samuel Solomon

Harry Spiera, M.D.

The
University of the State of New York

Amendment to charter of

Rabbi Isaac Elchanan Theological Seminary Association

This instrument witnesseth. That the Regents of the University of the State of New York

have amended the charter of Rabbi Isaac Elchanan Theological Seminary Association, New York City, which was incorporated as a membership corporation under the laws of the State of New York, March 20, 1897, and charter amended by the Regents of the University on March 27, 1924, by changing the corporate name of said corporation to Rabbi Isaac Elchanan Theological Seminary Association and Yeshivah College and by authorizing said corporation to give courses in liberal arts and sciences leading to the degrees of Bachelor of Arts and Bachelor of Science, provided, however, that such degrees shall not be conferred until the same shall have been duly registered by the State Education Department in conformity with its rules and regulations.

Granted March 29, 1928, by the Regents of the University of the State of New York executed under their seal and recorded in their office Number **3763**

Chancellor

President of the University

The 1928 issued Yeshiva College charter authorizing courses in "liberal arts and sciences leading to the degrees of Bachelor of Arts and Bachelor of Science." The charter amends the pre-existing charter of the Rabbi Isaac Elchanan Theological Seminary Association to include the soon-to-be opened Yeshiva College.

Table of Contents

A Note on Transliteration

Since Yeshiva encompasses so many different people who speak and write Hebrew with varying pronunciations, we chose to use a semi-academic/Modern Hebrew scheme of transliteration for Hebrew. Yiddish was rendered as we believe the speaker would have pronounced it.

School Abbreviations

AECOM	Albert Einstein College of Medicine
AZG	Azrieli Graduate School of Jewish Education and Administration
BGSS	Belfer Graduate School of Science
BRGS	Bernard Revel Graduate School of Jewish Studies
BTA	Brooklyn Talmudic Academy
FGS	Ferkauf Graduate School of Psychology
IBC	Isaac Breuer College of Hebraic Studies
JSS	James Striar School of General Jewish Studies
MTA=MSTA	Marcia Stern Talmudical Academy
MYP	Mazer Yeshiva Program
RIETS	Rabbi Isaac Elchanan Theological Seminary
SCW	Stern College for Women
TI	Teachers Institute
WSSW	Wurzweiler School of Social Work
YUHS	Yeshiva University High School

Editors' Preface

When we began compiling a list of authors to contribute to *The Commentator*'s (Volume LXIX, 2004-2005) literary celebration of Yeshiva College's seventy-fifth anniversary, the prospect of turning the project into anything beyond the newspaper articles was simply nonexistent. Our nascent YUdaica section — a play on words fusing Yeshiva's noted moniker with the word "Judaica" — was only to be a series of short, personal histories of college life, as well as profiles highlighting various personalities that made the YC education memorable. After sending out countless letters to selected alumni, we patiently awaited their responses, which, although originally few, soon grew in range and caliber. Only then did we realize we had tapped into an intellectual niche yet to be explored.

News of the section spread not only across Yeshiva's campuses, but also around the world. The feedback we received was simply tremendous, surpassing our initial modest expectations. Along the way, *The Commentator*'s online readership also exploded, quadrupling within the nine months the series ran. Not surprisingly, interest in it was not exclusive to the immediate Yeshiva University family; in the process, some of the most renowned names in Modern Orthodoxy agreed to participate, a sure indication of the implicit interconnectedness between Yeshiva and the world of contemporary Judaism beyond its walls. YUdaica was even credited with reuniting long lost friends, who rediscovered one another from reading about about their friends in *The Commentator*.

As such, the essays herein presented represent an amalgam of views, recollections, and expressions of intellectual, religious and social life at Yeshiva University, and at Yeshiva College in particular, over the past seventy-five years. It should be clear that the range of expression found in these essays is merely a reflection of those who responded to our invitations to participate.

In character and tone, the articles run the gamut of literary styling — from the boldly expository to the passively reflective to the hortative and critical. Some have been authored by former students, others by members of the faculty both then and now. Combined, these essays span three generations of Yeshiva leadership, from the early years under R. Dr. Bernard Revel, continuing through the university's ontogenesis under R. Dr. Samuel Belkin, and culminating with its recent years under R. Dr. Norman Lamm.

Given the format and manner in which we solicited these essays — and our own distinctive desire to explore a wide range of experience and opinion — this volume draws on various events, characters, and memories, subjectively described by those writing. The lack of uniformity among the collections, in content and style, reflect the objectives of each individual author in reproducing and developing their own conception of a Yeshiva College education rather than any attempt at objective historical research. While, in fact, some authors chose to employ a more scholarly approach, this volume in its entirety should be appreciated as memory rather than academic history. Historians of American Jewish history, and particularly of Yeshiva University, have done a far more comprehensive job, in detail and analysis, of cataloguing the intellectual and social trends of our institution. Most notably, but not exclusively, Gilbert Klaperman's *The Story of Yeshiva University*, Aaron Rakeffet-Rothkoff's *Bernard Revel: Builder of American Jewish Orthodoxy*, Jeffrey S. Gurock's *The Men and Women of Yeshiva*, and Victor Geller's *Orthodoxy Awakens: The Belkin Era and Yeshiva University* should serve as starting points for anyone curious of the historical record.

Nevertheless, the essays in this volume collectively highlight the inner spirit of the Yeshiva College experience and represent a defined sense of ideals remarkably maintained through an array of implementation and discovery. Each vignette reflects the intellectual and literary stamp of its author as simply one other manifestation of the multiple voices that have taught, lived, and learned at Yeshiva College. As such, we are hopeful this book will also be useful for future historians seeking to reconstruct and analyze the story — and ethos — of this great institution.

This volume could never have been written without the enthusiasm, support, and participation of the authors found within these pages. Their interest and eagerness to share with Yeshiva's current student body their reflections and considerations remains the core of this volume. Due to space and stylistic constraints, we could not include all those who contributed to YUdaica, though we are grateful to them for their articles.

Similarly, the actual publication of these essays in book form would never have come to fruition without the explicit leadership of President Richard M. Joel, a man who, in a short time, has made an enormous contribution to Yeshiva. It was President Joel who consistently inquired as to the project's status, and it was at his prodding that the most crucial aspects of this volume came to be. Our deepest thanks go to President Joel for his leadership and for writing the introduction to this volume.

Being that this volume is a project of the Board of Directors, Yeshiva College, we certainly express our gratitude to the entire board. In particular, members of the board Chairman Joshua L. Muss, Stanley I. Raskas (both contributors to this volume as well), and Samuel Solomon deserve particular recognition, as does Zev S. Berman, who was tasked with overseeing this publication. We also express our appreciation to Toby Stone, Esq., for her tireless efforts and attention to detail, to Daniel T. Forman, Vice President for Institutional Advancement, and Heidi Kuperman, Director of Institutional Advancement for Yeshiva College, for the many efforts they expended to find patrons for this volume, and to the all those who helped sponsor the volume. Our publisher, Gil Student of Yashar Books, should be commended for his patience, professionalism, and constant enthusiasm, even as our project went through many lives. We are grateful to former Yeshiva College dean Norman Adler, under whose watch Yeshiva College celebrated its Diamond anniversary, for his plethora of fresh ideas and boundless enthusiasm. We wish to acknowledge Noah Greenfield, Daniel Nagel, and Jeremy Stern for their assistance in putting together the index. And lastly, we wish to thank both Jonathan D. Sarna and Herman Wouk for their original contributions to this volume and for their interest in this project.

Personally, our sincere indebtedness goes to our parents and grandparents, as well as to our teachers, mentors, and colleagues at Yeshiva College, for continuously supporting this project and all our other *meshugassen*. In particular, we wish to thank Dr. Alan Brill, Dr. Jeffrey S.

Gurock, Rabbi Jacob J. Schacter, and our predecessor at *The Commentator*, Jamie Hirsch, for sharing with us their wealth of experience. Similarly, our thanks goes to the entire staff of *The Commentator*, for their continued efforts in creating an outstanding year for the newspaper, taking pride in their work, and for their eternal friendship.

Menachem Butler   Zev Nagel

A Message from the Board of Directors, Yeshiva College

It is with great pleasure that we present *My Yeshiva College: 75 Years of Memories*. Though nearly all the articles have appeared before in *The Commentator*, this first attempt to offer them uniformly constitutes a great achievement for Yeshiva University and American Jewish history. *My Yeshiva College: 75 Years of Memories* will remain a permanent icon of YC's personality as it grows in the twenty-first century.

A survey of the vast experiences portrayed in this volume demonstrates a remarkable irony worthy of our attention. While the Board of Directors, over the years, has taken great strides to improve the academic and social caliber of the college, the essays in this volume suggest the universality and timelessness of the Yeshiva College education; many of the character building challenges confronted by our students and faculty then are indeed the same as those explored today. As such, the YC experience can be considered a fluid one, where we have succeeded at inculcating a sense of shared values and purpose across the generational divide. Surely, we have done and will continue to do a great deal to improve both the cosmetic appearance and academic substance of Yeshiva College. But the mere fact that our current students and alumni can identify with the YC ethos presented herein is a testament to our continued success as a community.

We are obviously tremendously indebted to Menachem Butler and Zev Nagel for bringing "YUdaica" to the world, and, perhaps most importantly, for jumpstarting celebrations for YC's seventy-fifth anniversary. This volume is a testament both to their dedication and zeal, and to the enthusiasm and willingness of all the contributing authors. The latter, in particular, should be commended for sharing with us what Yeshiva College meant to them then and today. It is our hope that we can learn and grow from the vignettes and essays presented here, and appreciate together as a community our historic past and anticipate our seamless future.

Zev S. Berman, YC '82
Vice Chairman, "Yeshiva College@75" Anniversary Celebrations
Board of Directors, Yeshiva College

Introduction

It is my great pleasure and honor to write the introduction to this volume. Having avidly read the vignettes in the YUdaica section of *The Commentator* all year, I was struck by the diversity of opinions, and the passion to bring wisdom to life that characterizes Yeshiva College students, then and now.

This volume presents snapshots of the richness and breadth of Yeshiva College, and the energy and excitement that characterizes the Yeshiva College experience. Taken individually, these vignettes demonstrate the way YC students tackled all of the pressing issues of their day, whether they were economic difficulty, war, or societal change. Each generation of students faced their own challenges and distinct pressures, yet in each generation the rigorous intellectual pursuit of excellence in both Torah and *madda* shone forth to characterize the Yeshiva College student.

Yeshiva College students have always been idealistic. This idealism, driven by a pure commitment to Torah and desire to implement Torah values in life, assured that Yeshiva students would be involved in all the core issues of their day. In fact, Yeshiva students have always found their place together with the leadership of the social action movements. In the 1940s, Yeshiva students actively collected for the *Va'ad Hatzalah* and, as Dr. Lamm describes, they used their knowledge of science and their indefatigable energy to help the nascent Jewish State, even supplying it with much needed rifles. In the 1960s, student activists established the Yavneh movement and, later in that decade, began the Soviet Jewry movement, all the while continuing their firm support for Israel. Of course, there were times when the idealism of Yeshiva students put them at odds with the administration. One thing remains clear, however — whatever projects they embraced, Yeshiva College students were fueled by Torah values and the desire to use these values to improve and enrich the world. As I understand it, this represents the best of *Torah u-Madda*. Professor Joan Haahr's description of Vietnam War protests on campus interrupted for *Ma'ariv* is a wonderful example of the way our students are equally committed to the values of Torah and social justice.

Dr. Revel envisioned Yeshiva College as a small institution, and though we have grown considerably from the initial graduating class of nineteen students in 1932, the strength of Yeshiva has always been that, as a small school, our students were afforded numerous opportunities to participate in student life and to grow. A beneficiary of this has been Yeshiva's athletic department and drama society, both of which are described in this volume. However, as a small school, Yeshiva's facilities were oftentimes lacking. Josh Muss writes how "the facilities were lousy. At that time there was hardly anything that was 'good' and much that just 'wasn't'... But we loved Yeshiva." Despite the poor physical accommodations, or perhaps because of them, students fell in love with Yeshiva College. They loved Yeshiva then, as they do now, because of the warmth of its camaraderie and the depth and vigor of its intellectual heritage.

Not surprisingly, the greatest influence on Yeshiva College students has come from *Torah u-Madda* role models. Certainly, the first three Presidents of Yeshiva, Dr. Bernard Revel, Dr. Samuel Belkin, and *yibadel l'hayim tovim* Dr. Norman Lamm were rare individuals who excelled in both the tents of Shem and Yefet, and in turn, inspired many Yeshiva College students to think about the world in sophisticated and profound ways. Of course, the pervasive influence of the Rav, Rabbi Joseph B. Soloveitchik, was a major source of inspiration for our students to excel in both the *beit midrash* and the Academy.

A great testament to the strength and vitality of the Yeshiva *hashkafah* is how each of our first three Presidents interpreted *Torah u-Madda* in his own unique way, and all of the different interpretations can be found among Yeshiva students today. Dr. Revel spoke of "the harmonious union of culture and spirituality." Dr. Belkin spoke of an internal synthesis where "blending of science and religion is not to be in the disciplines themselves but in personality of the individual," and *yibadel l'hayim tovim* Dr. Lamm's rigorous text-based study of *Torah u-Madda* has transformed Yeshiva's motto from a slogan into a compelling academic discipline. The

outcome of these diverse approaches can be seen in the men of stature
and intellectual standing who graduate from Yeshiva College and assume
leadership positions in the Jewish world and the world at large, because
they can skillfully navigate the sea of *madda* with the compass of Torah.

For me, most striking about this volume is how many of the articles
tell the story of individual teachers and role models instead of the story
of Yeshiva College as an institution. Indeed, one of the great strengths
of Yeshiva has always been that as a small college our students were
intimately exposed to the warmth, caring, and valuable counsel of their
teachers, *rebbeim* and administrators.

We have been graced by a cadre of *roshei yeshiva* who deeply believed
that the highest levels of Torah can be taught in America. Rabbi Shlomo
Polachek, the Maichater *Ilui*, and Rabbi Moshe Aaron Poleyoff, Rabbi
Shimon Romm and Rabbi Shlomo Drillman were men of penetrating
intellect and profound integrity. In addition to their superior levels of Torah
knowledge, the *roshei yeshiva* described in this volume, and countless others
who are still waiting their due publicity, were inquisitive intellects who
inspired their students to be inquisitive and use their Torah knowledge to
make real contributions to society. In later decades, Yeshiva was graced with
great *rebbeim*, such as Rabbi Moshe Besdin and Rabbi Aharon Lichtenstein,
who themselves were emblematic of the *Torah u-Madda* ideal. We were also
graced by wonderful professors like Jekuthiel Ginsburg, Yitz Greenberg, and
Louis Feldman. Moreover, students were also exposed to the rare breed of
pulpit rabbi and communal leader, embodied by Rabbis Leo Jung, Joseph
Lookstein and Emanuel Rackman, who found time to share their wisdom
with students at Yeshiva College and RIETS. All these talented and erudite
men are described beautifully in this volume, and each of them had a
formative influence because of their love and warmth.

Of course, there are a few great men who had a profound influence
on Yeshiva students, and the larger Jewish world, who regrettably were
left out of this volume. This list includes Dr. Israel Miller and Mr.
Abraham Stern, two of my own mentors, to whom I owe so much. The
stories of these rare blends of Orthodox leaders and renaissance men will
undoubtedly inspire future generations to themselves pursue greatness.
To quote Rabbi Shalom Carmy in his tribute to Dr. Meir Hershkovics, "in
the end institutions don't count; it is individuals who matter."

Although each vignette is of great value on its own, when the
articles in this volume are viewed together as a unit, they become all the

more significant. As a unit, the snapshots found in this volume depict not only the growth and development of Yeshiva College, but the emergence of a strong, proud and vibrant Orthodoxy. Without question, the growth and explosion of the Orthodox world was provoked by Yeshiva College students. Yeshiva College is now an outstanding school that produces ambitious young men who serve humanity. It has grown from its humble beginnings, when the goal was to provide an education to immigrant youth and integrate them into the fabric of America while maintaining a firm grounding in Torah and Jewish values. Yeshiva College has grown at the same time that American Orthodoxy has moved away from its reticence and assumed a position of prominence.

Perhaps the overall message of this volume is that we have a sacred responsibility not only to recall, to remember, and to record, but to renew and look ahead into the next chapter of history and towards the next volume of YUdaica. I am certain that the next volume will reflect an even deeper engagement in core *Torah u-Madda* issues. Without doubt, the next generation of Yeshiva College students will take even more communal, professional and rabbinic positions of leadership as they proudly embrace a "*le-khathila*" vision of *Torah u-Madda*. Looking forward, I am certain that Yeshiva College graduates will proudly embrace their covenantal responsibility to enrich the world through the profundity and richness of their Torah values. I have no doubt that the near future will usher in a period of even greater academic excellence, as Yeshiva College attracts larger numbers of talented and dedicated students and we actualize our potential as the leadership incubator for *Klal Yisrael*.

I thank all the contributors who play an essential role in telling the story of Yeshiva College, as well as all of those who have engendered a conversation that will continue into tomorrow. I applaud Zev Nagel, the Editor-in-Chief of *The Commentator* Volume LXIX, and Menachem Butler, editor of the YUdaica Section and President of the Student Organization of Yeshiva, for taking the initiative to research and cull the history of our Yeshiva and for producing a work that will remain as a major contribution to the history of Yeshiva College and to the history of American Orthodoxy.

Richard M. Joel
President, Yeshiva University

PART I

THE REVEL YEARS

The Life and Times of R. Shimon Romm:
A Biography

By Zalman Alpert

Among the last European *roshei yeshiva* to teach at Yeshiva's RIETS was Rabbi Shimon Romm, my Rav and teacher, who served as a final bridge between the American students of Yeshiva and the great Lithuanian tradition of Eastern Europe.

Born Shimon Posniak in 1906 to a typically poor family in the town of Wysoki, Poland, R. Romm often spoke of the mixed heritage of his hometown; since Wysoki was located in Polish territory between Lithuania and Poland, the town was influenced both by the Lithuanian Torah tradition of the Gaon of Vilna and by the Hasidic culture of Polish Jewry, in this case the Kotzk dynasty.

At a young age, R. Romm lost his father and was sent by his mother to study at the *yeshiva* in Slonim. Although Slonim is now chiefly remembered for the Weinberg Hasidic dynasty that began there, it was in fact a real Mitnagdic town, with the greatest of Litvishe rabbis (among them, R. Mordechai Rosenblatt, known as the Oshmener Rav who, besides being a Talmudic giant was also a well known *poel yeshu'ot*, the last of the Lithuanian *ba'alei moftim*). In Slonim, the young R. Romm studied under the famed R. Shabsi Yagel and was exposed to the oratorical talents of the communal Rav, R. Yehuda Leib Fein. On numerous occasions, R. Romm spoke of R. Fein's impressive speaking abilities, even referring to him as the greatest rabbinical orator in interwar Europe. After some time at Slonim, R. Romm studied at the Mussar Yeshiva of Novardok before

Mr. Zalman Alpert is the Reference Librarian at the Gottesman Library of Yeshiva University.

moving to Kletzk, where he studied under the late R. Aharon Kotler, who later came to America and established the Beth Medrash Govoha and Kollel in Lakewood, New Jersey. Though he was close with R. Kotler, R. Romm never visited the Lakewood Kollel in the United States even while R. Kotler was alive, which I suspect had to do with issues of *hashkafah* and geographical distance.

R. Romm's final formal *yeshiva* years were spent in the Mir, the best known *yeshiva* in Polish Lithuania. There he studied both under R. Eliezer Yehuda Finkel (son of R. Nathan Tzvi Finkel, the famed Alter of Slabodka) and under the rabbi of the town of Mir, R. Avraham Tzvi Hirsch Kamai, who eventually conferred rabbinic ordination on Shimon Romm.

Despite the impressive list of teachers, R. Romm remarked on several occasions that his master teacher was the sixteenth century Maharsha (R. Shmuel Eliezer Eidels), a comment very much in tandem with that of another Lithuania giant, R. Avraham Karelitz–the Hazon Ish–who also bemoaned that modern post-Brisker *yeshiva* students were no longer steeped in the Maharsha.

Several years prior to the outbreak of the Second World War, R. Romm married Kaila Eisenbod, the daughter of R. Eliyahu Eisenbod of Vashilishok, a small town near Vilna with a strong tradition of Torah scholarship, even in modern times. The "Heiliger Hafetz Hayim," as R. Romm referred to him, had lived in Vashilishok for a while.

When R. Romm informed R. Hayim Ozer Grodzenski, the chairman of the Moetzet Gedolei Hatorah of the Agudath Israel, of his impending marriage to the Vashilishoker Rav's daughter, R. Hayim Ozer congratulated him and told him that he wished that the Agudah would have such rabbinic members as R. Eisenbod; the Vashilishoker Rav was a known Mizrachi leader. Indeed, it remains a little known fact that many of the Lithuanian rabbis in pre-war Poland were associated with Mizrachi. The Hafetz Hayim's eldest son, R. Yehuda Leib Poupko (who assumed the surname to escape from compulsorily army service) served as president of the Polish Mizrachi for a number of years leading up to 1939.

Following his marriage, R. Romm served as the associate rabbi of Vashilishok under his father-in-law, thus gaining experience in the fields of pastoral and practical rabbinics. He gave the daily Talmud *shi'ur* in the town's largest *beit midrash*. But in 1939, at the outbreak of the war, R. Romm fled Lithuania with his family and the rest of the Mirrer Yeshiva, making his way across the Soviet Union and eventually to Shanghai. While in Shanghai, R. Romm served as a teacher to the tens of thousands of German Jews already living there while continuing studying at the *yeshiva*.

Unlike most of his fellow refugees in Shanghai, R. Romm managed to leave prior to the conclusion of the war. In 1942, together with a small group of Jews from Shanghai, R. Romm left by steamer to Mozambique, then a colony administered by Portugal. In Mozambique he met a solitary Lithuanian Jew, who, in 1926, had built a small shul in anticipation of the Messiah, or at the very least, in case other Jews came. After a brief stay in Africa, R. Romm left for Palestine with the help of its chief rabbi, Dr. Isaac Herzog, whom he later befriended.

In *Eretz Yisrael*, R. Romm served as rabbi of the Gesundheit Shul in Tel Aviv. The Gesundheits were a prominent Polish family whose great-grandfather, R. Ya'akov Gesundheit, served as Warsaw's first chief rabbi. Although a small synagogue, many leaders of the *Yishuv* prayed at the Gesundheit Shul and were impressed by R. Romm's speaking talent. Among his congregants there were R. Isaac Mayer Lewin, son of the Bendiner Rav and son-in-law of the Gerrer Rebbe, R. Abraham Mordechai Alter, and Mr. Moshe Hayim Shapiro, a leader of the Mizrachi party.

After the establishment of the State of Israel, R. Romm left Israel for the United States for personal reasons. Although R. Herzog had promised him an important rabbinical position, R. Romm had already accepted an offer from his childhood friend from their days in Slonim together, Dr. Samuel Belkin, the second president of Yeshiva.

Once R. Romm arrived in the United States, Dr. Belkin made use of R. Romm's speaking abilities to fundraise, sending him off to cities across the country. Thankfully, Dr. Belkin and the other *roshei yeshiva* soon realized that R. Romm's talents could be better utilized in the *shi'ur* room, and he was appointed a *maggid shi'ur* at TI. When R. Mendel Zaks (son-in-law of the Hafetz Hayim) died after serving as official *bohen* for Yeshiva for many years, R. Romm took his place, and he became a full-time *rosh yeshiva* at RIETS soon thereafter. There he taught hundreds of students, delivering well crafted and scholarly *shi'urim* in a masterful Modern Hebrew.

The talents of R. Romm, however, extended beyond the walls of Yeshiva. He also served as rabbi of Congregation Noda Bi-Yehuda in

Washington Heights for many years. Although the synagogue was small, R. Romm's service in the shul was most impressive. His Shabbat morning *derashot* were masterpieces delivered in a beautiful Lithuanian Yiddish. His speeches focused mainly on the Holocaust and the renaissance of the Jewish people in terms of the creation of the State of Israel, and they often ran close to an hour in length. He loved to quote the *Midrash Tanhuma*, the *Torat Mosheh*, and *Meshekh Hokhmah*. His *derashot* on *Shabbat ha-Gadol* and *Shabbat Shuvah* always attracted large audiences from the neighborhood. During *seudah shelishit* on Shabbat afternoon, he would often morph into a Hasidic rebbe, relating Hasidic tales or exploring the teachings of the leaders of Hasidism.

The scholarly R. Romm also found time to be involved politically, especially in the Mizrachi movement in America. In the 1950s and 60s, the halcyon days of Mizrachi, R. Romm would often serve as the "warm up" speaker at its annual Lakewood convention, prior to the keynote address of his good friend, R. Joseph B. Soloveitchik. As a Mizrachi leader, he also delivered a weekly Talmud *shi'ur* at Yeshiva for laymen; this *shi'ur* was the last *Gemara shi'ur* delivered in Yiddish at Yeshiva.

Though R. Romm became disenchanted with the policies of the State of Israel in his later years and at times sounded like an Agudah leader, he always retained a passionate love for *Eretz Yisrael* and *Medinat Yisrael*. It should be noted that R. Romm's religious Zionism was not of the school of either R. Avraham Yitzhak HaKohen Kook or his son R. Tzvi Yehuda Kook; rather, he considered himself a proponent on the Zionism forged by R. Ya'akov Yitzhak Reines, R. Yitzhak Nissenbaum and R. Yitzhak Rubenstein. R. Romm was certainly no mystic, but he did believe in Israel as an important step in the realizations of Jewish messianic destiny.

Although R. Romm gave his *shi'urim* in Hebrew, he was a fervent lover of Yiddish and was well versed in the classics of Yiddish literature. At the same time, he was also quite familiar with the best of Modern Hebrew literature, particularly with the works of Hayim Nahman Bialik. On one occasion, R. Romm told me that Bialik's poetry was perfectly kosher, with the exception of some passages in two of his poems. He was well educated in secular studies and was familiar with world literature and psychology. I recall feeling shocked when, in the course of conversation, he mentioned the German-Jewish thinker Otto Weininger. R. Romm also kept up to date on world events and contemporary issues, including the Cold War, Israel, American politics, and Yiddish and Hebrew literature.

Despite joining RIETS, which culled most of its faculty from Lithuanian traditions, R. Romm had a soft spot for Hassidut from his days in Slonim and other cities in White Russia. While he was still in Israel, R. Romm maintained close contact with the fourth Belzer rebbe, R. Aharon Rokeach. He was also close to both R. Zalman L. Halberstam, the Klausenberger rebbe of Netanya, and R. Jacob J. Twersky, the Skverer rebbe, for whom he administered several complicated rabbinic functions. R. Romm also enjoyed a close relationship with the *Bais Yisrael* rebbe, R. Yisrael Alter of Ger, whom he met through the rebbe's brother-in-law, R. Isaac Mayer Lewin, head of the World Agudath Israel. Knowing my own Habad background, R. Romm always inquired into the health status of the Lubavitcher Rebbe when he was critically ill. Often he himself would personally make a *mi she-beirakh* for the Rebbe. When the Rebbe died, R. Romm dedicated his weekly *shi'ur* to the memory of the Rebbe.

Watching R. Romm walk with his *rebbetzin*, Kaila Romm, to shul on Shabbat morning along Bennett Avenue was always a lesson in spouse relations. R. Romm not only respected and honored his own rebbetzin, but on almost every Shabbat upon arrival in shul, his first order of business was at the *mehitzah*; there he inquired to the health and welfare of a number of elderly widows who were members of our shul.

R. Romm was fastidious in his appearance and was particular to present an image worthy of a *talmid hakham*, as was the custom amongst Lithuanian rabbanim in the twentieth century. A *rosh yeshiva* of the highest caliber who, at his death in 1997, was the oldest *rosh yeshiva* at RIETS, R. Romm also served his congregants in the Washington Heights community. But last, and certainly not the least, he was a good and loyal friend.

The Letter

By Abraham Avrech

My whole life has been bound up with Yeshiva. I received my high school education at Yeshiva, graduating in 1936. In 1940, after four wonderful years of study mixed with a great deal of Varsity basketball and pick-up softball, I graduated from YC. I received *semikhah* from RIETS in 1943. I worked practically my entire adult life in the Yeshiva, starting in 1949 as associate director of CSD, and then as director of Alumni and Rabbinic Alumni. I was also chairman of the Athletic Commission, and instrumental in building the Max Stern Athletic Center. Until my retirement in 1985, I was coordinator of Yeshiva's chaplaincy program.

It would be easy for me to write about the remarkable growth of the college and university. Where one building once stood on 186th Street and Amsterdam Avenue there are now a host of buildings. Yeshiva's outstanding growth and influence on the world Jewish community is unparalleled in American life and I am proud to have played a role in this continuing chronicle.

However, instead of writing about brick and mortar, expanding budgets, and the growth of *Torah u-Madda* in America, I want to tell you about a family — my family — and how Yeshiva contributed to its creation. For, in the end, it is Torah families that make up the heart and soul of Yeshiva University.

In 1943, I married Mina Keiler. Our early years were spent moving

Rabbi Abraham Avrech YC '40, RIETS '43, lives in Florida, where he is the unofficial rabbi of his co-op's minyan. He also plays golf every chance he gets. Rabbi Avrech is now married to Sylvia Lamm, who is a first cousin of Rabbi Norman and Rabbi Maurice Lamm. Thus, Rabbi Avrech's connection with Yeshiva University continues.

from army base to army base, as I was a chaplain in the U.S. Army. I also had my first position as the rabbi of a congregation in Maine, and my wife was nervously learning to fulfill the role of a rebbetzin — a difficult and demanding job for a young woman who did not come from a rabbinic family. Like all young couples, we looked forward to building a Torah family. But as the years passed, God did not bless us with children.

My wife and I decided to adopt. We applied to a Jewish adoption agency. We filled out dozens of questionnaires; we were interviewed by social workers and psychologists. Our home was inspected from top to bottom. It was exhausting, stressful, and was frightening beyond imagination. All around us, my wife and I saw our friends having children and basking in their growing families. Try to imagine the loneliness we felt as we contemplated the empty nursery in our apartment. Adopting a child is a nerve-racking experience for all couples, but Mina and I were determined to see the process through — no matter how long it took, no matter how strenuous.

The adoption agency finally told us that our application was "looking good," but one step remained — one final crucial step. We were instructed to submit a letter of recommendation from a community leader. It was whispered that the more important the person who writes the letter, the greater chance of the adoption being successful.

My wife and I sat down and made a list of the people we knew. In those days I was a young rabbi. I was not on intimate terms with any important or influential people. But our life, our family, was at stake and I made an appointment with the most important, most prominent figure on Orthodox Jewish life in America to ask for his help.

The secretary ushered me into his office.

"What can I do for you, R. Avrech?"

Haltingly, I explained everything. I was so nervous that I was literally trembling.

President Samuel Belkin rose and came over to ease my discomfort. He put his hand on my shoulder and said, "Don't worry about a thing, R. Avrech. I will take care of it."

Before I knew it, we received a phone call from the adoption agency. They told us that they had a baby for us — a boy. A healthy boy. Would we like to see him?

Mina and I stepped into the foster home where the orphan baby was lying in a crib. He stared at my wife with big brown eyes. He cried; he held

out his arms. We learned that the foster parents fed him, but otherwise
ignored him. This baby did not know what it was to be held in a mother's
arms.

"Poor thing," said Mina with tears in her eyes, "look how starved for
attention he is."

We took the baby home and several days later we named him Reuven
Ya'akov, Robert Joel.

Our social worker told us, in confidence, that Dr. Belkin's letter of
recommendation was so powerful, so supportive, that there was absolutely
no question as to whether my wife and I would be ideal parents. Dr. Belkin's
letter clinched the adoption. Who knows what would have happened
without the letter?

And so, yes, I have seen Yeshiva grow from an idealistic dream to an
influential reality. I have seen some of the greatest rabbis of our generation
pass through Yeshiva's *beit midrash*. I have seen the American landscape
change because of the brilliant philosophy of *Torah u-Madda*. But in the
end, Yeshiva University and Dr. Belkin in particular, are responsible for
giving me a family, allowing me and my wife to fulfill the *mitzvot* of rearing
Jewish children in a home infused with love of family.

Robert is a successful screenwriter and novelist in Los Angeles. He
is a leader in his community and active in his local Young Israel. My wife
passed away twelve years ago, but her gratitude to Yeshiva and to Dr.
Belkin was never forgotten and never diminished.

My son Robert tells me that the only time he has seen me break
down and cry uncontrollably is when Dr. Belkin passed away. My love for
Yeshiva and Dr. Belkin is impossible to measure. Most who think about
Yeshiva University end up marveling at its expansion. But for me, Yeshiva
University equals family — the very core of my life.

Seventy-Five Years at Yeshiva:
Reflections of a Son on His Father's Legacy

By Moshe J. Bernstein

It has been almost a quarter century now since my father, R. Michael Bernstein, was *niftar* on 23 Tevet 5741, and I am sure that my personal memories of the three decades before that date have been blurred and altered with the passage of time. So I write not as an historian, a checker of names, dates and facts, but as a reminiscer, considering what I remember and what I have been told about my father, from the perspective of one who has spent the last twenty-five years teaching some of the same courses as he did at the same institution at which he taught, often to the sons (and daughters during my twenty years at SCW) of those whom he taught. If some of my chronology, or a fact here or there, is inaccurate, I beg the reader's indulgence.

I am fond of saying, only slightly tongue in cheek, that I have been at Yeshiva for about seventy-five years now, the same number as the anniversary which Yeshiva College is now observing. Although I have yet to reach my sixtieth birthday, my effective "Yeshiva memory" reaches back three quarters of a century. From the day that my father entered MTA as a junior in 1930 as a transfer from Seward Park High School on New York's Lower East Side, we haven't been away from Yeshiva except for the years that he spent in *rabbonus* and *hinnukh* in the early 1940s. Together, we have taught at Yeshiva uninterruptedly since 1947; the fall

Dr. Moshe J. Bernstein, YC '66, RIETS '69, is Professor of Bible at Yeshiva College.

semester of 1980, my father's first semester as Professor Emeritus, during which he was taken from us at an all too young age after a two-decade illness, was my first as full-time Assistant Professor at YC and SCW.

Jewish education in the period between the two World Wars was so very different from what it has become today that it is hard to imagine. The flourishing Orthodoxy that we have all become accustomed to was not even on the radar screen; the Depression and acculturation, the need to be more "American," to become successful, and even just to earn a living, all took their toll on Orthodox observance in America. There were too many reasons to cast off the identifying marks of Jewish observance in order to integrate into American society. It is a byword today that the best defense of Jewish observance is Jewish education, but the opportunities for Jewish education in America were extremely limited at that time, and it was only the fortunate few who achieved it. After MTA, my father entered Yeshiva College in fall of the academic year in which YC graduated its first class; those early years of the College produced many of the rabbis and educators who do not get sufficient credit both for preserving Orthodox observance in America and for enabling the heightened levels of education and observance which my students of today take for granted.

Even in the distinguished company of the YC alumni of those early years, my father stood out. One of his *maspidim*, his life-long friend R. Moshe Besdin, spoke of him as the *yahid shebahavura*, the most distinguished member of the circle of serious *benei Torah* in the Yeshiva of those days. He majored in philosophy, not unusual in and of itself, but he took five years instead of four to complete his degree in order to spend more time on his *talmud Torah*. That was as unusual in those days as it would be today. I know that he must have interacted with more than one of the *roshei yeshiva* of those days, but the only one whose name I heard mentioned regularly, clearly his *rebbe muvhak*, was R. Moshe Soloveichik, whose name I bear.

Dr. Haym Soloveitchik of BRGS observed in a touching *azkara* for my father (printed in *Chavrusa*, April 1983) that he was the only American-born *talmid muvhak* of his own grandfather (it is often forgotten that my father was also the first American-born *Rosh Yeshiva* at Yeshiva University). That factoid, in a sense, characterizes my father; he was born in New York to immigrant parents, and his mastery of English was complete, but he also spoke elegant Yiddish like a European. For many of his European-born classmates and colleagues, his knowledge of English was a valuable asset. When they would go off into the rabbinate to those many American communities which were starved for *Yiddishkeit*, my father would write several generic sermons for them — bar mitzva, funeral, wedding, and the like — in English, but in Hebrew characters. I had always wondered whether this story was a myth until my mother returned from a visit to Israel for his *haqamat matzevah* and told me that she had met the widow of one of those classmates, who showed her the tattered remains of one of those sermons which her late husband had preserved. On the other hand, there is no surviving evidence of the love-letters that we were told he ghostwrote for one of his classmates who was engaged in a long-distance relationship with a girl who expected her young man to be fluent in English.

My father learned Torah classically, but was open to many of the paths to understanding Torah which then, as now, were not frequently walked by *roshei yeshiva*. My father was a seemingly paradoxical combination of a *lamdan* and a scholar, but the paradox was only superficial. For my father, his *lomdus* and his scholarship were simply different facets of his *talmud Torah*; there was no artificial distinction for him between his *lernen* and his *jüdische Wissenschaft*. Despite the fact that when he was trained in the 1930s there was an even greater fear of the "*maskilish*" than there is now, and academic scholarship was often seen as inevitably leading to defection from Orthodoxy to more liberal denominations, he did what he thought was right in this realm as in so many others. Not only did he see no conflict, but he found a harmony in the diverse elements of knowledge which he sought to master.

Yeshiva was his home, and my father's scholarship, like his Torah, was largely home-grown. He must have been one of the first students in the Graduate School (later to become BRGS, and his academic home for the last segment of his teaching career). I still have his notebook from the years 1937-1939 with carefully taken notes from teachers like Dr. Samuel Belkin, who was later to become Yeshiva's second president but was a scholar of distinction before that, Dr. Pinkhos Churgin, Dr. Solomon Zeitlin, and Dr. Joshua Finkel in courses ranging from Talmud to Second Temple Judaism to Philo to Comparative Semitic Philology to Biblical Versions and Ancient Semitic Inscriptions. There are even a couple — alas, only a couple — of pages of notes from lectures from "Dr. Soloveitchik" (the Rav of course) in Jewish Philosophy.

He left Yeshiva after receiving *semikhah* in 1939, and served as rabbi in congregations in Lynn, Massachusetts and the Inwood neighborhood of Manhattan, north of Washington Heights. It appears that teaching drew him more than the rabbinate, and he served briefly as the principal of the *Merkaz ha-Torah* yeshiva in Montreal. But 1947 found him back home at Yeshiva, and he never really left again. He began giving *shi'urim* in MTA and then progressed to the college level (as used to be the tradition), while at the same time teaching a full load in YC. He was doing what he loved to do, and for the next thirty-three years he left his mark on several divisions of Yeshiva University, teaching in the high school, the college, the yeshiva and the graduate school.

Yeshiva now became and remained his home in a literal, not just a metaphorical, sense. He lived down the block, a part of a Yeshiva community which in the course of time scattered over the years to Forest Hills and Flatbush, Teaneck and Monsey, Five Towns and Riverdale, and has only recently been reinvigorated. He lived in the vicinity out of choice, because he felt that it was not right that a rebbe should "teach and run." Yeshiva was my home as I grew up, and my father's home was part of the Yeshiva.

His higher education, however, had not yet been completed. He somehow found the time, while carrying a teaching load which boggles my twenty-first century academician's mind, to complete his coursework and thesis for the DHL degree at Revel. What is probably surprising to almost anyone who knew my father and his teaching career is that his thesis was in neither Bible nor Semitic languages, the primary fields which he taught for the last two decades of his life, but in the area of Classical Jewish History/Talmud on Rabbi Yehoshua ben Hananiah. After that, while teaching the load that he did and helping my mother raise me and my two siblings, he somehow found the time to attend classes at Columbia University to enhance his knowledge of Semitic languages further. The notion that the goal of study is the achievement of yet another degree or the publication of yet another article would have been beyond his comprehension. Knowledge had its own intrinsic value, with knowledge of Torah, of course, granted primacy, although not exclusivity. And we should not forget that his definition of Torah was far broader than many contemporary definitions would have it.

As a result of his maximalist approach to his academic training, the spectrum of subjects that my father taught ranged from Hebrew language, both elementary and advanced, to Bible and its interpretation, to Jewish history to Ramban to several dialects of Aramaic. In today's era of narrower and narrower academic specialization, he would have been a total anomaly, but even in his generation the range of his competence was astounding. He was a teacher, through and through, although without the sparkle and flash that often marks master teachers; his undramatic style was highly effective. He taught his children and grandchildren, and *semikhah* students and graduate students. He taught my sister and the women who studied with him in BRGS in the same way that he taught my brother and me and the men in Yeshiva. In that regard, he was perhaps a little ahead of his time. If you wanted to study Torah, he would teach you, and you would learn.

Unfortunately, my father never published any books or scholarly essays. Around the time that I came back to Yeshiva, having abandoned the field of classical languages for a career in Jewish Studies, he said to me that he had had the luxury of being able to read and teach only, while I had the obligation to publish as well. He operated in different times and at a Yeshiva with different standards from the one to which I returned to teach. He loved to read primary texts of every sort in their original languages; I rarely saw him spending much time on secondary literature, although it is clear to me that at an earlier stage of his career he had read both broadly and deeply. He wanted to solve the problem at hand, understand the passage which he was reading, no matter how difficult or complex. But the minutiae of scholarship, checking all the secondary sources and writing the footnotes, dotting the i's and crossing the t's, held no attraction for him. More than once I have "said over" my father's interpretation of some text to a biblical scholar who had never heard of him and who then asked me where it had been published. They have always been amazed when I tell them that his scholarship was transmitted only orally.

Whereas I am certain that he would have significantly enhanced the body of knowledge in his chosen fields by publishing his scholarship, I wonder whether he would have had the same impact in other ways if he had had to submit to the parameters of the academic world that govern me and my colleagues today. His Torah was a "*Torah she-be-al peh*," and it survives, with or without *shem omero* (about which he was never overly concerned) in the teaching of his students and his students' students. I have often wondered how many of our current students at Yeshiva College have been touched by him from a distance through that *shalshelet ha-kabbalah* without their ever knowing who he was. A significant number of *roshei yeshiva* over the years, *maggidei shi'ur* at MTA, *mehannekhim* all over the United States and in *Eretz Yisrael*, not to mention academic scholars of Jewish studies at prestigious universities, studied with him and now transmit his legacy to their *talmidim*.

When I learned with him, and of course when he taught in the Yeshiva, the focus was always on texts, biblical and rabbinic and medieval, some within the classic curriculum, and others ancillary to it. I don't know what his "*derekh*" was in giving *shi'ur* in *Gemara*, since I never heard him give formal *shi'urim*, but I know that when we learned together, especially during the summers, it was always *Gemara*, Rashi, *Tosafot*, Rosh and Ran, and occasional other *rishonim*. Mastery of the text was his goal, for himself and for his students. Although he was a product of the "Brisker *derekh*," that is not what he taught to me, at any rate. And what he chose to study with me privately in my early teenage years, beyond the standard *Humash* and *rishonim*, *Nakh* and *rishonim*, and *Gemara* and *rishonim*, was interesting. We studied *Iggeret Rav Sherira Gaon* and *Megillat Ta'anit*, neither of them a staple of the *beit midrash* curriculum, not because he was preparing me for a career in Jewish Studies, for I think that that was actually far from his mind, but because he thought that an educated Jew should have studied the primary sources of Jewish history. The core of all Jewish knowledge, for him, was the text, not the *sevara*.

Although he did not give *Gemara shi'urim* in the Yeshiva after about 1955, when a "new" *Semikhah* program was innovated with required classes in *Humash* and Ramban and in Jewish History that he taught, and although by the end of his life he was teaching only in BRGS and YC, my father was always a *rosh yeshiva*, both in his own self-image and in the view of others. His goal was to teach Torah and to enable others to study Torah; the fact that he occasionally did this by studying and teaching texts that were not part of the *beit midrash* canon somehow did not concern even our "rightmost" *roshei yeshiva*. This was due, in part, to a more open atmosphere which pervaded Yeshiva in the 1950s through 1970s, but even more, I believe, to my father's religious persona. It was inconceivable to those who knew him that any intellectual activity in which he engaged could be tainted.

I still occasionally hear Yeshiva old-timers using the term "*yeshiva mann*" — yeshiva man — to translate an untranslatable term. That is what my father always was, whether he was out in the rabbinate or back at Yeshiva teaching. His self-identification with, loyalty to and defense of Yeshiva University to the outside world were remarkable. He could not imagine my going to college anywhere else; after all, where else could I be trained in all the areas I was expected to master. But within its four walls he could be a very harsh critic of his beloved institution. His standards in learning, in teaching, in scholarship, and in ethics were very high, and those who fell short, and even his precious Yeshiva when it fell short, were subjected to trenchant and pointed criticism. Perhaps as a result, Yeshiva did not always treat him as well as it ought to have; it did not always keep its promises to him. Institutions cannot always afford to listen to their consciences. But he was "impervious," in the words of Haym Soloveitchik, to "the temptations of fame, power and finality." He took the high road, regardless of the personal or professional consequences.

When he was stricken with his long, lingering illness in the early 1960s, we realized that it was fortuitous that my parents had never moved from the Yeshiva neighborhood. He went to classes first with a cane, then with a walker, and later in a wheelchair, and ultimately, as the debilitating disease progressed, he taught his classes at home across the street, from his wheelchair, and eventually from a hospital bed in his bedroom. I don't think that there was anyone who saw him during that period who was not moved by his fortitude in the face of illness. I know that he would have dismissed this remark with a wave of his hand, because, as the Rav said, he wasn't just an *anav*, he was *nehba el ha-kelim*. But his students in those years learned more from him than the subject matter of their courses, as he became a model of greatness in the face of suffering. He had always davened with "the boys," as he affectionately called the Yeshiva student community, from the days that the minyan was in RIETS Hall (now Klein Hall), and later in its travels to Rubin Shul and then to Morg. When his illness reached a stage that precluded his going to shul, there was always a Shabbat minyan in his apartment. I often meet former Yeshiva students, including many who never studied formally with my father, who recall fondly that davening and kiddush (with cholent!), and the informal learning which followed them.

Although from a formal perspective, my father's influence on his *talmidim*, especially those who became rabbis and educators, began in the classroom, the impact which he had on a generation and a half of Yeshiva students went far beyond those four walls. From my childhood in the early

1950s and on, I remember students coming and going in our apartment, until the late hours of the night, seeking my father's and mother's advice and help, usually about matters far from the academic. He lived across the street from Yeshiva so that a student who needed his counsel regarding a job, a career, or a *shiddukh* could find it. My parents' door was always open to the students, and they took full advantage of that open-door policy. Many of those *talmidim* stayed in touch with my father long after they had left Yeshiva, continuing to ask for his advice and assistance. In later years, while he underwent the ravages of his lengthy illness, he appreciated the fact that many of them made a special effort to acknowledge gratefully all of the things that he had done for them; their visits and phone calls gave him strength and *sippuk ha-nefesh*. I think that I did not recognize the breadth and profundity of the impact which he had on his *talmidim* until I read what some of them wrote to us after his passing (a small selection of those letters appears in a memorial in the 1982 *Masmid*).

Although I had learned with my father from about age six, we had never talked much about teaching, as opposed to learning. But from the time that I began teaching at Yeshiva, about three years before he was *niftar*, we had many conversations about what to teach and how to teach it. I only wish that we had had more such conversations. I remember that when I taught Introduction to Bible for the first time we discussed the potential syllabus in detail, section by section, *mar'eh makom* by *mar'eh makom*, considering the value and potential significance to the student of each one. It was a sort of course that he had never taught, and I was teaching it to students who differed in significant ways from those whom he had taught for most of his academic career, but he tried to look at the issues from my perspective and at the goals which I had set for the course. I know that my students have benefited from the advice that he gave me.

My father's early study of Tanakh was not "literary" in the current usage of the term, but when I returned to Yeshiva to study, and then to teach, Bible, I would share with him regularly ideas about the literary approaches which were then becoming fashionable in biblical studies. Slowly at first, and then more enthusiastically, he began to think about Tanakh in this "new" way, and I remember very clearly his observing that these methodologies were among the things that Rashbam was alluding to when he talked about the *peshatot ha-mithaddeshim be-khol yom* — "the simple interpretations which are innovated daily." He did not believe that *hadash asur be-talmud Torah*, that novel approaches to the study of Torah were automatically forbidden, but that all of them were to be evaluated by rigorous standards. If they passed the test, they were admitted into the arsenal of the student of Torah. Rashbam's words, he felt, were meant to serve as an impetus to creativity in the study of *Torah she-bi-khtav*. Censorship of books, or of ideas, was anathema to him.

The dominant figure at Yeshiva during my father's teaching career was, of course, the Rav, and my father's relationship with him was legendary. He was a little older than the first generation of the Rav's *talmidim*, and about a half a generation younger than the Rav himself. They shared, however, a friendship whose nature I can only begin to imagine. Whence their "closeness" (and that was the Rav's word) stemmed, I don't know, but it was sealed in the 1940s, at a time, as the Rav said in his *hesped* for my father, that my father was willing to sacrifice his professional future and career in defense of the Rav at a time when others would not do so. I saw their interaction only when the Rav would visit my father at home, and retrospectively I would have liked to be a fly on the wall during those conversations. I also don't know what they talked about when they would take long walks down Broadway together as they did occasionally, sharing a little down time away from their *talmidim*. Their friendship, for I can find no other word to describe it, was manifest to all. I think that there were students who drew close to my father as a way of getting closer to the Rav, albeit indirectly, and there were others on whose behalf my father interceded with the Rav when they had incurred his displeasure.

We can see the relationship from the Rav's perspective in a small part of the *hesped* which he delivered at my father's *levaya*. Comparing him to the *ziknei ha-mikra*, he asserted that my father's place was with the generations of R. Saadia Gaon, R. Yonah ibn Jannah, Dunash ben Labrat and Radak. Seeing the role of those *rishonim* as preservers of the unity of *Torah she-bi-khtav* and *Torah she-be-al peh* with their linguistic skills against the attacks of sectarians like the Karaites, the Rav characterized their mission as "a gigantic task." Coining the term "*ish haiyyun*" to describe my father because of his philological acumen and perspicacity, the Rav said "I consider him to some extent as a teacher of mine...he sensitized my mind...he opened up to me another world.... I became more sensitive ...to interpretations by Onkelos that I did not notice before I met Michael Bernstein.... In this regard he was my rebbe, he gave me something which I did not posses prior to my meeting him." Although the Rav focused in these remarks only on a single aspect of my father's talents, it was that feature which attracted him as the *lamdan par excellence*, as the *maggid shi'ur par excellence*, the ability to understand how *derashot Hazal* were often deeply embedded in the language of the biblical text. Calling my father both a *gavra rabba* and a *gavra taqqifa*, he asserted that he was "a great man in many ways." Could anyone have asked for higher praise? But would the Rav have dared say it in his presence when he was alive, knowing that it would have made that humble, unassuming *talmid hakham* and scholar very uncomfortable?

At my father's funeral, R. Macy Gordon, representing my father's many *talmidim*, said that more important than the subject matter that my father taught his students, he taught them "to think, to reason, and to question." I should add that one of the most important lessons which he taught me, both as a teacher and as a scholar, was the ability to say, particularly to a student's question in the classroom, "I don't know, I'll have to look it up." In the student and the *ben Torah*, in the *lamdan* and the scholar, intellectual curiosity, intellectual rigor and intellectual humility have to exist side by side as they did in him. Those simple, yet profound, lessons are a significant and unforgettable piece of the legacy which he bequeathed to all of us who strive to follow in his footsteps, emulating both his efforts and his methods in the study and dissemination of Torah.

Professor Pinkhos Churgin:
A Personal Tribute

By Menachem Bloch

Few in his generation amassed as long a list of outstanding achievements in so many Jewish intellectual and administrative areas as Dr. Pinkhos Churgin (1894-1957), my beloved teacher and mentor.

Pinkhos Churgin was born in Belorussia into a rabbinic family. His father, R. Reuven Yonah, was the rabbi of Pohost, a shtetl near Pinsk. An ardent Zionist, his father decided to leave the secure life in Pohost and immigrate to Jerusalem with his family in around 1906. There, the young Churgin celebrated his Bar Mitzvah and studied in Yeshivat Etz Hayim before he left for study at the famous Volozhin yeshiva in Poland (later Lithuania), where he received his *semikhah* at the age of eighteen. Eager to receive a university education, he left Palestine in 1915 for the United States. He attended Clark College and Yale University, where he earned his PhD in 1922 in the field of Semitics as a student of the famous researcher Charles C. Torrey. His dissertation, "Targum Jonathan to the Prophets," was published by Yale in 1927 and has since become a classic. It was twice reprinted in the 1980s.

Dr. Churgin quickly entered the world of Jewish affairs and Jewish education, even before he received his PhD. Over the years, he published more than 200 articles in Hebrew, Yiddish and English, as well as two

Mr. Menachem Bloch, TA '42, TI '43, YC '47, was the first Registrar (1955-1959) and served as Senior Teacher of English (1970-1994) at Bar-Ilan University.

further books of great importance: *Targum Ketuvim* (1945) and *Mehkarim be-Tekufat Bayit Sheni* (1949). He also founded and edited the semi-annual journal *Horeb* (1936-55), devoted to research in Jewish history. Always concerned with Jewish education, he was an original member of the New York Board of License for Hebrew teachers and founded the *Va'ad ha-Hinukh ha-Haredi*, which later became associated with the Mizrachi Organization of America. He also spearheaded the movement for religious day schools in the U.S. and helped found the Hebrew Teachers Seminary for Girls, later affiliated with Yeshiva as the Teachers Institute for Women. He was active in the Jewish Book Council of America and the Jewish Book Annual, and was co-editor of the Hebrew journal *Bitzaron* (1949-55). Always active in the Mizrachi, he was a delegate to several Zionist congresses as vice-president, and then, in 1949, as its president.

The center of Dr. Churgin's activities for thirty-five years (1920-55) was at Yeshiva College and then what expanded into Yeshiva University. At the end of the second decade of the century, there was still no institution equipped to train qualified, Modern Orthodox Hebrew teachers. Mizrachi undertook the sponsorship of TI, affiliated with RIETS at Montgomery Street on the Lower East Side, to fill the gap. Dr. Churgin became a teacher in the fledgling *beit midrash le-Morim* in 1920. It was an entirely new experiment, and the total number of students was small, recruited from among graduates of Talmud Torahs and the three *yeshivot ketanot*. TI became the first higher school of learning to offer advanced studies in *Gemara*, *Tanakh*, and Hebrew in an *Ivrit be-Ivrit* environment, making its impact felt throughout the Jewish educational world and serving as an impetus to the eventual creation of *yeshivot ketanot* of similar orientation.

The first principal of TI was R. Ya'akov Levenson of Chicago. Dr. Churgin taught *Tanakh*, Jewish History, and Hebrew Grammar. At first TI was under the joint control of Yeshiva and Mizrachi, but this partnership was dissolved in 1921 due to financial difficulties, and full control remained in the hands of Yeshiva, which by this time had moved to 301 East Broadway. Not everyone associated with Yeshiva viewed its association with the Institute favorably, and many begrudged the use of the rooms in the far-from-spacious building for its classes, so that the rest of the *yeshiva* had to make do with minimal space. But Dr. Revel, the head of Yeshiva, lent his unwavering support, and in 1923 Dr. Churgin was appointed principal. At first, there were two classes, which Dr. Churgin gradually subdivided into four, always finding room to absorb in the staff gifted teachers recommended by Dr. Revel. By 1927, there was already a full four-year program of classes. In 1928, Yeshiva moved its headquarters to 186th Street and Amsterdam Avenue and opened its Yeshiva College, steps which enhanced the prestige of the *beit midrash le-Morim* as well, as there no longer was a need to struggle for students. There were already 150 registered students in 1930.

Although the period between 1930 and 1937 was a time of great suffering for everyone on the faculty as a result of the Great Depression, not only did work carry on but progress was made with plans for growth and expansion. The program of studies at TI was lengthened in 1942 to five years, and in 1945 it was extended and became a six-year curriculum. This became possible because of the existence of the college, which enabled the students to pursue their secular training in higher studies in the afternoon hours, as they did in their high school studies (at TA). This extension was vital, because the nature of the student body had been gradually changing. Most of the students in the 1920s were European immigrants, who had a better basis in Jewish studies. Four more years of training were more than sufficient for them to get a rounded and substantial Jewish education and definitely qualified them for teaching, whereas in the 1930s, most of the students were American-born and did not have such a firm basis in Jewish studies; they therefore required more years of study to qualify as teachers.

Dr. Churgin's activities at Yeshiva were not limited to the administration of the Beit Midrash le-Morim. At the request of Dr. Revel, he undertook to plan for the development of graduate studies at Yeshiva College. A special committee was subsequently formed, consisting of Dr. Samuel Belkin, Dr. Moses Isaacs and Dr. Churgin, and changes were made in salaries for the teaching staff, in the curriculum, and in the hours of classes, which were limited to seven in the evening, cutting down from the previous eleven o'clock limit. Eventually, Churgin became Senior Professor of Jewish History and Literature in the graduate school as well.

The death of Dr. Revel in 1940 created a crisis jeopardizing Yeshiva's continued progress. A vigorous attempt was made by the Agudath ha-Rabbanim to wrest control of Yeshiva from its leadership because it bestowed *semikhah*, which they felt should not be in the domain of Yeshiva College. They did not foresee the need for modern Orthodox rabbis who could take their place in the modern synagogues throughout the country. Dr. Churgin was a member of the committee that was appointed to deal with the emergency; it reconstituted itself as the central Board of Directors of the Yeshiva, preventing any takeover. It was decided to have Dr. Isaacs, Dr. Belkin, and Dr. Churgin elevated to the deanship, Dr. Churgin of the *beit midrash le-Morim*, Dr. Samuel Belkin of the Yeshiva, Dr. Isaacs of the College; Dr. Samuel Sar was appointed the Dean of Men. The Executive Board, consisting of the deans and the representatives of the chairmen (R. Joseph Lookstein and R. Leo Jung), and Dr. Churgin played an influential role in the decision to appoint Dr. Belkin as president of Yeshiva. Dr. Churgin remained his chief advisor for many years.

Dr. Churgin's crowning achievement, after more than three decades of service to Yeshiva University as one of its most influential leaders, was founding and serving as first president of Bar-Ilan University of Ramat Gan, Israel, the preparations for which are a remarkable saga in themselves. Before leaving for Israel on March 28, 1955 to take up his new post, Yeshiva University conferred on him the honorary degree of Doctor of Humane Letters. Shortly before this notable event, he delivered the following statement in an interview with Dr. Hyman Grinstein, his successor at TI:

> Bar-Ilan University represents actually an extension of what we were doing in the Yeshiva. We want, through Bar-Ilan University, to train a cultured generation in Israel, intellectual leaders, who at the same time will be based and rooted in Judaism, to guard the coming generations from an annihilating secularism. We believe that Judaism can go hand in hand with science and general culture, and we believe in the strength and the power of Judaism. It has enough strength in itself to not only recreate its past glories but to fashion new glories, and to bring new revelations, spiritual guidance, spiritual light to itself and to the world. And that is mainly the purpose of Bar-Ilan University. Personally, I believe that Bar-Ilan University will not only be a sister institution to Yeshiva University, but — I would not say part of it, because we cannot have a part in Eretz Yisrael — it will become a partner with the Yeshiva and a joiner with the Yeshiva in the great work of bringing about a great renaissance of the Jewish spirit.

Professor Pinkhos Churgin, outstanding figure of vision and practice, of learning and teaching, of planning and execution, an incomparable teacher, a personality distinguished by his personal warmth and magnetism, his love for his fellow-men, his support and encouragement of his many students, will always serve as a model of perseverance, dignity, and selflessness in his devotion to his people, their culture and their destiny.

Rav Moshe Shatzkes:
The Lomzer Rav

By Jonathan Hodes

R. Moshe Shatzkes, commonly known as the Lomzer Rav, was renowned for his scholarship, wit and ability as one of the pre-eminent *roshei yeshiva* of the early post-war period at RIETS. He was a close friend of R. Yitzhak Halevi Herzog, chief rabbi of Israel, and had been one of the *Gedolei ha-Rabbanim* of Poland, a close friend and confidante of both the Hafetz Hayim and R. Hayim Ozer Grodzenski.

R. Shatzkes was born in Vilna in 1882 to a scion of a centuries old rabbinic dynasty. His father, R. Avraham Aharon Shatzkes, was the spiritual leader of Vilna who was known as the *"Illui mi-Zhetel,"* one of the most famous *talmidei hakhamim* in Lita who was reputed to have been *baki* in Shas at the age of seventeen. His mother, Haya Resha, was the daughter of R. Avraham Abba Abelson of Vilna and granddaughter both of R. Hayim Dworetzky, rabbi of Zelve, and R. Yitzhak Sherwinter, *Av Beit Din* of Vilna.

Personal tragedy struck at an early age. R. Moshe's father, R. Avraham Aharon, died when R. Moshe was only three years old. Soon after, at the suggestion of her uncle R. Elya Eliezer Grodzenski (father-in-law of R. Hayim Ozer), R. Moshe's mother married R. Yitzhak Blaser (known as R Itzele Peterburger), one of the main *talmidim* of R. Yisrael

Mr. Jonathan Hodes is a director in the Real Estate tax practice of Deloitte & Touche in London, England. He is married to Karen, daughter of Jerry Shatzkes (YC '67, RIETS '70), son of R. Avraham Aharon Shatzkes (RIETS Rosh Yeshiva from 1944 – 1983) and grandson of R. Moshe Shatzkes.

Salanter. R. Moshe was brought up and educated by R. Itzele and was sent to study at the great Yeshivot of Slabodka and Telz; in 1904, at the age of 22, he received *semikhah* from R. Raphael Shapiro of Volozhin, R. Eliezer Gordon of Telz, and R. Eliezer Rabinowitz of Minsk.

R. Moshe's first appointment upon entering the rabbinate was in Lipnishuk, near Vilna, in 1909. This appointment marked the start of a career in which he excelled as a rabbi, leader, teacher, and friend. The community was immediately taken with him and within five years, in 1914, he was appointed rabbi of the nearby larger town of Ivye, in the district of Vilna.

He was a leader in all aspects of communal life, well known as an outstanding orator, scholar, and halakhic arbitrator. It was in Ivye that he demonstrated his skills in forging relationships with those who were able to make life easier for the community. He formed a cordial relationship with the German Commandant overseeing Ivye, and was thereby able to reverse some of the anti-Semitic decrees in place since World War I, gaining freedom of movement for the residents, and thanks to his efforts permission was granted to open soup kitchens for the poor and needy.

R. Moshe was arrested as a Bolshevik when the Polish army captured Ivye in 1920, but was released thanks to the entreaties of the local priest. This led to his increased standing in the eyes of the occupying forces, and he was able to serve as mediator on behalf of the community. Ultimately, R. Moshe was appointed as Vice Chairman of the *va'ad* that was set up to serve the wider Vilna district to aid refugees affected by the Great War. So began decades of rescue work that was to last until after World War II.

R. Moshe also excelled as a communal fundraiser. He was instrumental in forming a *gemah* for the needy and setting up an orphanage. The *beit midrash* and synagogues that had been destroyed in World War I were rebuilt. He established an educational network for Jewish children from elementary through high school, which gained a reputation as one of the best schools in the whole of Lita. He sought and found common ground with secular Jewish teachers; he understood the spirit of the time and was especially cherished for his rapport with the youth. He had a unique ability to capture the hearts of even the most unaffiliated, and was treated with uncommon *derekh eretz* by a very wide cross-section of the community.

He was also famed for his wit and wisdom, and he was regularly invited by the Hafetz Hayim to important rabbinic gatherings so that the participants could benefit from his teachings. His fame for Torah and wisdom spread throughout Poland through his vice-presidency of the Agudath ha-Rabbanim in Poland, and people turned to R. Moshe from near and far with questions. It is said that he was one of the great "*Meikilim*," using his encyclopedic knowledge of *Yoreh De'ah*, Talmud, and commentators to be lenient whenever possible in order to prevent financial loss to a Jew during those difficult times.

In 1929, a devastating fire consumed almost every building in the town, leaving hundreds of families without a roof over their heads. R. Moshe worked day and night, appealing to Jews throughout Poland and to *landsmen* from Ivye scattered throughout the world, to come to their rescue. Thanks to his efforts, generous help flowed in from Jewish communities around the world and communal institutions, new schools, and a *beit midrash* were rebuilt.

After the fire, he was approached by larger towns to head their communities. However, true to his principles, R. Moshe would not agree to leave his community in such a desolate situation. Within two years, most of Ivye had been rebuilt, and in 1931 he was asked to become *rav* and *Av Beit Din* of Lomza. He had been proposed for the position by his teacher, R. Hayim Ozer Grodzenski, to whom he was very close and who had nicknamed him "*Yismah Moshe*," on account of his sunny disposition.

R. Shatzkes was known for his neutrality, and this was a crucial factor in the ratification of R. Shatzkes by the whole cross-section of the Lomza community. The only dissenters were a group of Alexander Hassidim who opposed his election based on R. Shatzkes's annual subscription to *Keren ha-Yesod*, the implication being that he was a Zionist.

Shortly after his arrival in Lomza, R. Moshe was asked to give a *hesped* after the Hafetz Hayim's death in Elul 1933, both in his capacity as a close friend of the Hafetz Hayim and also as one of the outstanding speakers of the rabbinic world. Similarly, he was one of the *maspidim* at the funeral of R Hayim Ozer Grodzenski in Vilna in 1940. In fact, he was visiting R Hayim Ozer's sickbed with his brother-in-law, R. Hizkiyah Mishkovsky, when R. Hayim Ozer passed away.

R. Shatzkes's time in Lomza was not an easy one. It was marked by anti-Jewish demonstrations, the outlawing of *shehitah,* and a boycott of Jewish shops. Lomza Jews fled in droves, and the community gradually declined. With the Stalin-Hitler pact in August 1939 regarding the division of Poland, Lomza was transferred into Russian hands, and on *Hoshanah*

Rabbah of that year the Soviet tanks rolled into town. Community leaders pleaded with R. Moshe to escape before he would be arrested. R. Moshe was compelled to leave the city and escaped under cover of darkness across the Lithuanian border to Vilna, where he continued his work in relieving the plight of refugees who had assembled there.

Vilna, still neutral at that time, had become a magnet for *yeshivot* that had fled from their home towns. One of the *yeshivot* that had escaped en masse to Vilna was *Yeshivat Sha'ar ha-Torah* of Grodno, headed by R. Shimon Shkop. After the death of R. Shkop, R. Moshe was appointed by R Hayim Ozer Grodzenski to succeed R. Shimon Shkop as *Rosh Yeshiva*.

Apart from serving as the Vice Chairman of the Committee for Refugees, R. Shatzkes was an active leader of the *Va'ad ha-Yeshivot* in Vilna, a role that carried with it the enormous responsibility for the supervision (and financial condition) of the many *yeshivot* in Vilna and the surrounding areas.

After Vilna was captured by the Russians, R. Moshe traveled to Japan via Russia, having received a Japanese permit from Sempo Sugihara, the Japanese temporary consul in Kovno. Arriving in Kobe by boat in May 1941, R. Shatzkes immediately set about continuing his relief efforts for Jews. R. Moshe also worked to build a spiritual life for the almost five thousand refugees in Kobe, amongst them many *roshei yeshiva* and almost the entire Mir Yeshiva, who had fled Poland and Lithuania. He befriended the famous Japanese scholar, Professor Setzuso Kotsuji, a friend of Japan's Minister of Foreign Affairs, and with Kotsuji's assistance he helped thousands of refugees flee.

Owing to his reputation as a brilliant Talmudic scholar and his previous position as *rav* of Lomza, R. Moshe was selected by the refugee community as one of their two representatives (the other being the Amshinover Rebbe), who had been summoned to meet with Japanese government representatives in Tokyo to discuss their plight and to plea to stay in Japan until another place of refuge could be found.

R. Moshe finally reached the United States in 1941. He was immediately appointed a senior *rosh yeshiva* at RIETS. Having turned down the invitation of R. Herzog to join the chief rabbinate in *Eretz Yisrael*, he preferred to devote his time and strength to *harbazat Torah*. R. Moshe remained in this role for the last eighteen years of his life, during which time he also served as a council member of the Agudath ha-Rabbanim of the United States and Canada.

Along with R. Soloveitchik and R. Belkin, R. Shatzkes served as a member of the Rabbinical Ordination Board at RIETS, granting *semikhah* to 425 of its graduates. One recent biographer, Victor Geller, in his *Orthodoxy Awakens*, recalls the informal nature of the oral *semikhah* exams. The set-up invited distraction, with R. Soloveitchik and R. Shatzkes often ignoring the bewildered student and engaging in their own spirited, scholarly exchange, with R. Belkin often having to bring them back to the business at hand.

R. Moshe's wonderful sense of humor is manifested by one of the most famous stories about him, a story related by Yeshiva Chancellor Norman Lamm, who was in R. Shatzkes's class at the time. R. Shatzkes would usually look down the list of the names of his students and then at random would ask one student to read the day's *daf*. The students always assumed he didn't know the boys. One day, looking down the list, R. Moshe said, "Ok, Shapiro, *zug* the *Gemara* [say the *Gemara*]." Shapiro, who hadn't had time to prepare properly, piped up, "*Shapiro is nisht du* [Shapiro is not here]." R. Shatzkes looked up from his *Gemara* and with a twinkle in his eyes said to the trembling Shapiro, "OK, *du zog* [OK, you read]!" As you can imagine, the entire class fell to the floor in laughter.

After R. Shatzkes's death in 1959, the Kollel Rabbeinu Moshe Shatzkes was formed as a lasting memorial in Israel at Kfar Hassidim. It was attached to Yeshivat Kenesset Hizkiyahu, named after R. Moshe's brother-in-law, R. Hizkiyahu Yosef Mishkovsky, *Av Beit Din* of Krinki.

R. Moshe wrote many responsa and *hiddushim* on a plethora of subjects. Our tragedy is that the vast majority were destroyed when he left Poland in 1940 — indeed R. Moshe often said that his greatest loss in his lifetime of tragic misadventure was the loss of his writings, a loss from which he never truly recovered. His vast library of *seforim* was buried in the forests of Lomza for safekeeping before he left Poland and has never been recovered.

R. Shatzkes passed away in December 1959 (18 Tevet), at the age of 77. A crowd of more than two thousand gathered in the Lamport Auditorium of Yeshiva University as a final mark of respect to a person the Yeshiva press release referred to as one of the greatest rabbis and *roshei yeshiva* of the generation.

The *maspidim* included R. Samuel Belkin and R. Joseph Ber Soloveitchik, as well as R. David Lifshitz representing the Agudath ha-Rabbanim. From Yeshiva University, R. Shatzkes's body was taken to

Yeshivat Tifereth Yerushalayim, where the *maspidim* included R. Moshe Feinstein, R. Yosef Eliyahu Henkin, and R. Avraham Kalmanowitz. A large crowd of mourners headed by R. Aharon Kotler also gathered at the New Jersey airport, from where R. Moshe Shatzkes was taken to his final resting place on *Har ha-Menuhot* in Jerusalem. His funeral was attended by chief rabbis, Israeli *roshei yeshiva* and members of the Israeli Knesset.

Rabbi Shlomo Polachek:
The Unassuming *Illui* of Maichat

By Nathan Kamenetsky

In 1923, an attempt was made by R. Yehuda Levenberg to found a European-style yeshiva on the American shores, the Yeshiva of New Haven. But a year earlier, R. Dr. Bernard Revel, president of RIETS and later of Yeshiva College, had already brought over a prominent European *rosh yeshiva* to teach the highest class at the seminary. He was R. Shlomo Polachek, known as the *illui* of Maichat, favorite disciple of the master who had revolutionized the method of Talmud study in the *yeshiva* of Volozhin, R. Hayim Soloveichik. R. Shlomo had studied under R. Hayim for a total of over six years, from the fall of 1889 until the spring of 1896 — during the last two years of the Volozhin Yeshiva's existence and afterwards when R. Hayim served as rabbi of Brisk.

Before describing R. Polachek, let us define Dr. Revel's intention in bringing this great scholar to RIETS. Dr. Revel had an ambition: he believed that the Torah of Eastern Europe could be propagated in America, and he hoped to be the one to bring it about. Although there had been a tradition handed down by R. Hayim Yitzhakin (Volozhiner), who had died in 1821, that someday Russia would cease to be the world's Torah center and Torah would then wander across the Atlantic to America, there had been no conscious effort to transplant Torah to the New World until after the First World War. To be sure, there were European-

Rabbi Nathan Kamenetsky is a son and a son-in-law, respectively, of the late Torah sages R. Jacob Kamenecki of Mesivta Torah Vodaath, and R. David Lifshitz of RIETS. He has lived in Jerusalem since 1968 and is the author of the much-talked-about book about historical yeshiva figures, Making of a Godol.

trained rabbis in many cities on the North American continent who were great in knowledge, even before the war; they had come to America as individuals seeking safety or a livelihood. There had indeed been cases in which American congregations needed to infuse into their community the spiritual leadership that was available only in Europe — the bringing of R. Jacob Joseph from Vilna to head a short-lived union of New York congregations is an example of one of these situations. But neither the arrival of *gedolei Torah* to America on their own volition, nor the importation of great rabbinic figures to fill America's religious needs, was motivated by the desire to transfer Torah to a new home. Contrariwise, bringing into RIETS a man of R. Polachek's erudition was not to fill a need, for the level of knowledge that Yeshiva's students of that era had reached was much below the Torah plateau on which the Maichater *Illui* functioned; he could not be expected to create *talmidim* at RIETS — and Dr. Revel surely knew it.

It is interesting to note that when the Maichater's successor at RIETS, R. Shimon Shkop, an aged European trailblazer in the modern method of Talmud study, took over the post, he felt that he needed to bring to Yeshiva some of his former students at Grodno, Poland, in order to create a group which would understand his *shi'urim*. He invited students who were then still residing in Europe or had gone to Palestine to come to the United States to continue studying under him. Declaring, "Europe is *oisgespielt* [played out]!" he wanted to remain in America, but knew that the students present at RIETS were generally too weak scholastically to benefit from his tutelage. In fact, four of R. Shimon's former *talmidim* arrived from Palestine and three from Europe, and they were the mainstay of his class in RIETS.

The purpose of bringing the Maichater *Illui* to RIETS was a conscious effort by Dr. Revel to implant Torah in a new home, the United States. This 1922 act is not to be confused with what the founders of the Yeshiva of New Haven did a year later. There was a basic difference in the philosophies of R. Levenberg and Dr. Revel: the yeshiva that the former envisioned was totally European, effectively creating an extraterritorial locus on the new continent and reshaping a piece of America into a European entity; the latter was doing the very opposite, transplanting a chunk of Russian Torah onto the American environment — effectively a step in actuating the prognosis of R. Hayim of Volozhin.

When R. Eliezer Yehuda Finkel, a friend of the Maichater from the time they both sat at the feet of R. Hayim Soloveichik in Brisk, visited R. Polachek during a 1926 fundraising trip to the United States, R. Finkel told his host that R. Polachek had erred in leaving Europe because he could have been one of the most prominent *roshei yeshiva* there. R. Polachek replied that had he been a European *rosh yeshiva* he would also be in America now — just as his interlocutor, the *Rosh Yeshiva* of the Mirrer Yeshiva in Poland, was. Aside from seeing the Maichater's sharp retort as a sample of his *illuyus*, it is worthwhile analyzing the verbal exchange between the two Torah leaders. R. Finkel thought that the Maichater would not be utilized, nor appreciated, by the students in RIETS or by any *yeshiva* in America — so why did he leave Europe? R. Polachek answered that since Torah could no longer be supported physically in Russia (and in Poland, which had been Russia before the world war), Torah must already be seen as in a state of transition; Torah was on its way to America, and that is why he was there. The Maichater saw in the financial situation of the European yeshivot the beginning of the realization of the "prophecy" of R. Hayim Volozhiner.

Dr. Revel's attempt to bring Torah to America did not just begin with the hiring of R. Polachek. Four years prior, in 1918, RIETS was already busy trying to transfer the Torah center from Russia to America. As a result of the destruction wrought by the war, Vilna was thought to no longer be able to maintain its position as the publication hub of the Torah world, and a plan was drawn up by Dr. Revel for a joint venture together with the *Agudat ha-Rabbanim* to republish the Talmud in North America. The participation of RIETS in this project did not materialize because it was nixed by Yeshiva's Board of Directors; but Dr. Revel had tried. If he failed with the newly printed Talmud, he succeeded in bringing the "walking Talmud," R. Polachek, to America. Like the exiles at the time of the Second Temple's destruction who brought stones from the holy Temple to Babylonia to erect a place of Torah there, this visionary pictured the *Illui* as a cornerstone in the erection of the Torah structure in its new home. In 1928, the year R. Polachek died and RIETS moved from the Lower East Side of Manhattan to its present magnificent building uptown, R. Shimon Sivitz, rabbi of Pittsburgh since 1888 — a native of Tzitevian, Lithuania, where the author of this article was born seven decades after R. Shimon — wrote to Dr. Revel, "The first time I met you, I knew that... you were an angel sent by God to bring Torah... to the United States."

Who was R. Shlomo Polachek? Born at the end of 1877, this genius was discovered by a Volozhin Yeshiva student, Aaron Rabinowitz, on a farm near the town of Maichat shortly before his twelfth birthday. Aaron convinced the slight and bashful boy to accompany him to the Volozhin Yeshiva, and introduced him to the *Rosh Yeshiva*, R. Naftali Tzvi Yehuda Berlin, as a candidate for enrollment in the *yeshiva*. Surprised that Rabinowitz had brought a mere child to his world-class *yeshiva* which students usually joined at sixteen or seventeen, R. Berlin made a dig at Rabinowitz and said, "Why didn't you bring his crib along?!" Aaron replied, "Let the *Rosh Yeshiva* test him and decide what size crib he needs." As the brilliant Torah flashes flitted back and forth between the little boy and the wizened sage, the assistant *rosh yeshiva* R. Hayim Soloveichik, entered the room and joined in. R. Soloveichik then brought the entrance test to a close by asking Shlomo where he was from, and when he received the reply, "From Maichat," R. Hayim announced: "Then you are the Maichater *Illui*." The epithet stuck to R. Polachek throughout his lifetime; even his posthumously published *sefer* of *hiddushei Torah* was named *Hiddushei ha-Illui mi-Maichat*."

Upon his acceptance to the Volozhin Yeshiva, R. Hayim ordered him to cover ten pages of *Gemara* daily, and his roommates were assigned by the master to discuss with him each night before retiring the pages he had gone through that day. R. Soloveichik himself would test the lad for several hours weekly, on Friday nights. His peers at Volozhin could keep pace with the *illui* for not longer that an hour-and-a-half at a stretch, and Shlomo had to spend his eighteen-hour study day with twelve different study partners. His lightning-quick grasp and phenomenal memory made him the wonder of the *yeshiva*, but he remained as humble and unassuming as on the farm. When he became bar mitzvah, the Netziv made a festive breakfast in his honor one Friday morning — "possibly the first time the Volozhin Yeshiva celebrated a bar mitzvah of a student," according to the memoir of the Netziv's son — at which the youngster delivered his own *pilpul* in a demure fashion… and burst out crying.

When the Volozhin Yeshiva closed down in the winter of 1892, Shlomo Polachek spent a short time studying on his own in Minsk, the synagogues of which housed Torah students of various levels — he later recalled how hurt he had been when, in an effort to weed out irreligious elements among the students, he was asked by the rabbi to show that he was wearing *tzitzit* — but as soon as R. Hayim Soloveichik was appointed rabbi of Brisk, he invited his favorite student to join him there. Whenever a rabbinical guest visited the city, R. Hayim would proudly have him "speak in learning" with his student, despite Shlomo's personal distaste for flaunting his knowledge. He was especially loved by R. Hayim because their basic characters were similar; both were self-effacing and extremely sensitive to people's suffering. It is said that when Shlomo was in Volozhin, he would bring several shirts with him at the beginning of each semester, but never returned home with more than one; he had given the others away to students needier than himself. R. Hayim was, of course, carried away by the Maichater's unique cerebral powers, and was to say in later years that in all his life, he had never met as extraordinary a genius as R. Shlomo.

In the spring of 1896, eighteen-year-old Shlomo Polachek was convinced by his fellow student Eliezer Yehuda Finkel to leave Brisk for the famous Mussar yeshiva in Slabodka run by the latter's father, R. Nathan Tzvi Finkel. But the teenager did not take to the Mussar philosophy — not even after spending the month of Elul in Kelm in the proximity of R. Yisrael Salanter's prime disciple, R. Simhah-Zissel Ziv. After the disappointing Mussar experience, Shlomo continued his studies in the "*kibbuz*" (study group) operated by R. Hayim Ozer Grodzenski in Vilna. While learning Torah in that secular city, the young genius was introduced to the world of higher mathematics and Russian literature and developed an auxiliary lifetime interest in these subjects. He then married a wealthy young woman from the town of Ivenitz and tried his hand at business. After failing the profane venture, he returned to his holy studies in Vilna, from where he was invited in 1905 to head the Zionist Lida Yeshiva by its founder, R. Yitzhak Ya'akov Reines, rabbi of Lida and initiator of the Mizrachi movement. R. Shlomo stayed at this post until the outbreak of World War I; Lida turned out to be the locus where he remained for the longest duration in his lifetime. It is worth noting that despite R. Hayim Soloveichik's strong opposition to Zionism, his admiration for R. Polachek was undiminished by the latter's career choice.

The war saw R. Shlomo and his family exiled to deep Russia, wandering from place to place. One of his stations was Yelisovietgrad (renamed Kirovograd after the Communist Revolution), where he served as head of a small *yeshiva*. Another of his stops was Kremenchug, where several exiled Lithuanian *yeshivot* were located at the time. He lived through the battles of the Whites and Reds and the pogroms which killed an estimated 100,000 Jews in the Ukraine. He was finally repatriated in Bialystok, Poland in 1921, and he served as a lecturer in its Tachkemoni School for a year. R. Shlomo, always immersed in deep thought, did not commit his lectures to paper, but his *talmidim* in Lida would write down the *shi'urim* he delivered and give him a copy; the valise laden with the manuscripts was stolen during his wanderings in Russia, and he mourned this loss till the end of his life.

His final destination was RIETS, where he delivered his *shi'urim* four to five times weekly. He was also a distinguished member of the *Agudat ha-Rabbanim*, and his presence highlighted its conventions. He was active in raising funds for the assistance of destitute rabbis in Europe through the Ezras Torah organization, and he was a member of Mizrachi. When he once expressed his wish to go to Palestine and become "a *Gemara* teacher" there, but stated humbly that he did not know Hebrew well enough, someone remarked, "How can you judge what you know and what you don't know? You believe that you don't know how to learn [Torah], either!" Devoted to his *rebbe* until his own death, the Maichater was involved, together with several other great European and American scholars, in urging the children of R. Hayim Soloveichik to publish the master's *hiddushei Torah*. The volume "*Hiddushei Rabbenu Hayim ha-Levi*" finally saw the light almost two decades after the 1918 death of R. Hayim. Similarly, the Maichater's *hiddushei Torah* — gleaned by his survivors from the writings of his students both in Europe and in the United States — did not see the light until 1947, nineteen years after his demise.

The Maichater *Illui* was only fifty years old when he was summoned to the Yeshiva on high. In memoriam, RIETS published a gazette called "*Eideinu* [Our Tragedy]" mourning his loss to Yeshiva and the entire Torah world. No person could meet R. Shlomo Polachek and not be overwhelmed by his genius; the only one who did not comprehend his brilliance was the Maichater *Illui* himself. For as great as he was in Torah, he was equally great in character refinement.

A Glimpse at *Tziddkut:*
A Look at Rabbi Shlomo Drillman

By Benjamin G. Kelsen

How does one sum up or describe the life of an individual like R. Shlomo Elimelech Drillman in but a few pages? Were I to write five hundred pages, even a thousand, it would still be insufficient; I would still not be able to touch upon even the most simple description of the many events of note that occurred in R. Drillman's life, or reveal even a glimpse of his *gadlut* and *tziddkut*. Still, I will try, with a heavy heart and tears in my eyes, to make, what I assure you, is an inadequate and incomplete attempt in these few meager paragraphs to give a sense of this tremendous individual whom I am privileged to call *rebbe*.

R. Drillman's life was one that brought him into contact with, and placed him in the forefront of, so many of the historical events of the last eighty years. I remember how he told of his trips to Washington and his meeting Prime Minister Menachem Begin and Albert Einstein, as well as his experiences in the darkness of the Holocaust (several of which are recounted in Dr. Yaffa Eliach's *Hasidic Tales of the Holocaust*). I remember clearly how R. Drillman would tell over the story of how he became a student of R. Elchanan Wasserman, of his walks to the Hudson River with R. Joseph B. Soloveitchik, late at night, after *seder* was over. I remember how he related with such pride the time that he was given the privilege of accompanying his *rebbe* to the home of the famed *rav* of Vilna, R. Hayim

Rabbi Benjamin G. Kelsen, Esq., YC '94, Cardozo '97, RIETS '00, is a practicing attorney, noted speaker and lecturer, and author of The Wisdom of Solomon *and the forthcoming* From the Fruit of the Vine, *a conspectus of the sermons of Rabbi Chaim Yaakov Goldvicht, Rosh Yeshiva, Yeshivat Kerem B'Yavneh.*

Ozer Grodzenski, to visit with R. Grodzenski and R. Aharon Kotler.

I remember as though it were yesterday the story R. Drillman would tell us every year on *Pareshat Zakhor* of R. Elchanan's experience with a *dybbuk* in the late 1920s. When the story of R. Elchanan's death was related each year on the anniversary of his murder, R. Drillman would have tears in eyes as he would tell of R. Elchanan's last statements, and, invariably, the listeners would weep as well, because each of these stories were told in such a way that the listener could almost imagine themselves being transported into the actual events.

R. Drillman was a person for whom truth was the yardstick by which he would measure everything. A statement would never be made, a *sevarah* never suggested, a *hiddush* never put forth, unless it could be said that it was truthful. "*Emet atah hu rishon…*" he would tell me. I remember one time in the *shi'ur*, a moment of which I am still very proud, that I had suggested that perhaps we could understand a particular *aharon* in a certain way based upon a statement made in another *masekhta*. R. Drillman paused thoughtfully for a few moments and then began to nod his head slowly.

"I don't know if what you are saying is correct," he said, "because we can never know for sure what was in the mind of a person who is no longer with us. However, what you are saying seems *emesdik*."

I was puzzled by the use of this term until R. Drillman explained that too often suggestions are made that do not fit in with the facts as we know them, that people sometimes try to read things into the text that do not fit in with the facts. Such a *hiddush* was not "*emesdik*."

Those who were present at R. Drillman's eulogy for his *rebbe*, R. Joseph B. Soloveitchik, will remember a different facet to his pursuit of the truth when he became infuriated by those who pervert the teachings of the Rav for their own agendas, on either side of the spectrum. To attempt to usurp the Rav's legacy for one's own agenda was both unfathomable and repugnant to R. Drillman. In his eyes, one had to remain committed to truth even if it meant rejecting a particular outlook that was personally appealing.

However, R. Drillman was much more than simply an excellent story teller or a seeker of truth. He was an individual for whom the teaching of Torah was of primary importance, for whom being a teacher was everything. What is it that made him unique as a *rebbe*? What is it that made R. Drillman stand out among so many other *gedolim*?

R. Shlomo Elimelech Drillman, born in a small town in Germany, was a prodigy whose brilliance was discovered by the great R. Elchanan Wasserman, who brought him to his *yeshiva* at the age of twelve. R. Drillman became quite close with R. Wasserman, and the *mashgiah* at the *yeshiva*, R. Yisrael Ya'akov Lupchenski, and even lived in the *rosh yeshiva*'s home for several years. Several lifelong friends were made in Baranovich, among them R. Shmuel Birnbaum, the Mirrer *rosh yeshiva*. Shortly before the outbreak of the Second World War, R. Drillman went to learn with R. Baruch Ber Leibovitz in Kaminetz and remained there until the beginning of World War II. At the onset of the war, the Drillman family fled to Siberia, where they remained until the end of the war.

In 1946, R. Drillman came to the United States with his mother and siblings, and was reunited with his father, a *rebbe* in Yeshiva Torah Vodaath, who had come to the United States before the war. Upon his arrival, R. Drillman presented himself to R. Joseph B. Soloveitchik at Yeshiva University with a letter of recommendation from R. Elchanan Wasserman. He was immediately accepted into Yeshiva. Upon receiving *semikhah* from RIETS, he was appointed as a rebbe at BTA, the Brooklyn division of Yeshiva's high school. When BTA closed its doors, he was appointed as a *rosh yeshiva* at RIETS, where he remained until his first stroke, shortly after Sukkot 1997.

At RIETS, R. Drillman was the director of the fourth year *Halakha le-Ma'aseh* program, meeting every single one of his *semikhah* students and thereby touching the hearts of an amazing amount of people. R. Drillman was known for his tremendous intellect, spanning all walks of secular knowledge, in addition to his incredibly vast encyclopedic breadth of Torah knowledge. In addition to his intellect, R. Drillman was famous for the warmth he exuded towards those people with whom he came in contact.

I believe that R. Drillman's uniqueness was the way in which he became an absolute part of the lives of his students. This can be seen in the first real conversation that I had with him, one which I will never forget. It was the third day of the *zeman* in *Elul* of 5750 (Fall 1991), and I had started in the *shi'ur* two days before, having just returned from learning in Yeshivat Kerem B'Yavneh in Israel. I was having difficulty finding a *havrutah*. I had a friend in another *shi'ur* and I thought that perhaps I would switch *shi'urim* in order to learn with my friend. I went into R. Drillman's office in Furst Hall at approximately 10:00 a.m. that morning and said that I wanted to tell the *rebbe* that I would be switching out of his *shi'ur*. When he asked me why, I told him that I could not find a *havrutah* for the morning *seder*.

"Pull up that chair," he said, motioning to one of the empty chairs in his office.

"With all due respect to the *rebbe*," I responded, "I don't want to discuss the issue, I simply wanted to inform the *rebbe* myself of my plans."

"Who wants to discuss anything?" he said with that famous twinkle in his eye and that mock frown that quickly transformed into a beautiful smile on his face. "We have a lot of *mareih mekomos* to go through and not much time. Now, sit down and let's get started."

I was fortunate enough to spend the next six years learning with R. Drillman, privately, in his office. It was there that I was given the opportunity to get a glimpse into the nature of this person, this man who had dedicated his life to spreading Torah.

R. Drillman taught me to be an *ohev Yisrael*. He loved all Jews, regardless of their background or current level of observance. If he disagreed with someone or felt that there was something wrong with someone, his criticism always included at least one positive comment. "There are very few people who are truly all bad, so always look for the good in them, especially if you think that you see the bad," he taught me. In this he was a great role model. He was one of the first *rabbanim* to venture into the Flatbush section of Brooklyn in the late 1940s, when it was not considered a place for *benei Torah*. Dozens of shuls, *yeshivot*, *hessed* organizations, *mikva'ot*, and restaurants can be found in thriving Jewish community of the Flatbush that we all know today. What most people do not realize is that Flatbush might not be what it is today had it not been for the efforts of R. Drillman and his wife. In addition to his role at RIETS, he served as the rabbi and spiritual guide of the Glenwood Jewish Center, one of the first Orthodox synagogues in Flatbush, for almost forty years.

During *shivah*, countless people came to the Drillman home, each with a special relationship with R. Drillman that made them feel as though they we were truly important to him. Whether it was R. Shmuel Birnbaum, the Mirrer *rosh yeshiva*, who was R. Drillman's roommate and *havrutah* in Yeshivot Ohel Torah in Baranovich, or the doctor who was unaffiliated before R. Drillman took him under his wing (he is now observant and learned) — each had a story or *devar Torah*, each had been made to feel unique and special, and each felt a deep connection to R. Drillman.

After his family, which was of the utmost importance to him and of which he was so proud, came his *talmidim* and colleagues at Yeshiva. Those with whom he attended Yeshiva University and RIETS, with whom he learned in the Rav's *shi'ur*, and with whom he taught for the five decades during which he was associated with Yeshiva had a special place in his heart. When I would visit with him on Sundays and Wednesdays after the onset of his illness, he would always send me back to Yeshiva with regards to his many friends and colleagues.

R. Drillman was always very careful to make sure that I would go to R. Norman Lamm's office before the *Yamim Tovim* to give his regards. Despite my assurances that I would do so, he would call me at home the next day to make sure that I had transmitted the message exactly as he had given it to me. "But did you also wish Gladys [Chernin, R. Lamm's secretary] a *gut Yom Tov?*" He would demand. "Of course, Rebbe," I would tell him. Only then would he be satisfied.

Perhaps one of the most important lessons that I learned from R. Drillman was the concept of *kavod ha-Torah* and *kibud rav*. R. Drillman was fiercely dedicated to the honor and memory of his *rebbeim* and the Torah that they loved. Once, behind the closed door of his office while I waited in the hall, he chastised a well known rabbi for not visiting his *rebbe*, who was ill. "Everything you are, you owe to him! Everything that is yours is his! How can you not go?"

To understand the trauma of losing one's *rebbe* one need only speak to the *talmidim* of R. Drillman. "I have lost a father," one of my friends wrote to me after the funeral. The challenge to all of us is to ensure that R. Drillman's memory not be forgotten in our Yeshiva, that we not forget this giant who spent nearly fifty years in our *beit midrash*, that the sound of the *teki'ah* that he sounded on Rosh Hashanah every year from his retirement from his shul until his illness inspire us to fulfill and carry out his legacy, to strive for perfection in ourselves and our learning.

Years of Study, Years of Growth

By Earl Klein

My four years at YC, 1943-1947, were a defining period in my life. During those years I gathered the resources and established a course of action that directed my life. I wanted to attend Yeshiva because I wanted to function and be educated in an Orthodox atmosphere, and I wanted to continue my Talmudic studies. I came to Yeshiva from Los Angeles, where young Orthodox people were few. All of us who were observant and of high school age knew each other. I had attended Hollywood High School, where more non-Jews were absent on Rosh Hashanah and Yom Kippur because of studio work than Jews who were observing the holy days. In those days, many Jews would not acknowledge their Jewishness.

When I arrived at Yeshiva, it was a school in transition and poised for growth. The institution had earlier lost two prominent leaders, YC's first president, Dr. Bernard Revel, and R. Moshe Soloveichik, *Rosh Yeshiva* at RIETS and father of the illustrious R. Joseph B. Soloveitchik. Dr. Samuel Belkin was chosen as president in 1943 to fill Revel's post, and R. Joseph B. Soloveitchik took his father's *shi'ur*. Dr. Belkin had previously been a *rosh yeshiva* at RIETS, taught Greek in YC, and was an outstanding scholar. He made it his business to know every student in the school. I recall that when I was a senior, he called in every graduate and took an interest in each one's plans for the future. He often said he wanted the

The late Hon. Earl Klein, YC'47, was a California Administrative Law Judge for over thirty years. He was the author of five books on Jewish prayer, most recently Sabbath Prayer: Concepts and Customs published shortly before he passed away on December 23, 2005. He was buried in the Yeshiva University section of the Eretz ha-Hayim cemetery overlooking the hills of Jerusalem.

school to produce the "Yeshiva Man," a special kind of personality who would be recognizable as a product of YC.

California had furnished only a few students for YC up to that point. It was in those days a three-day trip to New York by train. I was not entirely prepared to compete with other students, especially with the New Yorkers, who had passed Regents Exams. Yeshiva requirements were demanding, and I am grateful for that. I was also not sure what studies I wished to pursue. One early subject that fascinated me was a "Survey of English Literature" course taught by a new professor, Dr. David Fleisher. I enjoyed his classes so much that I decided to major in English Literature. I took his classes in the Romantic poets, Victorian poets, and Milton's *Paradise Lost.*

I also took courses in Shakespeare with Professor David Klein. One of the stars in our class was Carmi Charney, who later, under the name T. Carmi, became a leading Israeli poet. He worked on Hebrew translations of Shakespeare and also edited and translated *The Penguin Book of Hebrew Verse.*

One of the most popular professors was Dr. Alexander Litman, who taught philosophy. He had a wonderful, although sarcastic, sense of humor and he bombarded us with teachings of the great philosophers and his own brand of philosophy. The class discussions were lively. When the students got out of hand, he would attempt to bring order by exclaiming, "You know I have a theory that in Egypt, the Jews were oppressing the Egyptians and not the other way around. Because Jews [he would say glancing around the classroom] can be very oppressive." Once, an unsuspecting student entered class with a Modern Library edition of Plato's *Republic.* Professor Litman, in mock horror, demanded: "Are you reading Plato in English?"

I took a course in *Tehillim* with Dr. Samuel Mirsky, a brilliant scholar. He taught me something that I have never forgotten. When we came to Psalm 118 (part of *Hallel*), his focus was on verse 17: "I shall not die, but live." That, he used to say, was the motto of the Jewish people.

There were numerous other outstanding members of the faculty, such as R. Leo Jung, who taught Jewish Philosophy, and R. Joseph H. Lookstein, who taught Jewish Sociology. R. Jung and R. Lookstein were associated with influential Orthodox congregations in Manhattan, and many of their congregants were major supporters of RIETS and YC. They were models for the younger generation of American Orthodox rabbis.

In 1922, R. Jung became rabbi of The Jewish Center on the Upper West Side of Manhattan, where he replaced R. Mordecai M. Kaplan, whose religious views did not comport with Orthodox tradition. His father, R. Meir Tzvi Jung, had been a rabbinical leader in London. In addition to his graduate degrees from renowned European universities, R. Leo Jung had three rabbinic ordinations, from R. Mordecai Schwartz, in London, from the chief rabbi of Palestine, R. Abraham Isaac Kook, who had taken a temporary position in London during World War I, and from R. David Tzvi Hoffmann of the Hildesheimer Rabbinical Seminary in Berlin. As a noted speaker and spokesman for Orthodox Judaism, R. Jung was a prolific writer and editor. He edited eight volumes entitled "The Jewish Library," starting in 1928, and he started teaching Jewish Philosophy and Ethics at YC in 1931. In discussing the rabbinate, he once said, "After the services, no one remembers what the rabbi said, but they will comment on whether he spoke well or not."

R. Jung was a friend of the famous author Herman Wouk. Wouk wrote that he had heard a sermon by the rabbi on Yom Kippur in 1937 that inspired him spiritually, and they soon thereafter developed a friendship during which they had many discussions about Orthodox practice. Wouk later said that R. Jung planted a thought in his mind, which grew in time to be his 1959 best-selling book *This is My God*.

R. Joseph Lookstein was rabbi of Congregation Kehilath Jeshurun, on the Upper East Side of Manhattan, and was a brilliant orator. R. Lookstein had founded Ramaz Academy in 1936 and was its principal for many years. He was also active in the establishment of Bar-Ilan University, along with Dr. Pinkhos Churgin, dean of Yeshiva's Teachers Institute. In 1957, R. Lookstein was appointed chancellor of Bar-Ilan University.

I will never forget R. Lookstein's eulogy of President Franklin Delano Roosevelt, a polio victim, who died on April 12, 1945 shortly before the Allied victory in Europe. It was delivered over the radio and later given at Yeshiva. FDR had led the country through the deep depression of the 30s and 40s, established many social programs to benefit Americans, and was also the great Commander-in-Chief during World War II. As best as I can recall, R. Lookstein said, "The man who could not walk showed us progress and how to move forward." Then, referring to the *Ma'ariv* prayers, he described President Roosevelt as a "*meshanneh ittim u-mahalif et ha-zemannim* [one who alters periods and changes the seasons]." He ended with a recitation of "O Captain, My Captain," a poem composed by Walt Whitman upon the death of Abraham Lincoln. There was not a dry eye in the packed Lamport Auditorium.

Another man of outstanding credentials was R. Emanuel Rackman. He returned from military service in the mid-1940s. I took his course in Jurisprudence. R. Rackman later became a vice president of Yeshiva, and eventually chancellor of Bar-Ilan University.

Yeshiva achieved university status in 1945. There was a special convocation, where an honorary degree was conferred upon Chief Justice Harlan Fiske Stone of the United States Supreme Court, who delivered an address. One thing that he said was engraved on my mind: "A college degree is a symbol, and man lives by symbols."

I often think about the essay, "The Idea of a University" by Cardinal John Henry Newman, that we read in English Literature. One of the points Newman made was that there is much to be learned beyond the course subjects. There are personal associations with faculty and students and the opportunity to hear words of wisdom from those we come in contact with.

In my senior year, I served as Student Body president. I prevailed upon the school and my fellow students to join intercollegiate student groups so as to broaden our relationships and gain recognition for the school. Dean Moses Isaacs was very supportive.

I must mention one of the most meaningful events I experienced at Yeshiva, hearing a lecture by R. Joseph B. Soloveitchik entitled "Sacred and Profane" in 1945. It was his custom to deliver a lecture on the occasion of his father's *yahrzeit*. He spoke for four hours to a rapt audience. He spoke of many things, but what remained in my thoughts from that evening on was the idea that Jewish religion does not necessarily purport to solve all problems of life, but it most certainly teaches a means whereby man can learn to cope with his problems.

With the education I received at Yeshiva, I always felt I was able to hold my own with graduates of other schools. Following my graduation from Yeshiva, I decided to go into journalism. My first job was at the Chicago bureau of Time and Life magazines, where I remained for twelve years. I returned to Los Angeles in 1951 and worked as a reporter and editor at legal newspapers while I continued to serve as a string correspondent for Time and Life publications. YC was good to me, and I will always be grateful.

Revel's Harmony:
Both "The Yeshiva" and "Yeshiva College"

By Will Lee

A pivotal figure in the preservation and growth of "Torah-true" Judaism in America and arguably the most significant educational leader of what would later be called Modern Orthodoxy, Dr. Bernard Revel founded the first *yeshiva* high school, advocated the major *yeshiva* day school movement that flowered long after he died, founded the small graduate school of Jewish Studies that later expanded and now bears his name, and founded Yeshiva College, the first college in America under traditional Jewish auspices. Throughout his career he envisioned, preached, and actively furthered the preservation, enhancement, and expansion of Eastern European Judaism. He argued for adapting it to the new world without compromising traditional values based on *halakhah*. The quest to understand the vision and motivations behind Revel's founding of three crucial educational institutions has led me to search through Yeshiva's archives for evidence in his writings, addresses, drafts, typescripts, and correspondence. In delving into these primary sources, I am pursuing my long-standing interest in, and hoping to deepen my understanding of, the blending of Jewish and secular education for which Revel was originally responsible. On the basis of my research, I have come to see Revel as a

Dr. Will Lee is an associate professor of English and director of the Jay and Jeanie Schottenstein Honors Program at Yeshiva College. The author expresses thanks to Dean of Libraries Pearl Berger, Curator of Special Collections Shulamith Z. Berger, and the authors of books featuring Revel: Gilbert Klaperman, Aaron Rothkoff, and Jeffrey S. Gurock. Comments by Profs. Alan Brill, Shalom Carmy, and Jeffrey S. Gurock have greatly benefited this article.

scholar and thinker who genuinely believed in the harmony of religious and secular wisdom.

Repeatedly in this essay, I emphasize Revel's choices of words, metaphors, and formulations because they reflect his thinking. In this age of press releases and PR, it's important to emphasize that Revel carefully wrote and revised all his own articles and speeches, starting with a draft manuscript that was then typed up. He would add hand-written revisions that would then be incorporated into a revised typescript, which he would then further revise until the process produced a clean final version. A remarkably consistent thinker and leader, Revel was nonetheless constantly striving to improve his positions, his strategies, and his choices of words.

Not only Revel's public addresses, correspondence, and proposals but his modes of thinking and his very language confidently exemplified the harmony he advocated. He spoke of "A harmonious union of culture and spirituality." "Educating both liberally and Jewishly"; "Education for the Jewish heart and will and mind"; "Spirituality and intellectual power"; "Faith and truth"; "Israel's Seers and Sages and modern thinkers"; "[I]nstitutions of light and learning"; "[O]ur spiritual, cultural, and scientific centers, sanctuaries of light, reason, and vision"; "[The] absolute unity of God and the essential unity of man." Revel originated "synthesis," "unification," and "integration," but he favored "harmony" as the best way of characterizing the ideal overarching relationship between the Yeshiva and the new college he had founded. He wanted each student, for instance, to develop "a harmonious Jewish personality."Only one qualification significantly complicates this interpretation of Revel's harmonious cast of mind. When required to reach a decision based on *halakhah*, Revel issued unequivocal, analytic responsa. No female vocalist at the Music Festival of 1926. No Reform Jews on Yeshiva's national board of directors. No mixed seating in synagogues. As the decisive issue in Revel's eventual rejection of a merger between RIETS and JTS, he pointed out in "Seminary and Yeshiva" that young rabbis trained by the Seminary often accepted counter-halakhic compromises such as mixed seating, and he underlined the vastly greater Talmudic learning of students at his own institution. Furthering their previous experience in European *yeshivot* and/or New York's *yeshiva* day schools, this formidable learning would deter them from making untenable compromises. A faculty member or student could read and think about materials outside halakhic boundaries, but a rabbi should remain entirely inside those boundaries when rendering a judgment based on *halakhah*. At the same time, while hoping that future trends would move in the right direction, in practice Revel often accepted or at least tolerated what he rejected in his responsa. Rabbis ordained by RIETS continued to accept pulpits in synagogues with mixed seating, for instance, and Revel never campaigned against the practice or discouraged his students from taking certain jobs.

Revel seldom dignified departures from Jewish ideals by mentioning them in public. Instead, he emphasized the positive in the here and now and pointed the way toward a better future. General religious language with positive connotations — "spirit," "morality," and "faith," for instance — came as naturally and easily to Revel as specifically Jewish religious language, which itself tended to remain rather general — most often "Torah," "Jews," "Jewish," and "Judaism." Ironically, Revel's wife's surviving speech to the Yeshiva University Women's Organization sounds more like the address of a *rosh yeshiva* than does Revel's address to the same organization. She used not only "Torah" but *"hurban," "Talmidei Hakhamim," "Gedolei Torah,"* and *"Torah ha-kedosha."* Her husband repeatedly invoked the Torah and once praised "Jewish traditions and idealism," but he also referred to "steadfast spirituality," "the soul of our people," "scholars and sages whose hearts were altars upon which burned the sacred fire of divine and human love and loyalty," and "the guiding hand of divine providence." In 1940, to another religious audience, the Rabbinical Council of America, he praised "the light of human reason," called on "the collective conscience of mankind," and asserted that "the ascending spirit of mankind will triumph." To religious audiences, Revel readily invoked the Torah and praised Jewish learning, but he virtually excluded both Hebrew and Yiddish. He tended to rely on general language in addressing all different kinds of audiences, including donors, entering and graduating students, the Union of Orthodox Congregations, and Young Israel. This consistent language reflects consistent modes of thinking based on consistent values.

Revel rejected American commercialism and materialism, but he didn't dwell on them. Instead he emphasized the relationship between ideal American values and traditional Jewish values. He quoted Franklin Delano Roosevelt: "American democracy has grown out of the spiritual soil of the Bible." American democracy represented the forces of light in the modern world just as religious Judaism had represented the forces of light ever since its foundation in the ancient world. He praised the vision of Abraham Lincoln. He praised the cultural pluralism of America, a concept he may have derived in large part from the writings of Horace Kallen. Like Kallen, Revel rejected the melting pot as the necessary and desirable result of American democracy. America stood for the freedom of each religious or ethnic or cultural group to retain its own special identity while contributing to the overarching ideals of truth, freedom, and justice for all. He predicted that in the future, if America lived up to its great promise and its ideals, "The true Americanism and the true Judaism will have achieved harmony."

In poring over Revel's drafts in Yeshiva's archives, I found phrases like "the supremacy and sanctity of the free human personality" and "the dignity and sanctity of unfettered personality" difficult at first to understand. The admixture of religious language and connotations notwithstanding, these formulations seem so Emersonian, so individualistic. Yet a thorough contextual understanding does place them under the broad umbrella of his syntheses. Revel assumed that each supreme individual had received an education at a *yeshiva* in Europe or a *yeshiva* day school in New York before entering his *yeshiva* and, later, Yeshiva College. He did not want to educate free-thinking intellectual atoms. Instead, religion, morality, and learning would infuse themselves into each "harmonious individual," who would think for himself within the framework of human and religious wisdom. In a note among his papers, Revel refers to the "ultimate perfection of the individual in the image of his Maker."

Why did Revel encourage students to continue working toward individual harmony and perfection by founding Yeshiva College, the most ambitious practical result of his thinking? What motivated him to climb the educational ladder upward from the *yeshiva* high school he had earlier founded? First of all, the college would inoculate students against assimilation "so that these men may not be lost to us." In other institutions, Revel was well aware, "Jewish students are led to efface their Jewishness." Why? Anti-Semitism ranging from mild to virulent would combine forces with the "strange fires" of non-Jewish value systems. Even at CCNY and NYU, which gladly accepted thousands of Jewish students, the campus atmosphere led to assimilation, to the loss of respect for Jewish traditions and values. Non-Jewish institutions tended to teach "Jewish antiquities," not a living Judaism. In Yeshiva College, by contrast, Jewish students would find "a congenial home, unhampered by real psychological restrictions, which stifle the spirit." Revel wanted to give the students the same knowledge they would receive elsewhere, but encourage them to harmonize all their knowledge within a Jewish intellectual, moral, spiritual, and religious environment.

Yeshiva College's original curriculum shows that beyond the centrality of learning Talmud within the *yeshiva*, Revel wanted every student to pursue a broad spectrum of Jewish studies. Why not rely on the Talmud alone? First, he wanted to compete successfully with JTS in offering Hebrew, Jewish History, and Semitics; whenever possible, he wanted to outdo JTS — for instance, by including Bible in his curriculum. Second, having accepted most aspects of the Zionist mission of preparing Jews to inhabit a new homeland, he helped make the thinking of a small minority of religious Zionists in Europe into what became the majority opinion in America by surrounding himself over time with like-minded colleagues. Third, Revel favored the dissemination and expansion of "*Judische Wissenschaft*," which would enhance the stature of Judaism as a world religion. For all three reasons, Revel sponsored the addition of "Jewish and Semitic Studies" to the classical and modern secular curriculum of other institutions. Accordingly, in addition to Talmud, students took Bible, Hebrew, and Jewish History, Ethics, Liturgy, Literature, Philosophy, and Education.

Somewhat surprisingly in light of today's curriculum, none of these Jewish Studies courses would contribute toward the 128 credits needed for graduation. Eventually students would graduate solely based on courses in a "standard curriculum" imported from liberal arts colleges elsewhere. The 104 credit fixed curriculum heavily emphasized English, speech, history, mathematics, science, and philosophy. Only one of seven concentrations of electives reflected the Jewishness of the new college. Clearly, Revel wanted to found a genuine college and looked far beyond the *yeshiva*'s walls for models to adjust to the needs and identities of his religious Jewish students. In doing so, he rejected a purely "'pre-professional' training" that would "prepar[e] our youth to 'make a living,' not to live." It was thanks to Revel that Yeshiva College joined the "Liberal Arts College Movement." At a fundraising dinner on behalf of twelve refugees from the European disaster, Revel referred to Yeshiva College as "the only college of liberal arts and sciences in the country under Jewish auspices."

Revel probably wrote portions of the first Catalog of Yeshiva College (1928-1929), and he certainly closely supervised its language; typescripts with his revisions appear among his papers. One key formulation reflects the centrality of a broad religious framework as the ideal source of direction for individual thinkers: "In pursuance of its aim to give its students a broad and liberal training for life, the Yeshiva College emphasizes the humanities in its curriculum. By the application of the group system of electives, it aims to secure both breadth and depth of thought, to combine the advantages of concentration and of wide survey, with *a spiritual outlook that will direct and properly sustain the acquired power*" [emphasis mine]. Thus, while genuinely adopting the mission of liberal arts education as a guarantor of "breadth and depth of thought," the Catalog placed a "spiritual outlook" based on Torah learning at the core of a Yeshiva College education.

If Revel and his colleagues considered the humanities most central to education, what about the major contributions to human thought within the sciences? Here Revel publicly expressed some major misgivings. Despite his admiration for scientists like Bohr and especially Einstein, Revel maintained that "mechanistic," deterministic principles produce "soulless science." Science and technology have "multiplied man's capacity for a life more free and happy, more just and purposeful," yet "science divorced from faith and humanity has multiplied man's capacity for evil and destruction." Whereas Revel believed in permanent, absolute values, "scientific theories . . . come and go." In his view, Jewish and general "humanities," not science, would provide direction, values, vision, and permanence. Only they could and would grant science a soul. Only the inclusion of sciences in sister institutions and among modern fields of knowledge guaranteed them a place in the curriculum of Yeshiva College.

Among the explicit "aims" for the new college, Revel underlined perhaps his most profound motivation: "the synthesis of the Jewish personality, bringing into harmony the mind of the Torah-true student youth and the modern mind." Revel wanted "an atmosphere where the age-old verities and the fruits of modern knowledge may be coordinated and compatibly absorbed." He wanted "a harmonization of spirit and culture, of faith and knowledge." A few years after YC opened, he proudly claimed that the college and the *yeshiva* together were already "blending the age-old faith and learning together with the tested knowledge of the world today." Jewish culture and religion represented an "integral phase" in the moral and spiritual development of mankind. The non-Jewish aspects of the "wisdom of the ages" therefore complemented Jewish wisdom.

During his administration, Revel advocated freedom of inquiry, thought, and expression. In a September 28, 1934 letter, he invited his in-laws Mr. and Mrs. M.P. Travis of Tulsa, Oklahoma to watch YC grant an honorary degree to Albert Einstein. Writing from the heart, he wrote, "Dr. Einstein symbolizes, to all thoughtful men, the spirit of free and unfettered research," and he signed the note "Bernard." Admittedly, after first agreeing to hire Samuel Krauss, a European star and evidently an observant Jew, Revel rescinded the offer because opponents objected to Krauss's "extreme Bible views." More characteristically, Revel continued to employ Solomon Zeitlin, a faculty member who did not always cleave to the rabbinic consensus. And he faced down opposition by more than one *rosh yeshiva* to the teaching of Bible and Hebrew. His belief in free, broad intellectual inquiry led him to produce a new curriculum in Jewish studies as well as in secular studies and to hire the best faculty he could find "regardless of religion." Many non-Jews and non-observant Jews taught the new courses. For Revel, freedom of inquiry had a religious dimension: "spiritual, cultural, and scientific centers" such as *yeshivot* and universities served as "havens of the free, inquiring, and aspiring human spirit."

Revel's confident founding of a genuine college reflected both his visionary idealism and his practical conclusions about the needs of traditional Jews, but it also reflected his own intellectual journey and his level of comfort with the pursuit of knowledge of all kinds. In Kovno, he and like-minded students discussed mathematics, he studied Hebrew and Jewish history as well as Torah and Talmud, and he was imprisoned for contributing to Bundist, reformist activities and publications. After arriving in America in 1906, he immediately enrolled in RIETS, but he later studied law at Temple University; ancient Hindu philosophy, oriental languages, and economics at the University of Pennsylvania; and comparative religion and philosophy at NYU. He was the first recipient of a PhD at Dropsie University for his dissertation on "The Karaite Halakah and Its Relation to Sadducean, Samaritan, and Philonian Halakah," which examines halakhic positions beyond the boundaries of normative Judaism. For several years, he actively helped rescue the oil business of his wife's family in Oklahoma, accumulating practical knowledge along the way. In his formative teenage years, he looked beyond his *yeshiva* training; in his graduate work, he looked beyond the boundaries of Judaism to other religions; in his scholarship, as opposed to his responsa, he often looked beyond the boundaries of the traditional consensus; in his responsa, he remained willing to quote Philo as well as rabbinic sources; and in his life in New York and Oklahoma, he interacted with people with widely varying beliefs and values. His are the considered actions of an intellectually free, inquiring mind following out lines of thought with discipline and integrity. His intellectual life and his life as a Jewish leader reflect the inspiring words of his second commencement address, "The goal of true education is [the] power and love of disciplined thought, the ability to envisage life as a great unity, in a binding frame of intellectual and moral truth, and the devotion and consecration of learning to the steadfast service of mankind."

Revel's "both/and" thinking, dedicated to harmony, may frustrate some interpreters because he embraces or avoids many apparent contradictions. Why didn't he pay more explicit attention to the difficulties of synthesis, to students' intellectual difficulties as they think through how to reconcile non-Jewish and Jewish viewpoints? His temperament, his confidence, and his own characteristic modes of thinking provide portions of the answer. In one of his most eloquent summaries of what students will learn in Yeshiva College, Revel intoned, "Theirs is a synthesis complete, profound. They appreciate that faith and science are parallels; that Judaism…does not deny grace to other creeds; that mankind is composed of many nations, moving in parallel directions; that various cultures are as the many nuances of the White Light." In terms of history, Revel believed that the Jews originated many of the moral and religious ideals of America and of mankind, and he believed that "love of light, learning, and liberty will forever remain our sacred burden until it becomes the heritage of all mankind." This is not Rav Kook's vision of an eventual mystical, transcendent unity; Revel anticipated the eventual historical convergence of all nations toward Jewish ideals of freedom, justice, and spirituality, uniting them all under the divinely inspired "White Light," which represents metaphorically the unification of the rainbow and the reunification of the spectrum.

As I Knew Him:
Memories of Rabbi Dr. Bernard Revel

By Moses Mescheloff

Seventy years ago, when I met the girl whom I later asked to be my wife, it was important to me to introduce her to Dr. Bernard Revel and get his blessing. He was my *rebbe*, role model and a very significant part of my life.

In 1906, at the age of twenty-one, a young Bernard Revel arrived in America. He was the brilliant son of the rabbi of Prenn, a neighboring town of Kovno, the great center of Lithuanian Jewish learning. Young Revel had a photographic mind and had proven to be a prodigious scholar of the Talmud and its commentaries. In the United States, at Dropsie College, he earned his PhD and became known as Rabbi Dr. Bernard Revel. The fame of his scholarship spread and he became known among Jewish leaders as a scholar of note.

That same year, 1906, my parents arrived in the "*Goldeneh Medineh*," as America was then known, with a young son and a daughter who was still a babe in arms. Foreseeing the expulsion of the Jewish community and feeling the endemic anti-Semitism of Russia, my father, a *yeshiva* educated descendant of scholarly forebears, left a comfortable lumber

Rabbi Dr. Moses Mescheloff, RIETS '32, served with distinction as rabbi in Congregation Machzike Hadas in Scranton, Pennsylvania (1932-1936), Congregation Sons of Israel, in North Adams, Massachusetts (1936-1937), Congregation Beth Jacob, in Miami Beach, Florida (1937-1954), and from 1955 at Congregation KINS of West Rogers Park, in Chicago, Illinois (emeritus since 1982) where he has spent his most recent 50 years as an active scholar and communal leader trade in Minsk to immigrate to the United States. Here, he first found a job at and then became the hardworking owner of a grocery and, later, a delicatessen store. I, the third child in the family, was born in America in 1909, when my parents lived in Manhattan. Although I was sent to public school through junior high school, my parents made sure that I had the finest and most knowledgeable Hebrew teachers they could find to give me private Hebrew lessons up to the study of the Talmud.

My third teacher, a knowledgeable young man, said that I was ready for entrance to a *yeshiva*. I passed a rigorous examination by R. Yehuda Weil, one of the *rosh yeshiva* at RIETS, and although I was much younger than the other boys, who had recently come from Europe and were all sixteen to twenty years old, I entered the *yeshiva*. In 1922, I began my studies with rabbi after rabbi until I reached the class of the R. Shlomo Polachek, renowned as the Maichater *Illui*.

While I was growing up, Dr. Revel married and moved to Tulsa, Oklahoma, where his in-laws asked him to run their prosperous business in industrial oil. In 1915, Mr. Harry Fischel, acting on behalf of the Board of Directors, asked Dr. Revel to come back East and take over as *Rosh Yeshiva* of the short-lived Rabbinical College of America, the result of a merger between Yeshivat Eitz Chaim and RIETS. Mr. Fischel wanted a learned and forward thinking educator to lead the *yeshiva* on the path to becoming a college. The *shiddukh* was made and YC was born in 1928.

For many of the ten years that I spent as a student at RIETS, Dr. Revel was my teacher, friend, and mentor. He was a fatherly figure who took an interest in every phase of the life of each of his *talmidim*. He met with our parents. He spoke to us in a concerned, friendly fashion, and he was interested in our interests. He was there to encourage and inspire us. He knew of my interest in books and in my project of researching the book stores and building a student library. He chose me to be the recipient of the golden medal for *hatmadah*, rewarded to the most studious student at the Yeshiva.

From the beginning, Dr. Revel had an agenda for the Yeshiva: to eventually make of it an institution of higher learning for Orthodox rabbis, *talmidei hakhamim*, as well as lay people born and educated in America. These would become religious leaders and speak to the American Jew in a way he could understand. Dr. Revel wanted to continue the tradition of learning brought from Europe by students and teachers. He wanted to halt the pattern of Jewish students attending classes in the Conservative or Reform Jewish Academies where true Jewish traditions, learning, and values were being bypassed.

In the *yeshiva* high school, which I entered in 1922 at the age of thirteen, I loved my studies and was very involved in the student government. I started a book store and continued to thrive in Torah; I was an American boy with a wonderful *yeshiva* background. I was bilingual; Yiddish was my "*mama lashon*" and I had no problem learning with my brilliant European *rebbeim*. With Dr. Revel's encouragement, I attended the City College of New York as a night student. The subways were my "Study Hall." I graduated college *Magna Cum Laude, Phi Beta Kappa*. No one was more proud than Dr. Revel of his student's accomplishments.

When Dr. Revel asked for a small class of distinguished students that he would teach himself, I was included, although I continued to be younger than my classmates. Dr. Revel's class was always fascinating. He had a remarkable ability to find material from many different sources and integrate it into the question at hand. He was a brilliant scholar and *posek*, and a class with him was a real privilege. Although he stuttered badly, his students agonized with him and tried even harder not to miss a word and to follow the sequence of his logic.

As his "American" student, Dr. Revel often sent me to represent Yeshiva in the developing Jewish communities. He felt that modern Americans would relate to me and what I had to tell them. He brought many visiting European Rabbis to the *yeshiva* to speak to the students; Dr. Revel felt there was so much that we could learn from these European *gedolim*. Years later, in my congregation in Miami Beach, Florida, inspired by Dr. Revel, I continued this tradition and invited many famous European rabbis who came to lecture and raise funds for their *yeshivot* to speak from the pulpit. It was important for the American Jews to feel some of that influence.

R. Herbert S. Goldstein was one of my professors of homiletics when I studied for my *semikhah* at RIETS. Among one of his pointers was, "Always be well prepared, but when you delivered what you had to say — sit down. Don't waste more time!" His classes were voluntary, and I attended them religiously every Friday morning. He taught us pulpit posture — not only what to say, but how to say it. He stressed the importance of making eye contact with the audience. "Keep your hands out of your pockets and above the waistline," he would frequently say.

My other homiletics professor was R. Joseph Lookstein, one of the great orators of his time. He taught us the majesty of the sweep of the hands and the importance of the use of the appropriate word. He was the installing officer and guest speaker at my installation in my Chicago congregation on January 9, 1955. Those who were there still remember the excitement that he generated.

In Miami Beach, I had the opportunity to get to know these highly regarded and dedicated men in a more personal way. R. Goldstein and his wife were frequent winter visitors. R. Goldstein, on these vacations, would work on behalf of the establishment of Machon Harry Fischel in Jerusalem. When he co-opted me to help him in raising funds from among the wealthy tourists, I had no way of knowing that one day my grandson would be a student there.

When, in 1936, Dr. Revel was deeply involved in his efforts to make YC a full fledged university, he desperately needed funding and contacted the famous Dr. Albert Einstein to lend his support. Dr. Revel also spoke to my father-in-law, Rabbi Dr. Lazar Schonfeld, a *musmakh* of the Pressburger Yeshiva and at the time the rabbi of a large congregation in the Bronx that had many recently immigrated Hungarian speaking members. Among his congregants were relatives of some of the movie greats, who were, even in those days of depression, able to support important enterprises such as that of Dr. Revel. R. Schonfeld spoke both German and Hungarian and was an acquaintance of Albert Einstein. Dr. Einstein wrote a beautiful letter in German to my father-in-law, in which he spoke of the importance of Jewish education and the need for Yeshiva, where the ancient Jewish beliefs, wisdom and traditions would be taught in tandem with modern, scientific knowledge, and where Jewish youth could learn without harassment or persecution. The letter was an introduction to and reinforcement of R. Schonfeld's mission.

Upon my father-in-law's death, the Einstein letter was willed to us and for many years was kept in its original envelope in our safety deposit box. Upon the urging of my brother-in-law, Frank Schonfeld, YC '39, we presented it to the Hebrew University in Jerusalem, where it is now part of the extensive archive of Albert Einstein papers. A copy also went to The Yeshiva University Archives, where it is made available to scholars who wish to study the thinking of the greatest scientist of the twentieth century about the importance of religion and faith. The "Einstein letter" is also part of the history of that great and modest man, Dr. Bernard Revel, of blessed memory.

As I think back to my formative years at the Yeshiva, I remember with affection and great respect the outstanding scholars and teachers, men of great wisdom, who influenced my life. Dr. Bernard Revel was primary among them. Of our three children, two are graduates of Yeshiva University. Indeed, Dr. Revel brought about a miraculous transformation in the landscape of American Orthodoxy. His memory will continue to be a blessing in the annals of American Jewish history.

Rabbi Moshe Aharon Poleyeff:
Rebbe to Three Generations

By Israel Poleyeff

In room 307 of Furst Hall, the teacher's desk stands on a specially constructed platform. It is the only one of its kind at Yeshiva, and dates back to the 1930s, when students of R. Moshe Aharon Poleyeff had it expressly built so that they might better hear their beloved *rebbe* as they crowded around his desk to hear every word of his *shi'ur*. From that time on, the platform was moved to whichever room in which R. Poleyeff was to give his *shi'ur* — until November 10, 1966, when he gave his last one. Four days later, on the 2 Kislev 5727, R. Poleyeff was called to his eternal rest.

On that day, a remarkable and unequalled career as *maggid shi'ur* for forty-six consecutive years came to an end. It was not length alone that set R. Poleyeff's *shi'ur* apart from others, but rather a combination of unparalleled *lomdut*, a clear presentation of the *shi'urim* and an unlimited love and concern for each and every one of his many *talmidim*.

Signs of R. Poleyeff's future greatness already appeared in his early life as a student in the *yeshiva* of Slutzk. He was born on Lag ba-Omer in the year 5648 (1888) in Timkowitz in Belarus (White Russia), a small town in the province of Minsk, to Chana and Yisroel Poleyeff. His father was a *melamed* in Timkowitz and it was from him that his son received his first Torah education. When he was twelve, R. Poleyeff left for the *yeshiva* at Slutsk, where he was to remain for almost ten years and was to become one of the *talmidim muvhakim* of its *rosh yeshiva*, R. Isser Zalman Meltzer.

Rabbi Israel Poleyeff, YC '49, RIETS '51, was a pulpit rabbi for over forty years and rebbe at Hebrew Academy of the Five Towns and Rockaway (HAFTR) for thirty years.

At Slutsk, he was the contemporary of such giants as R. Aharon Kotler, R. Moshe Tomashow, and R. Eliyahu Henkin.

As a student, he quickly earned the reputation as a *matmid* who would not rest if a section in the *Gemara* was not crystal clear in his mind. It is related that once, on a Purim day, when all the students were busy fulfilling the *mitzvah* of *"hayyav adam le-vesumei..."* he was nowhere to be found. His friends sought him out and found him poring over a *Gemara*. It seems that an unanswered question, raised during a recent *shi'ur*, gave him no rest. Before he could join his friends in the proper observance of Purim, he had to find some solution to the problem.

It was this characteristic pattern of an intense search for a clear understanding of a subject that he would retain the rest of his life. A problem would give him no peace until he had solved it or had established to his satisfaction that there seemed to be no solution.

His *Rosh Yeshiva*, R. Isser Zalman, early recognized this characteristic in his *talmid* when he wrote of him in the early 1900s that "he possesses straight-forward logic... a singular capability at developing new thoughts and concepts. He is blessed with a clear and thorough understanding..." Later, in 1910, when R. Poleyeff received *semikhah* from his *rebbe*, R. Isser Zalman added, "And may he become a *rav* and teacher, for he is verily a *gadol be-Torah* equal to the most distinguished and expert *rabbanim*." Prophetic words indeed.

After getting *semikhah*, R. Poleyeff, like so many others who received *semikhah* in his time, went into business because of financial necessity and due to the lack of rabbinical positions in Europe. He might have remained a businessman and the Torah world might have been denied the teachings of an outstanding *talmid hakham* and *rosh yeshiva* had world events not forced him to make a critical move. In the years following the Russian Revolution of 1917, the Bolsheviks swept the entire country and Jews fled the oppression of the communists by the thousands. R. Poleyeff and his family were amongst them.

Years later, R. Poleyeff would smile as he recalled those days. He remarked wryly that, "the Bolsheviks did not believe in any god, so they poured out their anger first and foremost against the religious leaders, whether Jewish or non-Jewish, arresting many and sending others to Siberia outright. I was doubly 'blessed' [*Tartei lerei'usa*, he would say]. Not only was I a *rav*, but my business made me a capitalist! We realized we could no longer remain in Timkowitz a moment longer."

In the spring of 1920, R. Poleyeff and his family left Timkowitz forever and headed for America. Months later, just before Sukkot, he arrived on these shores. An era of unusual success as *rosh yeshiva* was soon to begin.

Three weeks after his arrival he was appointed as a *rosh yeshiva* by Dr. Bernard Revel, then president of Yeshiva. It was the start of a record for longevity as *rosh yeshiva* in one *yeshiva* that is rarely matched in any *yeshiva* anywhere. For forty-six consecutive years, R. Poleyeff served with honor and distinction as *maggid shi'ur* to thousands of students. In many instances, he was *rebbe* to grandfather, son and grandson.

During those forty-six years, R. Poleyeff acquired the reputation not only as a *talmid hakham*, ranking among the greatest in his generation, not only as a brilliant *rosh yeshiva* to three generations of *talmidim*, but also as a humble and modest person and a *ba'al midot* of singular quality. Students of every decade still remember his gentle voice, his slow walk, his arm around the student while listening to his questions, and his readiness to help any student of any class. R. Poleyeff never condemned; he only used soft words of encouragement. On numerous occasions, he expressed his confidence in the American *yeshiva* student and in the future of Torah Judaism on these shores.

The goal of R. Poleyeff's *shi'urim* was first and foremost to understand the *Gemara*, Rashi and *Tosafot* well before proceeding to *rishonim* and *aharonim*. In this approach, he followed the pattern of such greats as R. Akiva Eiger, the *Tzelah* and the *Penei Yehoshua*. "Too many well-meaning students," he would say, "will give you a long *pilpul*, starting immediately with a Rambam, when they hardly know the *Gemara* on which it is based." The prime function of the *shi'ur*, R. Poleyeff scrupulously maintained, was to assist the student in the development of his individual ability to analyze and comprehend a section of the Talmud.

This teaching style, though not unique, was developed by R. Poleyeff to its ultimate perfection. Students could be recognized as his *talmidim* by how well they knew and understood the *Gemara*. R. Joseph B. Soloveitchik would often tell R. Poleyeff that at a *semikhah behinah* he could often recognize which students had been in his class by the clarity with which they answered questions on various *gemarot*.

R. Poleyeff also developed what was popularly known as the "Thursday *shi'ur*." Each week, a student was encouraged and guided to examine various *mefarshim* on a particular *sugya* and present it before the class. Following this presentation, R. Poleyeff would review it and then offer his own unique and incisive *hiddushim*, inviting comments by his *talmidim*. It was an experience in Torah research and presentation that every student would long remember.

The *hiddushim* presented in his *shi'urim* became the core of R. Poleyeff's published *sefarim* of *hiddushei* Torah. He valued the views of his *talmidim*, and every *devar halakhah* prepared for publication in his *sefarim* or in Torah periodicals first had to pass the critical comments of his *talmidim*. R. Poleyeff's fame grew even wider with the publication of these *hiddushei* Torah. Four *sefarim* were published in his lifetime — *Mahaneh Yisrael*, *Be'er Avraham*, *Orah Mishor*, and *Ohr Hashemesh* — and another in 1970, a three-volume set containing all previously published *hiddushim* and all remaining *kitvei-yad*, entitled *Orah Meisharim*.

R. Poleyeff's love for his students, his unwavering confidence in their ability, and his patience in imparting his knowledge to them combined to make him one of the premier *Roshei yeshiva* of his generation. In 1960, after R. Poleyeff had completed forty years as *rosh yeshiva*, Yeshiva conferred upon him an honorary doctorate, thus publicly recognizing his many decades of devoted service. In his presentation, R. Joseph H. Lookstein declared: "…rarely was there a more gifted, a more loving, and a more beloved teacher. His students became his children, and he their father… His sight is weak, but his vision is clear; the scholarly stoop is pronounced, but the personality is proudly erect. The voice is soft, but the pronouncements are bold…"

Dr. Samuel Belkin, in officially conferring the degree, stated: "…above all we respect him for his humility, his moral integrity, and for having dedicated his life and consecrated his energy to the study and to the teaching of the Torah and our sacred tradition without regard to honor and glory…"

On November 14, 1966 (2 Kislev 5727), the soul of R. Moshe Aharon Poleyeff was recalled to the *yeshiva shel ma'alah*. Lamport Auditorium was filled to overflowing with over two thousand mourners who came to say farewell to their beloved *rebbe* and friend and to hear R. Eliyahu Henkin come out of a sick bed and, in a voice hardly audible above a whisper, deliver a moving *hesped* of "his beloved and lifelong friend of over sixty-five years." His mortal body was brought to its eternal rest on *Har ha-Menuhot* outside Yerushalayim. Only fifteen feet away is the *kever* of his distinguished *rebbe*, R. Isser Zalman Meltzer, together again in death as they were in life.

Six Decades at Yeshiva

By Jacob Rabinowitz

My sixty plus year association with Yeshiva began in 1939 when, as a nervous high school sophomore, I came up to Washington Heights from the Lower East Side to take a *behinah*, in the company of Moshe Tendler and his father, my *rebbe*. It was Dr. Bernard Revel himself who gave us the exam, testimony to his own deep involvement in Yeshiva life, as well as to the size of the institution at that time. Unfortunately, that was virtually the only extended personal contact that I had with Yeshiva's first president. He passed away shortly thereafter.

I was extremely fortunate that, even as a high school student, I heard *shi'urim* from such world famous Torah luminaries as R. Moshe Aharon Poleyeff, who was later assigned to a college level *shi'ur* and who warmed us not only with his Torah but also with the love he radiated to his students, R. Aaron Burack, and R. Moshe Bick, who became the major *posek* for the Boro Park community after he left Yeshiva.

During my high school years, I was only dimly aware that there was a college on the premises. The war in Europe and the increasing involvement of the U.S. in World War II enveloped everyone, especially those who understood what was happening to our brothers and sisters in Europe. Thus, I do not have strong memories of the leadership void and difficult times at Yeshiva following Dr. Revel's passing. It took some three years for Dr. Belkin to be chosen as the second president of Yeshiva in 1943, and by then I was completing my freshman year at Yeshiva College.

Rabbi Jacob Rabinowitz, YC '46, RIETS '48, has held many administrative posts at Yeshiva and is currently an emeritus professor of Talmud. Upon his retirement, Rabbi Rabinowitz was awarded an honorary degree from Yeshiva.

The total enrollment in the college at that time was less than 300 students, and all of the college facilities were housed in the one building on Amsterdam Avenue, where I had spent my high school years. There were only two laboratories; one served all biology courses and the other was for chemistry offerings, and they were opposite each other on the fourth floor. There was also a room designated as a physics lab and lecture room. Since I was a major in chemistry, I spent a good part of my collegiate years on that floor. It seems that Dr. Levine, himself a YC graduate who taught virtually all the chemistry courses since required courses were offered only in alternative years, prepared us well because I was not at a disadvantage when I enrolled for graduate work at Brooklyn Polytechnic. The warm, personal student-faculty and interstudent relationships and small class sizes — very important for lab work — made up for the lack of extensive and sophisticated facilities.

One should also note that this warmth pervaded most of the institution. Student aid, for example, extended not only to tuition scholarships but also to weekly food stipends and even to distribution of suits at Passover time to needy students. This was all without government funding.

College courses began at three and, as today, *shi'ur* and *beit midrash* busied us until then. In college, as in high school, I was exposed to the best of the best, perhaps the finest group of *roshei yeshiva* in any institution at that time. There was R. Poleyeff again. And then Yeshiva's president, Dr. Belkin. He always cleared his calendar to offer a regular, brilliant *shi'ur*, which was marked by precise and clear formulations and applications of basic principles. Each *shi'ur* lasted exactly one hour and ended with a short summation. My last two years in Yeshiva were spent in the *shi'ur* of the incomparable and unforgettable Rabbi Joseph B. Soloveitchik, about whom so much has been written and will continue to be written as more and more of his teachings become available.

Semikhah was a two year post-college program at the time; one year was usually spent with R. Dovid Lifshitz learning *Hullin*, while the second was spent in self-study of *Yoreh De'ah*. An oral *behinah*, administered by the three giants of the Torah world at Yeshiva — R. Moshe Shatzkes, R. Joseph Ber Soloveitchik, and Dr. Samuel Belkin — based on *Yoreh De'ah* and two tractates of the candidate's choosing, was the final daunting task. It was a humbling, frightening experience, but it gave status and dignity to the entire process, and the successful recipient of *semikhah* could be proud of his achievement and confident of his scholarship and abilities.

While I was studying for *semikhah*, I served as a part-time laboratory assistant in chemistry and I had the pleasure of introducing students to a brand new laboratory, built in another section of the fourth floor. Faculty had been expanded and required courses were now offered every year. In 1950, with the appointment of Dr. Samuel Soloveichik to the chemistry department, I was no longer needed, and I left Yeshiva to teach at the Rabbi Jacob Joseph School and to pursue my graduate degree at the Polytechnic.

In 1957, Dr. Belkin called me back to Yeshiva to join the newly formed JSS faculty. The interview was really a student-teacher reunion. Indeed, all my life I addressed Dr. Belkin as "*rebbe.*" At our meeting's conclusion he asked me, "How much do you make at RJJ?" I told him, and he said, "I'll give you more." Only when I received my first paycheck did I know my salary.

In 1961, after receiving my Masters in Chemistry, Dr. Isaacs, who had been my dean at Yeshiva College and was now teaching chemistry at SCW, also asked me to join that faculty in addition to JSS. His family arrived in the U.S. early in the nineteenth century, and he and his six brothers were brilliant professionals. All seven were deemed worthy of *Phi Beta Kappa* election, a record which I believe still obtains for that organization. One of his brothers, Nathan Isaacs, a Harvard faculty member, is said to have been considered as a successor to Dr. Revel. Our Dr. Isaacs was a chemist with acknowledged expertise in water chemistry. As YC dean, he applied his own high standards and unwavering integrity, characteristics which the fledging college needed as it sought acceptance and recognition. When he came to Stern, he taught me to adopt his approach. I recall finding a worthwhile experiment in a lab manual which we were not using that semester, and I suggested that our students would profit from this exercise, and I wanted to copy it and distribute it. He agreed with my evaluation, but he then gently guided me to the opening page of the manual and the bold letters "copyrighted."

When David Ben-Gurion visited Yeshiva, Dean Isaacs was almost the only one who did not participate as a welcoming official in this ceremony for the noted Premier of Israel. He explained his absence to me: "All my life I've been against what this man stood for [referring to his own denigration of religion as a factor in the destiny of the Jewish people in the Land of Israel] and I'm not going to change now by honoring him."

He resisted all pressures to award college degrees when all requirements were not fulfilled. His was a totally honest administration.

Dr. Isaac's wife was the first Dean of Students at Stern and during the school year they resided in an apartment in the Stern Residence Hall. They were thus both readily available to students almost all the time.

My years at Stern came to an end in 1966. Dr. Belkin, reacting to the increasing activism and restlessness of students in American universities which was beginning to affect Yeshiva, asked me to become the first Dean of Undergraduate Students in Yeshiva's history. Dean Samuel Sar had been Dean of Men until his sudden passing in 1962, but his duties did not involve him with the undergraduate school to a great extent. I was to be responsible for all non-academic programs/activities at the undergraduate schools. To my pleas that the appointment be delayed for a year so that I could finish my doctoral thesis at the Polytechnic, Dr. Belkin replied, simply, "I need you now." I acceded and, as it turned out, gave up any chance for an academic career in chemistry.

To prepare for my new appointment, I had a long session with the Rav seeking guidance and direction on how to deal with religious issues and problems. He, of course, gave me invaluable advice emphasizing one basic principle: "Remember that you are an educator, not a legislator." I was to call upon him a number of times during my tenure as Dean of Students.

I was also anxious to be guided on keeping individual guidance records to preserve confidentiality because I wanted to expand and strengthen our efforts in that area. I went to Boston to spend an afternoon with the master of one of the dormitories at Harvard. He reviewed his processes, confirming my own emphasis on preserving confidentiality. When I asked what he would do if he received a court order to surrender student records he replied, "Well, I'd probably have to comply with it, but you can be damn sure I'll be up the night before going through them..." What was established at YC as a result of my efforts apparently had some value because Dr. Israel Miller, who succeeded me in 1968 with the title of Vice President for Student Affairs, continued the procedures I pioneered.

My two-year appointment as Dean of Students was by and large a period of introduction and acclimation to a new administrative structure in an uncharted area. But it also entailed YC's new attempt to cope with a student body that was beginning to reflect the seething student bodies on other campuses. One particular incident stands out. We had received word that students at Columbia were preparing to come uptown to "liberate" Yeshiva. The YC dean, Dr. Isaac Bacon, fearing physical confrontations, arranged to have the local precinct captain on hand in his office to help evaluate potential threats to student safety. A meeting of students was schedule for that evening in Rubin Hall. One of the student leaders who didn't want Columbia on the Yeshiva campus kept those of us who were waiting with Dean Bacon informed, periodically, of the progress of the meeting. Things were a bit tense until our contact came in at 10:00 PM and informed us "they're breaking for *Ma'ariv*." We now knew that there would be no violence that night and the captain went back to the station house.

In 1968, thanks to a major donation by Mr. Jakob Michael obtained through the efforts of the then Professor Norman Lamm, the university recast the Teachers Institute as the Erna Michael College of Hebraic Studies. TI had a new status and focus, and a thoroughly revised curriculum prepared by an outstanding panel of educators who labored for over a year and produced a structured yet innovative set of goals and objectives and the programs to achieve them. This new college would be empowered to award BA and BS degrees in the major fields of Jewish Studies. Its original mission to train teachers was not neglected and, in addition, it provided for a free tuition track for those who committed themselves to enter the field of Jewish education for a minimum four year period. An outstanding faculty was equipped and delighted to take on this challenge, and Dr. Belkin asked me to become a part of this effort by leaving my position of Dean of Students and becoming the first dean of this new college.

I was succeeding an enormously popular and widely loved director, Dr. Hyman Grinstein, and my appointment was not greeted with universal acclaim. Moreover, the degree granting tracks demanded greater academic rigor, and this was not received well by many members of the student body, who were accustomed to a more relaxed atmosphere. This, plus the introduction of a written entrance examination for admission and placement, combined to decrease enrollment at this new school. Over the years, however, we succeeded in graduating a most respectful number of highly educated men who have made and are making significant contributions as educators, academicians, and community leaders. We also introduced the first Sephardic Studies Program under the direction of *Hakham* Solomon Gaon and participated in the introduction of joint-degree programs with BRGS, FGS, and WSSW. Our education initiative, however, was not successful because other more attractive career doors opened at this time and drew more students.

My new position brought me into much closer, almost weekly, contact with Dr. Belkin because there were no layers of administration between us and I wanted to keep him abreast of all developments. I came to idolize him. He had a brilliant mind, a keen memory, and a clear understanding of the educational goals he wanted to pursue. At the same time, he had a realistic understanding of the interface between the school and its constituents: students, faculty, lay leaders, government agencies, and the community at large. Thus, he rejected a proposal, widely advocated at the time, to promote student recruitment for the colleges by sending college teachers to give credit courses at various high schools. "I don't believe in a college on wheels. A college is more than a teacher standing in a classroom. It's a daily interaction in all locales: the library, coffee in the cafeteria, a common club or activity."

He was also against building luxurious dormitory facilities, suggesting that students should spend time in *beit midrash* and library rather than playrooms and lounges. He supported other educational institutions unselfishly; when I complained that a new high school to be opened by a Yeshiva alumnus would impede recruitment, he replied simply: "The sun shines for everyone."

In dealing with government agencies, as well as the larger community, he was a proud and sharp advocate for Yeshiva and Judaism. I was present at a meeting between Dr. Belkin and a delegation of officials who came from Washington to discuss our admissions policy. One of the visitors said to him: "Now Dr. Belkin, I note your proximity to Harlem. When, and I say when — not if — you admit your first student from that area, what help are you prepared to offer that minority?" Dr. Belkin replied: "Jews are a minority and have always been a minority, although I know that your office does not classify them as such. But we know what it feels like and when the time comes we will know what to do."

Dr. Belkin never forgot that he was a *rosh yeshiva* by upbringing and training. His attitude towards members of the RIETS faculty was warm and sympathetic. It is true that the RIETS faculty salary scale was, by and large, lower than other faculties. This was due to the unrelenting financial pressures that always plagued Yeshiva. If one had to adhere to a market salary schedule to obtain qualified professors then there was no choice but to pay them more if quality education was to be provided. Yeshiva, which did not practice nepotism in employment, had a large pool of outstanding *roshei yeshiva* to choose from, and this dictated a lower range of salary to relieve the overall pressure on the institution.

But, in return for this sacrifice, *roshei yeshiva* enjoyed far greater job security. They were freed from the uncertainties of the academic world and did not live in a "publish or perish" atmosphere. Nor did they undergo periodic evaluation by peers in tenure reviews by internal and external academicians. I do not recall any appointed *rosh yeshiva* who was released by Dr. Belkin.

Moreover, Dr. Belkin sometimes withstood great pressure from lay leaders to end this practice. I recall an emergency meeting to deal with a financial crisis at which one prominent Yeshiva lay leader, a prince of a man and a close friend of Dr. Belkin, called out to him — in the presence of senior administrators and board members — "Dr. Belkin, we must cut down on our Yeshiva faculty. If you can't fire them then send them to me and I'll fire them." On another occasion, a similar request for cutbacks was withdrawn when Dr. Belkin sent in a letter of resignation after the meeting. When an astonished board member asked why Dr. Belkin had sent the letter, Dr. Belkin replied that he could not serve as a head of a faculty subject to such conditions. And that was the end of it.

And these feelings extended to individual faculty. With tears in his eyes, he once instructed me "always answer telephone calls." It seems that a *rosh yeshiva* had tried to reach him the day before, but Dr. Belkin was in a series of meetings and he was unavailable. The next day, when he was able to return the call, he was devastated to learn that "he needed me. His wife was in the hospital."

Dr. Belkin was also blessed with a sharp and ready wit, which sometimes was able to deflect or mitigate objections or resentment. To the interviewer from *Time* magazine who asked him at the age of 31 "aren't you rather young to be a college president?" he replied: "It's a fault which grows smaller with each passing second." When a *rosh yeshiva* came in to tell him that his daughter, fresh out of college, got a job with IBM at a salary which exceeded his, Dr. Belkin replied: "Tell her that her president also makes more than your president." When Dr. William Foxwell Albright, a non-Jew and one of the most distinguished archaeologists and historians of the Ancient Near East, was awarded an honorary degree at Yeshiva, Dr. Belkin greeted him and inquired about his health. He complained that his eyes were troubling him and that this was hampering his work. I heard Dr. Belkin's immediate response: "Dr. Albright, there may be something wrong with your sight, but there's nothing wrong with your vision."

Dr, Belkin's crowning characteristic, of course, was his humility. He even disclaimed the trappings of his office — the car, apartment, office furnishings. Once, when his grandson's application to an activity or facility (I forgot which) was somehow held up, Dr. Belkin asked me to find out what was wrong, and said: "Tell them I'll pay. I'll pay."

As the university grew and its budget and obligations expanded far beyond available resources, he opined that he lived by "divine optimism." And he would instruct a loyal Sheldon Socol: "Dr. Socol, you go home and get a good night's sleep. There's no sense in both of us being up all night."

But with all his hard work and total dedication, Dr. Belkin could not attenuate a deepening crisis. In the early seventies, Dr. A. Leo Levin, a vice president and trusted aide to Dr. Belkin, called me into his office to tell me that he was returning to his post at the University of Pennsylvania, but that before he left he was asking me to take on a "nasty" assignment. The university could no longer rely on individual departments and schools to cut their own budgets, and a university-wide budget committee was to be formed. This committee, which he asked me to chair, would be mandated to propose and implement reductions throughout the university, other than at AECOM, which was to have its own committee. It is always difficult to cut budgets, consolidate departments and eliminate offices. It is excruciatingly difficult when one deals, as we had to do, with a relatively small circle of administrators who are your friends and for whom you have the highest regard. But we set ourselves to gather data, decide priorities and, after months of meetings with all parties, achieved what we judged to be equitable reductions in budgets based on perceived priorities.

Scars of that process remain, and although the broadest reductions were made in non-academic areas and in schools which were deemed to be secondary to the university's mission, the faculties of the undergraduate colleges, which were given the highest priority, were deeply upset and hurt by some remedies which were considered. These feelings led to a diminution of campus collegiality, and faculty began to view themselves as employees rather than colleagues.

As the crisis continued, Dr. Belkin, debilitated by illness, discouraged by the divergence of funds and donors to Israeli causes, which caused a serious drop in fundraising for Yeshiva, wearied of the unending struggle, decided that he could no longer contribute as he had up to that point, and he resigned the presidency in 1975.

An executive committee was formed to administer the university on a daily basis. The Board of Trustees then decided to empower a university-wide search committee to identify and recommend candidates to succeed Dr. Belkin. The committee had fifty-three members and every constituency was represented. The Chairman of the Board, Mr. Max Etra, asked me to chair this committee. A recent book about Dr. Belkin alleged that two friends of Dr. Belkin helped him draw up a "short list" of possible candidates from which his successor was named. Our committee did not receive, nor was it guided, in any measure, shape, or form, by such a list. It did initiate an international search, contacting agencies and institutions as well as academicians and community leaders. It also directly solicited nominations from fifty-seven presidents of academic institutions. Internally, faculty, administrators, students, and alumni were approached by various means. This search was as thorough as we could make it.

More than a hundred responses were received and almost sixty nominations were presented. A working committee of fifteen, representing all constituencies of the larger search committee, analyzed all nominations using an evaluation chart of thirty-three criteria to quantify rankings. After many meetings of the working committee, the number of nominees was reduced to eight, whose names were presented to the full search committee. Of these, three declined to be considered and the conditions set by one nominee could not be met.

After a series of interviews and re-interviews, two candidates emerged as recommended by the committee. All in all, between December 1975 and July 1976 there were seventeen meetings of the working committee and nine of the full search committee.

At a final meeting in July 1976 the full committee approved a written report, which I presented for transmission to the board. This was to be supplemented by another report, also approved by the committee, which I delivered orally on July 14, 1976. The reports were well received. In August, the board elected Dr. Norman Lamm, one of the two recommended by the committee.

I do not know if Dr. Lamm was on the alleged "short list," but I doubt that such a list existed. I had made a private visit to Dr. Belkin in his hospital bed early in 1976 and I sought to benefit from his expertise and wisdom. I asked him directly if he had any guidelines to recommend to me. Mrs. Belkin was the only other person in the room and, because of our relationship, Dr. Belkin knew that I would respect a request for confidentiality should he decide to share something with me. There was no recommendation. Only a blessing that I shall always cherish, as these were his last words to me.

The new president brought his own style and strengths to the office. On the academic front, after a period of study, he revamped the traditional departments and divisions to cut across school lines. Student interest in Judaic Studies was helped by this change because interschool cross registration was now much easier. Faculty were also able to divide their course loads among different schools and campuses when invited to do so. Consolidation of administrative offices simplified schedule and program preparation. Lines of administrative responsibility were clarified.

In my view, Dr. Lamm's greatest overall contribution was putting Yeshiva's financial house in order. The new president, after surviving a nightmarish brush with an imminent bankruptcy, had no choice but to devote most of his time and energy to fundraising. He was rewarded with striking, historic success. When he took office, Yeshiva was about seventy million dollars in debt. When he left, the endowment stood at about one billion dollars. This is an awesome, unbelievable achievement. I think it is fair to say that if Samuel Belkin built Yeshiva, Norman Lamm saved it.

Of course, Dr. Lamm's presidency is marked by other accomplishments. He provided dignified leadership and his brilliant representation of Yeshiva to academic and lay communities through his speeches and writings helped Yeshiva grow and promoted the vital "Friends. Funds. Freshman" concept that Sam Hartstein, the venerable publicist of Yeshiva, used to emphasize. These facts are well known and need not be reviewed again here.

In all fairness, I would like to record that I believe that an important contribution to the successful attainment of financial stability at Yeshiva was made by Sheldon Socol. His indefatigable efforts on behalf of the institution that he truly loves, the skills which he brings to his work, as well as the fact that he is recognized and admired by the lawyers, bankers and financiers who have dealt with Yeshiva, contributed mightily to Dr. Lamm's success. I write this even as I note that I have often fought with him over what I thought were his false perspectives on the mission of Yeshiva and the role of faculty. There were times that I complained heatedly that his proper role was to carry out policy, not to make it. But, on balance, he was a vital part of the infrastructure at Yeshiva these many years.

My own administrative involvement with Yeshiva ended when I resigned as Dean of Undergraduate Jewish Studies in 1989 and I returned to my first love, teaching. I spent ten wonderful years in the classroom and, in my retirement, I miss my daily interaction with the bright, wonderful, sometimes maddening, Yeshiva students who are the future of our people.

Reflections on Those Years:
An Interview with Rabbi Emanuel Rackman

By Emanuel Rackman

The Rackman Family & Yeshiva

My father, Rabbi David Rackman, was a *rosh yeshiva* at RIETS in 1907. At that time, the *yeshiva* was at 156 Henry Street [on the Lower East Side of Manhattan]. At that time, there were only two *roshei yeshiva*, one of whom took ill and died. While he was sick, my father gave *shi'urim* for him.

My father was almost drafted to the army [in Slutzk] and instead came to America. They used to do what was called *Gemaravened*, when you don't eat, you fast day after day, and you became so underweight, so underfed because of it that they wouldn't take you into the army. My father was in that group. They were not drafted, but he had to run away because the army still would have taken him to the army. This was the late 1800s. And Slutzk then had the very famous Ridbaz [R. Ya'akov David Willowski] as a *rosh yeshiva*.

My father eventually gave up *rabbanut*; my grandfather didn't want him to be a *rav* in practice. It was also very difficult for him to speak. I

Rabbi Dr. Emanuel Rackman, RIETS '34, taught political philosophy and jurisprudence at YC beginning in 1947, and was named University Professor of political science in 1970. He received the honorary degree of Doctor of Divinity from Yeshiva in 1961, and was provost of Yeshiva University from 1970-1976. After leaving Yeshiva, Rabbi Rackman became president (1977-1985) and Chancellor (since 1985) of Bar-Ilan University. He currently divides his time between New York and Ramat Gan, Israel. This interview was conducted by Menachem Butler and Zev Nagel.

used to have to give the *devar Torah* to adults, from the age of eight or ten years old, and I suppose I became an orator under pressure from him.

Dr. Belkin

Dr. [Samuel] Belkin came to Yeshiva during the leadership and presidency of Dr. Bernard Revel, who also was *rosh yeshiva* and the head of the college. R. Belkin came because, apparently, Revel was told that there was an *illui*, an outstanding Talmudist, in the *yeshiva* of the *Hafetz Hayim*, and his name was Samuel Belkin. R. Belkin had a relative in New York who was willing to finance his trip to New York. R. Belkin's family owned the largest gasoline station in Manhattan. The day that he came to Yeshiva, he must have discovered that his family couldn't do much for him. They knew nothing; they didn't even have a kosher home and certainly did not observe Shabbat.

At that time, the head *rosh yeshiva* was still the Maichater *Illui*, Rabbi Shlomo Polachek. On the day they brought R. Belkin to the Yeshiva, Dr. Revel asked four students to schmooze with him in learning. I was one of the four. [Ed: The other three were a Mr. Wachtfogel, Aaron Levy — who later became a lawyer and an opinion writer for business journals — and a Mr. Chaifetz]. We spent an hour or two with Belkin. Dr. Revel specifically picked four of us who were involved in *lomdut*. We were learning then the first *perek* of *Ketubot*. The group regarded me as a Yankee — a native born American; my mother was also born in America. It was a very interesting experience.

We, the small group, continued to meet with Rabbi Belkin. He was a genius; in no time flat he learned the English language using a dictionary. He also managed to master Latin and Greek, which I hadn't yet; I knew Latin, but I hadn't yet mastered Greek. We urged him to try to get a degree in a hurry, and do it at [the nearby] Columbia University. He wouldn't be admitted to the regular program at Columbia. They had courses outside, exclusive of the regular programs. Belkin registered for them, and the *yeshiva* helped finance his studies since he had no money. [As said earlier], he did not stay very long with his relatives; they were highly Americanized.

After a while, Dr. Belkin mastered the English language. He was admitted to Brown University. It was amazing that Brown didn't ask him that he do anything to take a BA program. He had an "*illuisha kup*," he was that kind of a genius. The one book that he did publish was excellent — *In God's Image*; it didn't get enough recognition.

When R. Belkin was ready, Dr. Revel placed him at the head of a *shi'ur*. He had a group of fifteen to twenty more advanced students, close to *semikhah*; they were getting ready to learn *Yoreh De'ah*. It wasn't until a few years later that [R. Belkin] was ready to teach lessons in Greek and Hellenistic culture. Some of us became very close to R. Belkin, and I happened to be one of those who very much befriended him, particularly because I was helping him with his English. It was a period when the college was really in its infancy.

My Relationship with Yeshiva

I did not attend Yeshiva College. I was at the graduation of the Talmudical Academy in 1927. I was the valedictorian. I still remember the speech I delivered. It was held in Kehilath Jeshurun, on East 85th Street. Joe Lookstein was the rabbi already. Afterwards, I spent half a day at Columbia and half a day at Yeshiva. I started Columbia a year after my admission, since I asked for a leave of absence for a year and didn't want to start my BA training at Columbia before I was more advanced in my Talmudic studies. So I spent one year with nothing else but studying in the *beit midrash*. I was in the *shi'ur* of R. Moshe Soloveichik. R. Abramowitz was teaching *Yoreh De'ah* to some of the more advanced students, but that was during the time that the Maichater was still alive. Then there were R. Levine and R. Alishevsky, who both delivered advanced *shi'urim*.

The Maichater was brilliant; the *shi'urim* were phenomenal. I can tell you that there were times that chills would go up and down my back from the depth. We were learning *Yevamot*. *Yevamot* is a very difficult *Masekhta*, and it was a pleasure and privilege to be in his *shi'ur*. The Maichater died rather young, in the summer of 1928.

I felt that there were some of us who had studied so much *Gemara* that we didn't need *shi'urim* in *Yoreh De'ah*, which could almost be done by yourself with a little bit of guidance; I fought on principle that there was no need for it. It's true that the *rosh yeshiva* in charge would give *hiddushim* from some of the *mefarshim* on *Yoreh De'ah*, but not on the *Yoreh De'ah* itself. We also did not yet have examinations, as they did afterwards. When I took over the running of the rabbinical departments, so to speak, and Belkin was already president of the university, we did have very, very formal classes in *Yoreh De'ah*. It was quite different than our time. Then there was a group of us who felt that we'd learn by ourselves. We figured that whatever we would learn we would know, and whatever we didn't learn we wouldn't know.

I got *semikhah*, signed by Rabbi Moshe Soloveichik and Dr. Belkin much later. But by then I had not only received a few degrees at Columbia, BA — I was *Phi Beta Kappa* — I also earned my JD — the law degree, and I started in the philosophy of law program at Columbia.

I had very little to do with the Yeshiva [administration] until R. Revel died; then the fight began about a successor to Revel, who was an unusual president and a rich man himself. Once, R. Belkin and I saw R. Revel sign a check to buy a dozen overcoats for students [who could not afford them]. It was like a good, old fashioned *yeshiva*. And R. Revel had the money. But teachers weren't being paid. There were a lot of problems in those days, but nonetheless, we continued. It was an exciting school to be in.

In 1930, I was married, and R. Belkin was at my wedding. I remember that he was staying at the house of the Finers, who were hosting him on 187th Street, right opposite the dorms. And I remember that Mr. Finer saw R. Belkin getting ready to go to the wedding in a sweater. R. Belkin was still un-Americanized; he didn't know that he had to have a jacket to go to a formal wedding. Mr. Finer got him a jacket to wear to my wedding.

Rabbi Dr. Leo Jung was *mesader kiddushin* at my wedding at the Jewish Center. I married his niece, Ruth Fishman. I was twenty years old, and she was a few years younger. We had about eighteen rabbis under the canopy, including Dr. Revel and a number of the *roshei yeshiva* from RIETS.

R. Belkin eventually asked me to stay on and help him with the college. Our friendship remained until he died. It was my great loss. He was my *rebbe* and my *haver*, a genre of *rebbe-haver*. When one of the *talmidim* wrote a biography of Belkin recently [Victor Geller's *Orthodoxy Awakens: The Belkin Era*] he showed it to me, because he knew that I had been very close to Dr. Belkin.

The Torah and Rabbinics of the Early
Yeshiva College Years

By Aaron Rakeffet-Rothkoff

While I was no stranger to YC, since it was housed in the same building as TA, I approached the start of collegiate classes in September of 1955 with misgivings and doubt. A high school can be conducted in a parochial fashion as an adjunct to a Yeshiva. However, a college is different, since it possesses its own traditional character and outlook. Academic freedom in the pursuit of truth is an essential characteristic of the collegiate environment. This was certainly true of Yeshiva College, which was thus described by R. Joseph B. Soloveitchik, "The greatness of the Yeshiva is that it is a real Yeshiva and, on the second level, a proper academic institution. Both divisions function without synthesis and compromise."

A liberal arts curriculum calls for the study of subjects such as Darwin's theory of evolution and Freud's theory of psychoanalysis. These studies did take place at Yeshiva College, and there was complete academic freedom within its portals. The founder and first president of YC, R. Bernard Revel, maintained that the college should function as a true liberal arts college. He chose not to institute a controlled academic environment such as existed in most Catholic parochial colleges. Revel was confident that since the students were well grounded in the Torah classics, they would intensify their religious dedication as a result of the

Rabbi Dr. Aaron Rakeffet-Rothkoff, YC '59, RIETS '61, BRGS '67, is a rosh yeshiva and professor of Rabbinic Literature at Yeshiva University's Caroline and Joseph S. Gruss Institute in Jerusalem. This essay has been excerpted from the chapter on Yeshiva College in R. Rakeffet's forthcoming memoir.

collegiate challenges.

I was now about to start YC. I was not as confident as those who set the tone of the institution that I would succeed in coping with the challenges of a liberal arts curriculum. In Lakewood, I heard endless verbal assaults impugning such studies. I was not yet certain my decision to give YC a try was correct. My first class was a course entitled "The History of Civilization." When I arranged my schedule, the instructor listed for this subject was Professor Alexander Brody, a veteran faculty member. Right before the academic year began, a small notice appeared on the bulletin board disclosing that a new teacher, Dr. Louis H. Feldman, would teach the course. Trying to ascertain his background, we learned that Feldman had graduated *Phi Beta Kappa* in 1946 from Trinity College in his native Hartford, Connecticut. He was awarded the Master of Arts in classics from the same school the following year. In 1951, Feldman achieved his doctorate from Harvard University.

I entered the classroom with much diffidence among a group of boisterous students. Many were upperclassmen who simply signed up for the course to complete some secondary requirement towards their degrees. Soon, a short, slender, serious looking individual entered the classroom. He took his place behind the desk and opened his briefcase. He distributed a mimeographed sheet outlining the subject matter that would be discussed in the initial lectures. I quickly glanced at the page and was dismayed by what I saw. Among these topics were science and religion, universal traditions about the flood such as the Gilgamesh epic, and ancient law codes such as the Hammurabi, Hittite, and Assyrian. I started to shudder and felt the words of our sages dance before my eyes. The Midrash declared that when Esau came to Isaac to request his blessings after Jacob received them, "Isaac saw Gehenna opening beneath him." I fancied getting on the first bus back to Lakewood. Then the lecture began. "Religious Jews do not require scientific proof for their faith. Nonetheless, it certainly strengthens our commitments when universal concepts and scientific revelations confirm our traditions." Dr. Feldman then delivered a magnificent lecture illustrating the interconnection between the universal and the Torah traditions. The lecturer's span of knowledge was breathtaking and his insights were scintillating. Over the decades, I was to utilize the concepts that were engendered in this initial class in my own lectures time and again. When the hour and a half ended, I left the class in a state of euphoria. I mentally ripped up the imaginary ticket from New York to Lakewood. I had arrived at YC and I was not to look back.

The next day we learned from some of the dormitory students that the new instructor was spotted in the Yeshiva's dining hall at night. He was seen ritually washing his hands and pronouncing the appropriate benedictions before and after the meal. The following Sabbath, Feldman appeared to be an experienced worshipper as he joined in the prayer services at the Yeshiva. The word was out that the new faculty member was not only a unique scholar but also an observant Jew. Over the years, Professor Louis H. Feldman gained universal acknowledgment as a classics scholar and the leading American authority on Josephus. I wrote a term paper which compared the ideal in Plato's *Republic* to the religious kibbutz movement in Israel. I received an "aleph" for the course, which Feldman considered one grade above an "A." Unfortunately, the registrar's office did not see it that way; lacking a sense of humor or of proportion, the "aleph" was only credited as an "A" in my freshman collegiate average. Our senior yearbook, the *Masmid* of 1959, was dedicated to Professor Louis H. Feldman. The words of the dedication could well serve as a guide for attaining greatness in the art of teaching and imparting knowledge. It read:

> Love of learning can only be transmitted by a person who himself personifies in every aspect of his character, as a pedagogue and as an individual, the perfection attained through study. Dr. Louis H. Feldman, in the devotion he has shown towards his students has represented for us this perfection. His firm conviction in the truth and vitality of Orthodox Judaism, his vast erudition, his painstaking preparation of every lecture hour, his willingness to expend any amount of time and effort on behalf of a serious student; all of these qualities in Dr. Feldman inspired us to devote the fullest extent of our capabilities to gain mastery of the study we undertook with him. His challenge to our intellects impelled us to make use of our utmost potentialities, and simultaneously instilled in us a respect and admiration for the man who thus inspired us. We shall have pleasant memories of the laugh, we shall make extensive use of the knowledge, we shall never forget the man to whom we dedicate this, our final work, Dr. Louis Feldman.

Professor Samuel Soloveichik was another faculty member who enriched my knowledge and insight beyond the confines of the classroom. During my sophomore year, I studied chemistry with him to fulfill the requirement for a non-science major. (Reb Shmuel, as he was affectionately known, was the second-oldest child of R. Moshe Soloveichik. He was the younger brother of the Rav.)

I took a number of courses with Dr. Milton Arfa, who was a professor of the Hebrew language and its modern literature. Among the subject matter I mastered under his tutelage were the poems of Hayim Nahman Bialik and the essays of Asher Ginsberg, Ahad Ha-Am. There always was a sense of challenge in studying with Arfa since we knew that he was a 1945 rabbinical graduate of the Jewish Theological Seminary of America. We were constantly on guard to confront any inkling of Conservative Jewish doctrine in his lectures.

Dr. Hyman Bogomolny Grinstein was my professor of American Jewish History. Born in Dallas, Texas in 1899, he received his early education there and in Israel. A gentle soul, Grinstein was a link with the Yeshiva's earlier years. His affiliation with Yeshiva dated back to 1917 when as a student in the school he became a part-time secretary and aide-de-camp to R. Bernard Revel. Grinstein later continued his studies at Columbia University. Under the guidance of Professor Salo W. Baron, Grinstein achieved his doctorate in 1944 for his research in American Jewish History. His thesis, entitled "The Rise of the Jewish Community of New York: 1654-1860," was published by the Jewish Publication Society in 1945. Consisting of 645 pages, it was a model of punctilious research and documentation. Grinstein never married and his students constantly affirmed that his children and grandchildren were embedded in the text of his book. In his introduction, Grinstein described his study as taking "almost ten years of work." If so, his students' witticism may have indeed been valid.

Grinstein also served as the director of TI. He succeeded Dr. Pinkhos Churgin in this position when the latter left in 1955 to become the first president of Bar-Ilan University in Israel. Despite both administrative and teaching responsibilities, Grinstein always seemed at ease. His pleasant demeanor and rapport always came across in his relationship with the student body. In my junior year at YC a contest was announced for an original research paper in Jewish history. The prize for the best essay was to be a fifty dollar United States savings bond. This sum represented a small treasure for me at the time. I had long been intrigued by episodes that the *mashgiah*, R. Ya'akov Moshe Lessin, related about his 1924 visit to the United States. He came as the assistant to R. Moshe Mordechai

Epstein, the dean of the Slabodka Yeshiva. R. Epstein was a member of the rabbinical delegation which was sponsored by the Central Relief Committee to spearhead a massive fund-raising campaign for the *yeshivot* in Europe and Palestine. The other members of the delegation were R. Abraham Isaac ha-Kohen Kook, Ashkenazic chief rabbi of the Holy Land, and R. Abraham Dov Ber Kahana-Shapiro, chief rabbi of Kovno. The *mashgiah* once described the reactions of the delegation to the Sabbath desecration which they observed on the streets of New York City. In the midst of a discourse which decried the ability of the human to become insensitive to wrongdoing, R. Lesin declared:

> Our first Sabbath morning in America we were shocked to observe Jewish pushcart vendors when we left the hotel on the way to shul. We were distressed and sickened that our eyes beheld such wanton public Sabbath desecration. The second Sabbath we were still shocked but no longer as broken down as on the previous Sabbath. The third week we simply walked past the pushcarts with almost no instinctive negative reaction. R. Moshe Mordechai Epstein soon turned towards his colleagues and exclaimed that they were all candidates to become Sabbath desecraters! When the other rabbis probed his statement, R. Epstein explained that if they could become so indifferent to Sabbath desecration then their own piety was questionable.

Such concepts captivated my mind. Now was my chance to uncover the details of this rabbinical visit. I did the research and submitted the paper. I soon learned that my monograph was considered the best one among those entered. Yet there was opposition to my receiving the prize. Some of the faculty members felt that my essay was not acceptable since the paper had to be about Jewish History. They held that the saga of the Jews in America had not resulted in any positive achievements and that my paper did not qualify as Jewish History. Grinstein took up my cause and I was finally awarded the bond. My research later appeared in the 1959 *Masmid*, the Yeshiva College yearbook, under the title "The 1924 Visit of the Rabbinical Delegation to the United States of America." A more popular version became my first published article in the November-December 1963 issue of *Jewish Life*, the literary voice of the Union of Orthodox Jewish Congregations of America from 1946 through 1983.

My rabbinic studies were the focus of my collegiate experience. Our general studies did not usually begin until three o'clock in the afternoon.

The mornings and early afternoons were devoted to the sacred texts. From nine AM until noon, we studied on our own in the Harry Fischel Study Hall. I was to have only two *rebbeim* from the time I entered Yeshiva College until my ordination; in my Freshman and Sophomore years I studied with R. Shmuel Volk, who was rescued from the tribulations of the Holocaust by R. Revel, and later I studied with the Rav.

Reb Shmuel was a master of the Talmud, including the *Kodshim* and *Tohorot* divisions, which were not as widely studied as the other portions. He was a product of the Telshe Yeshiva and a leading disciple of its *rosh yeshiva* R. Hayim Rabinowitz. Volk's study partner for several years was R. Azriel Rabinowitz, the gifted son and successor to his father in the Telshe Yeshiva. In 1931 Reb Azriel was appointed to the faculty after his father's passing. He remained a focal personality on the Telshe scene until the Holocaust, in which he perished.

R. Volk was a master of the Telsher *derekh* or the Telshe method of rabbinic study. This approach stressed acuity and skill in profound logical analysis of the rabbinic texts. R. Revel and his right-hand man in administering the Yeshiva, Samuel L. Sar, had both studied in Telshe, and were therefore very favorably disposed to the new arrival. Reb Shmuel joined the Yeshiva's faculty shortly after reaching the American shores in 1939. He became a fixture on the Yeshiva scene for the ensuing decades. R. Volk was also to publish a multi-volume set of his Telshe oriented rabbinic novellas. Titled *Sha'arei Tohar*, these tomes were especially devoted to elucidating *Kodashim* and *Tohorot*. In a letter of commendation for these volumes, R. Samuel Belkin, the second president and *Rosh Yeshiva* of Yeshiva, declared: "I am sure that you know the name of R. Shmuel Volk who is one of our most distinguished *rosh yeshiva*. In addition to raising a generation of Torah scholars in America, he has literally committed his entire life to studying and writing monumental works on the Talmud. R. Volk is indeed a *gaon* of Torah learning."

Despite these achievements, Reb Shmuel was a prime example of those who were impaired by the Holocaust even if they were physically unscathed. In his presence, I always felt the frustration of what would have been and what was. Had the world remained sane, he would have been in the forefront of the Lithuanian *roshei yeshiva*. At Yeshiva, the students related to him as a European *rebbe* who never totally mastered western culture. His English was quite good, but Yiddish remained his native and preferred idiom of expression. R. Volk functioned in the shadow of the Rav, who had wholeheartedly and thoroughly mastered American mentality and contemporary enlightenment. Reb Shmuel Volk was a graduate of the gymnasium administered by the Telshe Yeshiva. Such a general educational curriculum under the auspices of an advanced *yeshiva* was unique for Lithuania. However, Reb Shmuel's formal general education ended with his gymnasium graduation. As high as the standards were in this school, in the eyes of his American students, his credentials were no match for a PhD from the University of Berlin.

Once in class, Reb Shmuel was involved in an erudite discourse based upon analysis of "Reb Hayim." Suddenly he thundered at me: "When I quote Reb Hayim, who do I mean?" I immediately responded: "Reb Hayim Brisker," the appellation for Reb Hayim Soloveichik of Brisk. My rebbe roared back at me with passion and more than a trace of annoyance: "Reb Hayim Brisker! Absolutely not! Reb Hayim Rabinowitz, Reb Hayim Telsher!" Only years later did I fully comprehend the academic differences and rivalries between the Telshe and Brisk approaches to rabbinic literature. How unsophisticated I was to have confused Reb Hayim Telsher with Reb Hayim Brisker. Yet here was my rebbe, Reb Shmuel Volk, a foremost disciple of Reb Hayim Telsher, teaching in a *yeshiva* where the dominant personality was Reb Hayim Brisker's grandson. Observing Reb Shmuel over the years intensified my perception of the Holocaust tragedies that affected endless millions physically, emotionally, and psychologically. R. Volk could justifiably paraphrase the rabbinic statement that once one does not attain his proper niche in the rabbinic world, he will always be at a disadvantage.

I was part of a group of aggressive and resourceful Yeshiva College students. Some were Holocaust survivors while others were American born. We were united in our incessant desire to attain unlimited Torah knowledge. We, perhaps arrogantly, assumed that we were ready to study with the master. We resolved that our next *rebbe* in the Yeshiva must be the Rav. However, a major obstacle blocked our aspirations. At this time the Rav was only teaching the advanced Codes of Jewish Law to post-graduate Yeshiva students. We began to petition the Yeshiva's administration. Our main interchange was with Norman B. Abrams. He conveyed our request to the Rav. I would imagine that the president, R. Samuel Belkin, was also included in the deliberations. After a few weeks of ambiguity, we finally got the word that we succeeded. Beginning with the semester of September 1957 the Rav would also conduct a class in

Talmud which would be open to undergraduates. With the initial flush of elation at our accomplishment there also came an awareness of our inadequacies. Next term would find us sitting in the same classroom with the Rav! How could we bridge the gap between own conventional Talmudic backgrounds and that of the world's premier rabbinic scholar?

The summer raced by and the new term was upon us. We began the study of the Talmudic tractate of *Sanhedrin* with the Rav. His *shi'ur* was breathtaking and his brilliance and insights motivated us to more dedicated study and preparation for the lectures. From the Rav's vantage point, I imagine he now faced a group of younger pupils for the first time in his Yeshiva classroom. The average age was no more than eighteen or nineteen. Perhaps he wanted to be certain that we were serious students and would strive to prepare the relevant texts in advance of the two weekly lectures.

Early in the semester, the Rav evidently decided to make this message clear to us. He met with us on Tuesday and Wednesday. That Wednesday, he began his lecture by announcing he wished to test us on our understanding of yesterday's class. He added that there would be three classifications. Either you knew, did not know, or you were a liar. If you raised your hand in response to his question and answered to his satisfaction, he recorded next to your name "*yada*" (he knew). If you did not lift your hand, he marked down "*lo yada*" (he did not know). However, if your hand was up and you did not respond and explain the topic in an acceptable fashion, the Rav recorded "*shakran*" (a liar). This quiz traumatized the class. We experienced the lecture that day in a state of distress. That afternoon, we discussed these events and the consensus was that we would not survive such classroom tension. It was decided to send a delegation to discuss the incident with the Rav's wife, Dr. Tonya Soloveitchik. My classmate, Gerald Blidstein, assured us that he could handle the situation. I can still see Jerry waving his hand in confidence as if to say "leave it to me." He led the entreaties to the Rebbetzin, as we referred to her.

Only years later did I come to appreciate my classmate's special relationship with the Soloveitchik family. Jerry was the grandson of R. Moshe Binyamin Tomashoff, known as the MaBiT. The latter was a preeminent Lithuanian Talmudic scholar and the author of impressive rabbinic tomes. The MaBiT arrived in the United States in 1912 and served as one of Brooklyn's leading rabbis. Jerry evidently enjoyed an informal relationship with the Soloveitchiks outside of the classroom due to their friendship with his grandfather.

The Soloveitchiks returned to Boston and we spent the weekend in a state of apprehension and stress. The next Tuesday, we glumly entered the classroom. The tension was palpable as the Rav took attendance. Everyone kept his head down. The Rav began his lecture with a simple but sagacious declaration: "You are a bunch of crybabies! Crybabies!" The tension was broken. The class laughed, and the master moved into the essence of his lecture. The Rav evidently made his peace with our youth. We understood that we had to extend our utmost abilities for the privilege of sitting before the Rav.

In the classroom setting, I only recall one incident when a student could pick up on the Rav's breadth of knowledge. In the midst of a lecture, he asked a student to bring him a cup of hot tea. The student dutifully went across the street and obtained the tea at the Greasy Spoon, a luncheonette located on Amsterdam Avenue that catered to the Yeshiva students. The tea came in a plastic covered cup. When the Rav removed the cover, he noticed that there were some foreign objects floating on top of the tea. He showed the cup to Ahron Batt, a student who was later to attain a doctorate in chemistry. Ahron looked at the cup and deduced that the pieces were part of the plastic cover that had melted due to the heat of the tea. Within seconds, he and the Rav were exchanging chemical equations to explain this phenomenon. This certainly was not an experience I encountered in any other Talmud class.

On June 18, 1959, I graduated *Summa Cum Laude* from Yeshiva College, first in a class of eighty-six. I received the degree of Bachelor of Arts, with a major in Hebrew and a minor in Education. My rabbinical ordination by the Yeshiva was granted on the fifteenth of *Tammuz* 5721, June 29, 1961. Fortuitously, my wife and I also became parents that very day. While I had officially graduated from the Yeshiva, I still retained an ongoing relationship with the Rav. He was to remain my inspiration and the paradigm for my own aspirations and deportment. His teachings and personality guided me throughout the myriad of situations that I encountered after I graduated from the Rav's formal classroom.

In addition to the formal classrooms in Yeshiva, there were additional faculty members who also impacted upon my perspective and understanding of the Torah society. Two such *roshei yeshiva* were R. David Lifshitz and R. Yeruham Gorelick. The former, popularly known as Reb Dovid, was a graduate of the Grodno and Mir *yeshivot*. In 1935, he succeeded his late father-in-law as the chief rabbi of the sizable Jewish community of Suwalki, a city in Poland. Although Reb Dovid succeeded in reaching the United States in 1941, he continued to be acknowledged as the Suvalker Rav until his death in 1993. When I entered the Yeshiva in 1951, Reb Dovid was already a central figure in the school. After his initial American years at Chicago's Hebrew Theological College, the Suvalker joined the Yeshiva's faculty in 1944. The Lifshitz family resided across the street from the school, and Reb Dovid was a constant presence on the campus. Dressed in the time-honored garb of the East European rabbinate, he was a tangible reminder of days gone by. His full beard was still black, except for a patch of gray in the center. Despite the brevity of his years in America, Reb Dovid appeared to be totally at home on the Yeshiva University scene. In addition to his prodigious Talmudic knowledge, the Suvalker was also an outgoing, friendly and warmhearted person. When he shook your hand, he grasped it with both of his. He communicated emotional commitment to those who sought his guidance. You felt Reb Dovid's heart and spirit when your hands met.

In contradistinction to the Rav, Reb Dovid emanated emotion. I will never forget his exuberance as we prepared to pray when daylight broke on Shavuot morning. We had been awake the entire night, engaged in the study of Torah texts. This is the customary comportment for observant Jews on this festival that commemorates the giving of the Torah. Reb Dovid gathered us into a circle, and hand in hand we danced before the recitation of the daily morning blessings. As we swayed, the Suvalker led us in the recitation of the liturgical poem which welcomed the dawn. Its refrain read: "I will thank the Almighty who scrutinizes all hearts, and has created the morning stars."

While the Suvalker personified serenity and composure, Reb Yeruham Gorelick was volatile and unsettled. A graduate of the Radin Yeshiva, he later studied for five years with R. Yitzhak Ze'ev Soloveichik in Brisk. Reb Yeruham arrived in the United States in 1941 and joined the faculty of Yeshiva Tifereth Jerusalem on New York's Lower East Side. In 1943, Reb Yeruham was appointed to the Yeshiva's faculty, where he soon became a focal and vocal figure. The Gorelick family resided in the Mount Eden section of the Bronx, which was then the heart of that borough's Jewish community. Reb Yeruham also became the rabbi of a local synagogue and organized both the Zichron Moshe Yeshiva for boys and the Beis Yaakov-Beis Miriam School for girls. At the Yeshiva he was a dynamic presence, appreciated both for his insightful Talmudic lectures and his pithy comments on contemporary issues. As much as he accomplished on the Bronx scene, he still was never truly at home in the United States. His close friend and my *rebbe*, R. Noah Borenstein, once remarked to me: "Reb Yeruham conducts himself in the Bronx just as if he is still in Brisk. His only accommodation with the new reality is that he allows his family to shop in Alexander's department store."

Reb Yeruham could be quite sharp at times, and we delighted in retelling his mischievous remarks. At the start of my high school senior year, I actually sat in on his class for a few weeks before the administration caught up with me. I was still in TA, and Reb Yeruham's class was comprised entirely of college students. During this period, I was witness to two incidents which reflect upon Reb Yeruham and his quests on the American Torah scene.

One Saturday night, Reb Yeruham's student was waiting for the D train at the local subway stop. He was on his way to a Bnei Akiva function. The young man was soon joined by a female acquaintance who was going to the same event. As they chatted, Reb Yeruham arrived on the scene, since he also needed the D train. Without exchanging a word, both the student and the *rebbe* caught a glance of each other. The next day, the hapless youngster confided in his classmates about his untimely experience the previous evening. "The *rebbe* will let me have it today. He saw me with a girl last night!" Being in the company of a young lady before you were ready for matrimony was not in conformity with Brisker deportment. The poor student was in a cold sweat as the daily lecture began. The Talmudic dialogue moved on, and Reb Yeruham did not say a word. The *shi'ur* ended, we prayed *minhah*, and the student was relieved. A few days went by and it seemed that all was forgotten. On Thursday, the final Talmudic class for the week, with minutes to go before the lecture's conclusion, Reb Yeruham peered at the errant pupil from the corner of his eyes. Without looking directly at him, the *rebbe* declared: "Such ugliness I have yet to see in my entire life." The class erupted in laughter, and the unfortunate student did not know whether to laugh or cry. He was zapped when he least expected his *rebbe*'s put-down. Worst of all, his male propriety was being questioned. Over the Sabbath, we all laughed with the victim as we put the incident into perspective. We resolved that the next time we would wait for the D train with Talmudic volumes in our hands.

The *roshei yeshiva* set the tone of the institution. At times it was in a monotone, but more often it was multicolored. Their own backgrounds, education, and personalities came to the fore in their outlooks on the issues of the day. Reb Dovid and Reb Yeruham were prime examples of the nuances of difference among the *roshei yeshiva* and their relationship with the student body.

As aspiring rabbis, we were also educated by New York's leading rabbinical figures in addition to the *roshei yeshiva*. The Rav acknowledged Rabbis Leo Jung, Joseph Lookstein, and Herbert S. Goldstein as the "heroes" of his students during the forties and fifties. The students alluded to them as "The Big Three."

R. Jung, a graduate of Berlin's Hildesheimer Rabbinical Seminary, also attained his masters at Cambridge and his doctorate at London University. In 1922 he became the spiritual leader of the Jewish Center on the Upper West Side of Manhattan. In 1931 he was appointed to the Yeshiva College faculty, where he taught a course in Jewish philosophy and ethics. One concept he expressed in class became a focal point of my own thinking. It was simple, but yet far-ranging. Dr. Jung declared that his life experiences taught him that "Judaism is perfect; Jews are not." I was to cite this aphorism endless times during the ensuing decades.

After college, while in the postgraduate *semikhah* program, we also took courses in homiletics and practical rabbinics. One year we studied with R. Herbert S. Goldstein and the other with R. Joseph H. Lookstein. Goldstein was the spiritual leader of the West Side Institutional Synagogue. A graduate of Columbia University and the Jewish Theological Seminary, Goldstein originally organized the Institutional Synagogue in Harlem. Years later, he gradually transferred his activities to the Upper West Side as the neighborhoods changed. Despite his reputation as a singularly successful, creative, and charismatic rabbinical leader, R. Goldstein comported himself as our colleague rather than as an elite professional. He understood our quests and aspirations. He taught us how to preach, and stressed clarity and conciseness. "If you cannot get the idea across in twelve minutes, do not get up to preach." Most memorable was the time he challenged a classmate regarding marriage. "How can you be studying for rabbinical ordination and not be married!" The young man shot back, "Find me a wife!" One week later, after the next class, R. Goldstein suggested a young lady who was a member of his community. Within a few months, the blissful couple stood under the *huppah*.

R. Lookstein was ordained by RIETS in 1926. His general education was acquired at the City College of New York and Columbia University. Already in 1923, Lookstein came to Congregation Kehilath Jeshurun as a student-rabbi. He went on to become its assistant rabbi and in 1936 he succeeded the late R. Moshe Zevulun Margolies as the spiritual leader. A year later, Lookstein established the Ramaz School under the aegis of Kehilath Jeshurun. The institution was named in memory of R. Margolies, with Ramaz being the acronym of his given names. The new school soon evolved into a modern day school which thoroughly integrated Judaic and general studies. The KJ synagogue and Ramaz were located on Manhattan's Upper East Side, one of the city's most fashionable neighborhoods. Into this area, Lookstein introduced an Orthodoxy that was graced with dignity and modernity.

In the classroom, R. Lookstein regaled us with the description of his struggles in doing away with the cuspidors in KJ. Some of the old-timers insisted that this removal was a violation of traditional synagogue deportment. Short in height, but tall in determination, R. Lookstein gradually guided KJ into a flagship synagogue of Modern Orthodoxy. Possessed of a golden tongue, R. Lookstein was acknowledged as the leading orator of the Orthodox rabbinate. He sought to guide us so we would be capable of discharging our rabbinical functions in dignity. The wedding ceremony, the funeral oration, and the weekly sermons were to be reflections of the new standards that the KJ rabbi pioneered on the modern scene. He also taught us the importance of well crafted titles for our sermons that would attract interest. Among his own sermons there were titles such as "Clothes Make the Man: A Religious Analysis of Fashion" and "Between Washington and Lincoln."

Years later, I heard of an incident which transpired towards the end of R. Lookstein's life. A young RIETS *rosh yeshiva* was invited to deliver a lecture under the sponsorship of the synagogue's adult education program. R. Lookstein learned that there was a poor turnout for this event. He subsequently met the young scholar and inquired as to the title of his lecture. The *rosh yeshiva* responded that it was about the unique analytical method of Reb Hayim Brisker, which was utilized in contemporary Talmudic study. R. Lookstein instantly remarked that with such a title it was not surprising that there was such a poor attendance. The *rosh yeshiva* asked what should he have headlined the lecture. R.

Lookstein immediately responded, motioning with his hands as if spelling the title out in the air: "There is more to Brisk than tea."

Pioneers of American Orthodoxy: Mr. Harry Fischel and Rabbi Herbert S. Goldstein

By Aaron I. Reichel

The names Mr. Harry Fischel and Rabbi Herbert S. Goldstein have found themselves mentioned in the same context time and again. Both were pioneers in the growth of American Judaism in general and in American Orthodoxy in particular, most notably during the dynamic, precedent-setting first half of the twentieth century. Mr. Fischel and R. Goldstein were both visionaries. Both played major roles in the history of the Jewish institutions of their era, not the least significant of which were YC and RIETS. When Fischel immigrated to America, his parents urged him not to exchange his religion for gold. Little did anyone imagine that, to the contrary, he was destined to help strengthen the religion of virtually all Jews in America in a wide variety of ways, not the least of which was by supporting the good works of his son-in-law, Herbert S. Goldstein.

Harry Fischel was born in Russia in 1865. He constructed a model version of the *mishkan* at ten years of age, mastered the basics of architecture by the time he was eighteen, became an architect and a builder at nineteen, immigrated to America virtually penniless at twenty, and earned his first million in real estate at a young age. When he became a director of the Beth Israel Hospital in 1891, he laid the groundwork for its kosher policy that still exists today; when he became a charter member of the American Jewish Committee in 1906, he persuaded his mostly

Rabbi Aaron I. Reichel, Esq., YUHS '67, YC '71, BRGS '74, and RIETS '75, is the author of The Maverick Rabbi: Rabbi Herbert S. Goldstein and the Institutional Synagogue. *Reichel's most recent book is* Fahrenheit 9-12—Rebuttal of Fahrenheit 9/11. *R. Reichel is a grandson of R. Herbert Goldstein.*

non-Orthodox co-founders to designate him to chair its second annual luncheon to assure that it and future events would be kosher; when he met with President Howard Taft in 1911, he successfully appealed to the President to order the installation of a kosher kitchen at Ellis Island so that Orthodox Jewish immigrants could have the opportunity to eat kosher food during a probation period and become strong enough to pass the test to avoid deportation.

The Harry Fischel Foundation, founded in 1931 and later renamed the Harry & Jane Fischel Foundation, has supported many institutions in Israel and America, most notably the Harry Fischel Institute (*Makhon Harry Fischel*) in Israel and Yeshiva University in America. True to form, Harry Fischel did not just give his money; he gave just as generously of his strategic thinking, planning, and implementation. At twenty-four years of age, this fast-track entrepreneur already became a director of the Eitz Chaim Yeshiva; then, in succession, from 1895 until 1927, he served as the hands-on chair of the building committee of virtually every successive campus of Eitz Chaim, as well as of the newly merged RIETS, and finally, YC, up until the period when the cornerstone was laid at the current main building of the main campus of Yeshiva in Washington Heights, between 186th and 187th Streets.

This last very public achievement might never have become a reality were it not for some work Fischel had done earlier, behind the scenes. In 1924 he had influenced the Lamport family into collectively making donations adding up to the then unprecedented sum of $100,000 to YC, and then promptly matched that donation single-handedly, as soon as it was announced, so that his donation was the largest donation to YC by a single individual during the college's formative years and for a significant period of time afterwards.

Fischel also donated the primary parcel of land for the construction of the main building of Yeshiva College at 500 West 185th Street, again in the main campus. After fifty-six years of leadership positions and initiatives in the university, Harry Fischel established the Harry Fischel Graduate School for Higher Jewish Studies at Yeshiva in 1945, which is now known as the Summer Program of BRGS. The main *beit midrash* at the main campus is known to this day as the "Harry Fischel Study Hall." A plaque in the main building of the main campus testifies that Mr. Fischel even served, for a time, as Acting President of Yeshiva College.

R. Herbert S. Goldstein (1890–1970) distinguished himself as a pioneering American born and educated Orthodox rabbi of national prominence, and as the only person in history to have been elected president of the Union of Orthodox Jewish Congregations of America, the Rabbinical Council of America, and the (now-defunct) Synagogue Council of America. The latter consisted of representatives of the rabbinic and lay arms of each of the three branches of Judaism. Notwithstanding Goldstein's role as a founder and president of the latter organization, he further distinguished himself by becoming one of the only leading Orthodox rabbis to publicly declare he was resigning from that organization after the members of the *Moetzet Gedolei ha-Torah* came out against participation in it in the late 1950s.

R. Goldstein's roles at Yeshiva and its affiliates also transcended the typical roles of a rabbi and communal leader. At a time when many Orthodox rabbis could not speak English fluently, he served Yeshiva not only as a teacher but also as an orator, fund-raiser, and toastmaster. R. Goldstein also headed the Homiletics Department at RIETS for decades, guiding virtually two generations of America's leading American-born and educated Orthodox rabbis. R. Goldstein joined RIETS shortly after he was ordained prior to World War I, and continued almost until President Kennedy sent advisers into Vietnam. R. Goldstein did not merely teach his rabbinical students how to preach in a technical sense, but he also inspired them to get their message out to the masses. In a recent biography of Yeshiva's second president, Dr. Samuel Belkin, author Victor Geller wrote that the RIETS men who "dared to try selling *Yiddishkeit* to their members... were following in the footsteps of an incurable optimist... Rabbi Herbert S. Goldstein."

To get an idea of what kind of an impact R. Goldstein had on his rabbinical students, R. Joseph B. Soloveitchik is reputed to have referred to R. Goldstein as one of the "heroes" of the rabbinical students of his era. I can vividly recall R. Lookstein's class on practical rabbinics, when he spoke of R. Goldstein's approach to sermonics in the present tense more than a decade after R. Goldstein had retired.

R. Goldstein encouraged his students to be brief. At one point, he suggested limiting their sermons to eighteen minutes, symbolizing *hai*, life. He commented that within the first eighteen minutes of a sermon, their ideas could come alive, and have an impact within the attention spans of most congregants. After that, they would increase their risks of dying out there in full view of their congregants! R. Goldstein encouraged his rabbinical students to figure out ways to keep their future congregants from losing interest and leaving the services early, suggesting that they point out, for example, "You wouldn't leave an important baseball game before the 9th inning, would you?"

As the president of the Union of Orthodox Jewish Congregations of America for close to a decade, R. Goldstein was the driving force in successfully getting Yeshiva recognized by the New York Board of Regents. In truth, the Orthodox Union did not have the money to actually guarantee Yeshiva's financial viability, but this daring and optimistic approach to Jewish communal and educational life was the hallmark of the *modus operandi* of both Fischel and Goldstein. Goldstein also used a similar strategy to save countless lives during World War II by assuring government officials that the congregants of his influential synagogue could easily guarantee jobs for people who wished to escape the Holocaust. Also, in his capacity as president of the Orthodox Union, R. Goldstein played a pivotal role in establishing the first national kosher food endorsement program in America — whose original seal bore his name on the wrappings of all Orthodox Union-endorsed products before the ubiquitous Orthodox Union symbol became universally used.

Perhaps the best way for people who did not have the privilege to get to know Rabbi Goldstein to visualize what he was like is to put him into the following frame of reference. When I asked R. Shlomo Riskin (founder of the Lincoln Square Synagogue in Manhattan) what he could tell me about R. Goldstein for use in my biography of him, R. Riskin responded that people who knew R. Goldstein well, in his youth, had told R. Riskin that he reminded them of R. Goldstein in his youth. R. Riskin then asked me whether I planned to enter the rabbinate. I told him that it seemed to me to be almost impossible to be three things as a rabbi — idealistic, successful, and happy. Usually, at least one has to give way to some degree. He smiled and pointed a finger at himself — another way in which he is similar to R. Goldstein. I hope all Yeshiva University rabbis will be able to reach and maintain all three of these career goals simultaneously and in perpetuity.

The Story Behind the
Benjamin Hurwitz Award

By Reuben Rudman

Each year The Benjamin Hurwitz Award for Excellence in Talmud is given to a deserving student of the Isaac Breuer College of Hebraic Studies of Yeshiva University. Who was Benjamin Hurwitz and why is an award given in his name?

R. Yekusiel Raphael Hurwitz, father of Benjamin Hurwitz, had been raised in Maitchet and studied in the Volozhin Yeshiva until it closed in 1893. R. Hurwitz, who received *semikhah* from the son of R. Yitzhak Elchanan Spektor, was a cousin and close friend of R. Shlomo Polachek, the Maichater *Illui*, and knew the Soloveitchik family from Volozhin. Like many students in Volozhin, R. Hurwitz was an *Ohev Zion*; he taught his American-born children to speak Hebrew and had purchased land in Raanana through the *Ahuzah Aleph* organization.

Born on May 4, 1910 in New York City, Benjamin Hurwitz attended Rabbi Jacob Joseph Elementary School, where his grandfather, R. Moshe Eliezer Gavrin, was one of the founders. As an orphan, R. Gavrin had been raised by the Shatzkes family, one of whose sons, R. Moshe Shatzkes, later became a *rosh yeshiva* and one of the three members of the RIETS *semikhah* testing board. Thus, in 1929, the Hurwitz family had many ties, past, present and future, with Yeshiva.

In 1927, Benjamin Hurwitz graduated from Yeshiva's TI and TA high school, where he had been president of the student's organization

Dr. Reuben Rudman, YUHS '53, YC '57, BRGS '61, RIETS '61, is Professor Emeritus of Chemistry at Adelphi University, NY, currently living in Jerusalem and lecturing in the graduate school of the Hebrew University of Jerusalem.

and business manager of the yearbook, *The Elchanite*. Soon afterward, Benjamin, together with his mother and two sisters, Deborah (my mother) and Leah (later Wachsman), left for Palestine. They resided in Petach Tikvah while Benjamin learned intensively with an older cousin, R. Tzvi Puchowitz, who had been a student at the Slabodka Yeshiva and a *havrutah* with the young R. Yitzhak Hutner. Benjamin Hurwitz's father remained in New York, with plans to join them after he could arrange his business holdings.

In 1928, R. Puchowitz notified the family that Benjamin Hurwitz was now ready to enter a formal *yeshiva*. He suggested the Yeshiva Knesseth Israel in Hebron, a branch of the Slabodka Yeshiva that had opened a few years earlier, headed by R. Moshe Mordechai Epstein, author of the *Levush Mordekhai*. Benjamin Hurwitz entered the Hebron Yeshiva in 1928.

On March 19, 1929, Dr. Samuel Sar — who in my time at YC, in the late 1950s, was known as Dean Sar — wrote to Benjamin Hurwitz's father: "I am delighted to inform you that the Faculty has decided to award the diploma of the Teachers Institute to your son, who is at present pursuing courses in Palestine... you are respectfully invited to be present and receive the diploma for your son."

The diploma awarded to Benjamin Hurwitz is in Hebrew, handwritten on parchment from the *beit midrash Le-Morim Shel Yeshivat Rabbeinu Yitzhak Elchanan* and declares him to be a "*Moreh u-Mehanekh be-Yisrael*." It is signed by Bernard Revel, *Rosh Yeshiva*, and by Pinkhos Churgin, *Menahel*.

Benjamin Hurwitz learned in Hebron until the fateful day of 18 Av 5789 (*Tarpat*), when the Arabs of Hebron rioted and killed sixty-seven people, including many *yeshiva talmidim*. Benjamin HaLevi Hurwitz was among those killed.

In a letter written only two days before he was murdered, Benjamin Hurwitz described his analysis of the situation, which was getting more serious with each passing day. The week before the riot in Hebron, an Arab had murdered a Jew in Jerusalem. Benjamin had been to Jerusalem and recorded his impressions, as well as his part in the preparations for his mother and sisters to return to the United States while he was to continue his studies in Hebron. The letter ended with the prescient words of consolation, "Your son who cries over the destruction of our Holy Temple." These words were the last Benjamin Hurwitz ever wrote to his father. Two days after this letter was written, and, of course, before his father received it, the Arabs of Hebron rioted and Benjamin Hurwitz was brutally killed at the age of nineteen years and three months.

The Arab rioting was front page news throughout the world, as it seemed that it would lead to a full blown Arab rebellion against the British. *The New York Times* carried Benjamin Hurwitz's name and some family details every day from August 26 to August 30, 1929.

On August 28, a telegram from a Mr. Knabenshue, the American consul general in Palestine, to Mrs. Hurwitz in Petach Tikvah said: "Regret report death your son at Hebron August 23. Mail report follows." The mailed report said exactly the same thing. A telegram from Henry L. Stimson, U.S. Secretary of State, to Mr. Hurwitz in New York, confirmed that information. Of course, by then the family knew; this was the official notification.

Among the condolence letters received by the family were those from Dr. Bernard Revel, R. Moshe Z. Margolies, several TI faculty members, the *Histadrut ha-Talmidim* of TI, the secretary of the June 1927 class, and a representative of the Young Israel Intermediates (Benjamin Hurwitz had been an active member). Three months later, a personal letter from R. Moshe Mordechai Epstein was received, as well as a formal condolence document from the Slabodka Yeshiva office in the United States presented in the name of leading rabbis in the United States at the time. Among the names listed are R. Barukh Ber Lebowitz (Kamenitz), R. Shimon Shkop (who, at that time, was delivering a *shi'ur* at RIETS), R. Eliezer Silver (president of the Agudath HaRabbanim), R. Bernard Levinthal (later Dr. Samuel Belkin's father-in-law), and R. Moshe Z. Margolies.

In concurrence with the memorial services a month later, on September 30, 1929, *The New York Times* reported that 500 people were at a memorial to the "students slain in Palestine...Last night at Yeshiva College at a meeting in memory of the slain students ... a resolution was passed for the creation of a library in memory of Hurwitz." On the first *yahrzeit*, the Young Israel Synagogue held a memorial meeting.

Needless to say, the Hurwitz family was devastated by the loss of Benjamin. Just a few years ago, I met someone who knew my grandfather before and after 1929. She remarked on the major transformation that had taken place in him after the death of his close friend and cousin, the Maichater *Illui*, in 1928 at the age of fifty and that of his son, in 1929 at the age of nineteen.

My grandfather probably kept every piece of paper he ever received, starting when he was a child in Europe. When his attic was cleaned out in 1963, I salvaged a couple of boxes of these papers. Inside were some materials that have never been published dealing with Yeshiva in the years 1923-1943. These papers shed some light on the Benjamin Hurwitz award that he endowed.

Chronologically speaking, the Benjamin Hurwitz award was the first Yeshiva-related response my grandfather had to the loss of his son. On March 31, 1930, Dr. Revel wrote: "It is with heavy heart that we accept your offer for the establishment of a memorial at the Yeshiva for your beloved sainted son, Benjamin... The income from the $500 you have sent will be used every year, as you suggest, as the Benjamin Hurwitz Prize (sic) to the best scholar of the Yeshiva Teachers Institute on the subject of the Bible or Jewish History (sic). The annual occasion of its award will provide an opportunity to bring vividly into the students' minds and hearts the example and inspiration of a beautiful life and heroic death of our beloved Benjamin, of blessed memory."

By May 6, 1931, the fund had been raised to $800 and by 1932 it had reached $1,000. This was commemorated by a panel on the bronze tablet on the wall of David H. Zysman Hall: "In Memory of Benjamin Hurwitz, created by Raphael and Esther Hurwitz." A photograph of this tablet appears in the 1934 Annual Report of the Yeshiva Endowment Foundation, Inc. When I was a student at Yeshiva in the late 1950s, the tablet was still there, although in need of some polishing.

For sixty years, the annual recipient of this prize would write a short note to the family acknowledging receipt of this award. When my mother, of blessed memory, moved to Israel in 1992, presumably without leaving a forwarding address, the letters stopped coming.

How the Rav Stayed With Me

By Fred Sommers

I was in the *shi'ur* of R. Joseph B. Soloveitchik, the Rav, for five years ending in 1947. In 1949, I began graduate work in philosophy at Columbia University and found to my astonishment that none of the lights in contemporary philosophy had his intellectual stature and power. This made things more difficult for me, since it was common for students of philosophy to become disciples of some major figure or to become closely identified with some school of philosophy. The Rav, who never himself preached or encouraged discipleship, had effectively spoiled me for all discipleships and schools of thought. The Rav always expected his students to criticize his assertions, and I was not in a mood to be anyone's *hasid*. In any case, after having studied with the Rav, there was no one around who could command from me the kind of respect I'd had for him as my mentor.

I had learned from the Rav — more by his example than by any explicit teaching of method — to treat each *sugya* with an independence of mind that was literally unorthodox. I had come to YC from Yeshivat Chaim Berlin, where I had studied with R. Yitzhak Hutner. R. Hutner was keen, but his method was standard. We learned the text with Rashi, *Tosafot* and other major commentaries, after which we might raise questions about the various positions and interpretations that had already thoroughly cooked the *sugya* for us in various ways. At no point were

Dr. Fred Sommers, YC '44, RIETS '46, was Harry Austryn Wolfson Professor of Philosophy at Brandeis University. He is known for several original contributions in logic and ontology. A Festschrift on Dr. Sommers, called The Old New Logic: Essays on the Philosophy of Fred Sommers, has recently been published by MIT Press.

we encouraged to look with our own eyes at the *peshat* of the *Gemara*, unfiltered by the major authorities. By sharp contrast, the Rav would approach a *sugya* in a notably objective, unencumbered way, without relying on the authoritative traditional interpretations. He did not explicitly tell us to approach the *Gemara* texts in this way, but those of us who were alert saw that this was what he did; even to those of us who were not methodologically self-conscious, the Rav's exemplary independence of mind was inspiring, if not contagious. *Shi'ur* after exhilarating *shi'ur*, we watched the Rav coolly, objectively, and incisively reason to achieve an interpretation of the Talmudic texts that was intellectually elegant and as consistent as possible with other texts. He did turn to the *rishonim* and *aharonim* as the *shi'ur* unfolded, but only after we all had a clear understanding of the issues and were in a position to see what was going on and why the various controversies among the *mefarshim* had arisen. He gave us the means to understand why the differing authorities said what they said, why they differed, and we also had the means to judge which one was more likely to be right. We were never encouraged to rely on the authorities as a substitute for thinking on our own. The Rav thus exemplified an intellectually independent approach and he respected this approach in any of his students who dared to take it. Indeed, he encouraged and expected it from us.

Please do not misunderstand me. When it comes to philosophy itself I am no disciple of the Rav. The Rav, who had studied philosophy in Berlin, was much too respectful of continental philosophy in the first half of the twentieth century; I never went along with him in his admiration for the existentialists or for philosophers of religion like Rudolph Otto. Where I remain forever in his debt was in his approach to the *Gemara* and *halakhah*. There he taught me what it means to be incisive, unafraid, and thoroughly honest. He taught me to be intellectually on my own, never to defer to authority in the face of reason, never to approach a text or a problem with an official point of view. *Lo ba-shamayim hi,* and also not in the *mefarshim*. He taught his students always to look at the problems without prejudgment and never to turn to authorities without having tried our best to fathom the issues on our own. That approach works wonders in any intellectual endeavor and it was to give me my way in philosophy.

It may sound odd that a teacher of Talmud should be more intellectually independent in his approach than the great secular teachers of philosophy in institutions like Columbia, Harvard, and Oxford, where intellectuals take special pride in being open minded, objective, and uncommitted to anything but reasonable and rational thinking. But the Rav's virtues were not to be found in these academies and I was not prepared for this. I'm now over eighty years old and I've known only one other person who was the Rav's equal in incisiveness, intellectual honesty and effortless brilliance. He was not a philosopher but the late scientist Francis Crick, whose name will ever be remembered as the co-discoverer of the DNA double helix.

The Rav himself had no pretensions; he had no ax to grind, and he never gave the impression that he had a personal stake in getting you to agree with him. He was passionately and dispassionately interested in the subject matter at hand. That subject might well be tradition-bound and we who studied it were committed to it as a practical ethos of faith. But given that constraint, the Rav's treatment of the subject was a brilliant paradigm of the unprejudiced and unfettered use of reason. He was also never less than professional; the Rav was masterful and we learned from him what it meant to be a master of a subject.

The effect of the Rav's example on me was decisive. It doomed me to do independent, solitary work on hard and controversial subjects and to work things out very much on my own. I had no desire whatsoever to join any school of thought or to commit myself to any particular approach or method, however popular. Independence. The Rav's example had left me with no option; if I was going to do philosophy as he did Talmud, I must be focused on the subject matter and not on the potential reader. Being a student of the Rav also gave me a taste for the most fundamental classical areas in philosophy; in the twentieth century this meant logic, the philosophy of language, and ontology. My own interests veered to logic and the theory of predication, and eventually I succeeded to make some original discoveries in these areas.

Certainly the Rav could be caustic and uncomplimentary in criticizing you. He wanted us to know the truth of the matter and when we got it wrong, he did not bother to be diplomatic or sparing of our feelings. His reprimand was always objective; it was never his purpose to put anyone down. He sharply criticized your argument, never your person. We understood that and took no offense. On the other hand, if you said something apt and right to the point, he would look at you with great love, appreciation, and gratitude. He would smile with delight. That was personal. I treasure the moments that brought him to that kind of reaction, even though it was not his custom to say more than a decisive and thundering "Gerecht!" Once — some two decades later — when I had solved a particularly vexing problem (it happened when I was in Israel on the first day of the Six Day War in June 1967), I too accorded myself the compliment of saying "Gerecht!"

The Rav's example inspired me to do careful, systematic work. If I had to put the Rav's influence on me in a few phrases and sentences that express the ideals I strove to emulate, they would be something like the following:

- Independence of mind and method.
- Be incisive, be bold, but also be meticulous, systematic, and careful.
- The problem you choose may be hard but it must allow for a systematic analytic approach.
- Don't tackle a problem if you do not have a systematic strategy for solving it. This meant to me that I must avoid some deep, clearly important and fascinating problems in philosophy. Some of these were fashionable and popular but if I could see no way to approach them with any prospect of solving them or even to getting close to a solution, I would not work on them. I later realized that not all important problems were ripe for a fruitful approach to solving them. Sometimes we just need to have more scientific knowledge. The Rav instinctively understood these limitations and he was always selective in his choices of *sugyot* to be tackled.
- Keeping the above in mind, make an effort to make some progress on some fundamental problem.
- Don't be seduced by metaphors. Keep to a common-sense interpretation and a sensible, reasonable line of approach. (The Rav, who loved *aggadata*, never let it intrude in his formal analysis of halakhic subject-matter.)

Some of you who read this will be doing intellectual and scientific work in fields outside Judaics. If so, you will be applying some of the powerful approaches you are now practicing in your study of the Talmud, especially if you study it in the inspiring and effective way the Rav taught us. The above rules would have been phrased far more elegantly by the Rav himself. But, they are roughly his rules as I learned them from listening to and absorbing him over many years. He was the teacher that influenced me most deeply. What cannot be put into words is the inspiration I got from constantly watching a pure, honest and effortlessly brilliant *gaon*, always unfailingly clearheaded, never ceasing in his joyful intellectual labors, day after day, week after week, an inspiring example of unpretentious genius who loved learning, loved argument, loved Torah, and was the embodiment of the maxim that a true scholar is never envious of his students. He took joy in us and long after we left his presence, we, his students, never ceased taking joy in him.

PART II

THE BELKIN YEARS

Reminiscences of the Past, Visions of the Future

By Steven Bayme

The Jewish people owe a debt to Yeshiva University for its role in Jewish history. Perhaps no institution in Diaspora Jewry matches Yeshiva's significance to world Jewry when it comes to Jewish education, scholarship, community service, and training of future Jewish leaders. For Orthodox Jews in particular, Yeshiva serves as the flagship institution of Modern Orthodoxy, charting a distinctive synthesis of Torah and western culture not as a compromise with the necessities of modern living but as an affirmative statement of vibrant and creative Jewish living in the modern world. For me, as for countless others, Yeshiva challenged my beliefs, expanded my horizons, and taught me the meaning and responsibilities of Jewish citizenship in the contemporary world.

As an entering freshman arriving in Washington Heights in September, 1967, I was excited — even dazzled — by the prospects of higher education at Yeshiva University. A product of thirteen years at the Maimonides Day School in Boston, Massachusetts, I considered myself well prepared to undertake the challenge of advanced study of two very different worlds and to weigh the relationship, as well as the degree of conflict, between them. Under the tutelage of its founder, R. Joseph B. Soloveitchik, Maimonides proudly defined itself as Modern Orthodox and as being rooted in a quest for excellence in both secular and Judaic studies. Particularly important to me was an East European *rosh yeshiva* who, over my junior and senior years of high school, assigned a series of

Dr. Steven Bayme, YC '71, serves as National Director, Contemporary Jewish Life Department, for the American Jewish Committee. Dr. Bayme taught in YC's History department from 1975 – 1979.

term papers to compare and contrast the accounts of creation in traditional commentaries with the perspectives of modern science, the varying ethical sensitivities of the biblical patriarchs, and, most surprisingly, the Joseph narrative in traditional commentaries with Thomas Mann's epic *Joseph and His Brothers*. The experience of sustained research and writing on two very different types of source materials both provided a capstone for thirteen years of Jewish day school education and a portal to the vision of *Torah u-Madda* represented by Yeshiva. Indeed, R. Yosef Blau, then associate principal of Maimonides and today *mashgiah ruhani* at Yeshiva, encouraged me to attend Yeshiva and commented that its strength lay in offering diverse avenues for fulfillment, such as rabbinics, secular studies, and social activism. He wisely predicted that I would focus on excellence in secular studies, albeit within the overall atmosphere of Yeshiva as an Orthodox institution.

Indeed, YC in the 1960s was an exciting place — known for its intellectual diversity and defining Modern Orthodoxy as open to plural perspectives, including those both controversial and challenging. The dominant voices on the faculty in that era were Dr. Yitz Greenberg and R. Aharon Lichtenstein. Although the differences between them were considerable, they shared a mutual commitment to excellence in both realms. Shortly after my arrival, I was treated to a symposium in Furst Hall, attended by over five hundred students, on defining *Torah u-Madda* for the future. The speakers included, in addition to Dr. Greenberg and R. Lichtenstein, Dr. Charles Liebman, rapidly becoming a world-class sociologist of American Jewry, Dr. Emanuel Rackman, "dean" of Modern Orthodox rabbis, and R. Yehuda Parnes, then a prominent RIETS *rosh yeshiva*. R. Parnes opposed the emphasis upon secular studies within the dual curriculum and student body, claiming that secular studies could be sanctioned only for the limited utilitarian purposes of earning a living — not as a source of values or *hashkafah*. The other speakers stressed the excitement of engaging alternative perspectives emanating from humanities and social sciences with those of Torah. Dr. Greenberg in particular came under harsh criticism for his openness to biblical criticism, his dialogue with Conservative and Reform rabbis and scholars, and his indebtedness to Christian theologians and thinkers. Yet all acknowledged his right to teach and, for many, his was the most influential voice on the faculty of that era.

In other words, the University and its administration recognized the significance of western culture for both personal and Judaic development. The then undergraduate dean, Dr. Isaac Bacon, greatly valued a liberal arts education for its own sake and consciously sought Modern Orthodox faculty who embodied the ideals of synthesis and constituted role models for students. Moreover, the intellectual tensions on campus so evident in the quest for synthesis underscored Yeshiva's uniqueness and strengths as flagship of Modern Orthodoxy and as intellectual center for training future Jewish leadership.

More generally, courses on the conflict of science and religion, Jewish intellectual history, the challenges of humanism in Western literature, to name a few, all served to challenge deeply rooted convictions and to develop a worldview integrating the traditions of Judaic heritage with the best currents of Western culture. In short, YC in the 1960s addressed a series of intellectual challenges while seeking to train students in critical thinking about the meaning of being a Jew in the modern world. The elusive goal of synthesis meant constant struggle to live with the creative tension between Torah and modernity, to search out and research difficult questions, and to acknowledge that simplistic answers provided no substitute for serious *hashkafah*.

To be sure, the 1960s were by no means trouble free, and in reviewing those years one must avoid the temptation to don rose-colored glasses. Academic departments generally lacked a critical mass of faculty and had to subsist with very few personnel. The double program in itself posed serious challenges to maintaining standards of excellence and demands upon student productivity. All too often, students cut corners, attributing this to the burdens of a double program. Issues of academic freedom were quite real and at times erupted in ugly forms, including assaults on character and personal integrity. Nevertheless, Yeshiva succeeded in opening the portals of intellectual inquiry, communicating that Jewish education was about the challenge of wrestling with ideas and that ideological conflict in fact reflected how deeply we cared about the future of Modern Orthodoxy and the Jewish People.

More specifically, one unresolved issue concerned both the degree and the limits accorded the academic freedom of the faculty, especially with respect to Jewish historical findings and teachings. Academic freedom protected the capacity of faculty to challenge prevailing views. It endured sustained attacks during the McCarthy period when, regrettably, some professors at American universities were actually dismissed for their "leftist" views. The concept of academic freedom is rooted in the assumption that higher education requires an open environment in which ideas can be freely debated and discussed, even if they are deeply challenging to the prevailing culture's sacred cows. The goals of higher education include teaching students to think for themselves through exposure to a broad array of scholarship and ideas. Although this last criterion of intellectual diversity has, all too often, been observed more in the breach than in reality within American university culture, the canons of academic freedom have generally served students well by exposing them both to a diversity of views and to ideas that may be politically incorrect yet intellectually compelling — or at least worthy of serious consideration.

Although Yeshiva had been somewhat immune to the controversies surrounding McCarthyism in the relatively benign 1950s, Yeshiva experienced its own tensions over academic freedom dating to at least the 1930s. The late Professor Solomon Zeitlin, who taught Second Commonwealth Jewish History, published an article on the Pharisees in 1939 that aroused considerable anger among the *roshei yeshiva*, who claimed that it undermined Oral Law. These tensions blossomed in the 1960s over questions of biblical scholarship, the impact of modern culture upon Jewish teachings, and the relationship of historicist findings to received tradition and texts. In themselves the tensions signaled Yeshiva's uniqueness, for in virtually no other Jewish institution could the dialogue between historian and believer take place with such profundity. The presence of the tensions signaled both Yeshiva's greatness as an Orthodox institution dedicated to the pursuit of truth and its desire to educate students through an open intellectual clash of ideas rather than the stifling of allegedly subversive opinion.

To be sure, most Judaic studies faculty acknowledged the need for some limits upon academic freedom. The *Faculty Handbook* underlined this clearly, although after 1970, when the university charter officially became "secular," the phrase to that effect was carefully blotted out. But the real question lay as to where to draw the limits. Was there a difference between the Pentateuch and the other biblical books? May one approach historical materials in the Talmud critically? Does the historicist temperament pose implications for our understanding of inherited tradition? Was the New Testament permissible for assigned reading and analysis? Ironically, only after the university became officially secularized were the boundaries drawn ever more tightly and the realm of dogma broadened significantly so as to constrain free intellectual discourse. Regrettably, Yeshiva's leadership, seemingly more concerned with maintaining institutional harmony, preferred that these controversies disappear rather than uphold them as the distinctive hallmarks of an institution that was simultaneously both a *yeshiva* and a university. These questions of approaches to biblical criticism, historical scholarship, rabbinic historiography, and the like, became relatively closed areas of inquiry rather than areas that could invigorate Yeshiva's students and future leaders of the Orthodox community. Although in subsequent years some of these questions would flicker occasionally, this aspect of Yeshiva's uniqueness and history would gradually fade, to the delight of some and to the dismay of others.

In joining the YC faculty in the 1970s, I was eager to continue what I regarded as the critical task of helping to educate and train Modern Orthodox Jews to confront the challenges of western culture. When Dr. Norman Lamm, a former professor with whom I had studied Jewish Philosophy and Mysticism, became president of Yeshiva, he tendered my first teaching appointment in Jewish and general history. Nervous at first, I was soon completely hooked on the experience of teaching YC students. A long day of classes left me only exhilarated and eager to return for more. Yeshiva's undergraduates were superb and a joy to teach, providing a natural forum to explore Jewish ideas and their intersection with western culture. My conversations with students, participation in campus politics, and my ongoing preparation for classes convinced me that I was blessed with a wonderful opportunity to help shape the Jewish community of the future and to articulate a distinctive vision of what being Jewish meant in the modern world.

Therefore, it was with great sadness that, for personal and professional reasons, I ultimately left Yeshiva's faculty and subsequently became a staff officer and spokesman for the American Jewish Committee. Upon leaving I noted how several trends at work within Yeshiva and American Orthodoxy could well shape a very different direction from the one with which I identified and from which I had so benefited. For one thing, the voices of the Talmud faculty had become increasingly outspoken and influential. Previously more restrained in their rhetoric, by the 1980s newer and younger *roshei yeshiva* began to define Modern Orthodoxy as, at best, a necessary accommodation for the purposes of earning a living.

This more narrow and isolationist view — one member of the Talmud faculty went so far as to equate Modern Orthodoxy with the "*Amalek*" of our time — increasingly became a visible, if not dominant, intellectual voice at Yeshiva. Once marginal voices, critical of the very endeavor of synthesis between Torah and *madda*, now became mainstream, or, as one senior colleague put it at one of the last faculty meetings I attended, "we are rapidly becoming a first class *yeshiva* with a few college courses attached to it."

Secondly, the near-universal practice of a year of study at Israeli *yeshivot* fundamentally transformed Yeshiva's intellectual culture. To be sure, I saw great value in the one-year post high school experience at an Israeli *yeshiva* and sent each of my own children to such an institution. However, within Yeshiva, the Israel experience meant limiting college to three years or less. By definition, undergraduate course work would be diminished by twenty-five percent or more. Moreover, the Israel experience signaled the ascendancy of *roshei yeshiva* as primary intellectual influences. Symbolically, the *beit midrash*, rather than the library, became the hub of Yeshiva's academic activity. Encouraging questioning and doubt gave way to a quest for certitude.

Perhaps nowhere was this more evident than in discussions concerning Middle East politics. I began to wonder aloud about the religious messianism of Gush Emunim and questioned why the late R. Meir Kahane remained a featured speaker on campus long after the rest of the Jewish community had ostracized him and his ugly messages of racism and hatred of Arabs, so chillingly reminiscent of the 1930s Nuremberg legislation.

Lastly, Yeshiva's culture was transformed significantly via the more general drift towards professionalism in higher education. As the cost of tuition rose, students and their parents increasingly were asking what professional skills they were receiving for their money. The traditional answer of the academy had been that learning how to read critically, think coherently, and write effectively were the hallmarks of an educated citizenry and skills necessary for effective communal leadership. This answer, however, now increasingly sounded hollow in a world in which students expected well-paying jobs shortly after graduation. The idea of college as time for individual growth of mind, body, and persona sounded to many as, at best, a luxury item that needed to give way to learning practical skills like budgeting and balance sheets. Moreover, Yeshiva itself confronted a serious decline in numbers of undergraduates, and its leadership was determined to increase enrollment rates, if necessary by fulfilling student desires for a more practical undergraduate education. Ironically, this emphasis upon professional skills suited quite well the worldview of the *roshei yeshiva*. They too wished to see their students engaged in gainful employment, while Talmud and Torah served as sources of values and ideology. Thus the "learner-earner" replaced the ideal of intellectual synthesis in communal discourse.

What then of the future? Returning to teach for a semester in 1999, I was again overwhelmed by the quality of Yeshiva's undergraduates. Without doubt, the best of Yeshiva's students easily match the best of Harvard's. I also witnessed the potential for developing a Jewish leadership that could be solidly anchored in the world of Jewish tradition and at the same time engaged with the challenges of modern scholarship and culture. Precisely at a time when Jewish communal leaders agonize over the ravages of assimilation and mixed marriage and struggle to secure future Jewish continuity, Modern Orthodoxy in particular can demonstrate both its success stories and its paradigm of integration of two very different yet powerful and attractive cultures.

For it to do that, however, major changes are required by all concerned. The delicate balance, and even tension, between secular and religious studies need to be expressed and not repressed. Some intellectual conflict is indeed preferable to a non-aggression pact, for the conflict itself demonstrates precisely how passionately we care about these issues. Spokesmen for Modern Orthodoxy need to reassert their vigor, independence, and verve in defining Modern Orthodoxy as paradigm rather than as concession. A quest for synthesis between Torah and *madda* necessitates a *weltanschauung* that has its own compelling strengths and integrity and does not require us to look to leadership on either right or left. University officials need to acknowledge that faculty and courses that embody Modern Orthodox values and ideals are likely to have the most positive impact upon students and university culture generally. Lastly, and perhaps above all, students need to recognize the need for sacrifice and deferred expectations. The college experience cannot be a simple matter of accumulating credits from diverse sources. It needs to be a coherent and sustained program of core requirements, advanced electives, serious reading, and independent research. The demands for such a program will, without question, be quite heavy, but the long term rewards will far outweigh the efforts required.

Transformations

By Ruth A. Bevan

Before the earth was created, God dreamed about building a very special place on earth. This very special place would be called Yeshiva University. It would be nestled in Washington Heights, overlooking the East River, where the captain on the Circle Line circling Manhattan each and every day would point out to his passengers the golden Byzantine dome designating this very special place. The sun would shine. All would be well.

There would be so many yarmulkes swirling atop Jewish heads attached to Jewish bodies frantically scurrying to and fro that, in their knitted and woven mass, they would appear like a magical flying carpet with fringes over Amsterdam Avenue in these Washington Heights. This magical flying carpet would carry *mitzvot* and *berakhot* near and far. Awe-inspiring!

The plan was laid. It even included a kosher pizzeria. Eventually, hopefully, a Chinese restaurant. Or, at least, a sushi counter.

And then the earth was born. It wasn't exactly according to plan, but close enough. As for the very special place in Washington Heights, the pizza could have less sauce and more cheese. Sometimes the Circle Line skipped a beat. The magic carpet got weighted down; too many responsibilities. But it carried on. Furst Hall, adorned in kindergarten pastels, throbbed with activity both intellectual and bureaucratic. A rather unhappy mix.

Dr. Ruth A. Bevan is the David W. Petegorsky Professor of Political Science at Yeshiva College and the Director of the Rabbi Arthur Schneier Center for International Affairs at Yeshiva University.

The garage on Amsterdam Avenue housed the library. Next door, thespians performed on a make-shift stage. Morg and Rubin dorms sported a lawn, now forgotten, where every year commencement took place under the grueling summer sun, over the years bleaching the colorful academic robes of faculty. On the lawn, parents came to glow with pride, to shake hands with esteemed faculty, to enjoy afternoon tea and to wonder at this special place specially created in Washington Heights. The sun shone, as planned. And all seemed well.

Years later, commencement exercises moved to Madison Square Garden. Its air conditioned theater gave younger faculty the color edge. Their robes did not bleach out. In Madison Square Garden, parents disappeared unseen in the crowd while faculty, equally unseen, wondered how they slipped through the cracks of official, that is to say, bureaucratic self-congratulatory recognition of bureaucratic accomplishments at commencement ceremonies, meant, after all, for faculty and students, at this very special place. Even those with unbleached academic robes wondered why they felt so blanched. A cloud eclipsed the sun.

During the days of the great lawn, where students played soccer, where bare feet greeted the springtime earth, where the sun shone on commencement, my path wound its way to YC. I was twenty-six, still in graduate school and trying to get the hang of New York City after studying in Europe for two years. New Yorkers told me I had an accent; one cabbie asked me where I learned to speak English so well. In Boston, I replied. He seemed satisfied with that. To my relief no question about my supposed accent cropped up at Yeshiva, since virtually everyone there at that time had an accent.

Dean Isaac Bacon, a gentle, gracious man, spoke with a German accent from Prague. President Samuel Belkin, the rabbis, all of them brought the Old World to Washington Heights. Even the seemingly sole American-born administrator, Morris Silverman, the punctilious Registrar, spoke with an accent, albeit one from Brooklyn.

In these years immediately after JFK's assassination, when young Americans, in particular, remained determined to keep alive the Kennedy Peace Corps vision, YC students remained determined to make it in America. These were first generation Americans at best. A few had been transported in the womb from Displaced Persons camps in war-ravaged Europe to this New World. More than their edges were rough. Middle class mores remained beyond reach. They spoke with the mainly East

European accents of their immigrant families and reflected their families' belief that the world at large worked against them as Jews. These same families feared that New York's first Jewish mayor, Abraham Beame, would spell disaster for all Jews everywhere. What if he makes a mistake? They'll take it out on the Jews, you'll see.

For this generation of students, Yeshiva University appeared like a mythical kingdom. Where in Europe did such a place exist? How many of their parents had been able even to dream about going to college? Now these students, their children, read old English literary texts, dissected frogs in the biology lab, and put on plays under the spirited direction of that new, young speech professor. What kind of a name is Beukas? Moreover, a young woman now taught them political science. What kind of a science is that? What kind of a name is Bevan?

Studying politics in their minds meant finding out how to survive in a world where other people, non-Jews, exercised power. And for a woman to teach political science at that time meant teaching how men use power. Women voted, but that pretty much covered it. No one thought of women as powerful. Women in political science graduate schools lacked visibility as a tiny minority. After giving my very first paper at the American Political Science Association meetings in 1969, a male member of the audience remarked that I was a "rare bird on the lecture platform." So here we now were, YC students and I, studying about the world of power, our other.

At best five years separated me in age from my oldest student. I called everyone "Mister" to create distance. In our own separate ways, we all were struggling to find our voice. Being heard was another matter. We lived rich interior lives. In those vibrant interior spaces, doors miraculously opened; drawers revealed their contents — like the drawer of my classroom desk that I opened to search for chalk only to find a hidden message: "Dr. Bevan, I love you!"

A stately group of full professors stood at the College's helm — David Fleisher (English), Arthur Tauber (Speech), Irving Linn (English), Joseph Dunner (Political Science), and Samuel Goldberg (Sociology). Louis Feldman was an up-and-coming young Classics professor. They all came dressed in suit and tie and created an air of authority wherever they went. (Most of my early students also dressed in suits — black suits and black hats.) Faculty meetings took place evenings in Furst 535 behind closed doors. *The Commentator* reporters waited outside for the scoop of the day.

Gravity found its center in the Rav. Berlin educated, he encapsulated *Torah u-Madda*. His aura gave life and distinction to the campus. Students, faculty, anybody and everybody packed into Lamport Auditorium of the Byzantine building for the Rav's annual *Yahrzeit Shi'ur*. Nervous excitement filled the air of the vaulted auditorium as everyone awaited "The Entry." Some, seated in pairs, contested points of text, lifting their yarmulkes and replacing them on their heads in a twirling gesture of intellectual exasperation. Others sat passively, waiting to be stimulated. The Rav entered to a reverential standing audience. And, in his quietly measured voice, he began his *shi'ur*, sitting at a table on the stage. To hear his wisdom in his inwardly resonating voice against the handicap of poor acoustics in the auditorium, the entire audience became one gigantic ear bent as far forward as possible to catch the vibrating sound waves.

In May 1967, Yeshiva College in effect closed. Israel was under attack. Students volunteered. Joseph Dunner, head of the Political Science Department and my husband, departed for Israel along with students. After the war, we journeyed to the newly liberated Mt. Scopus. Israel had turned a corner in its modern existence.

The pressures of war in the Middle East defined our lives. We lived with a sense of constant emergency. For the post-Holocaust generation of Jews, this war extended the threat of the Holocaust. It meant the Holocaust had not ended — only one phase of it had terminated. Racial unrest in New York City that produced a new outcropping of anti-Semitism brought the sense of a two-front war. In those days, political science classes and offices were on the fifth floor of what I still call the Byzantine building, Muss Hall. In those days, too, we had several former Israeli soldiers. In my classroom we had two exit doors, one in the front and one in the back. From a military point of view, these double doors posed defense problems. Fearful of a neighborhood possibly besieged by anti-Semitic ideological gangs, these Israeli students organized a defense system of my classroom. And so we lived for some years.

And then came the Jewish Defense League. At first they appeared reasonable, before it got out of hand. "Never again" is a credible post-Holocaust objective, and self defense certainly a human right. But the JDL became dysfunctional. Some students of mine got arrested and, deserted by JDL leadership, called me desperately for help. One mindlessly asked me during such a telephone call if I had a picture of the Arch of Titus of which I had spoken in class, on which is depicted the Roman enslavement of Jews with the caption *"Judea capta."* "Why do you want it?" I asked. "To show the Judge how persecuted Jews have been throughout history," he replied. "That does not justify your defacing United Nations property," I answered.

The Vietnam War invaded YC. Students wanted a piece of the action but did not know how to achieve it. A major debate was staged on the pros and cons of the war. Some students wore armbands and headbands signifying protest. Others watched others protest on TV. The RIETS enrollment swelled as students sought refuge from the draft. Moshe Dayan waded through the swamps of South Vietnam to show solidarity with America. Rebellious students desired to ape Columbia University by sitting in on President Belkin's office for a brief sit-down. Demands for New Left student democracy arose! The University Senate was created to give students a voice in decision-making. Faculty meetings went into suspended animation.

Belfer Hall was built; then the library building. The theater in the garage moved to Schottenstein. Rubin lost its lawn to a gym with an indoor swimming pool. Rumors abounded of transporting YC and Stern to a bucolic campus in New Jersey.

Returning one fall, I noticed a snazzy yellow Lotus parked by Furst Hall. The neighborhood now being Dominican, it was unlikely that the owner of the Lotus came from the neighborhood. Even the resident drug dealers weren't that flamboyant. Some research revealed a YC student owner. He wore no black suit and hat, but Bermuda shorts with an emblazoned T-shirt and a knitted yarmulke. He had spent the summer in Israel, planned to return for the winter break, and otherwise lived in the Five Towns.

A new crop of young professors replaced the former stately elite. Those of us who were mid-generation now had to take up the leadership slack. Some heroically fought the union battle that the Supreme Court squashed. I remember the gentle but perseverant professor of physics, Ralph Berens, who devoted himself to the cause of faculty rights and of justice. I would also like to recognize the unstinting devotion to the faculty cause of Prof. Manfred Weidhorn. In the Supreme Court's brief, only Justice Brennan's dissent got the issue on the nose. It didn't matter; it was a done deal. That did not make the faculty's cause any less valid or any less urgent. We suffered. Some of us left, as I did shortly before the decision was rendered. My husband and I packed all our belongings and moved to the Stanford area of California, where I had a position at the Hoover Institution at Stanford University. We did not expect to return.

Then our dreams of a new life collapsed. My husband, who had undergone an unexpected cancer operation shortly before our departure, required chemotherapy treatment that specialists in California did not administer. I urged our return. I had taken a leave from Yeshiva, so I was able to reconnect.

On the one hand, that was for me a fatal professional step. On the other hand, it produced its own rewards. What I sacrificed in professional advantages I gained in rich student associations. Students close to my heart can not be enumerated here. They know who they are and how grateful I am for their involvement in my life and in that of my husband's. An active Zionist since his Blauweiss days in Germany, my husband had created the YC Political Science Department in 1964 as a department devoted to Israel and to Jewish well-being, to activism. Elected to the German Reichstag, blacklisted by Hitler, and escaping Germany in the dead of night with only a backpack, a member of Patton's occupation army in Germany after World War II, court-martialed for countermanding Patton's order to send all Jews back to their East European countries of origin, where Communism awaited them, and saved by President Harry Truman from this court martial, my husband well understood politics and the need for political activism to protect one's rights. That was the tradition he inspired and carried on at Yeshiva College. How many students he touched in the process! How many students touched us as we worked together!

In the 80s we had a particularly active program, emphasizing leadership training and involvement in active politics. Accents had largely disappeared on the Yeshiva campus. We now dealt with second and third-generation American Orthodox Jews who felt as entitled as any other American citizen to basic rights and to expectations about the good life. Oddly enough, my accent now stood out. It became a matter of curiosity. One foreign student told me, "You pronounce whole words!" Professor Linn of the English department, in his declining years, speculated suddenly, breaking ranks with the silence of all those years, that he thought he traced my accent back to the Mississippi Delta, which, as someone born and bred in Massachusetts, I knew little about even from books. The yellow Lotus became commonplace as Orthodox families moved into middle and upper middle class America. YC no longer represented a fantasy kingdom but reflected the arrival of American Orthodox Jews in American society, both economically and in terms of power.

No Yeshiva student today assumes he has no power potential. No Yeshiva student, or, probably, his parents, would question the viability of a Jewish political candidate or the wisdom of electing a Jew. Since the days of my arrival at the age of twenty-six, Yeshiva has undergone its own Americanization. It has arrived. We have students who are in public office. Our present American Ambassador to Israel, Daniel Kurtzer, was a political science major and later dean of YC. We now have students contemplating campaign management positions or running for elected office.

The intifada notwithstanding, Israel remains safe. We worry less about Israel's survival than about Israel's security. But success on the home-front and on the Israel-front brings with it complacency. We lost our edge of difference and insecurity; our accents gave way to hip. We don't feel the same need for activism as we loll in front of the TV and otherwise enjoy the good life.

Cell phones, iPods, laptops and Walkmen give us the illusion of a qualitatively better life and thus, by false deduction, of a more secure life.

And the captain of the Circle Line pointed out to the passengers the golden Byzantine dome that signified YC. And he swept his finger in the air from the golden dome to the Belfer Building skyscraper to the dormitories, Revaya, and Time Out. And a great wind stirred the waters, causing the Circle Line to sway back and forth.

The passengers grew anxious. Objects fell about the gyrating ship. Overhead, students walked about Amsterdam Avenue, holding onto their *kippot* in the curling wind, but otherwise oblivious to the waters below. Tomorrow would begin the weekend; they would retreat to their homes. Out-of-towners and foreign students would find a weekend haven. God looked upon his very special creation quizzically.

A *Torah u-Madda* Intellectual Autobiography

By Jack Bieler

When I think back to my Yeshiva College years (1964-69), I realize that the undergraduate experience was chiefly responsible for the development of the *Torah u-Madda* perspective with which I have approached my career in Jewish education and the rabbinate. As a veteran educator with an interest in the philosophy of Jewish education, I am accustomed to reflecting upon concise educational strategies that can contribute to advancing particular perspectives and orientations in students. Since of late there has been much discussion regarding the increasing paucity of self-conscious and proactive educational contexts within which the interdisciplinary and integrated approach championed by Dr. Bernard Revel is unabashedly advanced, I have decided in this essay to focus upon my own experience and consider how my personal *hashkafah* evolved, in the interests of possibly providing implicit recommendations to those interested in assuring that *Torah u-Madda* remains a viable option for students of Judaism in Yeshiva and elsewhere.

Nothing prior to my arriving on the Washington Heights campus in the fall of 1964 provided me with even an inkling of the *hashkafah* that is so intrinsic to the Modern Orthodoxy that I have espoused. My late parents had immigrated to the United States from Europe and never so much as completed high school. Shabbat and Yom Tov services, as well as

---

Rabbi Jack Bieler, YC '69, RIETS '74, Ferkauf '74, has been Chairman of the Talmud Department at The Ramaz School and a permanent Scholar-in-Residence at Congregation Kehilath Jeshurun. Rabbi Bieler has served as Assistant Principal and member of the Judaic Studies Faculty at the Melvin J. Berman Hebrew Academy, and is the rabbi of the Kemp Mill Synagogue in Silver Spring, MD.

my memories of the Talmud Torah in the Conservative synagogue which my family attended, can hardly be credited with offering a sophisticated intellectual approach. As for the bulk of my formative education, I am a product of the public schools of Queens, N.Y. which, while offering me a solid *madda* background, was hardly a source of Torah.

My first encounter with *Torah u-Madda* was not so much in terms of a concept or abstract idea, but rather in the embodiment of such an outlook and lifestyle in many of the instructors of the *shi'urim* and classes at Yeshiva. A general observation that struck me deeply early on was how many of my teachers in both general as well as Judaic studies were also congregational rabbis. While in some cases, this may have been the result of an individual needing to increase the relatively inadequate financial compensation that he was receiving from his synagogue community, or even vice versa — meager payment for teaching part-time on the college level could be augmented by serving as a part-time congregational rabbi. Nevertheless I was impressed that a person could bridge the worlds of academics and communal service and serve in both domains with distinction.

The very first college class that I ever had, during the first afternoon period of the first day of classes, propitiously allowed me to encounter one such unforgettable personality, R. Dr. Maurice Wohlgelernter. In addition to impressing us with his erudition, analytical expertise in dissecting short stories, and ability to critique and hone our writing skills, Dr. Wohlgelernter, or the "Reb" as he demanded we refer to him, later in the year invited the class to attend the celebration at his synagogue honoring him for the book that he had just authored on Israel Zangwill, *The King of Schnorrers*. The numerous "hats" that the "Reb" wore, English professor, author, synagogue rabbi, served to broaden my understanding of what a fully engaged and multi-dimensional religious and academic life might entail.

R. Dr. Irving "Yitz" Greenberg, by means of his class on the *Mussar* Movement in general and R. Yisrael Salanter in particular, reinforced the impression that the "Reb" had made upon me. By the time I participated in his class, R. Greenberg had achieved a significant reputation as a masterful synagogue rabbi with regard to his great contributions to the Riverdale Jewish Center and his advocacy for and input in the cutting-edge SAR Academy in Riverdale, as well as a radical thinker, unafraid to challenge many of the "orthodoxies" of Jewish Orthodoxy. The fact that he had a PhD in history from Harvard and taught courses in Yeshiva College intrigued me, and I decided that it was important to see how these various roles contributed to a college course. I remember being powerfully stimulated by not only R. Greenberg's lectures — I remember and cite to this day some of the material about R. Salanter that I first learned in this class some thirty years ago — but by the exchanges between the instructor and several knowledgeable students who regularly challenged R. Greenberg's assumptions. Due to my public school background, I was still a student at JSS during my junior year and was hardly in a position to evaluate the extent to which R. Greenberg was combining some of his controversial theological ideas with the class' subject matter. But some of my classmates rose to what they considered the regular challenges posed by the teacher. I do not recall another class which was so electric, and not only did I come away with many thoughts about how Judaism and general history could, and even should, be integrated, but I also never forgot how the provocative "gadfly" Socratic approach to teaching could be so powerfully memorable and educationally effective. I have tried to emulate the stance of teacher as "agent provocateur" in my own career, due in no small measure to experiencing the give-and-take in a true *Torah u-Madda* context.

  A third seminal example that is emblazoned in my memory is R. Dr. Moshe Tendler's introductory biology class. By this time, it was clear to me that the humanities were my destiny, and I would enroll in science and mathematics classes only to fulfill distribution requirements. Although I did not expect to be enthralled by studying biology, R. Tendler's approach and general persona captured my attention and interest. Here was another individual who was a community rabbi in Monsey, a *maggid shi'ur* at Yeshiva, and a distinguished biologist and medical authority. During the course of his lectures, R. Tendler would often regale us with accounts of his varied and profoundly interesting experiences and interchanges with all sorts of memorable personalities, not the least of whom was his father-in-law, R. Moshe Feinstein. Sitting in R. Tendler's class, it was unmistakable to all that he was looking at biology through the lens of Torah and vice versa.

  In addition to the intriguing modeling provided by synagogue rabbis who, possessing wide interests and knowledge, also taught secular college classes, certain other instructors, although not necessarily personally *benei Torah*, nevertheless conveyed to their students the possibility and necessity of bridging the worlds of *Torah u-Madda*. As an English major, I studied with Dr. David Fleisher for six semesters. Dr. Fleisher was another memorable instructor whose sardonic humor was unmatched. He also was a master of literature, and it was a privilege to study with him. In contrast to the teachers that I mentioned above, some of whom peppered their presentations with references from both the world of Torah as well as a particular general studies discipline, Dr. Fleisher rarely let on regarding the extent of his own personal Jewish knowledge and observance. This is why I was quite taken aback when the three hour examination for his "Art of Drama" course consisted of the following single question: "You have been commissioned to write a musical about either the life of Moses or David. Which would you choose and why?" I can say with assuredness that I had not expected to be called upon to integrate biblical studies with what I had learned and been thinking about concerning the structures, contents, and dramatization of plays. Furthermore, throughout "The Art of Drama" nary a reference had ever been made to any biblical character, let alone Moses and David. Dr. Fleisher was challenging each us to "think out of the box," to cross disciplinary lines and develop ideas that would be cross-pollinated by contributions from the worlds of Judaic and secular studies.

I am fairly certain that this question at least in part motivated me to pursue the same sort of thinking within the contexts of topics of papers that I wrote for other courses. In the Shakespeare course taught by Dr. Manfred Weidhorn, one of the papers that I submitted was a comparison of the interpretations of the biblical verses that Shylock cites in *The Merchant of Venice* with how Barabas understands Torah passages in *The Jew of Malta*. While biblical texts were not an area of Dr. Weidhorn's expertise, he encouraged me to write the paper, and commented upon it as seriously as any that other students submitted. In another of Dr. Fleisher's courses on 17th Century British Literature, I wrote about John Milton's essay concerning censorship, "The Areopagitica," and compared what he says with regard to the censoring of religious writings and the general state of religion today. Consequently, in addition to whatever else I learned in "The Art of Drama," the implied lesson from the question on the final left a deep impression.

Another source of modeling *Torah u-Madda* thinking for me while at Yeshiva was the student publications that were produced during my college years. The *Gesher* annual contained a number of articles, including one entitled "Synthesis" by a young R. Aharon Lichtenstein, which constituted written exercises wherein the authors grappled with reconciling assumptions between their Yeshiva and college studies. *Hamevaser*, which was published several times over the course of each academic year, also strove to clarify and explore contemporary Jewish issues by accessing a wide variety of materials and disciplines. I remember reading R. Joseph Soloveitchik's essay "Confrontation" on the issue of ecumenical interchanges with representatives of other religions, a subject that has recently been revisited at conferences and in journal articles, in *Hamevaser* shortly after the Rav presented it in lecture form in Lamport Auditorium in 1964. Even *The Commentator* literary supplement gave me an opportunity to review I. B. Singer's collection of short stories *A Crown of Feathers*, an assignment that challenged me to evaluate a volume containing a plethora of traditional Jewish themes from the perspective of both traditional Jewish thought as well as literary sensibility.

By the time I entered R. Aharon Lichtenstein's *shi'ur* during my final year in Yeshiva College, my sensitivity for *Torah u-Madda* was already considerably developed. Nevertheless, R. Lichtenstein demonstrated from time to time, particularly during *mahshavah* discussions at the end of the Thursday afternoon *shi'ur*, in a very overt and unapologetic manner, how great works of general literature and philosophy can be smoothly integrated and intertwined with Jewish primary and secondary sources. I remember very clearly discussing a personal issue with him one day in the Rubin Hall cafeteria, and his rejoinder based upon a quote from Nietzsche. R. Lichtenstein not only presented the possibility of *Torah u-Madda*; he continues to personally embody the conception in a most impressive and inspiring manner in his writing and oral presentations, which I, for one, am very drawn to emulate on my own modest level.

There have been those who have maintained that the only responsibility that Yeshiva should have with respect to *Torah u-Madda* is to provide students with exposure to the various disciplines "on both sides of the curriculum" and then leave it up to them to reconcile and integrate what they have learned. I disagree with such an approach from an educational philosophy perspective — in my estimation, Yeshiva College students, let alone younger individuals attending day schools, have hardly the maturity, sophistication or breadth of knowledge that will allow them to successfully and meaningfully integrate the often ostensibly antithetical ideas that they have been taught. In addition, reflecting upon my own personal educational experience leads me to conclude that *Torah u-Madda* can best be conveyed and promoted by means of living examples of teachers — both *magiddei shi'ur* and secular studies instructors — who actually think and live such a life in "real time," as well as by means of writing assignments, papers, and publications that demand and provide opportunities for students to be encouraged to engage in this type of thinking in serious and ongoing manner.

Fifty Years and Still Going Strong:
Professor Louis Feldman at Yeshiva University

By Jay Braverman

Thursday evening, September 8, 1955 was an auspicious day in YC's history. A young scholar, armed with a PhD in Classics from Harvard and four-years teaching experience (including two courses at Hartford Theological Seminary on the original Greek of the Gospels and Paul's Epistles) joined the faculty of YC.

At that time, I was beginning my sophomore year at Yeshiva and received permission from the instructor to audit Dr. Feldman's History 19 course in Roman Civilization, which met at the ungodly hour of 9:30 PM on Thursday nights. I vividly recall the first lecture. Before he began lecturing, Dr. Feldman distributed a typed outline (which I still have today) with an annotated bibliography of seven works. The bibliography included: "*The Foundation of Roman Italy* by J. Whatmough, my most dogmatic teacher at Harvard, and *The Etruscan* by Walthari, a recent bestseller; really gory." The eleven suggested topics for the term paper included one that intrigued me, "Jews in the works of the Church Fathers, e.g. Jerome." I had previously taken a course in the History of Western Civilization and never came across the term "Church Fathers." That first lecture dealt with, among other things, Virgil's *Aeneid* and the legend of Romulus' founding of Rome in 753 B.C.E. (one hundred and sixty-seven

Jay Braverman, YC'58, RIETS '61 and BRGS '70, currently teaches Classics and Humanities at Montclair State University. He has specialized in Jewish Day School and Supplementary School Education since 1955 and served as Educational Director of the United Talmud Torahs of Montreal from 1970-88. Rabbi Dr. Braverman's honors from Yeshiva University include the Bernard Revel Memorial Award and the Educator of Distinction Award.

years before the Babylonian destruction of the First Temple, I quickly calculated). Why did these names and facts "draw a blank" with me? I didn't even know that Rome existed as a world power before Herod asked it to intercede in the affairs of Judea, approximately one hundred years before the destruction of the Second Temple. Weren't the Greeks and Hellenists dominant in the Ancient World until approximately 165 B.C.E. (Hanukah)? What were the Romans doing from the 8th century B.C.E. until the first century B.C.E.?

Who was this Dr. Feldman who shook the foundations of my comfortable capsule knowledge of the Ancient Near East? By the end of the lecture, after referring to many Latin terms, the professor simply stated that without knowledge of Latin, one cannot understand the basics of English, and is really not educated. I went home quite upset to learn how ignorant I was.

This was my introduction to a teacher who has become my most important academic mentor for the past fifty years, who guided me through the Latin complexities of Cicero and Virgil, enlightened me concerning the influence of Classical Civilization on the world in general and on Judaism in particular, initiated me on the path of serious scholarly research, encouraged me in my choice of Jewish education as a professional career, directed me in the research for my doctoral dissertation at BRGS: "The Influence of the Rabbis on the Church Fathers (especially Jerome) in their Interpretation of *Tanach*," and painstakingly checked every jot and title in the manuscript prior to its publication by the Catholic University of America. Best of all, he remains both a mentor and a close friend to the present day. The only way I can repay my debt to Dr. Feldman is by continuing to teach others in his footsteps.

My experience as Dr. Feldman's student was not unique. One could contact (extemporaneously) any of his students during the past fifty years and ask about their impressions and remembrances, and the stories would be quite similar, whether they took Latin or Greek, Classical or Intellectual History, or Masterpieces in Western Literature. Our individual memories of him are sharp despite the passage of time; our collective memories have added layers to the "Feldman Lore," which has become the "Feldman Legend."

As students, we were not aware of his stature in the academic community outside of Yeshiva. His humility disguised his rapidly developing reputation as a world-renowned authority on Josephus. When I found out, quite by accident, that Louis Feldman translated Books eighteen to twenty of the prestigious Loeb Series of Josephus' Antiquities, I was amazed! This series was the accepted gold standard of the translations of classical Greek and Latin texts. During his fifty years at Yeshiva, Dr. Feldman has compiled an astounding number of scholarly publications: four books edited, twelve books written, and one hundred and sixty-eight articles in scholarly journals. He has been awarded many academic honors including an Honorary L.H.D. from Trinity College, Fellow of the Guggenheim Foundation, Senior Fellow of the American Council of Learned Societies, Fellow of the Annenberg Research Institute for Judaica and Near Eastern Studies, and Fellow of the Institute for Advanced Study, Princeton. He has served as visiting professor at many leading universities, including Bar-Ilan, Dropsie College and Mount Holyoke College. He has been courted by many universities offering positions with substantially higher remuneration, as well as considerably less teaching and administrative responsibilities, to allow him the opportunity to devote more time to research and publication. Because he is committed to the ideals of Yeshiva University and prefers to teach the type of student that it attracts, he has declined every offer.

Dr. Feldman's devotion to students comes first, even if this interferes with his research and publication. Throughout his long tenure at Yeshiva, he made sure to teach each term, in addition to his required full-time assignments, any extra classes needed to complete a sequence in elementary, intermediate, and advanced Latin and Greek. He does this frequently without remuneration. Once a student of Dr. Feldman, always a student. He maintains files on the accomplishments of every student, always ready to write meaningful recommendations and advise them, even if he hasn't had contact with them in decades. He revived the *Eta Sigma Phi* Classical Honor Society and continues to hold annual meetings in his home for inductees.

Professor Feldman's reputation precedes him. Only those students willing to submit themselves to a demanding taskmaster dare enroll in his language classes. He does not compromise in pushing his students to pursue excellence. (I am told that he has mellowed somewhat since the 1950s, but it is hard for me to imagine Dr. Feldman's version of "mellowed.") There was never a moment wasted in class; he even begins the first class session of the term at a rapid pace — *in medias* race [sic]. Each class session of Latin 1, which is devoted to the mastery of basic

Latin grammar, began with a short quiz, which lasted precisely the amount of time that Dr. Feldman expected a student to answer the questions, and not a second more. As the term progressed, we were expected to translate more rapidly. The tests were graded in percentages, carried out to the nearest seventh. The final exams were unusually creative. I remember the first question in the Intellectual History final: "*Rabosai*, you have been chosen to sit in Heavenly Judgment to evaluate the following great thinkers: Plato, Aristotle, Augustine and Thomas Aquinas, as far as their contributions to Western Civilization. Grade each one, followed by a detailed justification of your grade." The term papers were just as creative. In Latin 4 each student was given ten lines of the *Aeneid* together with six famous translations of these lines: Three in English (from the eighteenth, nineteenth, and twentieth centuries) one each in French, Spanish and Italian. We were asked to evaluate the positive and negative aspects of each translation, grade each, and then indicate what aspects of the original Latin no translation could capture. When we protested that not one of us knew French, Spanish and Italian, Dr. Feldman answered, with a straight face: I will give you a week to familiarize yourself with all three languages!

When a term paper was due on a specific day, Dr. Feldman graciously offered to accept the paper in his apartment until 11:59 pm on that day. I once attended a seminar in his home on an evening that a term paper was due for another class. As the clock approached midnight, papers were slid under the front door. (A paper that was late lost several points per day). Dr. Feldman claimed that "deadlines bring out the best in us." Whatever he demanded of us, he demanded even more of himself. In all my undergraduate and graduate experience, he was the professor most prompt in returning exams and papers, graded with copious annotations. In his pursuit of excellence, he brought the world-famous standards of Harvard University to Yeshiva. It is no wonder that his students have been accepted to the best graduate schools, received the highest academic scholarships, and found the demands and academic load of graduate school relatively easy.

There was a lighter side to Dr. Feldman, as well. We imagined that he looked like an ancient Roman with his aquiline nose and jutting jaw, and he sounded like a vestige of classical antiquity when he would seriously declaim one of his favorite phrases: "I would argue that...." When he found something amusing, we were treated to the unique and famous

"Feldman chuckle." This certainly must have been how the ancient Romans laughed! He began every class exactly on time, even though there might be only one student present. To determine what he would do if no one showed up, one day the five of us hid in the closet in back of the classroom before the teacher arrived. At precisely the appointed time, he began the lecture by stating that the class would be responsible for everything he said and he would not repeat one word whenever we arrived. He could not have known that we were in the closet!

When Dr. Feldman arrived at Yeshiva in the 1950s, the academic atmosphere in the school was permeated with its motto, *Torah u-Madda*, which at that time was understood as the "synthesis of Torah and worldly knowledge." The academic leaders of Yeshiva themselves espoused this cause. President Samuel Belkin was an *illui* and classics scholar, with a PhD degree in Greek from Brown University and author of a famous work on Philo. R. Joseph B. Soloveitchik had a PhD in Philosophy from the University of Berlin. R. Dr. Moshe David Tendler served as an awesome *Torah u-Madda* role model to the students, successfully juggling three careers: A *rosh yeshiva* giving a daily *shi'ur*, a professor of advanced biology directing medical research, and an active pulpit rabbi! Synthesis of Torah and *madda* was not debated — it was part and parcel of the ethos at Yeshiva. However, the individual task of each student was to strive for his own unique balance between Jewish and general studies, to enable him to learn and appreciate the inter-relationships between universal values and the particular Jewish ideas and ideals.

Given the above background, it is quite appropriate that in 1955 Dr. Belkin recruited Louis Feldman at the suggestion of Dr. Bernard Lander, who was then teaching in the sociology department of Hunter College, to join the YC faculty. Dr. Feldman more than blended into the academic and religious atmosphere of Yeshiva. He thrived in it and enriched it — all to the benefit of his students in particular, and the student body and faculty in general. He is also a consummate *talmid hakham*, who is as much at home with Abaye and Rava as he is with Homer and Virgil. He is therefore well qualified to delineate and assess the interaction between the Ancient Greco-Roman world and Judaism. All of these qualities make his scholarly contributions to the students of Yeshiva both unique and essential.

Dr. Feldman, in his classes, took every possible opportunity to "introduce the beauty of Japheth into the tents of Shem." We began to realize that the history of the Jews during the Second Temple period was inextricably intertwined with that of Ancient Greece and Rome. We were amazed at the large number of Greek and Latin terms preserved, in the original, in the Talmud. The many *midrashim* citing Alexander the Great's visit to Judea caught our attention. It became absolutely necessary to understand the relationship of the Hellenistic world to the Jews at the time of Hanukah, just as it was imperative that we understand the entry of the Roman Empire into the affairs of Judea after Herod the Great. The history of the Septuagint and its influence on early Christianity was of the highest priority. And the works of that prolific enigma, Josephus, were essential to the understanding of the entire Second Temple period, down to the Great War with Rome. Dr. Feldman gave his students all of the above keys to open the doors of study and contemplation for the rest of our lives.

As I now look back on my years at Yeshiva, I can clearly see how the demands that Dr. Feldman made upon me in my pursuit of scholarship prepared me for the rigorous regimen required by R. Soloveitchik. The Rav demanded absolute commitment in the meticulous preparation before his *shi'ur* and his students required many hours reviewing it. Each reference in the commentaries on the text of the Talmud had to be carefully studied and traced back to its origins. The intellectual demands of the Rav were uncompromising. Every verse from the biblical Prophets and Writings quoted in the Talmud had to be examined in its original context. Nothing could be assumed or taken for granted, even if its meaning seemed obvious. Unknowingly, at the time, it was to my great advantage that I had experienced the rigorous standards of Dr. Feldman's classes prior to entering the Olympian heights of the Rav's *shi'ur*.

Louis Feldman left me with a legacy far greater than a classical language, insight into classical thought, and an approach to scholarly research: He prepared me for life. He related the ancient Classics to the contemporary scene. Later years may have dulled my memory of much of the specifics he imparted to me, but subsequent experience of life has affirmed the universal truths he taught me. The Classics are alive today — one just has to know where to look. He succeeded in merging in my life "the wisdom of Japheth within the tent of Shem."

It and Not About It:
The JSS Education

By Steve Brizel

From its beginnings in 1956, Yeshiva University featured one of the finest *yeshivot* for students with little or no background in Judaic studies — the James Striar School of General Jewish Studies. JSS owed most of its success to long-time director R. Moshe Besdin, one of the finest and, sadly unacknowledged, Jewish educators in the United States. Before coming to JSS, R. Besdin served congregations in Scranton, PA, and in Washington Heights and Kew Gardens, NY, and he was also a teacher and administrator at Yeshivat Dov Revel in Forest Hills, Queens. In JSS, R. Besdin impressed upon my classmates and me the importance of becoming literate in the basic traditional sources of Torah and in showing honor for *talmidei hakhamim*. I firmly believe that any Torah proficiency I gained was a direct result of my four years at JSS.

It was in 1971, as part of the admissions process, that I first met R. Besdin. We briefly discussed my level of observance. I felt as if I was in the presence of someone who was both a kindly father figure and a demanding teacher. R. Besdin asked me to read from the *Siddur* and inquired as to my textual level. At that point, I was unable to translate a verse in *Humash*, read Rashi, or understand even the simplest *mishnah* or passage of Talmud. I also became acutely aware of a very important factor. I realized that although NCSY had provided me with an inspiration to become observant, I was missing the intellectual basis that would be the building block of a Jew's life — the ability to learn and to appreciate the

Mr. Steve Brizel, YC '76, JSS '76, Cardozo '79, lives with his family in Kew Gardens Hills, Queens.

profound and sweeping nature of *Talmud Torah*. Thus, in 1972, I enrolled in YC and JSS.

I quickly learned that R. Besdin frowned upon the use of any crutches in the classroom, such as a linear *Humash* and Rashi or the Silverman translation. In contrast, R. Besdin encouraged us to buy and use R. Charles B. Chavel's works on Ramban. We learned how to translate a verse in *Humash*, and to learn Rashi, Ramban and Ibn Ezra from the text. R. Besdin emphasized that we first had to master "It," meaning textual proficiency, before we could talk "about It," in the sense of expounding upon our then meager knowledge of the philosophy of Judaism.

Under R. Besdin's leadership, JSS was one of the main addresses for *ba'alei teshuvah* of all orientations. Our class included many alumni of NCSY, some Habadniks, and others who sought to gain textual proficiency in *Humash*, *Mishnah*, Talmud and *Halakhah*. R. Besdin also accepted students who had a formal day school education but who had not been given the proper tools and motivation in "learning how to learn." For those of us who had never formally learned Torah in a classroom, we understood that JSS presented us with an opportunity to literally transform ourselves via "learning how to learn." This process would be accomplished by being exposed to some of the finest minds in the American Orthodox community. The students who arrived with some background realized that they could learn and be inspired to learn as never before in their lives.

R. Besdin treated all of us alike in class and insisted that we prepare and study as if we had never opened a *Humash* before we had entered his class. Regardless of our educational level, R. Besdin treated all of us as equals who were expected to approach *Humash*, Rashi and Ramban with excitement and on an adult level. Although we read the *pesukim* together, we were all expected to prepare the *pesukim* and textually based commentaries on our own. We spent many hours preparing so that we would be ready to read and explain the *mefarshim* if R. Besdin called on us to read in *shi'ur*.

To this day, whenever I open *Humash Bereishit* and go through Rashi and Ramban, I hear R. Besdin and his voice urging a class of "trumpenickers" to work on "It" as opposed to "about It." R. Besdin believed strongly that the exposure of a challenging mind to Torah would serve as the basis for change in *hashkafah* and attitude, rejecting the belief that one must adopt a way of dress and only then dive into learning. In other words, R. Besdin knew that change for a motivated JSS student was a lifelong process that was always underscored by a commitment to Torah study and observance. In this regard, R. Besdin was unimpressed by students who appeared *yeshivish* but who were unable to grow in their abilities to handle the text. The emphasis on learning "It and not about It" set JSS apart from other *yeshivot* that attracted *ba'alei teshuvah*. This educational philosophy was based on the attitude that one taught a child first to crawl and only then walk and run through life. In other words, one first had to become literate in the classic Torah sources before one could expound upon the philosophy of Judaism or the Jewish approach to any subject.

Although we did not have a dress code, R. Besdin had an ingenious way of detecting whether you wore *tzitzit* without you being aware of his inspection. If you raised a question that was excellent but tangential in nature, you were a *darshan*. R. Besdin also reviewed the material that would be covered on his tests. When I look back on those test pamphlets and my notes, I am amazed at the commentaries that R. Besdin utilized. In retrospect, this approach enabled many of us to crawl, walk, and then run as we gained more confidence in Torah study.

If you were in the late morning class, the class ended with *Minhah*. A crowd of students always escorted R. Besdin back to his office, where he would always be available for discussions on a wide range of issues, even as he discussed *divrei Torah* with other JSS and other Judaic studies faculty members. I recall that many faculty members, such as R. Louis Bernstein, R. Norman Lamm, R. Jacob Rabinowitz, and R. Joseph Wanefsky, were frequent visitors to the JSS office.

R. Besdin was also a wonderful administrator and faculty talent scout, who brought in R. Mordechai Willig and R. Hershel Billet. It was only many years later that I discovered that the JSS *shi'urim* on *Berakhot* served as the foundation for R. Willig's book *Am Mordekhai*. When we switched to *perek ha-Mafkid*, we seemed lost, especially since we thought that we had just gained some basic Mishnaic skills. Part of the problem was that we just did not realize that our *rebbe* had to water down a very difficult Talmudic portion. We also did not realize that our *rebbe* also expected us to act, walk, talk, and dress as *benei Torah*. One morning, R. Willig devoted an entire *shi'ur* to this rapidly growing communication gap between us and discussed these issues. After that morning, we all noticed that we understood our *rebbe*'s "lingo" and the *shi'ur* with fewer difficulties.

We were also exposed and treated to R. Benjamin Blech and R. Shlomo Riskin, two of the younger up and coming stars in the American Orthodox rabbinate. In R. Riskin's *shi'ur*, in which we learned *Massekhet Shabbat* and *Massekhet Beitzah*, he brought in a *frum* physics professor from BGSS to discuss the scientific aspects of fire and electricity. We covered the later ninth and tenth chapters of the *massekhet* in a more traditional manner with Rashi, *Tosafot*, Rambam, Rosh, and Rif. My notes from those *shi'urim* include references to the *hiddushei Torah* and various views of R. Joseph B. Soloveitchik, R. Moshe Feinstein, and the *Eglei Tal*.

If you had the temerity to ask a question in a way that showed a lack of respect towards a *rishon*, R. Riskin would let you know very clearly that you were not fit to shine that *rishon*'s shoes, let alone ask a question in such a presumptuous manner. I distinctly recall that R. Riskin encouraged all of us not to become "Riskiner Hassidim," but to develop as *benei Torah* and to find time to learn Torah, whatever our choice of career. R. Riskin also impressed upon us that the study of every detail in a *sugya* that dealt with what seemed an obtuse *av* or *toldah* was a uniquely halakhic way of sweating the details because these details defined the essence of Shabbat as refraining from work. R. Blech had a masterful approach to hashkafic issues. In addition, R. Blech also had an amazing and encyclopedic approach to *Humash Shemot*. R. Riskin and R. Blech also were available for help in aiding many students in their striving to become fully observant and to deal with their parents in a respectful manner.

In retrospect, R. Besdin had an enormous impact on us students both inside and outside of the classroom. Many of us in JSS went on to careers in the rabbinate, Jewish education, and other professions. I will always recall my years in JSS as the building blocks of my Jewish education. Those four years gave me a love and appreciation for learning "it," as opposed to "about it." During those years, I developed a fundamental love for Torah and appreciation for its scholars.

An Interview in Autumn

By Shalom Carmy

Thirty years ago I was a *semikhah* student with no prospects and with a father whose time was running out. A couple of YC Bible courses were open for the spring semester. Having been recommended, I was sent to Dr. Meir Hershkovics, a senior Jewish Studies professor.

After the barest civilities, Dr. Hershkovics produced his agenda: he had been asked to evaluate my suitability for the position. Having gotten this far, I presumably knew something. He could easily expose my areas of ignorance, but that would prove nothing. It was his considered opinion that anybody with half a mind could humiliate any job supplicant at will; no doubt, if I were in the driver's seat, I could embarrass him. He therefore proposed to dispense with the "gotcha" part of the interview and concentrate on more important issues: my outlook and approach to teaching. My father, in the last month of his life, would experience the dubious pride of hearing that his son was a college teacher. And I had the first of many conversations about Bible, about teaching, and about teaching Bible with my new senior colleague.

There was then considerable agitation for more colorful, more collegiate sounding, offerings in Bible. "Doc" Hershkovics, as he was dubbed by the numerous TI students for whom he frequently served as a father figure, ensured that I was assigned the task of teaching the pilot section of "Introduction to Bible." A series of courses on interesting topics, rather than dull *sefarim*, was introduced; he saw to it that I took charge of these as well. One course was "Prophecies about the Nations."

Rabbi Shalom Carmy, YC '71, RIETS '73, is Assistant Professor of Bible at YC and Editor of TRADITION.

The texts it dealt with were a virtual *terra incognita* in terms of theology, and seemed to require a daunting technical knowledge of regional history. I asked my senior professor how he would contend with such a challenge. He answered that he would identify a resourceful, energetic young person and devolve the work on him.

Dr. Hershkovics' death, two years ago, went largely unnoticed at the institution he graced for over twenty years, much loved as a teacher and mentor, and where he produced his most significant books and articles. For him, I suspect, it was a substantial interlude in a long life. Yeshiva followed the infernal years of Holocaust Hungary and subsequent relocation as a Yeshivah of Flatbush teacher. He left Yeshiva for a long and fruitful scholarly and educational career in Jerusalem, to which he retired. Though I had little contact with him in recent years, his son-in-law informs me that he knew what he had done for me, and the extent of my appreciation.

I have recounted the interview for a reason. When I knocked on Dr. Hershkovics' door, I was apprehensive about my ability to survive in the community I had chosen to enter, not least because life in the academic world is often morally dispiriting. This is one reason for my father's mixed feelings about my vocational direction. In academia, the mediocre take comfort in gratuitous exhibitions of pedantry and compulsive assertions of superiority. Lust for status trumps the yearning for solid achievement; the intricate choreography of snobbery apes the dance of illumination; bullying, subtle or transparent, becomes a way of life. The assurance that at least one veteran scholar with the power to affect my future was beyond that kind of pettiness meant not only that I had one person less to be afraid of, but even more important, that there was one more person I was not afraid of becoming like.

Another lesson: I shared with Dr. Hershkovics an interest in biblical study; I admired his work on nineteenth century Jewish intellectual history without any desire to emulate it. But my primary preoccupations were not his. He had not been molded by the Lithuanian tradition of conceptual Talmud study, nor by the theological concerns and analytic standards of contemporary religious philosophy in its various forms, and I don't think he cared much for general engagement in the liberal arts. My connection with him was fortuitous; had I not attempted to teach at YC, I might well have passed out of the institution without learning what I did from him. One advantage of a medium-sized school is that it's small enough for personal relations and large enough so that you may obtain friendship and support from individuals whose primary interests are not the same as yours. It is sad that we are prone to squander these opportunities.

Lastly, a reminder that in the end institutions don't count; it is individuals who matter. If professional spokesmen for Yeshiva make the institution all-important, that is what they get paid to do. We should know better. We are not educated, religiously, morally or intellectually, by the institution, but by individual teachers, students and friends. Truth be told, greater awareness of this point would be better for institutional morale, too. The *Mishnah* does not tell us to look for an ideal institution. If instead of all the hand wringing and kvetching endemic to the Yeshiva University atmosphere we concentrated on "make for yourself a teacher, acquire for yourself a friend," and then worked on expanding the circle of our teachers and friends ("Who is wise? He who learns from all human beings") we would not expect the institution to provide what can only come from other individuals, and we would emerge better educated and less cynical about the institution that makes our education, and our fellowship, possible. If we did so, then you, who probably hadn't heard of Dr. Meir Hershkovics until a few minutes ago, would become a link in his continuing legacy.

Inside and Outside the Classroom

By Donald S. Davis

I arrived at Yeshiva College in September 1961 after a seven hour drive from Montreal, Canada, a trip that traversed worlds and changed my life. Of all the incoming freshmen, I was the only "Montrealer," although there was one other Canadian from Ottawa. The vast preponderance of our class came from the greater New York area. While the "New Yorkers" tended to stick together, the "out of towners" quickly became close friends, developing life long relationships.

At the time, the college campus consisted of the Main Building (now called Zysman Hall), Furst Hall, the library (and its adjacent barrack style buildings), and the Rubin Dormitory. We all lived in the Rubin Dorm, about twenty-five rooms to a floor, two or three to a room, with paper thin walls and one payphone on each floor. Life, to say the least, was interesting. The dorm emptied out for the weekend on Thursday night when the "New Yorkers" went home, but we "out of towners" remained. We created our own Shabbat atmosphere. We ate Parker's food. We explored the sights of New York, it culture, theater and kosher restaurants; most of us, if we were lucky, had one kosher restaurant in our hometown.

During my sophomore year, along with five other "out of towners," I rented the top two floors of a brownstone on Washington Terrace,

Mr. Donald S. Davis, YC '65, is an attorney in Montreal and currently is an officer of and sits on the Executive and Board-of Federation CJA (the Montreal Federation), the Education Committee of the Jewish Agency for Israel, and the board of Keren ha-Yesod. Mr. Davis is a past president of the Presidents Council of all Jewish Agencies of the Montreal Federation, past president of Hebrew Academy, and past president of the Association of Jewish Days Schools of Montreal.

(the dead end street behind the library off 186th street). We were the first students to live on campus, but not in the dormitory. We were three sophomores and three juniors in the apartment. In my senior year, together with my roommate Michael Chernick, I returned to the dorms and took up residence in Morgenstern, which opened in the fall of 1964. We brought our television set along. It was the first and only one in the dorm.

When I reflect back on my four years at Yeshiva College, I remember not only my classmates, the friends that I made and retain to this day, but also the extra-curricular activities and experiences and our *rebbeim* and professors.

My Yeshiva experience extended well beyond the classroom. I remember with nostalgia the late Thursday night bridge games, heart games, and early (4 am) Friday morning breakfast at Ratners on the Lower East Side. In the main building, the gym — if you could call it that — had a ceiling that was no more than eight feet high; the basketball team practiced and played its home games at Powell Memorial High School, swimming was at Washington Heights High School, and tennis practice was at the armory. The social highlight of the year was the Dean's Reception and the Dramatic Society Play.

The most important and influential extra curricular activity for me was the Debating Society and the Debate Team. Dr. David Fleisher was our team coach. Each year, there was a national topic debated across the United States. Since we were unable to attend debating tournaments that took place on Shabbat, we went on a two-week tour across the continent every March, around the time of Purim. There were four tours: the Northeast, the South, the Midwest and the Far West. I was fortunate to be selected as president of the Debating Society and captain of the Debate Team in my senior year I had the opportunity to represent Yeshiva in the Northeast (Boston, Philadelphia, Baltimore, Washington), the Mid-West (Chicago, Dayton, Kansas City, St. Louis, Madison), and the Far West (Denver, Los Angles, San Francisco, Waco). Yeshiva debated the major universities in each city. We were Yeshiva's ambassadors to the world.

Above all, what made our education at Yeshiva so great was our exposure to giants of the Jewish world, *talmidei hakhamim* and professors who traversed both the secular and religious academic spheres each day, combining knowledge and expertise in both areas attempting to inculcate into us the unique philosophy of *Torah u-Madda*. First and foremost was

R. Joseph B. Soloveitchik. He lived in the dorm two days a week. We were exposed to the Rav as he walked the halls, ate his meals in the cafeteria (lining up like us with his tray), and took out his own garbage. Praying with him at the morning *minyan* in the dorm was an education in itself on how to pray.

Steven (Shlomo) Riskin was my dorm counselor during my freshmen year. His backslapping and good wishes as we left the dorm Saturday night was not encouragement to have a good time, but his *tzitzit* inspection.

My Jewish studies *rebbeim* inculcated in me a lifelong desire and commitment to learning. R. Moshe Besdin, R. Moshe Chait, R. Pesach Oratz, R. Leonard Rosenfield and R. Israel Wohlgelernter all had a lasting impact on my life. R. Besdin's insistence on "the text, the text" and carrying with you a pocket *humash* at all times has remained with me to this day.

My college professors exposed me to the *Torah u-Madda* philosophy by example. Dr. Irving "Yitz" Greenberg, Dr. Emanuel Rackman, and Dr. Moshe D. Tendler connected us to both worlds by example in their personal and professional lives. I majored in Political Science. Professor Charles Liebman arrived at Yeshiva in my sophomore year, and having taken "Poli Sci 101" in my freshman year I was able to take advanced courses in my sophomore year. I signed up for three of his courses; I was the only sophomore in the class. After having "aced" all my mid-terms in his class, we became close friends. I spent time at his home, had Shabbat meals with his family, and maintained a relationship with him for many years after I graduated.

In my senior year, together with nine other students, I took an innovative course offered for the first time, "Politics, Morality and Religion." There were three professors giving the courses, Dr. Charles Liebman, Dr. Aharon Lichtenstein, and Dr. Martin Goldman (a visiting philosophy professor from Columbia). The course was given as a seminar once a week for three hours. All three participated in each class. The exposure to these three, all *talmidei hakhamim* and brilliant professors, interacting together in a classroom and traversing both the secular and religious academic worlds and texts was exhilarating. Not only was the course intellectually stimulating and challenging, but it allowed me to develop a personal relationship with each of these teachers. My relationship with R. Lichtenstein continued for many years and gave me the ability, when I was president of a day school, to call him on a regular basis to discuss issues on which I had to make decisions that impacted the school. R. Lichtenstein was always available and always encouraged me in my community commitments and endeavors.

Dr. Louis H. Feldman taught, and continues to teach, Classics. Very few students took his courses. I was just like them; I also did not. He prepared the exam schedule for Yeshiva College. He always had two assistants, a senior and junior class member, working with him. As one of his assistants for two years, I spent time with him and got to know him as an individual. Dr. Feldman's integrity and commitment to fairness in attempting to create an exam schedule that best suited all the students was remarkable; we agonized together for weeks on end. A true *ben Torah*, Dr. Feldman transmitted the mission of Yeshiva to me in a non-academic environment.

All of the above professors and rabbis encouraged me to take a year off between graduation and law school to spend learning in Israel. I spent that year at Yeshivat Merkaz Harav Kook in Jerusalem, and this served as a form of graduate school in Jewish learning and experience. In those years it was not the norm to spend a year in Israel. I don't think there were fifty foreign students in Israel at the time.

Yeshiva College changed my life; it was the best four years of my life. I am eternally grateful to my parents for sending me to Yeshiva, to my rabbis and professors for the education that I received, and to my fellow classmates for their friendship. I have tried to remain connected to Yeshiva and repay it for everything that I received from it.

My involvement in Jewish community life, locally in Montreal, nationally in Canada, and internationally through *Keren ha-Yesod* and the Jewish Agency in Israel, is due to the education that I received at Yeshiva and the role models that I was exposed to. Jewish leaders from around the world with whom I sit on various committees and boards all know that I am a graduate of Yeshiva, and that my *weltanschauung* was shaped and molded by its outstanding teachers, rabbis and professors.

Inspiring the Love of Mathematics:
The Legacy of Jekuthiel Ginsburg at Yeshiva

By Hillel Furstenberg

To me, as undoubtedly to many who attended YC in the early 50s, the subject of mathematics was identified with one remarkable individual, Professor Jekuthiel Ginsburg. Renowned for his scholarly work in the history of mathematics, he was no stranger to the arcane frontiers of modern mathematics. But his fondest desire was to make mathematics accessible to a broad public. In the classroom, he communicated to his students the innate beauty of abstract mathematical ideas. (Who has forgotten Fibonacci and his endlessly intriguing series of numbers?) When possible, he would call on the inventiveness of geometric imagination to give concrete form to this beauty. At one point, *Life* magazine picked up on this and, featuring Jekuthiel Ginsburg on its cover, offered this vision to a very wide public. But the undertaking that would enable Jekuthiel Ginsburg to share his appreciation of mathematics with a large — but modestly sophisticated — audience was the publication of *Scripta Mathematica*, the journal founded by Professor Ginsburg in 1932 and published by Yeshiva University.

Throughout the twenty-five years that Jekuthiel Ginsburg served as its editor, the journal was "devoted to the philosophy, history, and expository treatment of mathematics," and, as emphasized in the first issue, "a special effort will be made to have the articles free from such

Dr. Hillel Furstenberg, YUHS '51, YC' 55, has been a Professor of Mathematics at the Hebrew University in Jerusalem since 1965, and has also taught at Bar-Ilan University. He dedicated his book Stationary Processes and Prediction Theory *to the memory of Jekuthiel Ginsburg. Dr. Furstenberg moved to Israel with his wife Rochelle in 1965, and currently lives in Jerusalem.*

technicalities as would repel the intelligent reader who has not had a thorough training in mathematics." A later issue of *Scripta Mathematica* included a statement by Yeshiva's first president, R. Dr. Bernard Revel, alleging that "the policy of the journal is in agreement with the ideal of 'learning for the sake of learning' which inspired the founders of Yeshiva College." The early issues of *Scripta Mathematica* were indeed devoted to philosophy and history of mathematics, and included some now classic essays: a eulogy by the distinguished mathematician Hermann Weyl of Emmy Noether, one of the outstanding female mathematicians of the previous century, and a disquisition by Professor Abraham Halevy Fraenkel on the "crisis of the excluded middle," treating the challenge of the infinite to mathematical logic. With the passage of time the journal broadened its appeal, enabling its readers to play a more participatory role, and sharing with the less sophisticated mathematical reader the enjoyment of mathematical creativity.

This was done by including among the journal's departments "mathematical recreations," "notes," and "curiosa." These were open to a wide spectrum of "*hiddushim*," original observations on all levels that might be worthy of attention. The volumes of *Scripta Mathematica* found in most good libraries today remain as a testimonial to Jekuthiel Ginsburg's vision of mathematics as a many-sided humane enterprise.

Professor Ginsburg's love and appreciation of mathematics were matched only by the personal interest he took in his students and the attention he lavished on those he felt could someday seek a career in mathematics. My own good fortune was not only having Professor Ginsburg as mentor during my college days, but also in the proximity of his office to the classrooms of TA during my high school years. So when my friend Shlomo Sternberg and I, after an extended effort, had succeeded in cracking an unusually hard high school geometry problem, the two of us gathered up the courage to ascend the flight of steps that led to Jekuthiel Ginsburg's office, in order to show off our first fruits to a real mathematician.

We modestly made the admission that our success came after many days of fruitless effort, to which Professor Ginsburg consoled us with "but then others have worked longer and didn't succeed." He then proceeded to show us a pamphlet he happened to have in his office that had twenty-six other solutions to this famous conundrum.

This began my acquaintanceship with the kindly professor who would stimulate and feed my mathematical curiosity for many years. By the time I entered college, the personal tutelage I had received made most undergraduate courses unnecessary, and Professor Ginsburg saw to it that I was left with as much time as possible to pursue higher mathematics at my own pace. Aware of my need to earn spending money while attending college, Professor Ginsburg arranged to have me work for *Scripta Mathematica*, translating papers submitted in French or German to English and drawing diagrams that would appear in the journal. Much of this was probably more for my edification than fulfilling real needs of *Scripta Mathematica*. I know some of my diagrams did appear, but I'm not sure my translations were ever made use of. What was achieved was a reduction in my college language requirements, leaving me more time for mathematical pursuits, and the experience also provided me with a fluency in French and German mathematical writing, at that time indispensable for a broad knowledge of mathematics. Finally Professor Ginsburg, availing himself of his friendship with Max Stern, set up an arrangement whereby I would receive an additional monthly stipend, freeing me further from financial concerns and enabling me to devote all my free time to my studies. As I recall, the Hartz Mountain Bird Food factory was not far from the Barnes and Noble bookstore that carried the latest mathematics books, and so my personal mathematics library owes much to my benefactor, Mr. Stern, and his friendship with Jekuthiel Ginsburg.

Already the beneficiary of the personalized care and tutelage at the hands of Professor Ginsburg, I was to benefit substantially from another important development that Jekuthiel Ginsburg brought about in his effort to enhance mathematics at Yeshiva University. This was the expansion of the undergraduate program in mathematics at YC into a full-fledged doctoral program, a first step in the establishment of the Belfer Graduate School of Science. It was my good fortune to be present at the initial stages of this development, so that while still an undergraduate I was exposed to a series of high-level lectures in advanced topics given by prominent professors who visited from a number of institutions. These included Samuel Eilenberg and Ellis Kolchin from Columbia University, Jesse Douglas from City College, and Abe Gelbart, who traveled from Syracuse University.

It is hard to imagine a professional career that owes more to one individual and to one institution than my own career owes to Jekuthiel

Ginsburg and Yeshiva University. Over and beyond the mathematics I learned, I experienced the love of mathematics blended with human-kindness, an experience I can only wish I could replicate for others.

Jekuthiel Ginsburg, Abe Gelbart, and the Beginnings of the Belfer Graduate School of Science

By Stephen Gelbart

My father's association with YC dates back to 1928, the year of its founding, when he was seventeen years old. It was then that he met Dr. Jekuthiel Ginsburg in the math section of the New York Public Library at Fifth Avenue and 42nd Street. Dad had dropped out of school in Paterson, New Jersey when he was fourteen and had gone to work in order to help bring home much needed money for the family. That left weekends free for studying alone. Having mastered the material in math and physics that was available at the public library in Paterson, he went on to the wonderful library at 42nd Street in New York.

It was there that he had met Dr. Ginsburg. After several weeks of reading together at the same table, Ginsburg approached my father and said, "Young man, I see you're here every weekend. I'm presently chairman of the Mathematics Department at Yeshiva College, and I come here to read books I don't have. Why do you come here?" My father told Dr. Ginsburg that he was very interested in math and physics and found the New York Public Library the only source he had for continuing his education in that field. Ginsburg's curiosity was piqued, and he began asking my father questions about how much he really understood. "If you're so eager to learn about these subjects," Ginsburg asked, "I'll make you a proposal you can't refuse. Instead of coming to this library, why

---

Dr. Stephen Gelbart, a son of Abe Gelbart, is the Nicki and J. Ira Harris Professor at the Department of Mathematics, The Weizmann Institute of Science (Rehovot, Israel). This article is based on a few chapters from Abe Gelbart's unpublished (and unfinished) autobiography.

don't you come to my house, and I'll tutor you there." This offer, of course, overwhelmed my father, who was amazed that anyone could make such a suggestion. So he told Dr. Ginsburg he would gladly accept his offer, and thanked him for his generosity.

My father began visiting Dr. Ginsburg on weekends at his home. When he mentioned the visits to his family, they were well aware of the name of Jekuthiel Ginsburg, and they were especially aware of the name of his brother, a well known Hebrew scholar. Dr. Ginsburg proposed that he and my father take Wilson's Advanced Calculus and start going through it page by page. This textbook contained chapters on advanced calculus, differential equations, differential geometry, and some partial differential equations. Ginsburg's proposal was for Dad to start from the beginning of the book, studying a section each week and solving the problems at the end of each section. If Dad didn't manage to do these problems, they would discuss them together at the next meeting. In this way, my father covered most of the advanced topics of mathematics that were normally covered in undergraduate study of that day.

After a few years of working together, Dr. Ginsburg told my father: "Now you'll have to pay a price for what I have done for you!" My father realized that because of his kind, gentle, wonderful personality, whatever Dr. Ginsburg might ask of him would not be a heavy burden. It turned out that Dr. Ginsburg had started a mathematics journal some years earlier, and was suggesting that my father proofread its galley proof as each issue appeared. The journal was called *Scripta Mathematica*, and was published by the Yeshiva College Mathematics Department. My father felt that this was not only a fair price to pay for what Dr. Ginsburg had done for him, but would also be a wonderful opportunity to become acquainted with articles that were in the forefront of modern mathematics. My father was very excited about this project. In addition to doing what he could to help proofread the galleys, he also made suggestions about the articles that were about to appear.

At about this same time, Dad also found a new construction of an ancient problem that had fascinated him for some time: given three arbitrary circles, how do you go about constructing a fourth circle that would be tangent to the three? Dr. Ginsburg read the proof my father had given and agreed to publish it in *Scripta Mathematica*.

Dr. Ginsburg's initial help, as well as help he gave my father in later years, was crucial in the progress of my father's education. From 1935, when he left the United States for college at Dalhousie University in Canada, to 1957, when he was an established mathematician at Syracuse University, my father and Dr. Ginsburg kept up a close relationship. My father got his PhD at Massachusetts Institute of Technology in 1940 and continued his work on *Scripta Mathematica*. In the late forties, at Dr. Ginsburg's request, he prepared a program of courses for the Master's degree at Yeshiva. A draft of the program was approved by the State of New York, and the first courses leading to the Master's degree were offered in 1952. Dr. Ginsburg then approached Dad about giving a graduate course at Yeshiva in the program Ginsburg was thinking of developing, which would lead to a PhD degree. Dad like the idea — he felt he should do whatever he could for Ginsburg's developing program. He flew down from Syracuse one day a week to help in the teaching of courses.

In my father's unpublished autobiography, he mentioned one incident that occurred during the class in set theory that he was giving. This class was attended by one undergraduate student and several other graduate students. My father had given a proof that the set of all subsets of the integers was a set of higher order of infinity than Aleph zero. Having given the proof, my father made the remark that for any infinite set the set of all its subsets is an infinite set of higher order. He also commented that that was a little harder to prove, and he would therefore skip over it. Slowly, the undergraduate in the class raised his hand and said "I think the proof is not that hard." Dad immediately asked him to come to the board and show what his thoughts were about it. The young man struggled for fifteen minutes and then came up with the proof. My father was deeply impressed with this student and knew that he would have a great future in mathematics. As it turned out, this student went on to Princeton to get his PhD and soon took a position in Israel; today, Harry Furstenberg is one of the most outstanding mathematicians in Israel.

When Jekuthiel Ginsburg died of a heart attack in 1957, my father was asked by President Samuel Belkin to replace Dr. Ginsburg. By then Dad was also associate editor of *Scripta Mathematica* and was quite familiar with the program that Dr. Ginsburg was trying to develop. After several discussions with Dr. Belkin, it was decided to develop a graduate program leading to the PhD degree in the physical sciences as well, in addition to mathematics. Since Yeshiva already had a graduate program in the life sciences associated with AECOM, this would not overlap in any way with that program. My father was willing to leave Syracuse University and come to Yeshiva to establish the graduate school of science. He was also asked to become editor of *Scripta Mathematica* and he agreed to accept that position as well.

Dr. Belkin was interested in convincing Mr. Arthur Belfer, a successful businessman in New York, to support the university in some way. He approached Belfer and asked him whether he would be interested in funding the proposed graduate school that my father had talked about, and told him that with a suitable gift the school would be named in his honor. Mr. Belfer responded with a large gift that provided the key to financial support for the school.

The Belfer School of Science began with a rather dilapidated war surplus frame building. It had facilities for a few offices and a couple of classrooms. My father was very fortunate to be able to get Professors Atle Selberg and Deane Montgomery to act as visiting professors from the Institute for Advanced Study in Princeton. A series of classes that launched the graduate program for the PhD, which got approval from New York State, was in the areas of mathematics, physics, and chemistry. When the Middle States Association accreditation team came to visit in 1958, they found the school to be unbelievably high-quality. Their report began, "There is nothing but praise." They were amazed at how such a distinguished faculty could have been assembled in such a short period. In the years that followed, my father also invited Noble Prize winner Paul Dirac and the later Wolf Prize winner, Freeman Dyson, to act as visiting Professors of Physics.

While the growth of the school in its early years was quite encouraging, its development could hardly have continued without laboratory facilities. Without means, however, my father was only able to dream about a new building; the dreams had to be restrained, and the first plans for a new building at the campus made no new provisions for the laboratory sciences. Had they been restricted to these initial plans, the scope and variety of university's academic programs would have been severely limited for the indefinite future.

Of course, there was a very serious need for better facilities: This was a short time after Sputnik was launched by the USSR, and the United States increased its interest in supporting basic sciences. It was not long after that substantial grants from the government to support additional facilities came to Yeshiva; plans for a new, bigger, structure were made — plans that called for a twenty story structure that would contain laboratories as well as offices and lecture halls.

My father spent two years working almost daily with the architect on the plans for the Belfer School of Science. During that period, he moved the school from the dilapidated war surplus structure to some space received from the New York Telephone Company. Then, in 1970, after acquiring a very impressive faculty in the areas of mathematics, physics, chemistry, and even astronomy, the new building for the Belfer School of Science was dedicated.

In addition to their normal program, the Belfer School ran a series of national conferences attended by scientists from all over the country and published many books under the auspices of *Scripta Mathematica* that resulted from these conferences. All in all, the school of sciences had a rewarding beginning. The dreams of an older mathematician, Dr. Jekuthiel Ginsburg, and — first his student, then mathematician — Dr. Abe Gelbart, had come to fruition.

How the Maccabees were Born

By David Gleicher

What's in a name? For some sports teams, the answer can be quite controversial. You can't have a team name that will engender controversy. Thus, the St. John's Redmen became the St. John's Red Storm, the Marquette Warriors became the Marquette Golden Eagles, and the Elon (North Carolina) Fighting Christians became the Elon Phoenix. Sometimes, however, a college team will change its name for reasons other than political correctness. Such was the case with the Yeshiva Maccabees.

Our story begins in the fall of 1934, when YC's basketball club became an official school team with an intercollegiate schedule. Two years later, it hired Milt Trupin as its first coach, compiled a 7-10 record, and ran out of money to pay Trupin for a second year. Sophomore Irv Koslowsky, YC '40 — later known as R. Irving Koslowe — became the player-coach for the next two years until Yeshiva scraped up enough money in his senior season to hire Hy Wettstein as the team's next coach; Wettstein later became MTA's coach for several decades.

It was sometime in the late 30s that the team's name of the Mighty Mites was adopted. Earlier in the decade, the varsity had been called the Quinthooplets. One of these "Quints" was a short, quick guard named Julie Mager, nicknamed "The Mighty Mite." Eventually, Mager's moniker caught on and the whole team became the Mighty Mites, and "Quinthooplets" was relegated to the dead file.

Mr. David Gleicher, YC '76, is a writer in Cleveland, and the author of Louis Brandeis Slept Here: A Slightly Cynical History of American Jews. He is currently working on a book about the origins of the American Jewish community in 1654.

Over the next thirty-five years, the Mighty Mites had some great years — 16-2 in 1956, 14-4 in 1959 — and some great stars — Marv Hershkowitz, Abe Sodden, Red Blumenreich, Stuie Poloner — but by the early 1970s, the team was in a deep slump, punctuated by its worst season ever, 1973-74, when it went 1-19. That year, while center Paul Merlis was learning in Israel, the team's offense consisted of Bruce Wenig's passing the ball to Dave Wilzig. And a two-person offense leads to a one-win season.

The next year, I became Sports Editor of *The Commentator*. One evening in November, I stood in line at the cafeteria with Steve Reisbaum, the paper's Editor-in-Chief and my predecessor at the sports desk. We discussed our high hopes for the team. Wilzig had graduated, but Wenig was back, Merlis had returned, senior Ira Scharaga had found his shooting touch, and promising freshman Robbie Rosenbloom was joining the team. I was worried about one thing, though. Steve asked, "Foul shooting?" "No," I answered, "the team's name: Mighty Mites." Is there any college team in America with a wimpier name? Maybe if the team changed its name, it would play harder, more aggressively, and with more pride. Steve asked what the name should be. I suggested something tough like MTA's name, the Lions.

Steve disagreed. An animal name is too generic; we need something unique to us, like Maccabees. I liked it immediately. I told him, "That's it. From now on, the team will be known as the Maccabees." He laughed and said, "You can't just change the team's name. You have to get permission, though I don't know from whom — maybe from Red [Sarachek] or Jonny [Halpert]." I said, "No, I'm just gonna do it."

In my sports column on November 20, 1974, I announced that from this day forward, the team's name would no longer be the Mighty Mites, but would now be the Maccabees. As Sports Editor, I made sure that only the new name appeared in the articles. The next year, I prepared the athletic department's media guide, and the team's name was listed as the Maccabees. I never got permission from Red or Jonny or even Mrs. Miller, who really ran the athletic department back then; I just did it.

Unfortunately, the name change didn't immediately influence the team, which won only five games that year and three the next. But eventually, the spirit of the Maccabees permeated the team, which began racking up successful seasons; of course, getting better players and hiring assistant coaches helped too.

During my student years at Yeshiva, I contributed to the institution by serving on the 1976 Presidential Search Committee that eventually chose Norman Lamm. But I have always felt that my unique contribution to Yeshiva was changing the name of its sports teams. Whenever I read a university press release or an article in *The Commentator* about the success of the "Macs" or "Lady Macs," I get a singular feeling of pride.

Yeshiva in the 60s

By Irving Greenberg

I taught at YC from September 1959 until June 1972. In retrospect, the atmosphere and influence of the 60s shaped the dynamic of those years.

In the 60s, the dominant American White Anglo-Saxon Protestant paradigm was overthrown by the eruption of long-repressed ethnic/ religious minorities. I went to Harvard to fulfill the American dream: to get a PhD and become an academic. Most of my Brooklyn College Jewish classmates were assimilating in fulfillment of this dream. Luckily, I was deeply rooted in *Yiddishkeit* by my home — my father's *misnagdishe lomdus* and my mother's elemental piety — and my life-transforming encounter with Bais Yosef-Novardok Mussar Yeshiva, which shifted my undergraduate plans from RIETS/YC to Bais Yosef/Brooklyn College. Still, I was discussing staying on at Harvard with a fellowship in the Center for American History when the incoming Dean of YC, Dr. Isaac Bacon, called and offered a job as assistant professor of History. Acting intuitively, I accepted almost immediately. Although I did not fully realize the implications of the step then, my Jewish impulses — inspired by Bais Yosef's missionary emphasis on spreading *Yiddishkeit* — won out over my *drang nach* America.

Dean Bacon's main pitch was that he had a mandate to invigorate

Rabbi Dr. Irving Greenberg is the President of Jewish Life Network/Steinhardt Foundation. He taught at YC from 1959-1972. From 1974 through 1997, he served as founding President of CLAL - The National Jewish Center for Learning and Leadership, a pioneering institution in the development of adult and leadership education in the Jewish community. Rabbi Greenberg served as Chairman of the United States Holocaust Memorial Council from 2000-2002.

Yeshiva's vision of *Torah u-Madda*. The college was weak; the undergraduate concentrations were heavily skewed to sciences and pre-med. A more challenging college experience could deepen the students' religious lives. There would be allies in the attempted transformation. R. Aharon Lichtenstein would come to teach English Literature and Talmud — another important model of *Torah u-Madda*. Charles Liebman was coming from the University of Illinois. Dean Bacon said there would be others. When I arrived, I found R. David Hartman teaching Jewish Studies. He shared many of these ideas and quickly became my *havruta* and soul mate. Yeshiva was the national leader in outreach; the Torah Leadership Seminar was the jewel. R. Moshe Besdin was running the Jewish Studies Program to bring in non-observant Jews.

We newcomers thought we could improve the Yeshiva, not just the College. We gave continuous input to the *roshei yeshiva* and administration, including recommendations to switch all *shi'urim* from Yiddish to English, to pick a more relevant *masekhta* for study, to put less stress on *pilpul* and more on *bekiyut*, to expand RIETS study beyond *Gemara*, to pay the *roshei yeshiva* better, and to give students more personal counseling. Throughout the decade, we — husbands and wives — got together for "salons" to develop our thoughts on Modern Orthodox issues; the meetings were held mostly in the apartments of the Liebmans and the Lichtensteins at 17 Fort George Hill. In short, like the 60s, we were filled with the conviction that we were going to change the world.

In 1959, I became spiritual guide to the founders of Yavneh, a pioneering organization serving Orthodox students on general college campuses, by dealing with the challenges of Torah confronting modernity. I truly believed that the tradition had the capacity to cope with the toughest questions — even in a university's "no holds barred" atmosphere. In the early 1960s, Jacob Birnbaum arrived with his historic call to rescue Soviet Jewry. Most of the *roshei yeshiva* opposed demonstrations, lining up with the Agudah leaders in upholding *shtadlanut*. We, the "Young Turks," came out strongly for direct action. In the atmosphere of that decade, we won that argument with the *Gedolim*. YC students provided many of the shock troops for SSSJ demonstrations. Of course, contact with the outside world opened many students up even more.

In April 1966, there was a disastrous fire in the library of the Jewish Theological Seminary. Countless books were burned; tens of thousands of volumes were soaked by the water that put out the fire and they were rotting away. JTS reached out for help. To be rescued, each book had to be opened gently, pages separated, dried, etc. We organized YC students to go to 3080 Broadway and help; they saved thousands of books. The statement of friendship and *areivut* crossing denominational lines was inspiring.

Mitzvah goreret mitzvah; friendships were engendered by the helping hand. In 1969, a group of JTS graduates were key organizers of the student take-over of the General Assembly of the Council of Jewish Federations. The demonstrators demanded a turn from the non-sectarian, universalistic agenda of the Federations toward a new priority investment in Jewish education. I and other Yeshiva people were invited to join. That assembly was an important turning point in community policy. The event brought me personally into the world of philanthropy and community leadership. This encounter eventually led to the founding of CLAL, with its agenda of Jewish education for community leaders and dialogue for the sake of religious pluralism and unity.

In 1969, the national anti-war movement called for a demonstration in Washington, D.C. Many YC activists were moderate opponents of the war. Because I was Orthodox and the son of fiercely patriotic immigrants, I — like most YC'ers — avoided the extremism of depicting America as Amerika, an imperialist, abusive power. As the decade wore on, more Yeshiva leaders were recoiling from the radicalizing cultural environment — "make love not war." They feared that students would be tempted and make the wrong choices. In the face of warnings that we would embarrass religious Jewry as well as undermine personal observance, we decided that Yeshiva students should join in the demonstration. This posed great challenges in terms of Shabbat observance, providing kosher food, etc. After sleeping and staying within walking distance of the Mall site, we participated in the Mobilization Weekend while making Shabbat together. The experience — shared with other young Jews, religious and non-observant alike — turned out to be simultaneously an inspiring religious expression and a morally uplifting form of outreach.

Throughout the decade, I was undergoing a spiritual odyssey — moving not toward withdrawal, if you will, to *haredi* or pre-modern approaches, but toward greater involvement. I wrote then: "Orthodoxy must change its identity from a fundamentalism to a religion, from preserving Judaism to affirming it and its sovereignty in modern culture." I urged "applying religious values and practices to all areas of secular life.

But this can only be done when Orthodoxy actually works through, in depth, the modern experience..." The view went counter to the growing failure of nerve vis-à-vis modernity in many up-and-coming *lomdim* and Modern Orthodox leaders.

The driving force for my move was an encounter with the Holocaust. In 1961-62, I went to Israel to teach American history as a visiting Fulbright Professor at Tel Aviv University, but soon was immersed completely in study and reading about the catastrophe. The agony of the suffering in the *Shoah* created a personal religious crisis far beyond the conflicts and doubts generated by modernity. I struggled to understand anew the relationship of God, the world, and the Jewish people. Orthodoxy did not have all the answers. My conclusion: all Jews carried the message of God and the Torah (which is why Hitler tried to wipe them out); all Jews were heroic for having decided to go on living as Jews in whatever form they did. I also concluded that I wanted to refocus directly on Jewish studies and work in healing the Jewish people.

YC did not share my feelings. Yeshiva President Samuel Belkin said: "But, Greenberg, we are so proud of your PhD in American history...why would you want to change to Jewish history?" Dean Bacon objected that an un-academic course on the Holocaust would damage the transcripts of our pre-med students. He finally relented and agreed to a course called "Totalitarianism and Ideology in the 20th Century."

Nor did YC share my priorities. Over the years, I discovered that at Yeshiva, salaries were inversely proportional to the Jewishness of the subject. Albert Einstein College of Medicine's salaries were highest in the university; RIETS's were the lowest; YC was the second lowest, etc. Years later, R. Shlomo Riskin gave the best critique of this arrangement. The poverty of Jewish educators constituted *mesirat ha-guf* — which is wrong. Salaries should be raised to dignified levels. Then *roshei yeshiva* should be asked for *mesirat nefesh*, i.e., total devotion to students, wrestling with the challenges of modernity, risking their souls by reaching out to connect to the most alienated and even heretical people. I came to realize that the Yeshiva administration had so prioritized creating a university — higher standing for the American and the modern — that they would not raise salaries among Judaic scholars, not even to keep the best — like R. David Hartman and Dr. Gerald Blidstein, whom we lost.

Modern Orthodoxy's institutional leadership did not measure up to its challenge. Some administrators and *roshei yeshiva* argued that to lighten the burden of the dual curriculum, college studies should be diluted. Such an approach betrayed YC's outstanding student body. I believed that a shallow college education would weaken Modern Orthodoxy. Not understanding the depth of the questions, students and religious leaders would be satisfied with shallow, cultural backwater answers. In my courses, I tried to apply the same standards for content, sophistication, and readings that I had encountered at Brooklyn College and Harvard — if not higher. The students flourished. Sadly, RIETS and YC were shortchanged. During those years, there was never anyone in charge of RIETS who was qualified to assess religious quality or to scout *ramim* and promote *lomdim* committed to "synthesis." YC did not keep increasing its investment in quality professors either.

YC's glory was the quality of its students. I loved teaching such bright, hard-working, idealistic and highly absorbent students. In every class, there were a disproportionate number of brilliant students who could have been stars in the Ivy League, but who came to Yeshiva because of religious search and commitments. Yeshiva failed its covenant with the students by skimping on salaries and failing to recruit the brightest and the best to teach. Adding to the injury, YC's administrative procedures were often needlessly difficult; they often were enforced in arbitrary, bureaucratic, and tormenting ways.

By 1965, R. David Hartman persuaded a wealthy lay leader to underwrite a week of learning together for a group of scholars. We invited the best Orthodox thinkers we knew and — there being money left over — invited some Conservative and Reform thinkers as well. I came with my burning interest in the *Shoah* and ignited Emil Fackenheim and others. Fackenheim and other Reform rabbis inspired me to go back and look again at Covenant and see how central it is to the Jewish tradition. We formed deep friendships.

Those were heady days. One year Jakob Petuchowski came with a *ger tzedek* — a German Protestant minister, Aaron Schmidt, who had won a scholarship set up for Christian clergy to come to Hebrew Union College. Schmidt actually came to study for conversion. In accordance with Jakob Petuchowski's *shitah*, he was prepared to be a *shomer mitzvot*. However, he was not content to convert as a Reform Jew; he wanted to become a *Klal Yisrael* Jew. We set up a *Beit Din* consisting of an Orthodox, a Conservative and a Reform rabbi — all *shomrei mitzvot* — to do the *gerut*. Afterward, we greeted the *ger* and danced ecstatically together. R.

Aharon Lichtenstein and R. Walter Wurzburger, who did not sit on the *beit din*, nevertheless, joined in the dancing. People hugged and kissed for joy. While I was somewhat troubled by the fact that none of what was going on at the Canadian Center for Jewish Studies, as it was now called, was being talked about and taught to the YC world, I was so enraptured with the group that I did not complain. Nor did I pay much attention to the beginning of the reaction to the 60s — a drift to the right.

In 1966, I sat in my office for hours talking with a student about my thinking on Modern Orthodox issues. I spoke unguardedly with an open heart because he was a seeker. The student never told me that he was writing up the conversation with intent to publish. Actually, the interview appeared in *The Commentator* without being reviewed or vetted by me. This was highly improper behavior.*

In an environment where I was moving to the "left" and toward affirmation of non-Orthodox as my response to the *Shoah* and Israel while Yeshiva was beginning its drift to the right, the interview burst like a bombshell. Furthermore, I was orienting myself to a *Klal Yisrael* community of Orthodox-Conservative-Reform rabbis, whereas the religious leadership of Yeshiva was still insular and inward-looking. When I saw the headline: "Greenberg Discusses Orthodoxy, YU, Vietnam and Sex," I knew there would be trouble. All my life I respected the Rambam's teaching that, even in Torah, revelation is only up to the capacity of people to hear. Therefore, I would have spoken more restrainedly had I known the views were to be published. I believed in what I said, but the printed words went considerably beyond what many people were prepared to hear. In my written response to the furor, I disingenuously tried to soften and minimize the implications of my words — which convinced no one.

The RIETS leadership sought to condemn my views but realized that they personally had little credibility because of the perception that they did not understand or confront modernity as I had. As the uproar grew, I went to see the Rav. We always had a limited but special relationship. He recognized and was pleased by his strong influence on my thinking. He also respected this thought even though many of my controversial views grew out of pushing his insights farther than he was willing to go, at least

---

* *Publication of this article led to a heated exchange in the pages of* The Commentator. *See letters to the editor in* The Commentator *69:12, Monday, May 16, 2005, pgs. 4-5, and R. Greenberg's response, page 5, 12. R. Aharon Lichtenstein's letter and R. Greenberg's response are printed at the end of this volume.*

publicly. R. Soloveitchik heard me out respectfully. He deplored the lack of discussion of these issues at Yeshiva, and then said: "You know, they pressured me to speak out and denounce your views. They pressed me very hard. But I want you to know that no matter what they do, I will never denounce you publicly." I was moved by his words because I knew that the Rav found it hard to take pressure; this silence was his way of giving me *hizuk*. Yet I felt a burning desire to say to him: "Why don't you speak out and make clear how much these controversial views are rooted in yours?" But my courage failed; instead I urged that he speak out more himself on these topics. At that he launched into a jeremiad against his *lomdishe* students. They were only interested in Talmud and *lomdus*; they were tone deaf to matters of spiritual meaning; they did not come or would not listen when he wanted to talk *hashkafah*; that is why he talked about these topics less and less. I wanted to tell him that if he spoke out publicly that he would set the agenda and no one would dare resist. Again I could not get myself to say it. I was relieved by his assurance and feared offending him.

The opposition found the only other person at Yeshiva who had the credibility to "refute" my views: R. Aharon Lichtenstein. Although vigorous debate was a good thing, I was disappointed by R. Lichtenstein's article in *The Commentator*. It served the political purpose — appearing to contradict my views. But that was misleading. Written with R. Lichtenstein's characteristic style — highly complex, with subtle distinctions and abstract boundaries — only highly trained, sophisticated readers (which the Yeshiva students and teachers mostly were not) realized that he actually conceded the essential validity of most of my views. His agreement was concealed by his repeated criticisms of the tone of the interview — the too sweeping or too open nature of my formulations.

In its effect, the article reinforced those who insisted that even discussing these issues was not acceptable. R. Lichtenstein ignored my call for the needed response to the *Shoah* and Israel reborn. Nor did he acknowledge Orthodoxy's need "for self-criticism, self-questioning and exploring." The argument that to work effectively on the intellectual challenges of modernity, "there must be leeway to make statements wide of the mark," he dismissed as "a nice nineteenth century notion...[with] a pleasant liberal ring about it." R. Lichtenstein passed over in silence my plea that "I speak as an impatient lover not an outsider," although he knew there was a lot of delegitimation going on. He rejected the warning of an unhealthy atmosphere at Yeshiva in which "criticism is identified with rejection" and that "the net hysteria...would foreclose serious consideration of these problems," blaming the reaction on my language, not on any tendency toward censorship or repression. To this day, I believe that R. Lichtenstein's tolerances for exploration are so tight that they handicap Modern Orthodoxy's capacity to deal with issues such as historical-critical studies and feminism. Notwithstanding the above, R. Lichtenstein spoke with respect toward me and I continue to admire his personal model combining *gadlus be-Torah* and Modern Orthodox values and thinking.

For the most part, over the next two decades, discussion of frontier issues was tolerated less and less — and, except for R. Emanuel Rackman, the institutional leadership of Yeshiva and Modern Orthodoxy stood by and let the swing to the right and the silencing of discussion proceed. From Riverdale Jewish Center to CLAL, I became more and more preoccupied with professional tasks. To my great frustration, I had less time even to be present, let alone to defend my views and policy directions. After another year at Yad Vashem from 1974-75 and in the years of CLAL, my views moved to full religious pluralism and toward affirmative theological dialogue with Christianity. The religious right aggressively moved to delegitimize these views and to cut off any chance that I could speak for them at Yeshiva. Again, the moderate leadership, except for R. Rackman, stood by or joined in the process.

In 1970, I made an abortive attempt to create a Center for Jewish Survival that could deal with the needed response to the *Shoah* and Israel and with the growing challenge of freedom and choice. All Jewish groups were needed to accomplish the task, but Riverdale's lay leaders were hung up on the participation of non-Orthodox. I concluded that one cannot turn an Orthodox shul into an intellectual/theological think tank open to all groups. Although I loved the Riverdale Jewish Center, I was determined to go back to academia, where I would have the time and professional need to write and publish my views. I thought of returning to YC, although I sensed the growing isolation of my views. However, I saw no indication that they would let me teach full time in the field of Jewish Thought and Theology.

Then City College — where I had taught the Holocaust as an adjunct in 1970-72 — offered me a full professorship to start a Department of Jewish Studies. CUNY offered a salary — a standard academic full professor salary — which so outstripped the YC scale, it even outstripped my RJC salary, that I was stunned. In a flash, I realized the extent of the disrespect for religious teachers/rabbis at YC and my own financial naïveté — a product in part of the false spirituality imparted in most *yeshiva* education that denigrated the material.

I felt conflicted. I realized that I would miss the incredible quality of YC students and their deep involvement in the religious issues that I passionately cared about. Also, despite its failure to cultivate *roshei yeshiva* and *poskim* who would combine *Torah u-Madda* and to recruit outstanding college professor role models, Yeshiva still had the largest concentration of teacher/thinkers and students wrestling with these issues. But nothing in life comes without trade-offs. Academia was the *avi avot* of the confrontation between Torah and modernity; I also hoped for another chance to start the Center for Jewish Survival there. As it turned out, in 1975, CCNY received a bequest that funded CLAL's start-up. I accepted the City College offer. Sadly, my teaching days at Yeshiva were over.

An Open Letter to My Children

By Lawrence Grossman

Dear Boys:

Over the years, you have often asked me why I've raised you in a way that's somewhat out of synch with the approaches you have encountered over the course of your *yeshiva* educations. I've explained to you that I grew up in a different era. This is my opportunity to go into some detail, to explain how and why.

In the 1960s, strange as it may sound, there were a good many Orthodox young men committed to Jewish life and the study of its texts, and also insatiably curious about the world, its culture, its history, and its literature — not for the purpose of *parnassah*, but to understand the truth and beauty inherent in God's creation.

Orthodoxy, at the time, seemed poised to throw off its earlier defensiveness and engage intellectually with modern culture. The primary avenue of the transformation was the printed word. The Rabbinical Council of America's fledgling *Tradition* journal, each issue eagerly awaited and quickly devoured by us, contained many articles exploring the implications that Torah and modernity posed for each other. The Orthodox Union's magazine *Jewish Life*, now defunct, also featured material along these lines, and Orthodox thinkers were beginning to contribute significant pieces to non-Orthodox periodicals, such as *Judaism* — a sure sign that Orthodoxy was shedding its parochialism and starting to get a

Dr. *Lawrence Grossman*, YC '66, RIETS '69, *edits the* American Jewish Year Book *and is associate director of research at the American Jewish Committee. Dr. Grossman taught history at YC and Stern from 1972 through 1982.*

hearing in the broader Jewish community. On prestigious campuses across the country, a new Orthodox Jewish student organization, Yavneh, ran programs geared specifically to address the intellectual interface between Torah and the secular disciplines.

But Yeshiva was ground zero for *Torah u-Madda*, a marketing slogan that became almost a palpable reality during the decade. First, Yeshiva's dual program — including serious social science and humanities requirements — strongly encouraged the inquisitive student to relate the disparate curricular components to one another. And even more important, its faculty included a wide variety of Orthodox role models who proved that the term "Orthodox intellectual" was not necessarily an oxymoron.

The overarching figure, of course, was R. Joseph B. Soloveitchik, who had a PhD in philosophy from the University of Berlin and was a prime exemplar of the possibility of combining Torah and *madda*. His *shi'urim*, delivered in professorial English, were pure Brisker analysis; anyone experiencing this extraordinary man solely in the classroom or through the selective memory of some of his students would have no idea of the breadth of his mind. Suffice it to say that it was in the 60s that his dazzling combination of encyclopedic knowledge and shrewd understanding of the real world and of human nature became known to a wide public. *Ish ha-Halakhah*, virtually ignored when first published in the 1940s, became *de rigueur* reading for the intellectually sophisticated Yeshiva student. *Tradition* published the Rav's two primary English-language essays, "The Lonely Man of Faith" and "Confrontation," and his regular talks in New York and Boston on Jewish texts and issues, open to the public, drew large crowds that included people far removed from Orthodoxy. Ironically, this great exponent of halakhic Judaism consistently eschewed the use of halakhic arguments to decide public-policy issues, declaring, for example, that the question of whether to demonstrate against the Soviet Union over its treatment of Jews was best left to the Sovietologists and that territorial decisions after the Six Day War were not to be made by rabbis but by the Israeli government.

Two of the Rav's close relatives also had a major impact on students. His younger brother, R. Aharon, who, like the Rav, taught Brisker Torah in English — he had a law degree from NYU — was so convinced of the need for Orthodoxy to confront modernity that he devoted one *shi'ur* weekly to *hashkafah*, Jewish perspectives on contemporary issues. The

Rav's son-in-law, R. Aharon Lichtenstein, started giving *shi'ur* in 1963, armed with a Harvard PhD in English literature. It was from him, way back then, that I first heard that the methods of textual analysis used by literary scholars could be fruitfully applied to the Bible, a notion that Robert Alter and others have since brought into the cultural mainstream. When he headed the RIETS *kollel*, R. Lichtenstein would host monthly get-togethers for the members at his apartment, where a previously announced contemporary issue — poverty, the Vietnam War, civil rights, etc. — would be discussed from a halakhic perspective. I can recall one somewhat otherworldly *kollel* boy asking me in a panic, just a few hours before the monthly session, to fill him in on Biafra.

The college faculty included several memorable figures who demonstrated, in their disparate fields, the confluence of Torah and *madda*. There was R. Emanuel Rackman, embodiment of a species now extinct, the pulpit rabbi/Jewish communal leader/academic, successful in all three fields. In his course on political theory, he analyzed the thought of Maimonides along with that of Machiavelli, Hobbes, and the other great theorists — I will never forget this class, since the great blackout of 1965 occurred while I was sitting in it. And there was the late Dr. Meyer Simcha Feldblum, a great *talmid hakham* who showed us how to analyze rabbinic texts critically, with an understanding of their historical development. I once told him that having been exposed to his methodology, it would be hard to go back to the traditional way of learning. He replied that I would quickly revert, but that "something will remain." He was right.

I have left for the end the two men who most profoundly influenced my life: R. Irving "Yitz" Greenberg and Dr. Charles Liebman. Both were barely 30 years old when I was their student at Yeshiva. Virtually everyone has heard of Greenberg, largely through what he did after leaving Yeshiva — his work at CLAL, pioneering Jewish-Christian dialogue, and presiding over the United States Holocaust Memorial Museum. But few, beyond those directly involved, know what he meant to the intellectually inquisitive YC students of the 60s. Greenberg swept us up in the excitement of intellectual history, providing a broad perspective for understanding the Jewish experience. He was the first, as far as I know, to frankly pinpoint the ways that the shock of modernity challenged Orthodox Judaism to its core, raising serious problems especially for young Jews on college campuses. His articles from that era resonate today with their original freshness because the problems have not disappeared.

Greenberg's subsequent estrangement from Yeshiva University circles has been unfortunate for American Orthodoxy and, I believe, for him.

Charles Liebman was a fascinating character. He came to Yeshiva in 1963 to teach political science, but he hated teaching and was in the process of changing his field of interest to the sociology of religion. He loved to schmooze in his office — he had a wicked sense of humor — where he had a wonderful collection of books. I remember Liebman taking down Peter Berger's *The Noise of Solemn Assemblies*, handing it to me and saying, "I think you'll enjoy this." I did, and my appreciation of religion's embeddedness in historical and social reality dates from that moment. Liebman was then working on "Orthodoxy in American Jewish Life," the first of his path breaking studies of American Judaism, which appeared in the 1965 American Jewish Year Book; last year, as editor of the Year Book, I wrote his obituary. After leaving Yeshiva, he taught at Bar-Ilan for many years and wrote several important books and articles on American and Israeli Jewry. He died just months after receiving the 2003 Israel Prize, the country's most prestigious award.

For a host of reasons related to shifts in American cultural values and developments within the Jewish community, the Yeshiva of the 60s collapsed like a house of cards. As early as 1972, when I returned to join the faculty, the institution had changed drastically. Rabbi Lichtenstein and Professors Greenberg and Liebman were gone, and R. Rackman, fated not to become the next president of the university, would soon follow. All would achieve great success within other institutional frameworks. The prevalent mood among the students was pre-professional. Pressure was mounting for loosening the liberal arts course requirements and instituting majors in business, accounting, and computers. A year of study in an Israeli yeshiva was becoming increasingly popular; the college credit given for it further cut down on exposure to liberal arts, and a *"yeshivishe"* mindset took root among many of the students. American-born men who had studied at Yeshiva were being appointed *roshei yeshiva* and, unlike their European, Yiddish-speaking predecessors, they could tell their students in good faith that they had gone to college and therefore knew that it was of little value beyond *"parnassah."* YC, it appeared, was no longer competing for students with Columbia, but with Ner Israel and Telz.

But the legacy of the 60s has not disappeared. A highly disproportionate number of YC students of that era — far more, I dare say, than among older or younger alumni — chose careers in academic Jewish studies or as Jewish communal professionals, reflecting the overarching ethos of that time and place — that the "real" world and the Jewish world form a seamless whole. We, the dinosaurs, still think of ourselves as embodiments of what Yeshiva was intended to be.

And so, my children, I hope you now understand my alienation from the Orthodoxy in which you have been educated — it's a generational thing. But I have exposed you to a different path, one that YC blazed for me. Will you, like Robert Frost's walker in the snowy wood, take the path "less traveled by?" For me, at least, "that has made all the difference."

Love,
Dad

The following pages are from an early brochure about Yeshiva College (circa late 1920s), featuring a description of the educational philosophy and goals of the institution, and an artist's rendition of the proposed campus design and layout. Though not all the building plans came to fruition, a number of similar structures still stand today. The brochure, appearing here in its entirety for the first time since originally being published, is used with permission of the Yeshiva University Archives.

The Yeshiva College

What It Is and What It Stands For

A Challenge and a Promise to American Jewry

The Yeshiva —
A Tradition of 2000 Years

NO word in any language, ancient or modern, which in its use is associated with the terms of education and learning, can compare with the dramatic significance of the Hebrew word—Yeshiva.

It is a simple word. In Hebrew it means a "meeting", a "session". Since early times it has been applied to the meetings of scholars who have sought the truth through education, through interpreting the law of God, through searching for the light of understanding in the avenues that lead to justice, righteousness and inspiration for a higher life. "Yeshiva" also means a "class", a group of students who seek instruction from the elders, from the scholars and sages, in short, an Academy for Jewish learning.

Long before any of the oldest colleges and universities, famous today, came into existence, Yeshiva was a familiar and potent word to the non-Jewish as well as to the Jewish world, signifying the distinctive Jewish institution of higher learning, a particular type of culture and world outlook. Long before any of the existing forms of civilization, states and governments in the western hemisphere were established, there was not a continent of the then known world, where a Yeshiva could not be found. In all climes, under all political, social and economic conditions, the Yeshiva carried on the old tradition, in accord with the divine inspiration derived from the Revelation at Sinai, shaping the character of the Jewish people and their culture. In Palestine, in Babylon, in Persia, in Africa, in Spain, in France, in Germany, in Poland, in Russia and today in America, the Yeshiva continued the uninterrupted tradition.

Throughout the ages, whether under the most cruel persecution or under the most luring prosperity, the Yeshiva remained a smithy where Jewish character was wrought and hardened, where the principles of that tradition which has made its indelible impress on the mind and culture of the civilized world, were interpreted and expanded.

A single historic fact, of the tenth century, envisages the majestic story. At a time when all established forms of government and society were declining, when the world of antiquity was shaken to its foundations, giving way to a period of chaos, restlessness and bloodshed, four Jewish men of letters were taken into captivity by the field marshal of the Califf. The four were sold as slaves in various parts of the world. Thrown into a new environment, where there were but small Jewish communities, each of the four, succeeded, despite slavery and suffering, in establishing a Yeshiva. These new centers of learning continued the thread of the glorious Jewish tradition and laid the foundation for a new Jewish life on new continents.

The Yeshivas of all ages have been the centers of learning, the reservoirs of knowledge, of spiritual strength and idealism, the instrument for a continued transmission of the divine light of Sinai. Out of the Yeshivas have come the scholars, the sages and the standard bearers in Jewish life. In them the soul of Israel has found its truest and noblest expression.

The story has continued for centuries and centuries, the Yeshiva being ever a bulwark of strength, building character, spreading learning, interpreting the law, producing leaders, sustaining Jewish life until—

American Jewry entered.

General View

American Jewry at a Turning Point

THE entrance of American Jewry, the youngest Jewish community in the world, lasted fifty years. Although the history of the Jews in the United States dates back 270 years, the history of American Jews as a community began only a century ago. The most important developments, which led to the congregation of four million Jewish men, women and children in the United States, have enfolded almost before our eyes. It has been mainly during the last forty years that the turn of events in world history created conditions and factors that determined and shaped the component parts and the character of American Jewry. It was a sturdy, pioneering generation that carried the burden of the period, overcoming the greatest difficulties, against all possible odds. During that most difficult process of adaptation to the economic, cultural and political conditions, the Jews in America, in the main, continued the line of Jewish tradition.

Philanthropy and social work, essentials of the Jewish conception necessarily had to absorb the major attention of the Jewish communities in all parts of the land. This sturdy, pioneer generation, strengthened by the spiritual equipment which it had brought from the other side of the ocean, emerged successful. It has gone through a most remarkable process of transformation, unequalled and unprecedented.

With its material adaptation drawing to an end, the question of cultural and spiritual adjustment has become the vital issue that confronts American Jewry today. With Jewish immigration to the United States practically closed, with the conviction growing that all methods applied in the various Jewish schools, have brought very little, if any, satisfactory results, the query arises now on every tongue: "Watchman, what of the night?" What of the future of Judaism in America? In what manner will the otherwise rich and fully equipped American Jewish community, solve its perplexing problem of spiritual self preservation and make its distinct contribution toward American culture? By what means and methods will it reach a standard that will lead to the creation

Group A Buildings—High School, Auditorium and Dormitory

of the real type of American Jew in the truest meaning of the two terms?

Peter Wiernick, editor and author of the "History of the Jews in America", thus sums up the result of fifty years experience in the field of Jewish education in America: "The experience of nearly half a century with Talmud Torahs, Hebrew Institutes and similar institutions under different names has not produced results to which one could point with pride or even with qualified satisfaction. In these schools the methods are not entirely new and the student cannot be given enough Jewish instruction to produce Jewish scholarship. And without a supply of indigenous Jewish learning of the good old traditional sort, Judaism will wither even under the most flourishing material conditions."

The question is one of vital importance not for American Jewry alone, but for Jewry the world over. By the will of a tragic fate, American Jewry is the only part of the Jewish people today that has emerged from the World War and the post war period, with its material strength preserved. Many centers of Jewish learning in the old world have been uprooted.

Some of the historic Academies and Yeshivas in European countries, where the continuity of Jewish tradition was guarded, where Jewish thought was preserved and expanded, where the principles of the Torah were interpreted and handed down to the coming generations, have become disintegrated.

All students of Jewish history for the past two thousand years know of the unique phenomenon that whenever an old established center was destroyed, a new center and haven of refuge for the Jew sprang up. Dr. B. Revel, distinguished scholar and leader, president of the Faculty of the Yeshiva, has defined the situation in the following few words: "American Jewry is destined by Providence to play a dominant role in the history of world Jewry and Jewish culture. The mantle of responsibility and opportunity is descending upon American Jewry."

What can American Jewry do to meet this great opportunity?

What will American Jews do, that the mantle of responsibility which, by the grace of destiny, is falling upon its shoulders, may become for it a mantle of honor and fulfilment?

Interior of Auditorium

The Challenge; The Men Who Made It Possible

AS in times of old, the four captives, transplanted into new regions, emerged from their state of material poverty to establish new centers of Jewish learning, the Jews in America, who came to the shores of the new world as refugees from persecution, soon emulated this example.

When in 1881 the stream of Jewish immigration began to flow from Czaristic Russia, the new arrivals, had only one object in mind: to find relief from persecution, and to enjoy religious and material freedom. In such a state, individuals lose sight of the interests of the community: personal need demands their single minded efforts. Notwithstanding that, communal efforts were made, necessarily limited to philanthropic activities, bringing relief to the poor and needy and the sick, providing employment for the waiting "hands".

However, history repeated itself. A generation ago, in the midst of this chaotic condition, a small group of pioneers recognized that in order to maintain Jewish life and to provide for the development in this country of a Jewish

culture as a real and living force, the continuity of Jewish learning and of Jewish tradition, must be guarded. The first thing that had to be done was to transplant into this land, the historic home of the Torah, the Yeshiva.

With meagre means at their disposal, they founded the first Yeshiva on the American continent. They named it the Rabbi Isaac Elchanan Yeshiva following the old Jewish adage that "when a great man dies a Yeshiva is to be founded in his memory". The perpetuation of learning is the greatest monument that can be erected to the memory of a great man. In 1897, Rabbi Isaac Elchanan, a sage and leader in Israel, died in the city of Kovno. The small community of East European Jews who lived in New York at that time, received this news with great sorrow and true to Jewish tradition, they established the first American Yeshiva in memory of this great scholar.

In the whirlpool of modern American life where the pressure of the torrent constitutes such a tremendous danger for the growing Jewish youth, where antagonistic social and economic forces, tend to create a cleavage between the old and the continually new, the Yeshiva became a rock of strength for the few who were to assume the leadership in the growing communities.

And so this work continued for a generation. During this period, the Yeshiva has sent forth many rabbis, and teachers, several thousand students passing through its doors. These graduates have become the torchbearers of traditional Judaism and leaders in their communities. In a short span of time the Yeshiva has established itself as the worthy successor to the great Jewish centers of learning of all ages. With the Torah as the guide, Orthodox Judaism, as interpreted in the Yeshiva, made for itself a place in American Jewish life and in the life of America.

Situated in the midst of the most crowded section of the world's most tumultuous city, with building and equipment most inadequate, the Yeshiva continued its daily struggle for existence, aided by a small group of loyal and devoted pioneers. Under these restricting conditions the Yeshiva could not, however, take in Jewish life the place which it deserves and which it most vitally requires.

The challenge issued by the early pioneers found its dramatic climax on December 20, 1924. Orthodox Jews, so long dormant, found themselves in the Yeshiva College Building Fund. Generous and active individuals in every important fund raising movement, Orthodox Jews in America never before united to achieve something big for themselves. When the proposal to create a Five Million Dollar Fund to strengthen the Yeshiva as an institution for higher Jewish learning was first broached, it was greeted with a smile of scepticism. Small wonder! Such a proposal was unprecedented!

Samuel Levy, chairman of the Executive Committee of the Yeshiva College Building Fund who has himself contributed the amount of $50,000, gives the following narrative of how and when the Yeshiva appeal took its present form.

"On December 20, 1924, the leaders of the campaign held their initial function, nervous, hesitant, afraid of the results. On that date Orthodox Jewry was reborn, revitalized in America. A small group of about 125 attended a dinner in the Hotel Astor. The devoted leaders of the campaign hoped that at most

$100,000 might be subscribed, towards securing the future of Traditional Judaism in this country. The unexpected happened! The magnitude of the proposed institution—the arresting significance of the movement, heretofore considered a nebulous dream—the responsibility resting upon this small group of earnest men and women for their children and their children's children—all these emotions crystallized and before the meeting was over nearly $1,000,000 had been pledged as the initial contribution toward the $5,000,000 Building Fund.

"It began with the venerable Nathan Lamport, Acting President of the Yeshiva, who announced a contribution of $100,000. Then came Harry Fischel, another stalwart champion of the Yeshiva for many years, who also made a $100,000 contribution. These announcements were electrifying. They swept through that small group and contributions poured in, in amounts never before given for Jewish educational endeavors.

"Nearly a million dollars from 125 contributors in one night. It was almost beyond belief. It was commented upon by the press of the world. It showed the world the tremendous potentialities of Orthodox Jewry in America. The smiles of scepticism disappeared. American Jewry had been shown what Orthodox Jewry could do. Most significant of all, Orthodox Jewry had shown itself what it could do.

"With the first million dollars raised, Harris L. Selig, executive director, set about devising a new way to secure the second million. Dramatic as had been the raising of the first million dollars, Mr. Selig knew that an even more dramatic idea would have to be the central theme of the campaign for the second million dollars. And so he proposed a Million Dollar Dinner, a dinner at which one thousand guests would each pay a thousand dollar cover charge to realize the Building Fund's second million. It was a revolutionary proposal. Leaders of the campaign said it had never been done and it could not be done. Of Hundred Dollar Dinners there had, of course, been many for various fund raising campaigns. But a Thousand-Dollar-Dinner! True, a small group of Yeshiva leaders had raised a million dollars among themselves. True, Orthodox Jewry was beginning to realize its own potentialities. But to raise one million dollars

College of Liberal Arts and Science—Teachers Institute—Physical Culture Building

through a thousand dollar cover charge? Thus the campaign leaders reasoned, but in the end the proposal of Mr. Selig was agreed upon and the rest is history.

On May 26, 1925, at the Hotel Astor, almost twelve hundred men and women sat down at a dinner, historic, but for the fact that each of them paid a cover charge of one thousand dollars for the privilege of attending. It was undoubtedly the most brilliant dinner ever held in the annals of Jewish fund raising in America."

On December 19, 1926, the Executive Committee of the Yeshiva College celebrated the 70th birthday of the President of the Yeshiva, Mr. Nathan Lamport. On this occasion, Mr. Lamport raised his subscription from $100,000 to $200,000. Many leading members of the Committee have, as a token of appreciation to Mr. Lamport, given substantial increases.

The Promise —
The Yeshiva College for Higher Learning

TO the group of the early pioneers, humble in purse and in influence, but rich in vision, there were added men of devotion and determination to make the hope of the pioneers a convincing reality. True benefactors of American Jewry, recognizing that the problem touches the very core of its existence, they undertook the effort which up to the present has produced more than two million dollars toward the five million dollar fund necessary for the construction of the buildings of the Yeshiva of America. The challenge which was so boldly issued to the community at large by this group contained also a pledge and a promise which has to be redeemed.

The eight buildings which will soon be erected on the three city blocks on upper Amsterdam Avenue, New York City, foreshadow a new era in Jewish life, not alone in America: A Yeshiva College—an institution

Students' Congregation

devoted to the pursuit of higher Jewish learning on a scale and magnitude heretofore unparalleled. The spiritual confusion which obtains in the life of the Jewish communities, the chaos which exists in the various types of Jewish congregations throughout the land, will be cleared away with the establishment of the great Yeshiva, with the return to the authentic sources of the Torah.

The query vibrant on the lips of all thinking American Jews, of every father and mother who care for the future of their children, the disturbing anxiety of "Watchman, what of the night?" the general uneasiness and deep concern as to the future of Jewish life and the Jewish contribution to America's spiritual development and culture, will be relieved and find a solution in the laboratory of the Yeshiva College.

The challenge and the promise embodied in the Yeshiva College of America are a matter of concern not only to American Jewry at large; they concern every individual Jew and Jewess.

It is a matter that holds promise also for you. The Yeshivas of old were not limited to the training of rabbis, teachers or preachers. The Jewish conception of knowledge and cul-

ture is that they are not the heritage of the chosen few alone, but the treasured possession of the entire house of Israel. The Yeshivas of old were accessible to every qualified young man irrespective of his future activity in the community as a rabbi or a layman, merchant, physican or lawyer. According to Jewish conception, the ultimate aim of education is not in the mere acquisition of knowledge, the mere training of the intellect, nor the mere preparation of an individual for a particular task in life. The ultimate aim of education is the building of character and the harmonious development of the faculties of man. Its background is spiritual and cultural, its goal is the strengthening of the will and the inculcation of an appreciation of nature, of love and reverence for the Creator. Its goal is finally to imbue the pupil with a passion for all that lifts man to God, inspires love for his fellowmen, for home and country.

"The Yeshiva's conception of Jewish education is based upon the conviction that we serve our country and humanity best by training the growing generation to live in the ways of Israel's Torah, its moral standards and cultural values," Dr. B. Revel states.

The Yeshiva will be a center from which the

Yeshiva Rabbi Isaac Elchanan—Library and Court

Jewish spirit will radiate once more, where new leaders true to the Torah will be raised and where a new Jewish meaning will be given to the life of American Jewry.

The Yeshiva is authorized to confer the Divinity degrees and the degrees of Doctor of Hebrew Literature. The Teachers' Institute is authorized to grant a diploma qualifying its possessor to teach in Hebrew Schools.

The work of the high school, Talmudical Academy, recognized by the New York State Department of Education as of full high school grade, will be extended and developed into a college which, together with the Yeshiva, will constitute the Yeshiva College. The record of the Yeshiva High School and the gratifyingly large number of state scholarships awarded to its graduates are indicative of the scholastic attainments.

The course of study in the Yeshiva includes the comprehensive study of the Bible and Targumim, and the reading of important Jewish medieval and modern commentaries on the Bible. The Halachic Midrashim are studied in connection with the Bible. The course in the Talmud and Codes comprises the study of the Babylonian and Palestinian Talmuds, Codes, early and later Commentaries and the Responsa literature. The course in Jewish history includes the study of historical texts and documents. Particular stress is laid on the historical material contained in the Talmud and Midrashic literature. The vast Responsa literature is utilized in the study of Jewish history. Research work along these lines is encouraged and provision is made for such work. In the course in Jewish literature, the reading of Jewish philosophical and ethical works is included.

Dr. Bernard Revel, president of the Faculty of the Yeshiva, thus outlines what the Yeshiva College will stand for:

"The proposed Yeshiva College of Liberal Arts and Science is intended mainly for its own students. It will dedicate its energies to the education of a number of American Jewish young men of ability and high ideals, who wish to prepare themselves for the rabbinate, for Jewish social service, for teaching in or the supervision of Jewish religious schools, for Jewish scholarship or communal leadership.

"As the college develops, it will extend its usefulness to Jewish youth who consider Jewish learning part of the mental and moral equipment that they wish to obtain through a college education, and who are prepared for

Classroom in High School

such a combined education as the Yeshiva College will offer.

"The college will help bridge the chasm between intellectualism and faith. It will present to at least a portion of our academic youth, in a proper setting, the spirit and vital message of Judaism, and make it a potent force in their lives; and will thus help bring back the days when our great thinkers and intellectual giants were at the same time our religious guides. The interaction of Jewish culture and philosophy of life, and all knowledge of mankind, the harmonious development of the human and the Jewish consciousness, will help to create harmony in the heart and the mind of the Jewish youth and will help develop a complete Jewish personality. The college will, as it grows and advances, become a distinctive intellectual and spiritual center of American Jewry and will help advance Jewish culture, together with the dissemination and increase of general knowledge. Such an institution of higher learning can mean only added strength to American civilization.

"The college will attract a group of creative personalities to its faculty and will, in time, help create a demand and help supply the demand for constructive Jewish educational forces with a Jewish perspective, to whom nothing Jewish is alien.

"The Yeshiva stands for a closer unification of the forces of education. It aims to enhance by simultaneous human and religious appeal to the mind and the heart of the child, its moral consciousness, to develop a mind that is spiritually integrated and capable of seeing the harmony of life, its duties and opportunities. It stands for a system of Jewish education which will widen the spiritual and moral horizon of our youth, will help them to live anew Israel's glorious millennial yesterday, that of the Prophets, Maccabees, Hillels, Akibas, Maimonides—of Israel's countless martyrs and heroes, and will prepare them to live the life and hopes of Israel's Messianic tomorrow, which embraces all mankind."

High School Library and Reading Room

What American Educators and Leaders Say Concerning The Yeshiva

THE great benefit which will accrue to American Jewry through the firm establishment of the great Yeshiva in the proposed Yeshiva College, has found the appreciation not only of Jewish, but of the leading American educators, statesmen and thinkers.

Jewish learning is an integral and vital part of humanity's knowledge and experience. The creation of a home for higher Jewish learning in America, will add strength and glory not only to the Jewish community but to America, too. The blending of a general high school and college training with the spiritual values of Judaism will introduce a *new note* into the American educational system.

It is hoped that through the Yeshiva College of America on the rich background of an harmonized Jewish and general education, a lasting contribution to the culture of America, will be made. By training the rabbis, the teachers, and the leaders for Jewish communities, equipped with the advantages of a higher general education combined with a knowledge of the ideals and the truths of historic Judaism, based on the original sources of the Torah, the Yeshiva College will constitute a new and unique force in America's spiritual structure. Its influence will bring the name of American Jewry and of America into the far off corners of the world.

This view is not the property or the cherished hope of farsighted Jewish leaders alone, but is likewise the hope of the most outstanding American educators, statesmen and leaders.

NICHOLAS MURRAY BUTLER, *President Columbia University*, says: "The undertaking is plainly one of value to the intellectual and religious life of our city and country, and I trust that it may meet with the success which it deserves."

WILLIAM HOWARD TAFT, *Chief Justice, Supreme Court of the United States*, says: "I wish the men and women engaged in this work the greatest success."

Dormitory Room

J. H. PENNIMAN, *Provost of the University of Pennsylvania*, says: "Any institution, which has for its purpose the disseminating of truth and the cultivating of the minds of the people in their youth is welcome in America. There are certain special literatures about which all American citizens should be informed, and there are certain subjects of study which concern only particular groups of our population. The study of Hebrew literature and Jewish civilization are of the utmost importance."

ELMER E. BROWN, *Chancellor New York University*, says: "The placing of Jewish learning upon the highest plane of scholarship is certainly a thing to be desired. It should be of interest to scholarly minds generally, regardless of race or creed."

SIDNEY E. MEZES, *President of the College of the City of New York*, says: "Every branch of learning and almost every field of human activity has been quickened by the contribution of the Jewish scholar and the Jewish thinker. There are minds that cannot attain their fullest possibilities in an environment that is not altogether emotionally and spiritually sympathetic. This, it seems to me, is one of the chief justifications of parochial education in a democracy. Your Yeshiva will un-

doubtedly provide an opportunity for the American youth whose religious allegiance is intensely Jewish to make his contribution to the cultural development of America."

FRANK J. GOODNOW, *President the Johns Hopkins University*, says: "I recognize the desirability of the establishment of seminaries devoted to the study of Jewish philosophy and history. Anything that you can do to bring about the establishment of such a seminary would be of great advantage to the cause of higher education in America."

J. R. ANGELL, *President of Yale*, says: "So far as I understand the project, I should be very sympathetic to it, if it could be guaranteed that it would be conducted in the spirit of modern, liberal education."

RAY LYMAN WILBUR, *President of Stanford University*, says: "The rich history of the Jews, particularly in religious and cultural subjects, will, I am sure, be a real contribution to the intellectual life of America. The study of the Torah, Talmud, Jewish philosophy, theology, history and literature should certainly attract leading scholars both to the faculty and to the student body."

WILLIAM LOWE BRYAN, *President of Indiana University*, says: "I can have no other feeling

Reception Room in the Dormitory

than one of great satisfaction at the founding of a Jewish college in America. The eminent scholars of your race in many lands and times make a glorious background for the group of scholars who will constitute your faculty."

WALTER D. SCOTT, *President Northwestern University*, says: "The step which you have taken is a most important one for the country, and for Jewish culture, and stands with the establishment of the new Hebrew University in Jerusalem as one of the outstanding recent contributions to education."

H. N. MACCRACKEN, *President Vassar College* says: "Several years ago I became very much interested in the establishment of just such an institution as the Yeshiva College. It seemed to me then, as it does now, that there is a great field for its activities and that the ideal of transmitting the cultural heritage of the Jewish people in its integrity is one which ought to be a concern of modern education.

FRANK AYDELOTTE, *President Swarthmore College*, says: "I am firmly convinced that a Jewish institution of learning maintained up to a standard commensurate with the outstanding intellectual achievements of the Jewish race would enrich the cultural and academic life of America in a most valuable way."

GEORGE FREDERICK KAY, *Dean of the State University of Iowa*, says: "As a result of the establishment of this Jewish College, I feel sure that a great contribution can be made in enriching the cultural and academic life of America. There never was a greater need than now for the cooperation of Protestants, Jews, Catholics and other organizations in the development of the higher values of life."

FRANK L. SPEARE, *President Northeastern University*, says: "The Jewish people have a great ancestry. They have done much for the world's work and your future should be safeguarded by the establishment of institutions where the high ethical and moral standards of your church can be taught and exemplified and the oncoming generation may have available the best thought and practice of their ancestors."

W. H. P. FAUNCE, *President Brown University*, says: "The establishment of such an institution would be of measureless benefit to the Jews of America, and indeed to all our citizens, regardless of religious faith. Only through the higher education, permeated with faith in the unseen, can the varied peoples of America be lifted above prejudice and party spirit and attain that intellectual leadership which will lead us into an ever broadening future."

View looking North from 186th Street

Building a Sanctuary of Learning
for American Jewry

A GREAT deal of the indifference displayed in some quarters toward Jewish learning and the institution which is its embodiment, the Yeshiva of old, was due to the fact that full regard has not been paid to the external form.

Since early days on Palestine soil, when, under the persecution of a mighty world regime, the substance of Jewish culture and learning was reduced to the status of "flying letters", the orientation of Jewish learning became introspective. The wandering Jew was accompanied by the wandering Torah. With the exception of brief periods of comparative rest, the Yeshiva was a "floating university", with its center in the minds of individuals, scholars and students, often more an idea than a physical actuality. No record is available today that would indicate a deliberate planning and building of a center for Jewish learning, a Yeshiva on a munificent scale and a high plane, as

the one planned and being built for the Yeshiva College.

American Jewry has spent huge sums in the last few decades on the erection of synagogues, centers, hospitals, orphanages, old age homes, and the like. Millions are being spent every year by the Jewish communities throughout the land for the maintenance and expansion of Talmud Torahs and religious schools for our children. Equally large sums have been invested in the erection of buildings to house these necessary and vital institutions. Of what ultimate avail is all this expenditure of funds and effort if it reaches no further than the elementary grades? Of what avail, if no adequate provision is made for training leaders and producing scholars of a high calibre?

It was with the coming into being of the Yeshiva College Building Fund that the Jewish community in the United States could point with pride to the fact that for the first time a

Students Dining Hall

free and prosperous Jewry has undertaken the gigantic task of creating a great Yeshiva College, planned and designed not only to serve the needs of the present but to provide for development and expansion in the future.

"Builders for tomorrow." This is the name of the new roster, the roll of honor, the register of the aristocratic families of American Jewry, those, who have made possible the progress up to the present and of those who will join in this historic work.

The Yeshiva College, as visioned and designed by the builders for tomorrow will be a distinct contribution to the architecture of America and constitute a departure in the mode of construction of American Jewish public buildings.

In planning the material expression for the idea of the Yeshiva College of America, its builders had no precedent to follow. In fact, the impelling command was, away from precedent. In laying out its plans and in their execution, the Building Committee of the Yeshiva College Building Fund, under the chairmanship of Harry Fischel, made a notable record.

The Building Committee purchased 85 city lots comprising three blocks on Amsterdam Avenue between 186th and 188th Streets, New York City. The sum of $370,000 was paid for the site, the largest sum paid by any Jewish educational institution. On this site eight buildings will be erected to provide proper accommodations for the Yeshiva College in its various departments.

The series of buildings will consist of three groups.

Group A includes (1) the high school, (2) auditorium and (3) the first dormitory building.

Group B will consist of buildings to house the (1) College of Liberal Arts and Science and a (2) physical education building.

Group C will contain: (1) the Yeshiva building; (2) the library; (3) the Teachers Institute; (4) the Department of Semitic languages and post graduate research, and (5) the gardens and courtyards.

The first group of buildings is now in process of construction. The high school will provide for 2,500 students, the dormitory for 250 out-of-town students. The auditorium and assembly hall will have a seating capacity of over 2,000.

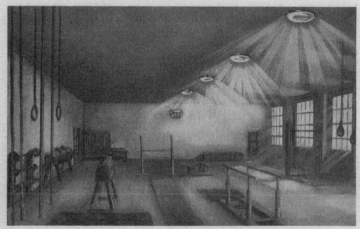

Gymnasium

In this magnificent home, with adequate facilities in serene surroundings, the Yeshiva College of America will attract thousands of students from all parts of America. The truth seeking Jewish youth, hungry for spiritual development, for the message of the Torah, will receive the opportunity for harmonious development as Jews and Americans and prepare themselves in a thoroughly Jewish environment for a life of usefulness in the community.

The American Jewish youth will be brought in direct contact with the sources of Jewish faith, with Jewish culture in all its manifestations which will deepen their understanding and loyalty to the Torah and the ideals of eternal Israel. The Yeshiva College will prepare the youth for their role as true citizens, will bring them nearer to the faith of our fathers, mustering them as true guardians of the continuity of Jewish history and Israel's incomparable contribution to the progress of mankind.

In the Yeshiva College of America, the American Jewish youth will find the great opportunity which it has been denied until now.

THE SCHOEN PRINTING COMPANY
17 VANDEWATER ST., NEW YORK

My Yeshiva Career

By Joan G. Haahr

I was twenty-nine years old in the fall of 1969, fresh out of graduate school and with a brand new PhD in hand. My husband, small son, and I had moved from Cambridge to Riverdale, in the Bronx. With a three-year-old at home, I was looking for a teaching job no more than half an hour's drive away. I had written letters to a number of nearby institutions, asking about openings in medieval literature — my field of specialization — and had received positive responses from a few. YC was certainly within that half-hour radius, but it hadn't occurred to me to apply there, as I was unaware that women were welcome on the faculty. When, however, I discussed my job search with my good friend and fellow Harvard graduate student, Charles Persky (YC '62), he suggested that I contact David Fleisher, his beloved professor and mentor at Yeshiva. I mailed David my curriculum vitae, was asked to come in for an interview (held in the very office that, a few years later, became my own), and after a warm discussion of things literary — devoted mostly, as I recall, to the recently published *Portnoy's Complaint* — I was hired. However, before we went downstairs to see Dean Isaac Bacon, David, with only a small sign of embarrassment, added a little postscript: "I hope you don't mind," he said, "but we already have someone teaching medieval literature. How would you feel about teaching the English novel?" I gulped and, after a moment's hesitation, responded, "Well, I've always liked reading novels." And so began what was to turn into thirty-six years at Yeshiva.

Dr. Joan G. Haahr is Professor of English at YC. After thirty-six years of teaching at Yeshiva, she retired in the spring of 2005.

The change from Harvard, my only prior teaching job, was dramatic. Not that the students were not as good as those I had taught in Cambridge. Some were, in fact, as bright and talented as the very best of my Harvard students. Nor was there any difficulty in getting used to all male classes: Harvard, in the 1960s, was still predominantly male, and all my classes there had been "men only." However, there was no question about the difference. Harvard faculty meetings were formal and restrained; Yeshiva's, in contrast, were like family gatherings, both intimate and contentious. The Harvard students' polite reserve was replaced by Yeshiva volubility, with students freely offering opinions on every issue, often without bothering to raise their hands. Yeshiva students also (and this is something that I still can't get used to, even after so many years) freely wandered in and out of class — a holdover, I came to realize, of their customary practice during the morning program. My biggest shock, however, occurred in my first Freshman Composition class.

In order to make the first year's preparation of eight new courses a bit easier, I had decided to assign a textbook I had used in one of my Harvard classes. In those days, we usually taught composition by asking students to read essays, discuss their ideas in class, and then write papers inspired by what they had learned. The textbook I assigned was divided into units focused on broad subjects such as "Heroes and Great Men;" "The Concept of Virtue;" "About University Education;" "Is the Will Free?" All went smoothly until we got to a unit (which I had taught without any problem at Harvard) called "Does the Theory of Evolution Have Ethical Consequences?" To me, the readings, by writers like Thomas and Julian Huxley, seemed stimulating but innocuous. To my considerable surprise, however, what I had anticipated as an exciting discussion of "ethics" turned into a heated battle about "evolution," with the class divided about 50-50, pro and con. Today, with the conflict over "Darwinism" and "Creationism" a commonplace, this might not seem surprising. However, in the late 1960s — before the dramatic growth in fundamentalisms worldwide, when those of us from the secular world thought *Inherit the Wind* the last word on the subject — the furor raised in my class astonished me, making me realize that hitherto unexercised tact and caution were sometimes required at my new institution.

Always in the background, that first year, was the Vietnam War. Although considerable antiwar feeling existed on campus, there was little open protest, for, as declared "divinity students," most Yeshiva students had draft exemptions and did not feel immediately threatened. All that changed, however, shortly after midterm examinations in the spring of 1970 (semesters, at that time, commonly ended in mid-June). Although American forces had been secretly bombing Cambodia for months, on April 30 President Nixon announced publicly that American troops and B-52 bombers would enter Cambodia. Campus protests erupted immediately all over the United States. On May 4, inadequately trained National Guardsmen, who had been called in to quell protests at Kent State University, fired blindly into a large group of students — not all of them demonstrators — injuring thirteen and killing four. Campuses everywhere exploded in protest against the killings; classes stopped and most colleges and universities held all-day antiwar teach-ins to discuss the unpopular war. At last, YC joined the protests. On May 5, classes were cancelled and an antiwar rally held on Amsterdam Avenue. The campus was covered with NYC police as the students marched and the college administrators huddled nervously in the Dean's office, fearing a student occupation as had occurred on some other campuses. Their relief was evident when, late in the afternoon, a genial police officer entered with the welcome news that there was no need to worry as the demonstrators had broken up for evening prayer. Nonetheless, much of the remaining semester was spent at teach-ins and antiwar protests, led by faculty members — Professor Manfred Weidhorn always in the forefront — and packed with students. I took my small son to some of these, wanting him to understand, even at an early age, the importance of political action. Many classes never resumed at all that term, instructors basing final examinations solely on work done up to the midterm.

In those days, there was still a considerable amount of prejudice against women in "the Academy," a point that one was certainly well aware of at Harvard, where one of the libraries was, by statute, off-limits to women and a few professors made it known that women were not welcome in their classes. I was determined to be an exemplary professional and was pleased by my unexpected nomination, by YC, for a National Endowment for the Humanities Summer Stipend for the following summer. I was therefore somewhat dismayed (though, of course, very happy, too) when, just two months into my first full-time teaching job, I found myself in the rather awkward situation of being pregnant. Fortunately the baby was due in July, so there would be no trouble completing the school year. However, I knew it would be difficult, if not impossible, with an eight-course teaching load, to resume full-time teaching the following year. Even so many years later, I remain grateful to Dean Bacon for the way he took the news. Though unmistakably surprised, he at once asked my preference and then supported my request for a part-time schedule, designating it a "partial leave" so that I would not lose full-time faculty privileges. Indeed, that schedule proved so comfortable that I kept it for eight years, having a third child four years later. I then slid easily back into full-time teaching upon the retirement of Yeshiva's long time medievalist, Professor Irving Linn, when I was finally able to begin teaching courses in my area of specialization. Incidentally, I did win the NEH fellowship, which I was able to defer until the following summer.

I have many fond memories of my students — and if I cannot always remember their names, I never forget their faces. Some have stayed in touch through the years, and I have had the pleasure of hearing about their families and careers. In some cases, I have had the opportunity to teach their sons and am always delighted to hear from a current student, "My father sends regards. He took your class [many!] years ago." Have the students changed? In the early years, more students came from public schools, and, of course, it is no secret that Modern Orthodoxy itself has changed, so that many students are probably more dedicated to Torah studies than were their predecessors. But I find it as difficult to generalize about my students now as I did then and can only note that they remain as lively, intelligent, and fun to teach as they always were.

Having chaired the English Department for twenty-one years, I am well aware of the many changes in the department. It is, of course, considerably larger than it was when I arrived, with a far greater variety of courses, many of which would have been inconceivable in the canon-based curriculum of the early 1970s. The department has also become increasingly professionalized, as has the university as a whole; no one would now be hired as I was, on the basis of a single, casual interview. In fact, the department has just successfully completed an intensive search for my successor, consisting of a nation-wide appeal for candidates, off-campus interviews by a departmental committee, on-campus interviews by all tenured and tenure-track members of the department, and an on-campus presentation for both faculty and students.

Yeshiva University, as an institution, has also undergone considerable change. I arrived during the presidency of Dr. Samuel Belkin, when the institution was still finding its identity as an amalgam of an old-world *yeshiva* and an ambitious American university. The presidency of his successor, Dr. Norman Lamm, was, in many ways, shadowed by the near bankruptcy that had threatened its early years, and the effects of that threat unfortunately persisted throughout his tenure, especially when it came to issues of faculty welfare. For example, it was not until Dr. Norman Adler arrived as dean of YC that department chairs (now called cluster heads) began to be compensated. They had previously received no compensation for their work, either in time or money — a situation that certainly created considerable hardship for me during the fifteen years I simultaneously ran the department and taught a full complement of courses. Despite much progress, some of the effects of Yeshiva's long-past fiscal crisis are still with us in the form of the still too-high teaching loads and too-low salaries of many senior faculty members, although both have improved in recent years, thanks to faculty persistence and administrative support, notably from Academic Vice President Dr. Morton Lowengrub. Nevertheless, as founder and president of the university's chapter of the American Association of University Professors, and as a senior faculty member now preparing to retire, I am especially conscious of the continuing penalty paid by those faculty members who served the university longest, in the form of low retirement income commensurate with our low salaries. Fortunately, President Richard Joel seems determined to continue improving faculty compensation, and younger faculty members will not, it is to be hoped, have to suffer as the older ones have.

Despite the frustrations of these bread-and-butter issues, my years at Yeshiva have been happy ones, for which I am grateful to both my students and my colleagues. Many of the latter have become close friends, and I can hardly imagine my life without them. I am thankful, too, for the warm welcome I have always felt from the Yeshiva community in general. As a secular Jew (married to a secular Christian), I was not, initially, entirely at home at Yeshiva, and during those early years, I was sometimes astonished to become suddenly aware that I was the only woman in a roomful of men. Now, however, I think of Yeshiva as my community, too. All through the years, students have been generous and affectionate, starting with those who, in 1970, presented me with a bottle of pink champagne on the birth of my daughter. Wherever I go, I meet former students who greet me warmly, eager to reminisce about our classroom explorations of *Beowulf* or Chaucer, of Milton, Austen, or Joyce, and to tell me their own news, both professional and personal. Moreover, my perceptions of the literature I love have unquestionably been influenced by my students, and I can hardly read a familiar text without recalling the particulars of one or another lively and intense classroom (or e-mail) discussion. As I now begin to loosen the ties that have bound me to Yeshiva for so many years, shedding my full-time position for one of greater flexibility, I know that Yeshiva will remain for me a continuing source of friendship and intellectual renewal.

Fragments of Memories and Reflections

By Jerry Hochbaum

At the fiftieth anniversary of my graduating class from Yeshiva College last May, I shared with my classmates memories of things past that took place within the four cubits of the Yeshiva. My classmates were a remarkable group of "*zeidena Yidden*," as the Yiddish expression has it — "silken Jews." I cherished our chitchat and the warmth of that encounter.

In my imagination that afternoon, I found myself a freshman again in the *beit midrash* of the *yeshiva*, preparing for a *shi'ur* with my *havruta*, Izzy Goodman. It was lunch hour, when the *beit midrash* was almost empty. We were struggling with some question on *Pesahim* 14A when a gentleman approached us. He asked us what our difficulty was and helped clarify our concerns. Before he left, he queried us again to be sure we understood the matter under discussion.

A rabbinical student rushed over to us when he left. "That was the Rav, R. Joseph Ber Soloveitchik!" he told us. We were awed.

Fifty years later, we are no longer the naïve, innocent-eyed students we were then. We certainly have changed. What of the Yeshiva?

Torah was, in the years I attended Yeshiva College, the central focus of the institution. This, I believe, has remained the case. But we cannot assume that this centrality is inevitable unless the Yeshiva family strive collectively to assure that condition.

When we were students in the early 50s, the dominant educational philosophy articulated by Yeshiva's second president, Dr. Samuel Belkin,

Dr. Jerry Hochbaum, YC '54, RIETS '56, is Executive Vice President of the Memorial Foundation for Jewish Culture. He taught Sociology at Yeshiva College in the 1960s.

was synthesis. In Yeshiva's curriculum, *kodesh* and *hol* were separate domains. It was each student's responsibility to integrate these two distinct *weltanschauungs* within his own personality. As I recall, there was neither at the *yeshiva* nor the college support systems to assist students in this complicated and potentially frustrating enterprise. Coming from a very caring ambiance in the Rabbi Jacob Joseph School, where I attended high school, I found it hard sometimes to adjust to what appeared to be a less caring institutional environment.

But there were also sparks of personal concern, not always expressed in institutional terms or settings, from the faculty and administration, and certainly from among the students. One story that I heard decades after I graduated expressed the *hesed* that could inhere in the institution. A rabbi's wife whose family could barely make ends meet sought and obtained a meeting with Dr. Belkin. She earnestly explained that her oldest son was graduating high school and she hoped he and her other children would be able to attend Yeshiva College. Dr. Belkin assured her that all her children would receive scholarships to attend Yeshiva University, and he promised that they would also have the opportunity to complete their rabbinic ordination there. The oldest of the siblings who related this story to me confirmed that this was exactly what happened.

The synthesis that Dr. Belkin espoused was achieved by some of the classmates who attended our class' fiftieth anniversary, but it required many years of intellectual struggle and reflection, continuing long after graduation. In my view, that accomplishment is therefore all the more meaningful and enduring. The "synthesis" that we accomplished was not simply the result of our attendance at Yeshiva. We, in a very important sense, made it happen through a Herculean effort and an unwavering persistence over many decades.

When I taught Sociology at YC in the 60s, I developed a special appreciation for its students. It was a real joy teaching them. During those years, I once served as one of the hosts of a luncheon for a delegation of officials from the Middle States Association, who were engaged in the accreditation of YC. Someone in the group asked me about the variety of colors, designs, and shapes of the skullcaps that the students were wearing and how they related to the "orders" they represented. I responded that there were no "orders" at the Yeshiva. Their skullcaps represented their individual tastes and styles. The personal diversity and individualism of the students during the years I taught at the college was one of their most pronounced and charming attributes. I often thought that this individualism and diversity provided some helpful definition and coloration for the institution.

There was another, even more important, example of the impact of the student body on the ideological configuration of the college. In the years that I studied at YC, I cannot recall ever hearing any serious mention of the teachings of the late R. Abraham Isaac Kook. After receiving *semikhah*, I immersed myself in his work and found it to be exceedingly helpful in facilitating a synthesis between *kodesh* and *hol* and relating Jewish thought to aesthetics; this was in addition, of course, to the profound impact his writings had on my thinking about Israel and Zionism. Looking back, this was a stunning omission in my studies.

The administration of YC during my years at Yeshiva was also only lukewarm in its formal support of Israel. The strong Zionist impulse that characterized the institution in the 50s and 60s emerged from the students themselves. And it was no small accomplishment.

Today there are many more options for Orthodox students for study here and in Israel than there were in my day. We were the children of immigrants who were trying to find their place in American life and were concerned that their offspring make it economically and vocationally while remaining in a Jewish environment. That immigrant syndrome hardly exists any longer among the parents of the current generation. Orthodox parents today are usually fully integrated into American life and are cognizant, and oft-times supportive, of the new options from which their children can choose. To that regard, I hope that my grandchildren will choose Yeshiva, as my three daughters did in attending Stern College.

To be successful in the future, Yeshiva will need to do a better job of defining the vision of the community it represents. The Jewish world, Orthodoxy in particular, has greatly changed in the last half-century. Yeshiva needs to create and articulate its own vision of what it believes should shape contemporary Orthodoxy. Only then can it commit and contribute to securing a viable future for American Judaism, well into the twenty-first century.

Social Mores of Yeshiva College Students

By Morris Kalka

Whatever else they may think of him, most people would concede that Bill Clinton is an astute observer of the American political and social scene. In his book tour, Clinton repeatedly made the comment that "if you think the 60s brought more good than bad, then you're probably a Democrat and if you think the 60s brought more bad than good, then you're probably a Republican." Yes, the era called the 60s, comprising roughly the years between the civil rights movement and the end of the Vietnam War, looms large in the minds of those who lived through it, especially those who were college students at that time. What was it like at Yeshiva? Well, along with my classmates, I spent the years 1967-1971 as a student at YC. We saw the tumult of the period through the prism of Yeshiva. Was it so different for us than for the students a few miles down Broadway at Columbia? Probably so, but no matter. Yeshiva as an institution and Yeshiva students as individuals were affected by the societal changes.

It is always a mistake to ascribe qualities to an institution that deny the diversity of opinions and outlooks that make a university such an interesting place to be. I have come to understand, after nearly thirty years of teaching at universities, that what faculty members bring to a university is not just their knowledge of a subject, or even their ability to help students learn that subject; they bring themselves — their personalities and way of looking at the world. Students try us on for size and see who among us suits them best. In the 60s, there was no dominant

Dr. Morris Kalka, YC '71, is Professor of Mathematics and Chair of the Department of Mathematics at Tulane University in New Orleans, Louisiana.

voice on campus, but lots of faculty and students speaking and listening to each other. To some it was the Modern Orthodox, *Torah u-Madda* voice; to others it was the voice of those who were less comfortable with the secular world; while to some it was the completely secular voice of some members of the college faculty. I believe this is a point worth emphasizing, since many who have written in this volume thus far have been men who have made their careers either in the rabbinate or in Jewish communal service. They see their religious training as the dominant feature of their time at Yeshiva. I have another perspective.

I came to Yeshiva from a high school where going to college was viewed as unacceptable for religious reasons (some would call it a "black hat *yeshiva*," a characterization I eschew because identifying people by their clothing smacks of identifying gangs by their colors). As you can imagine, we received the bare minimum of secular education needed to meet New York State standards. I sensed that there was more to be learned and I sought out books in the public library and went to some of the museums in New York, in an attempt to expand my horizons. When I arrived in Washington Heights in September, 1967, I was anxious to begin my secular education in earnest and was in active rebellion against the kind of religious training that I had received until then. Though I was well prepared from high school for RIETS, I enrolled in EMC. As I look back on it now, I do not find it surprising that I can recall every single course that I took at YC, but only a few specifics from EMC come to mind.

At YC, I majored in mathematics, availing myself of the excellent faculty then of the Belfer Graduate School of Science. In my year, out of a class of roughly 250 students, four of us went to graduate school in mathematics. I know that three of us got PhD's and became faculty members at research universities. This was very much in the spirit of post-Sputnik America, where great emphasis and prestige was placed on science, and Yeshiva had a graduate school in physical science and mathematics but no business school.

One of the few faculty members at EMC who remains in my memory is R. Aron Kreiser. It is a sign of the respect and admiration we had for him that he was voted the Senior Professor by the class and invited to address us at the Senior Dinner at graduation time. It was also completely in character that he declined the invitation. That I became close to him is an indication of just how magnetic a personality he was. That an EMC rebbe would be held in such high esteem in such a secular time in the history of the College is not surprising to those who knew this remarkable man.

But a secular time it was for many students. In the 1971 edition of *The Masmid* — itself the cause of much controversy — I found an article by my classmate, Heshie Billet, in which he posed the questions "Does profane reality desecrate the Yeshiva of my dreams? Has it placed the secular idol of Mada [sic] on a pedestal making it but a poor attempt to maintain the façade of a Torah institution? ...Is it possible that the Yeshiva I attended is not a link in the tradition of great Ycshivos [sic]?" It is important to emphasize that I do not mean that a large percentage of students were not observant Orthodox Jews. The great majority were. It is just that to many, Yeshiva was a place where one could get a good liberal arts and sciences education in a Jewish environment.

What about the social turmoil of the times? In the popular mind, the 60s are associated, among other things, with the civil rights movement, the loosening of sexual mores, the women's movement, opposition to the war in Vietnam, a drug culture among young people and, on campuses, increased demands for student participation in decisions regarding academic matters. How did these things play out at Yeshiva? The landmark civil rights laws were passed before my time at Yeshiva. During my time there, Martin Luther King was assassinated and there were riots in some major cities, notably Newark, Washington, D.C., and Detroit. I cannot recall these events evincing any particular reaction at Yeshiva, perhaps because they occurred over *Pesah* break, when everyone was at home. I do recall a discussion of canceling classes in tribute to King, but this was not overly controversial.

Generally, I think the students at Yeshiva were sympathetic to the civil rights movement. The estrangement between Blacks and Jews was beginning and R. Meir Kahane did speak and have some followers on campus, but I do not recall him stirring the passions of a large number of students.

I am not sure to what extent Yeshiva students participated in the sexual revolution, or to what extent the sexual revolution consisted of anything more than young people feeling free to talk more openly about their sexual activities. As far as the movement towards equality of various sorts for women, this was not a topic which engendered much discussion. Certainly there was no discussion of the religious dimension of this issue.

Drugs? You bet. There were illegal drugs widely available in the dormitories. It was an open secret that the administration chose not to deal with. I know of no special effort made by the administration to deal with students who were selling, much less those who were using, illegal drugs. The extent of drug use was probably less than on other campuses, and though some students used LSD and mescaline, the majority of recreational drug users used only marijuana.

The war and the draft were, I believe, the most important and emotionally charged issue both at Yeshiva and across the country. At Yeshiva, there was a special dimension to the discussion, reconciling U.S. involvement in Vietnam and U.S. support for Israel. Nevertheless, YC students took part in antiwar activities. The most radical thing that happened was that YC classes and final exams were cancelled in response to the U.S. invasion of Cambodia and the subsequent killing by National Guardsmen of four students on May 4, 1970. These debates are still fresh in my memory: While I recall R. Dr. Moshe Tendler telling an audience of students during the October 15, 1969 anti-war moratorium that "we should fight Nixon, but we should fight him like Yeshiva students," I did not understand what he meant. I remember R. Louis Bernstein and Dr. Moshe Carmilly of EMC giving passionate speeches tying support for Israel to support for the Vietnam War and warning about rising anti-Semitism if Yeshiva students become identified with the antiwar movement. I remember vividly Dr. Simon of the French department saying that after the Six Day War, the "young sabras" in Israel would want us to act independently. All of this has been written about extensively.

What I would like to emphasize, however, is the draft. As Yeshiva students, we had available to us a divinity deferment, called a "4D deferment." To get such a deferment, all one had to do was sign a statement asserting that he was studying for the rabbinate and that once he became ordained it was his intention to enter the military as a chaplain. For most of us, this was dishonest, but it was widely viewed as a safe deferment. It was also widely used at *yeshivot* all over Brooklyn and elsewhere, some which were especially set up for this purpose; a person would register, pay the head of the *yeshiva* some money in tuition, get his deferment, and proceed with his life. To my knowledge — and I hope that I am wrong about this — no rabbi at Yeshiva ever spoke out against this dishonesty. I used to feel especially angry at those Yeshiva faculty members who would speak out for the war as being in Israel's interest but would never encourage any Yeshiva students to enter the military. Quite the contrary; they were complicit in a scheme where their students were dishonestly avoiding the draft. This contributed to my feeling at the time that the war was becoming racist in character — "as long as Blacks are fighting against Asians why should I care?"

Among the lasting effects of the time were demands by students to have a greater say in their education. Thus was born student evaluation of teaching at Yeshiva and everywhere else, as well as the Yeshiva College Senate. Such things are so routine now and it is difficult to believe that there was a time when they were controversial.

Were those times so different than today? I would argue that they really weren't. We live in a time where fundamentalist religion is ascendant in the society at large and pre-professionalism has replaced liberal arts as the norm in higher education. Is it so surprising that these trends are reflected at Yeshiva?

The Way We Were

By Barry J. Konovitch

We were students at Yeshiva University at a moment of significant political and cultural transition in American Life. It was 1959, and the Beat generation was coming to an end, soon to be replaced by the Hippie generation of the late 1960s, molded by the Vietnam War.

We frequented the coffee shops in the Village and the second hand book shops on 4th Avenue, looking for every book that Professor Leo Taubes — who served in the YC English department for forty-two years until his retirement in 2002 — casually mentioned in his English literature class. It was his first year at the college as well as ours; we were impressionable freshman and we hung on his every word. Occasionally he would "beg" a cigarette, and smoke would wreath the latest "Taubes idea" still hanging in the air. He wasn't much older than we were and we considered him one of our generation. He spoke to us as equals; he was literate, erudite and clear. He was one of those teachers who make an impression and is always remembered.

The student body was split along religious and cultural lines. We were the "TI boys" who explored the full range of Jewish thought from literature to philosophy to *Tanakh* to Talmud. Opposite us in the student body were the "RIETS boys," who confined their textual study to Talmud and whose intellectual curiosity, at least in our eyes, was also confined to the *daled amot* of the *beit midrash*. Other divisions existed, drawn along the lines of our academic pursuits. The pre-med and science boys were

Rabbi Barry J. Konovitch, YC '63, RIETS '67, is the rabbi of the Aventura Turnberry Jewish Center in North Miami Beach, Florida. He is also the author of two books: From Idealism to Realism *and* Rabbi in the Strike Zone.

different from us, the liberal arts majors. We considered ourselves superior; we dealt with ideas, they dealt with facts and figures. They would fix the world; we would change it.

The pre-meds didn't have much time for anything other than organic chemistry and biology, much to the chagrin of Dr. Hyman Greenstein, director of TI. But he was a kind and beautiful man who understood the academic realities and always empathized with our overworked science majors. For those of us who paid attention, TI was a source of great Jewish scholarship. Professor Lief was the soft-spoken editor of *Ha-Do'ar*. Dr. Norman Lamm was the newly minted PhD who taught philosophy. R. Shimon Romm was our brilliant Talmudist. The list included many luminaries of Jewish learning and culture.

TI was the address for the progressive, Zionist, liberal, Modern Orthodox, future leaders of the Jewish community. We looked upon the RIETS students as the center of pre-World War II European-style Yeshiva life, transplanted to the United States but out of touch with the reality of contemporary American life.

In addition, the student life of the Parker Dormitory boys was different from the commuters. From the outer reaches of the Bronx, it took me two buses and a free transfer to reach Washington Heights. Pelham Parkway was as close as you could get to suburbia, but we paid for the privilege with the long ride down Fordham road, up University, and across the old George Washington Bridge. It was certainly better than our MTA days, when it took six train transfers to go from the Yeshiva station on the IRT all the way to Pelham Parkway (I was always so proud and excited to see "Yeshiva University" inscribed in yellow mosaic on the subway wall). Why, you ask, didn't we take the shorter and faster bus? Because we had a free train pass; the bus cost good money. Bus passes came later.

By our senior year, many of us were licensed to drive, and a few of us were lucky enough to have access to a car. My dad presented me with his old Oldsmobile, newly repainted battleship gray, and it quickly became the transportation of choice for the fencing épeé team. The "gray ghost," as we referred to it, traveled around the metropolitan area transporting Yeshiva "Taubermen" to the far reaches of New Jersey, Brooklyn, and Manhattan.

We looked askance on the dormitory residents who came from such far away and snooty places as Connecticut and Massachusetts. We were New Yorkers, the real McCoy, and I was from the Bronx, home of the

Yankees and the Salanter Yeshiva gang, who knew how to manufacture a "zip gun" and how to deal with the local Italian toughs.

Looking back on those years, I realize that the Orthodox movement was slowly but surely radicalizing to the right, a reaction to the rest of the Jewish community, which was moving to the liberal left. We thought of ourselves as at the center on the spectrum of Jewish religious life, even though the term Centrist only came into use decades later. When R. Lamm suggested the term to identify the Yeshiva philosophy, the center had already dropped away. There was no longer a center, only an extreme right and left.

Nowhere else was our Yeshiva life represented so sharply and clearly than in the lecture room of R. Irving Greenberg, in later years called "Yitz" by his students and colleagues. He effectively synthesized the Yeshiva motto of *"Torah u-Madda."* His command of all academic disciplines from philosophy to literature to art to history superbly equipped him to influence young minds.

Dr. Alexander Litman was the enfant terrible of the faculty. He challenged our assumptions in the first course we ever took in Greek Philosophy. Poorly thought-out answers to his sharp Socratic questions were dismissed as "sub-gartelian" — below the *gartel* — logic. His sharpest critique was always reserved for the "common traitor," as he labeled the Yeshiva newspaper, *The Commentator*, and its censored editorials.

Yeshiva sports life centered around the basketball team that occasionally made it to Madison Square Garden. But for the rest of us who didn't have the time to invest in long practices, or who resented playing in the basement of the main building where any shot from beyond the foul line had to follow a straight line trajectory due to a fifteen foot high ceiling, other teams offered a good alternative. I can only remember a tennis team and a fencing team; we chose the fencing team.

Coach Arthur Tauber was as handsome and swashbuckling as Zorro himself. With his pencil mustache and lighting quick sword arm, he could easily have taken his place on the silver screen. He was the greatest fencer in the history of New York University, where the greatest teams garnered the collegiate championships year after year. He went on to coach the Pan American team and the Olympics and eventually agreed to coach at Yeshiva.

Twice a week, down in the smelly, dank basement of the main building, we went for our dose of Tauber torture. Advance and retreat;

lunge and back. He drilled us until we were so charley horsed that we couldn't walk the steps for two days. But he created champions. In 1962, I was privileged to captain the team that presented Coach Tauber with his 100th victory. A presentation gold foil marked the occasion and the picture appeared on the front page of *The Commentator*. Several of us went on to be designated as Yeshiva all stars selected by the editors of *The Commentator*. We fenced some of the finest teams in the New York area, but we delighted in whipping the blue bloods at Columbia University. Even the cadets at West Point got the point.

I look back on my days at YC with great fondness and nostalgia. The heady intellectual atmosphere, along with the camaraderie and the idealism, was a wonder to behold. I am forever grateful that my formative years were spent at 186th Street and Amsterdam Avenue, an address forever etched in my memory.

God, Torah, and Yeshiva in the 60s

By Eugene Korn

I entered the world of Yeshiva University — and Orthodox Judaism — in September 1964, studying at YC and JSS from 1964-1968, and at RIETS from 1969-1971. I came from an elite all-American public high school and Yeshiva introduced me to the world of authentic Jewish life and its best articulations throughout Jewish history. For the first time, I encountered the texts and personalities of Torah and our *mesorah*, from *Humash* through *Gemara*, from *rishonim* and *aharonim* through twentieth century *gedolim*, from the works of medieval Jewish philosophers through the ideas of twentieth century Jewish thinkers. Just as important, Yeshiva made me feel welcome in Orthodox life and community. I will be forever grateful to my alma mater for these gifts and acts of *hesed*.

It was a time of agony and ecstasy in America: the unrest over the Vietnam War, the assassinations of Martin Luther King and John and Bobby Kennedy, the civil rights movement, the Peace Corps, and America's bold conquest of outer space. As Jews, we were also caught up in the campaign that liberated Soviet Jewry, shaken to the core by Israel's existential crisis leading up to the Six Days War in 1967, and later deliriously joyful at Israel's lightning victory and new-found sense of security.

Those days were also the Golden Age of *Torah u-Madda* at Yeshiva. Our religious culture was invested in a very fundamental way in Torah's

Rabbi Dr. Eugene Korn, YC '68, JSS '68, RIETS '68-71, is Director of Jewish Affairs at the American Jewish Congress and editor of The Edah Journal. *After Yeshiva, he went on to earn a PhD in moral philosophy from Columbia University and semikhah from the Israeli Rabbinate.*

engagement with all human wisdom. *Torah u-Madda* was no tired slogan, but a fountain of living values, a *weltanschauung* for students and rabbis who were searching intellectually and religiously. Similar to today, Yeshiva had no formal courses to bridge Torah and *madda*, nor any explicit programs to address the synthesis, but the philosophy had produced enormously gifted and charismatic models who circulated around the campus daily, R. Aharon Lichtenstein, R. Norman Lamm, R. Moshe Tendler, R. Shlomo Riskin, R. Irving Greenberg, R. David Hartman, and R. Moshe Besdin, to name a few. They exerted profound influences on our young and thirsty minds.

Of course, the primary source of this vision and *hashkafah* was R. Joseph Ber Soloveitchik. The Rav was an exquisitely cultured person, a man of the world who could discuss *Gemara*, medieval church architecture, Newtonian physics, Russian literature, and John Paul Sartre in the same lecture. He taught us to believe that Torah was something of cosmic importance that should contribute to humanity and to the critical social and ethical issues of the day. R. Akiva and Rambam could live in a healthy tension with ancients like Aristotle, with moderns like Locke, Kant, Mill, Einstein, Freud, and with contemporaries like Isaiah Berlin and John Rawls — and we students tried to bring these thinkers together in dialogue. The Rav taught us that the best human culture was motivated by spiritual impulses and that Torah was part of a great universal drama.

Retreating to the cave — the rejected ideal of R. Shimon — was an abdication of spiritual responsibility, a religious cop-out. Torah and Jews showed their best when interacting with high culture — low culture was either silly or decadent even back then — and Torah could even be deepened by this interaction. As a result of this empowering religious vision, many of the college's best students studied the humanities, despite their career disutility. Many of Yeshiva's best went to study for PhD's in Jewish studies, history, philosophy, political science and literature at Ivy League graduate programs.

We were filled with a sense of youthful challenge regarding our interconnected religious and intellectual lives. We sought to think new thoughts and to blaze new trails, since our creativity was a way to imitate the way of our Creator. This sense of optimism also inspired quite a few graduates of that period to make *aliyah*.

Certainly there were prosaic elements of Yeshiva then, as well as detractors of the dream of *Torah u-Madda*. The college and its professors were undervalued and under funded, and students felt they deserved more in the way of serious college courses and first-rate professors. And human relations at Yeshiva were often severely deficient. I remember until today how stunned I was during my first day at Columbia University when the Registrar of the Graduate School of Arts and Sciences addressed me by name, invited me into his lavish office, and spent thirty minutes with me to resolve my problem, all the while treating me with graciousness. Was that place on the same planet as Yeshiva? But in the end, the cynics, the nay-sayers, and those who longed to retreat into the past didn't define Yeshiva.

We students sometimes jousted with the administration — not out of some nihilistic motivation a là the Berkeley student revolution that was taking place at the time or with destructive actions a là the Columbia riots that were also occurring then. Our most public protest was a rather innocuous sit-in; our most violent actions were dormitory water fights that sometimes spilled over onto Amsterdam Avenue. These actions helped to sublimate our frustrations. Our most strenuous demands of the Administration were that it work harder to make our college education first rate — we felt that we didn't deserve less than those at Harvard and Yale — and that it ensure that the religious image of Yeshiva University was consistent and honest. It was during this period that RIETS had to separate legally from the university because of federal requirements regarding non-discrimination in religion. Sometimes, this embarrassed the administration, but I cannot help thinking that, deep down, the President and vice presidents of Yeshiva understood that the students were correct in our uncompromising ideals and that they respected us for it.

Yeshiva fostered a strong attachment to *Klal Yisrael* that both strengthened and transcended our Orthodox identity. Perhaps because of our commitment to Soviet Jewry and our passion for Israel and her citizens during those difficult days, we understood that our Torah values had a trajectory that extended beyond the walls of the *beit midrash* and Orthodox Jews. Something greater than Orthodoxy was at stake: *Am Yisrael* and God's plan for a chosen people within universal history were at stake.

Times and Orthodoxy have changed. The humanities are no longer in vogue; Jewish women now clamor for voice, dignity, and empowerment; most of the *Torah u-Madda* giants mentioned earlier are no longer at Yeshiva; Israel is in a different place; and general culture has been transformed from what it was in the 60s. Yet it seems to me that the deeper religious challenges of Yeshiva today remain the same as what we saw as Yeshiva's spiritual questions then: How do we critically accept high culture and be true to the halakhic and meta-halakhic values of our *mesorah*? What is the proper dialectic of intellectual rigor and moral sensitivity? How can we retain our Jewish identity, yet not become just a curious and isolated sect? How can we relate to *Klal Yisrael* in a real, not merely rhetorical, way? And finally, what do we have to contribute to God's world, the future, and to all humanity whom He created *be-tzelem Elokim*?

Looking Back on Those Years

By Henry Kressel

In 1951, YC was not the first choice of students seriously considering a career in physics — except for those like myself who were interested in combining a Jewish and secular education. Having made that choice, however, I look back fondly on my college years. I acquired a rigorous education in mathematics and the basic sciences, a command of the English language, the habit of self-study, and the ability to speak in public. All of these have served me well in my professional life.

Preparation for a medical or legal career was the objective of many of the students at Yeshiva at that time. A career in physics was of interest to very few students. These were the early years of modern electronics, and vacuum tubes were the enabling components. Computers were just emerging from the laboratory, the transistor had been invented only a few years back, and nobody dreamed of the Internet. The computing tool of choice was the mechanical calculator or the slide rule. Career options in physics were limited to employment in a few laboratories, such as Bell Labs or RCA Labs, and academia. Of course, a PhD from a top school was essential. Therefore, the focus of the college program had to be preparation for the prestigious graduate schools, of which Harvard and MIT were on top of the list. It is not surprising that the number of physics majors was small — I don't think that it exceeded half a dozen in an

Dr. Henry Kressel, YC '55, is Managing Director at Warburg Pincus, a global venture capital firm, where he is responsible for investments in high technology companies. In July 2004, Dr. Kressel was elected to the Board of Directors of the Sy Syms School of Business of Yeshiva University and in November 2005, he was elected to the Board of Trustees of Yeshiva University.

average class during the 1950s. There were a dozen mathematics majors. and I took many courses with them. Dr. Henry Lisman and Dr. Jekuthiel Ginsburg taught the advanced mathematics courses with great distinction. Noteworthy among my classmates was Harry Furstenberg, who received his PhD from Princeton University and went on to a brilliant academic career at the Hebrew University of Jerusalem.

Physics majors benefited from almost private instruction. The only physics class with a significant enrollment was the introductory course taught by Dr. Perez Posen, which was mandatory for pre-med and chemistry majors. This course included a lab of a relatively rudimentary sort that was not taken seriously by the physics pros, but was torture for most of the pre-meds. Since the pre-meds needed A's in the course but usually demonstrated only modest interest in the subject matter, Dr. Posen had a challenging teaching mission.

The more advanced courses were taught by Dr. Arnold Lowan. The classes were small, the students dedicated, and the standards much more demanding. It was in those classes that serious work was done. Among these students were enthusiasts who actually enjoyed solving physics problems not on the assigned list, and I remember fun problem solving sessions lasting late into the night. Dr. Lowan added a very valuable dimension to his teaching: Each student was expected to prepare a full lecture on a new topic to present to the class. Having to prepare a lecture on difficult new material was a very valuable lesson in self-study. In fact, the acquired habit of self study made my life a lot easier in graduate school and later on as I had to master new fields of knowledge.

Crowded as the schedule was, we had the opportunity to take non technical courses with outstanding teachers. Dr. David Fleisher's introduction to the English literature classics was unforgettable, as were his jokes, which did not change from year to year. The standard ritual was to stay up the night before finals in group reviews of the material. The system worked — I have continued my interest in English literature. However, the course with greatest impact for me at Yeshiva was the one taught by Herman Wouk, the famous novelist. During my senior year, he gave a course in composition to a small class of selected students. The class assignments consisted of reading world literature classics and of creative writing assignments. He then carefully edited each piece and met with each student in his home to review the papers. I have never forgotten the lessons learned from one of the greatest contemporary masters of the

English language. I must also mention the French literature course taught by Dr. Sidney Braun, which introduced us to the classics and gave us the opportunity to contribute to a student publication called *Le Flambeau*. Here again, I have a maintained a life long interest in French literature as a result of that exposure.

Extracurricular activities were an important part of my education. As a freshman, I quickly gave up any ideas of participating in sports after a short attempt at fencing, and I joined the staff of *The Commentator*. I eventually became Features editor, with the privilege of frequently writing feature stories on topics that I found interesting. Among these was a story about my visit to the Packard Junior College facility that later became Stern College for Women. Writing features was a great experience in professional, creative writing. I also benefited from my stint as editor-in-chief of *The Masmid*.

After graduation, many of the pre-meds had the good fortune to enter the first class of Yeshiva's Albert Einstein College of Medicine. I left Yeshiva for Harvard University's Applied Physics graduate program, following in the footsteps of Arnold Knoll. The first semester proved difficult — the amount of material covered in each course was large, the teaching pace fast, teacher expectations very high, and competition from fellow students was fierce. Thanks to my solid grounding in math and physics, however, the adjustment period was short and the second semester proved to be much less stressful.

I began my professional career doing electronics research at the RCA Laboratories. My first project in 1960 was developing a silicon transistor, which became the core electronic device in early computers. This was just the start of microelectronics, of course. Over time, using new technologies, I helped develop integrated circuits, which eventually contained millions of transistors on one chip. These devices made possible desktop computers with many times the processing power of the mainframe computers of the 1960s. It is important to remember that technological advances always leverage fundamental physical and chemical principles.

In the 1970s, I had the opportunity to participate in Yeshiva University activities as a part time lecturer at the Belfer Graduate School of Science and sponsor of one of the PhD level students, Yehuda Juravel. As luck would have it, I met him by accident at Ben Gurion Airport on one of my trips to Israel. He made *aliyah* after graduation and worked for one of the leading electro-optics company in Israel.

I look back to my years at Yeshiva with great appreciation for the secular and Jewish education I received. Thanks to devoted and talented teachers, I acquired the intellectual tools that prepared me for my career.

There is Only One Yeshiva College:
A Memoir

By Norman Lamm

The four years I spent at Yeshiva College (yes, four full years — no AP, no summer school, no credits for the year I spent learning between high school and college) were some of the happiest of my life. Some of my fellow students tempted me to share their cynicism about Yeshiva, a hoary tradition of YC students, but I resisted simply because I loved the place. It was everything I wanted at that point in my life: concerned *rebbeim* and teachers, intellectually alert classmates, a philosophy of life that I soon came to identify and cherish as *Torah u-Madda*. Everything was precious despite the inedible food, the unwashed washrooms, the uppity secretaries, the understaffed libraries, a gym in which the mice walked hunched over, and the Teutonic tutelage of the unattractive dormitories by Mr. Bear. None of this counted for much when I had the likes of Dr. Samuel Belkin, R. Moshe Shatzkes, R. David Lifshitz, and, of course, the Rav, as my *rebbeim* and the intellectual companionship of the likes of Willie Frank, Joe Gold, Louis Bernstein, and Matthew Katz, all gone now, along with Shmuel Schoner-Sprecher (he was then called Milon Schoner and later, as Professor of Chemistry, head of the Natural Sciences, and then Rector at Bar Ilan, he somehow became Shmuel Sprecher) and Pesach Oratz, who were both my *havrutas*, and a dozen others.

My YC experience has much to do with how and why I originally chose

Chancellor Norman Lamm, YC'49, RIETS'51, BRGS'66, is Rosh Ha-Yeshiva of RIETS and was president of Yeshiva University from 1976-2003.

to enroll at Yeshiva. I graduated from Mesivta Torah Vodaath in 1944. The times were ominous. It was the penultimate year of the Holocaust, and a period of uncertainty and a profound, unspoken awareness of how really dreadful and dangerous life was for Jews, reawakening the deep and usually unarticulated fears of American Jews. Unfortunately, there was no State of Israel then, and my desire for a year of total immersion in Torah had to be satisfied locally. I decided to continue learning at Torah Vodaath until 3:00 pm, and then repair to the home of my sainted grandfather, a renowned Galician *ga'on*, there to wander through his library and learn, for the first time, of the wonders of the Responsa literature. In the evenings I read Freud and Adler, Schopenhauer and Meade and Durant, and wherever my curiosity directed me.

One scene remains indelibly inscribed in my otherwise imperfect memory. I was visiting the home of my uncle, the founder and rabbi of the Crown Heights *yeshiva*, and noticed in his library the then standard English translation of the Rambam's *Guide of the Perplexed*. Perplexed I certainly was, but frightened as well. I had it drilled into me that it was strictly forbidden to read the *Guide* because it was dangerous to my spiritual health, because it posed questions without providing simple answers, and because it would lead me astray into the study of philosophy and other such abominable heresies. But suddenly, with the *Guide* in my hands, I could not resist this heterodox temptation, and I began to leaf through the recondite volume. I recall that I was particularly interested in angels — "was there or wasn't there a rational explanation?" — and so kept on reading furtively, afraid that at any moment some adult would walk in, catch me in the act, and publicly reveal my shame.

I knew then and there that I would no longer be satisfied with the narrow and restricted education I was receiving at Torah Vodaath, and that there must be some other way that a student could be exposed to the total wisdom of Torah and the world without jeopardizing his *yir'at shamayim*. The thought of transferring to "Yitzhak Elchanan" never entered my mind. Luckily, at just about that time, my father began to speak of Yeshiva College as a possibility. The major breakthrough came when my grandfather expressed his support for the idea because, as he put it, it would give me an opportunity to study under "the young *ga'on* Soloveitchik."

My Torah Vodaath mentors tried in diverse ways to dissuade me from my incipient sacrilege, and did so in the crudest fashion. I was basically shunned. When I went to learn in the *beit midrash* of Torah Vodaath the following *Shavuot* evening, intending to spend all night in study of Torah, the *mashgiah* asked me how I liked it "up there." When I replied politely that "it's nice," his riposte was, "a church is nice too." My decision to stay with and identify with Yeshiva College was now confirmed. Nevertheless, so brainwashed was I that at my first venture to Washington Heights, when I witnessed one student being hailed by another with the words, "*Sholom Aleichem*, Yankel," I was pleasantly surprised to hear such blatant "Jewishness" in the place that was "nice, like a church." To this day, I look back upon this experience with a degree of annoyance mixed with understanding. Their methods, in this instance, were coarse and unsophisticated, but their intention was probably *le-shem shamayim*, if compounded with more than a bit of institutional envy. This attitude remained with me into my adult life; I remained critical of and unintimidated by the *Haredi* world. I believed then and believe now that we have nothing to be ashamed of and that, on the contrary, our *Weltanschauung* is more legitimate in its comprehensiveness and therefore deserving of unabashed and unapologetic advocacy; but I understand those who disagree, respect them, and even support them. I will always remain indebted to Torah Vodaath for the Torah I learned there, although I experienced much Torah but little *da'at*.

I majored in Chemistry at YC, where Dr. Eli Levine reigned supreme with an occasional assist from Dr. Joseph and the then dean, Dr. Moses Legis Isaacs. Dean Isaacs was a total paradox to me. He was the first Jewish Republican I ever met — and a confirmed *Agudah*-nik at that! R. Jacob Rabinowitz, whom I later appointed as dean of IBC and who remains a dear friend to this day, was the lab instructor. I gained much from this immersion in science. The scientific method became a living reality for me, much more so than merely reading about it, although I wonder to this day if I might have better spent my years at Yeshiva College in some other major. Indeed, after my sophomore year I enrolled as a philosophy major. I attended two classes with a long-time senior member of the philosophy faculty (of which he was the sole member) and I was annoyed, even repelled, by his obsession with criticizing the administration, the Talmud faculty, and almost everyone else who came to his mind. In these first two lectures I heard only *letzonus* and no philosophy. He was a man who was admired by a certain faction of the student body, but I was not ready to risk two years of college with a self-important and self-appointed resident cynic. Maybe I was naïve, but he did not fit my image of a philosopher as the incarnation, or at least the heir, of Aristotle and Plato and Kant and Descartes — and certainly not Maimonides and Yehudah Halevi. It was only when I attended classes at Revel that I was formally introduced to philosophy without the mediation of idiosyncratic personality traits.

I stayed with chemistry for a while, and even came to use it somewhat when, in the spring of 1948, I persuaded a few of my friends, all chemistry or physics majors, to offer our services to the nascent Jewish state. Schoner and I were assigned by the Jewish Agency to a fairly primitive redoubt in upstate New York. It is there, in East Fishkill, NY, that we met Dr. Ernst Bergmann, who headed the research program at, and later became the head of, the Israel Atomic Energy Commission. Our work resulted in the preparation of a bullet that could be manufactured on a shoe string in an embattled country with no significant natural resources. It was a heroic time for *all* YC students, almost all of whom volunteered to pack blankets for shipment to Israel; in between the folds of the blankets were rifles — rather clumsy ones, but the best under the circumstances of siege and boycott. YC students shone, and I never will forget their readiness to serve under difficult conditions — almost everything we did was technically illegal. They were magnificent and their successors remain so even today, well over fifty years later.

I did not stay long in chemistry, although I did do a year of graduate work at Brooklyn Polytechnic Institute. It was an excellent school for working scientists, but not my first choice. I had applied to Columbia and was granted an interview. The interviewer was an elderly physical chemistry professor whose aura of alcohol filled the room and made a young and naïve visitor feel inebriated. The man didn't have the courtesy to offer me a seat while he glanced casually at my YC transcript. After a few moments he looked up and asked me, shamelessly, "Why do you people want to come to Columbia?" I had little experience with anti-Semitism, but I was irate. I bent over, grabbed the papers from him, tore them in half and literally threw them in his face. I told him I'd never set foot in his school unless officially invited, and urged him and his university to forthwith repair to a place of infinitely high temperatures. I should note that I did not set foot in Columbia until, when I was already President of Yeshiva, I was invited to a meeting as a colleague by the then President of Columbia — who happened to be a Jew.

Some of the humanities professors at YC were distinctive and interesting personalities. Prof. Braun treated us like elementary school children — but we learned our French, and learned to love it. I even managed to write an article in French for *Le Flambeau*. David Fleisher of the English department was an institution in his own right, and we laughed at his jokes even though we had been prepared for them by an informal *mesorah*.

I never had political ambitions as a student. I refused to run for office — I was too busy keeping up with our dual program — but I once succumbed and became vice president of the senior class. I have no recollection of why I allowed myself to be nominated, nor do I remember having contributed anything at all to justify the faith of my voters. This reluctance to accept such official responsibilities accompanied me throughout my rabbinic career, which lasted for twenty-five years. The one time I yielded and went back on my principles was when I accepted the offer of the presidency of Yeshiva University. I regret neither my previous aversion to politics, nor my later change of heart.

By the standards that prevail today, our quality of life then was, well, awful. We were a much smaller school, crammed into one building (today, Zysman Hall) and one dormitory (RIETS Hall). I mentioned above some of the inadequacies under which we labored. But those of us who were serious students loved it, and we managed to survive without the burden of envy of other college campuses. Life in the dorm was exciting. The arguments and debates in the dorm rooms were mature, adult, and scintillating. The late R. Louis Bernstein and I exchanged sharply divergent views on school policy in the pages of *The Commentator*, and eventually became very good friends. I probably learned more from my dorm experience than from my formal classes — in the spirit of *u-me-haverai yoter me-rabbotai*.

It should not be assumed that we were a collection of humorless nerds. Or, more accurately, even if we qualified as nerds, we were not without humor. Shlomo Poupko and Charlie Bahn formed a twosome of creative clowning that kept the rest of us cheering at their antics. Willie Frank was as much a genius at humor as he was in mathematical physics and almost everything else. Once, Dr. Belkin was escorting Prof. Albert Einstein through the building when he noticed Frank across the hall. He beckoned to him to come to greet his eminent guest, and told Einstein that Willie Frank, a physics major, was one of our most gifted students. Prof. Einstein offered his hand in greeting, and red-faced Willie extended his hand — from which fell a yo-yo.

Guest scholars often lectured, and many were quite good. Dr. Raphael Gold expounded on the "Jewish neurosis," writer Ludwig Lewisohn told of his personal adventure from assimilation to Zionism and Judaism, and a Franco-Jewish poet read from his own works.

I enjoyed the laboratory, I enjoyed the classes in French and English, but my heart lay in the *beit midrash*. We studied at the feet of giants, and we grew *shi'ur* by *shi'ur*. The orderly *shi'urim* by Dr. Belkin, the magisterial *shi'urim* by R. Moshe Shatzkes, the proactive piety of R. David Lifshitz, and the unparalleled intellectual excitement of a *shi'ur* by the Rav — these are the unforgettable legacies of my Yeshiva College experience. No fancy campus, no elaborate scientific equipment, no prestigious Ivy League university could give us what Yeshiva College did. They were great years of growth and sensitivity as our *roshei yeshiva* and mentors introduced us to the thought of the masters of our sacred tradition.

In those days there was a significant attrition by YC graduates to the Jewish Theological Seminary and the Conservative movement. With some rare exceptions, it was not the best students who undertook this denominational hegira. In recent years, this trend has changed considerably. Now we often see the reverse pattern: Conservative rabbinical students applying to RIETS and seeking our Orthodox *semikhah*.

The culmination of my undergraduate life at YC was not the graduation exercises, at which President James Conant of Harvard spoke and which was important in a way, but the assembly that took place in Lamport auditorium shortly after the announcement of Israel's independence. I do not recall if it was the administration or my fellow students who appointed me to preside at the assembly and introduce the guest speaker, but I do know that in the heat of mass enthusiasm, anything I might have said remains utterly insignificant. The speaker was Menachem Begin, then leader of the opposition in the Knesset and formerly head of the *Irgun*, who was later to become Prime Minister. This slightly built and conservatively dressed man of quiet demeanor had us mesmerized by his majestic oratory and the palpable sincerity of his presentation. Begin spoke in Yiddish — many or even most of us understood Yiddish in those days. He reached the acme of his speech when he railed against the internationalization and division of Jerusalem. Holding his arms outstretched and pointing in opposite directions with his forefingers, he proclaimed, "There are no two Yerushalayims." And then, bringing his hands together over his head, he proclaimed, "No two Yerushalayims. There is only one Yerushalayim!" The audience in that packed hall was almost berserk with enthusiasm. My admiration for Begin was and remains boundless. And the students at that assembly felt that he was in so many words saying what we had been taught and what we believed.

I often feel like offering my own proclamation: There are no two Yeshiva Colleges. There is only one Yeshiva College!

My Experience at Yeshiva

By B. Barry Levy

In September 1963, after graduating from Haddonfield Memorial High School in New Jersey, I attended my first class at YC, as it happened, a course entitled "Poetry in the Torah" in TI. Able to function in both biblical and modern Hebrew but poorly prepared in Talmudic and medieval rabbinic texts, I was shocked when told that the assignment for the next meeting of that two-hour a week course was *Parashat Ha'azinu* with the commentaries of Rashi, Rashbam, Ibn Ezra, Ramban and Seforno. While I had some experience with Rashi, the rest of these writers were essentially unknown to me, and I had never heard of the *Mikra'ot Gedolot*, the seemingly magical volumes that contained them.

Hours of preparation every night left me totally baffled — in those days, almost none of the commentaries existed in translation, and no honorable student would use one anyway — and when the professor called on me the following week to answer specific questions about the material, I could contribute nothing worthwhile. Sensing that a lack of knowledge indicated a failure to prepare, he wrote "zero, unprepared" in his record book, and called on me the subsequent week, with essentially the same results. This continued well into the semester, until in desperation I went to see him and explained the situation. "If you must, you can give me a zero for not knowing the answers," I said. "But please stop writing 'unprepared.' I spend at least two hours every night on the homework for this one class." In fact, I had spent so much time doing this work

---

Rabbi Dr. B. Barry Levy, YC '67, BRGS '71, RIETS '71, is Professor of Biblical Studies and Dean of the Faculty of Religious Studies at McGill University.

that, when I returned home and was asked to read the Torah without preparation because the *hazan* was sick, I found I had inadvertently committed the *trop* to memory.

That was during the 1963-64 academic year. By September five years later, that teacher was my close associate, and I was a member of the faculty, teaching Bible and how to use those same commentaries, and lecturing on the history of Bible interpretation and related subjects. I had completed an MA at BRGS, begun as a senior at YC, but it was really the four undergraduate years that changed my life and prepared me for my academic career.

As a student of Jewish Education in TI and a Hebrew major in YC, I had the option of taking every Judaica course offered in both schools and in BRGS, but I could not be a Bible major because the concept did not exist; Bible was simply not deemed a topic worthy of undergraduate specialization. In those days, almost no Yeshiva Bible professor had a degree in Biblical Studies. Most had *semikhah* and a doctorate in history or some other field, and that was the preferred path for anyone so misguided as to want to follow in their footsteps. Indeed, during my junior year, I went to discuss my career plans with one of my Bible professors, Dr. Menachem Brayer, but before gaining entrance to his office, I had to provide information on my health, relations with my parents and brother, and similar matters; Dr. Brayer was also the Yeshiva psychologist, and neither he nor anyone in his office had ever encountered a student who wanted to talk about being a Bible professor.

In any case, Hebrew became my college major because it seemed the closest and most flexible option and it enabled me to devote myself fully in both YC and TI to Bible and Jewish Studies. This brought me into constant contact with rabbis, professors, and teachers like Michael Bernstein, Menachem Brayer, Moshe Carmilly, Mayer Feldblum, Mayer Hershkovics, Arthur Hyman, Aron Kreiser, Norman Lamm, Hayim Leaf, Shimon Romm, Aaron Skaist, Israel Wohlgelernter, Abraham Zimels, Eric Zimmer, and many others, who trained me in the fine points of Hebrew, Aramaic, Ugaritic, Bible, Talmud, Jewish history, classical *parshanut*, Talmudic criticism, philosophy, and the like. Contrary to other models of study at Yeshiva, these men taught both texts and how to think about them, which, even if inadequate by some standards, provided a much broader form of education than received at the time in either RIETS or JSS. Thanks to the teaching of these men, a lot of independent reading

— based on their advice and my future wife's syllabi from religion courses at Barnard — and the wonderful environment they all helped create, by the end of my senior year I had accomplished four things.

The first was largely personal and a function of Yeshiva's relatively small size, which gave me numerous opportunities to participate in student life and to grow. I was a four-year varsity wrestler and captain of the team; I also played intramural volleyball. I was involved in student government and helped create the first EMC curriculum evaluation. I continued to develop the religious lifestyle that had brought me to Yeshiva in the first place, receiving *semikhah* from RIETS in 1971. I was engaged to my wife a few months after graduation from college, and we have since been blessed with three sons, three daughters-in-law, and four grandchildren. Except for the lingering death of my father during my final semester, the four years at Yeshiva were simply wonderful. Hebrew major or not, I never went to study in Israel because I did not want to miss what would have been left behind.

Second, I mastered the textual skills needed to work with the ancient and medieval primary sources on which my studies were based. This happened largely by the second half of my freshman year, when, while taking an open book exam, I suddenly realized that I could make sense of almost any new text I was asked to read. When groups of *yeshiva* high school graduates gathered at exam time to listen to me recite *Gemara* as learned in my remedial class so they could take exams in the more advanced courses, I knew I had arrived. Aramaic remained a nuisance for a while longer, but years of studying it with Professor Michael Bernstein and a subsequent PhD in Aramaic at NYU put the handicap to rest permanently.

A lot of effort had been invested in my philological training, but not as applied to medieval rabbinic texts. Then Professor Isadore Twersky of Harvard flew in to lecture every second week, and he taught me exactly that. During those years, Professor William Foxwell Albright lectured at BRGS for a brief time and, after being injured in a fall, he was replaced by Professor Moshe Held from Columbia. As a member of the faculty, I was forbidden by the BRGS administration to attend the last mentioned classes. Albright did not object to my participating; Held actually helped me avoid the pusillanimous administrator who hunted weekly for unauthorized auditors.

Third, I prepared for a career in teaching. As my own level of education rose, so did my aspirations, so what began as interest in informal work with teenagers concluded with the goal of teaching in graduate school. I had been teaching continually since age sixteen — and have been ever since — but formal preparation was designed to give me the credentials to teach, in case my graduate studies were ended prematurely and I needed to support myself. I never did hold a full-time job as a day school teacher, but I did serve as a principal for two years, and I have been a consultant for schools in Canada, the U.S., and Israel for thirty years. I write Judaica curricula, and I served as director of the McGill program that trains Jewish Studies teachers for well over a decade. Perhaps the most rewarding outcome of this early training was the pride in teaching that I developed, which has led to two teaching awards, one from McGill and one from a synagogue in the U.S.

Finally, and perhaps most importantly, my undergraduate years gave me the opportunity to develop a personal *modus vivendi* for negotiating the legendary synthesis of *Torah u-Madda*. This was the ideological issue uppermost in most people's minds in those days, but the range of traditional and modern-critical courses I attended allowed for their approaches to be integrated into my intellectual, professional, and spiritual makeup in a very natural way. Together, they helped me understand that, optimally, *Torah u-Madda* differs from the sum of Torah plus *madda* as water differs from hydrogen plus oxygen. This seemed obvious then; now many critics wish to reverse the process and separate the elements.

After four undergraduate years, I had my BA, BRE, and teacher's diploma; I was an experienced *ba'al koreh* (of inestimable value for a Bible professor), and I was ready to study for *semikhah*, to do Talmudic criticism, to teach the Bible and the ancient Near East, and to take all of these things very seriously as part of my life. I had studied Latin (in high school), Greek, Aramaic, Ugaritic, Arabic, French, German, and more Hebrew than anyone might have thought possible. And what did we read in Hebrew? Everything imaginable, not just sacred texts. While we were learning *Gittin* in Talmud class, Dr. Hayim Leaf had us reading Yehuda Leib Gordon's *Kotzo Shel Yod*. This seemed perfectly natural at the time; only in retrospect do I chuckle at what Leaf was up to.

The four years I spent teaching at EMC before leaving to teach at Brown and subsequently at McGill were as much a part of my education as my undergraduate experience. The opportunity to share what I had learned and the pressure to teach what I wanted to teach in the way I believed it should be taught, in short, to strike out on my own — even as the youngest EMC faculty member by a generation — was invaluable. I owe a huge debt to the former Dean, R. Jacob Rabinowitz, who gambled on a young and enthusiastic but essentially untried teacher and gave me my first academic job. No less responsible was the other (for now unnamed) senior administrator who, against all odds but not all precedents, admitted that the value of what I was doing by teaching outweighed the need to be in the *beit midrash* in the morning and permitted me to teach at that time and to prepare for *semikhah shi'urim* in the afternoon. As a Dean at McGill I do everything possible to ensure that graduate students start teaching as soon as they are ready. Undoubtedly the most challenging part of my experience was the 45 seconds when I had to walk from my faculty office on the second floor of Furst Hall up the stairs to the *semikhah* classroom on the third floor. For several years, at exactly 12:59 pm, I underwent a daily metamorphosis from young, exciting, creative teacher to quiet, passive, and often bored *semikhah* student.

Fluency in languages and mastery of lots of text are not enough to produce a professor; one also needs various teaching, administrative, and research skills, as well as creative drive, the ability to think critically, and the commitment to continue growing. And one can count the many ways in which taking a double or triple academic program seriously for years prepares one for working, surviving, and succeeding under pressure outside the *yeshiva* world. Still, without the basics, it is impossible to advance, and my undergraduate education served me very, very well. A line modeled on a commercial for Salem cigarettes that was popular during my student days, and that one still hears from time to time, quips, "You can take the boy out of the *yeshiva*, but you can't take the *yeshiva* out of the boy." While it is often applied to the childish or improper behavior for which some *yeshiva* students are notorious, in my personal case it has a very different meaning. In response, all I can say is, "Thank God."

Looking Before and After

By Aharon Lichtenstein

A wealthy and patriotic Texan, the father of two talented sons, wanted them to attend West Point. They, for their part, very much sought to learn at a *yeshiva*. They compromised — so the word ran at Chaim Berlin, where I learned prior to coming to Yeshiva University — and the sons went to Yitzhak Elchanan. It was a pallid joke, reflecting the brand of condescending chauvinism, then very much in vogue, whose diminution could much enrich the Torah world; and, from an objective standpoint, it was, in many respects, offensive. No one questioned the stellar *lomdishe* credentials of the RIETS staff. Its members having, collectively, mostly come from premier Lithuanian yeshivot — Radin, Telshe, Slabodka, Mir, et al — were acknowledged to be fine *talmidei hakhamim*, including disciples of the Hafetz Hayim, R. Shimon Shkup, and the Brisker Rav, as well as the erstwhile *rabbanim* of Lomza and Suvalk. Above all loomed the towering figure of the Rav, regarded by the *talmidim* at Chaim Berlin with a measure of ambivalence bordering on suspicion, but unequivocally referred to by the *Rosh ha-Yeshiva, mori ve-rabbi* R. Yitzhak Hutner, as one of the *gedolei ha-dor*. Moreover, it was clear that the great scholars at "Yitzhak Elchanan" taught much Torah to serious *talmidim*; and, finally, at a time when so many of those learning at the major Brooklyn *yeshivot* also went to college, the quest for higher secular education *per se* did not disqualify for entry into the world of *benei Torah*. Why, then, the

Rabbi Dr. Aharon Lichtenstein, YC '53, RIETS '59, is the son-in-law of the late Rabbi Joseph B. Soloveitchik and the Rosh Yeshiva of Yeshivat Har Etzion in Alon Shevut, Israel. He is a Rosh Yeshiva at the Rabbi Isaac Elchanan Theological Seminary, where he lectures at the Joseph and Caroline Gruss Institute in Jerusalem.

putdown?

And yet, judged retrospectively, by the standards to which we have become accustomed, the remark was not utterly without foundation. For, indeed, many of the ingredients endemic to the identity of a *yeshiva* and essential to maximal spiritual realization of its *talmidim* were then woefully inadequate at Yeshiva. Personally, together with many other budding *benei Torah*, I benefited immensely from the YU of the fifties, both spiritually and materially, and I am deeply indebted to all, from R. Dr. Samuel Belkin down, who sustained the institution and to those, within the *yeshiva* and within the college, who taught there. Jointly and concurrently, they put me on the road to *lomdut* and enabled me, upon graduation, to earn a doctorate during a four-year interlude at Harvard. However, inasmuch as I perceive this book as more history than autobiography, I feel bound to relate to a broader canvas. Nevertheless, I trust that these remarks will not be viewed as reeking of base ingratitude, but rather as retrospective evaluation.

If space permitted, I ought perhaps have attempted an analysis of my total venue, academic as well as of the *beit midrash*. Inasmuch, however, as it does not — and, in any event, my expectations of the college were and are more limited, and my knowledge of its course far less familiar — my predominant emphasis shall be upon the *yeshiva* proper.

Undoubtedly, at mid-century, at a time when the Torah world was perceived as having its shaky back to the wall and sociologists projected the bleakest of futures for it, YU contributed immeasurably to the cause of *Yiddishkeit*; woe would have befallen large segments of American Orthodoxy in its absence. And yet, internally, there is no question that the *yeshiva* side — particularly as regards its experiential and existential component — left much to be desired. Institutionally speaking, Shabbat and *Yom Tov* were virtually nonexistent. During a period of over six years, I spent exactly one *yom mo'ed*, the Shabbat of an *aufruf*, at Yeshiva. Generally, the only ones who stayed with any frequency were the out-of-towners (I lived in Brooklyn) who were, in effect, incarcerated. On *yamim nora'im*, the local *ba'alei batim* appropriated the *beit midrash* and Lamport Auditorium for their *tefillah*, while the incipient and still miniscule Yeshiva *minyan* was held in a moderately sized classroom in Graduate Hall (since demolished) across 186th Street. The room was more than adequate, inasmuch as the great majority of the older *bahurim* took leave to officiate in outlying shuls, many with mixed pews — in part in order to service communities, but also, in part, in order to earn some money.

On another front, the level of religious commitment at Yeshiva often left something to be desired. By way of example, it might be noted that one of the hottest issues raised during my freshman year in 1950 concerned an annual play presented by the Dramatics Society under the aegis of the dean. The vehement debate did not focus upon the drama proper but rather upon its character, that is, its serving as a social event to which dates would be brought *en masse*. The president of the Student Council was vigorously opposed. He had come to Yeshiva out of a secular high school in Bayside but had been turned on to Torah, and now found himself regarded by many peers as *farfrumt*.

As regards *talmud Torah*, there was much serious quality learning going on and some fine *talmidei hakhamim* being developed; but here, too, the scene was far from optimal. The entire library of the *beit midrash* was housed in the glass-enclosed bookcases at the southeastern corner. As to its population, the evening *seder* was woefully weak, with only a relative remnant staying on after 10:00 *ma'ariv*. There was no meaningful *kollel* presence, with less than a *minyan* of RIETS students having joined a small group of European refugees who came to learn, pretty much as an independent unit, in the aforementioned Graduate Hall, and from 1954 to 1961 there was no *kollel* at all. For all intents and purposes, no one beyond the age of 24 could be found in the *beit midrash*. Prior to the introduction of the *semikhah* program in the mid-fifties, upon graduating from college, one learned *Hullin* and *Yoreh De'ah* while also learning and/ or reviewing ninety *blatt* over a two-year period, and then underwent a two-hour make-or-break oral *behinah* before leaving.

Some of these deficiencies were signs of the times, barely intelligible to today's generation. In 1950, Chaim Berlin did not yet have a *kollel* either, and the *rosh yeshiva* explained to me that he often had to present concepts to as yet unseasoned *talmidim* because if he waited till they ripened, he would discover that so many had left at age twenty-two. Of my 1948 high school graduating class, it was internally anticipated that only roughly half would remain *shomrei Shabbat*.

At RIETS, however, there were additional aggravating factors. The most pressing was probably the issue of direction, personal and institutional. The cultural divide between the staff and the students was frightening. The *mashgi'ah*, a disciple of the Alter of Slabodka, was a genuine *oved Hashem*, but he never realized he had left Lithuania. He was shocked to discover, for instance, that *talmidim* had radios in their dorm rooms. Many of the *rebbeim* did not identify with the institution and exerted little effort in seeking to mold it (staff meetings were a great rarity) or its denizens, whose language they simply could not fathom. It wasn't a question of the King's English — although that, too, could be a barrier. (One of the *rebbeim* once asserted that he knew enough to read the Post or the News but not the Times.) The divide was, rather, cultural. They had simply never heard of Robinson Crusoe or of Jackie Robinson. Some, like R. David Lifshitz, cared passionately about their *talmidim* and reached out to them with all their heart and soul. Many, however, were either indifferent or in despair, and left their students to fend for themselves. Of these, some groped successfully, but many either floundered in confusion or were beset with spiritual schizophrenia, torn between Torah and secular values and identity.

At the apex were the two individuals who, each in his own way, both represented and articulated the ideology of *Torah u-Madda* — or, as it was then more commonly denominated, synthesis — the Rav and Dr. Belkin. Both were committed to the ideal, both sought to develop and initiate strategies for its implementation; and both regarded it as defining the character of Yeshiva University generally, and of RIETS and YC in particular. And yet, impressive as their pronouncements and achievements were, the students' thirst was only partially slaked, and many of the hungry sheep looked up and were not sufficiently fed. Dr. Belkin, for his part, was burdened with overseeing the university and meeting its financial needs, and was driven by a passionate impulse to extend its bounds. The fifties saw the founding of SCW, JSS, AECOM, BSS, and AZG. These were notable achievements, but they consumed time and energies which were not available for regular contact with *talmidim*. Earlier, Dr. Belkin had been a stellar *maggid shi'ur*, and in 1950-1 he sought to revive this position with a regular *shi'ur* on *Yoreh De'ah*. However, he had to give it up in fairly short order, and he remained, sadly, captain of a ship with whose crew and passengers he had little dialogue.

The Rav's situation was, of course, entirely different. He was, as the *melamed* of his favorite self-image, peerless, and his contact with those of us fortunate enough to learn from him was not only direct but electrifying. He was at or near his zenith and the pace could be exacting. During my first year in the *shi'ur*, 1950-1, in just four weekly hours, he covered all of *massekhet Niddah*. What we heard, as well as the sheer experience of being in the *shi'ur*, was inspiring. Moreover, he was sensitive to his *talmidim*'s basic existential concerns and the complexity of their cultural situation. I don't know whether he could have identified Jackie Robinson, but of Robinson Crusoe he not only knew but eventually wrote. Hence, he could and indeed did serve as a spiritual polestar.

And yet, at the plane of institutional leadership, his role was also limited. He set a tone but he did not take charge. He did not conceive of himself as the head, titular or practical, of RIETS, and even if he had, it is questionable that he could have discharged the duties of the office effectively. He conceived the *semikhah* program and initiated its implementation in mid-decade, but, on the whole, the demands of such a role — overseeing faculty, tracking *talmidim*, the nuts and bolts of curricular planning, periodically addressing the student body, and, consistent and meaningful interpersonal contact with a wide range of individual students — were not his cup of tea. He knew all this was important, but that was not his strength. And even if it were, the role simply could not be filled in the course of a weekly twenty-eight hour sojourn in New York. Hence, at that time, his impact beyond his own *talmidim* was limited, and many boys found themselves meandering from one *rebbe* to another, developing no ongoing relationship with any spiritual mentor — in effect, having, in the broader sense of the term, no *Rosh Yeshiva*.

I do not present this summary catalogue in order to be *pote'ah bi-genut*, *per se*. I do so, rather, in order to lay the groundwork for being *messayem bi-shevah*. As I enter the main *beit midrash*, filled from pillar to post with eager *talmidim* poring over a *Gemara* or a *Rambam*, their excited exclamations filling the air with cacophonous discourse, in my mind's eye I recall so many late hours spent in the solitary company of Sam Aronson, the janitor who cleaned the *Beit Midrash*; as I survey the treasure trove of the *sefarim* lining the walls in serried rows and compare them to the paltry resources at our disposal, as I confront a phalanx of multilayered *kollelim*, each plowing through and mastering one or more *hadrei Torah* and headed by a senior *rebbe*, my memory flashes back to our humble birth. I recall opening the resuscitated *kollel* with seven members, with myself, barely five years older than they, *primus inter pares*, in charge, and my heart distends with pride, with joy, and with hope. Indeed, *messayem bi-shevah* — first and foremost, to the *Ribbono Shel Olam*, and, at a very different plane, by reflecting on a number of salient factors which, over a period of time, enabled the remarkable transmutation to which I, *inter alia*, can bear witness. At the risk of omission of some deserving persons or forces, let me note some of the more prominent.

Several go back to the late 50s and early 60s. At the general plane, it was around that time that the efflorescence of Torah study, accompanied by greater commitment to *dikduk* concerning halakhic observance, began to be felt across a broad front, including that of modern Orthodoxy. This has unquestionably been a major impetus for enhancing the Torah level of our camp; while some insist upon denigrating this development as a "drift to the right," *benei Torah* should be able to appreciate its positive aspect.

On our home turf, I would single out, in addition to the consolidation of the three-year *semikhah* program, at least three factors. The first is the gradual escalation in the Rav's involvement in *talmud Torah* proper at Yeshiva. From two weekly *shi'urim* for a single class of some thirty students, he moved, upon the initiation of the *semikhah* program, to having two weekly *shi'urim* for each of two separate classes; even when, largely for reasons of health, he eventually reverted to a single class, it included, for many years, close to a hundred participants. Subsequently, he started saying a *shi'ur* three days a week. Still later, after his wife's untimely death in 1967, he became even more deeply immersed in *harbatzat Torah*, saying almost daily *shi'urim* for *talmidim* who would come to Boston to learn during the summer, and lengthening many of the regular New York *shi'urim* to three hours or more. It was during the sixties and the seventies that most of his premier students developed (I won't list any names for fear of offending an oversight, but serious Yeshiva University *benei Torah* know whom I have in mind), and this reflected the changed climate in one sense and contributed to it in another.

Second, the advent of R. Ahron Soloveichik to the RIETS staff in 1960 had a powerful effect upon the *yeshiva*. His great learning and impeccable *zidkut* contributed much, but one should take particular note of his weekly *hashkafah shi'urim*, which dealt with basic issues, on the one hand, and with contemporary problems, on the other. While he only stayed for six years before moving on to Chicago, these discourses, attended by many who were not necessarily in his regular *Gemara shi'ur*, charged the atmosphere and molded many serious seekers. Just ask Daniel Tropper in Jerusalem or David Berger in New York.

Third, the revival of the *kollel* in 1961 had a multiple positive effect. Its members were almost all in the Rav's *shi'ur*, and that constituted their primary commitment. However, inclusion in the additional framework enriched and intensified their learning, provided a forum for self-expression, infused *esprit de corps*, and raised the demands they made upon themselves in the present and the hopes they entertained for the community for the future. Suffice it to note that almost all of the current Yeshiva *rebbeim* of the relevant age group entered the *kollel*'s portals in the sixties.

Beyond the decade, the gradual and natural changing of the guard, through the appointment of American-bred and Yeshiva-trained *rebbeim*, had a cumulative salutary effect. To the chagrin of some, the transition did not necessarily usher in the more liberal climate they had anticipated upon the retirement of the European cadre. On the contrary, the molding of a faculty which, as compared to the relative laissez-faire attitude of is predecessors, was more engaged, knowledgeable, and articulate with respect to the college and the university, opened up the prospect for increased tension no less than for rapprochement. Nevertheless, from the students' perspective, they now had the benefit of mentors who, by and large, were familiar with their language, shared their concerns, and understood, although not evenly so, their cultural needs. Many *talmidim* still complain of the lack of rapport, but, on the whole, their *rebbeim* are far better attuned to them than in the previous generation, and this has provided spiritual stimulus. Moreover, the faculty, despite methodological and ideological differences, has melded as a group, so that, while none of its members are within hailing distance of the Rav, it has a collective impact greater than in his day. Indeed, it is entirely possible that the absence of an overpowering figure has hastened the process of staff consolidation.

With respect to personnel, a word should be said — and I hope it can be uttered without flattery and without inviting invidious comparisons — about the role of the administration. I refer, particularly, to R. Norman Lamm and R. Zevulun Charlop. I know that the former has, at times, been at ideological loggerheads with some of the *roshei yeshiva*, and I understand their reservations about some of his decisions and pronouncements. And yet, if only for his remarkable success in keeping the institution afloat and solvent, American Orthodoxy is very much in his debt. But not only for that — in the spiritual realm, while he, like Dr. Belkin, has been more removed from the *beit midrash* than he would have liked, he has presided over a period of its growth and has contributed to it. He has projected a vision consonant with the religious needs of a broad spectrum of his community, encouraged *talmidim* to learn in *Eretz Yisrael,* and significantly extended the bounds of Torah at Yeshiva by enabling the establishment of a range of *kollelim.*

R. Charlop, for his part, has provided much-needed ongoing direction. Given his own variegated background, he has come remarkably close to being *razui le-khol ehav,* serving as a cohesive force between faculty, students, and general administration, and he has enjoyed the confidence of various constituencies. With shrewdness and efficiency, he has contributed incalculably to both stability and growth for over a generation; this, too, has enhanced the RIETS environment.

Finally, as R. Lamm has noted on various occasions, the influence of the Israeli experience has been crucial. Back in the fifties or even the sixties, very few went to study in Israel. However, since the early-to-mid-seventies, going to learn for a year or longer in Israel has increasingly become almost *de rigueur;* this has, in turn, impacted powerfully upon the American Yeshiva University scene. The decision to go constitutes, in itself, an expression of commitment, and in the course of a concentrated period of *talmud Torah,* with relatively few digressions, that commitment is hopefully deepened. Hence, students return with greater zest and, especially, with different conceptions concerning what serious learning entails, and, consequently, with different habits. This element is most manifestly in evidence in the evening *sedarim* — and it is, perhaps, then, that the cacophony sounds most melodious.

"Tho' much is taken, much abides," proclaimed Tennyson's Ulysses. That is, in our case, self-evident. With respect to the quality and the scope of *yir'at shamayim* and *talmud Torah,* internally, there is never enough. Externally, much greater momentum needs to be generated with regard to our involvement with the broader community. In mid-century, modernists envisioned themselves as encamped at the center of Orthodoxy and reveled in the flattering thought that they were both leading and communally connected, while *haredim* were confined within their cloisters. However, in short order, and before Yeshiva circles took true notice, the latter seized the initiative and Yeshiva found itself in arrears. We certainly ought not begrudge the *haredi* world its accomplishments, but we need to do much more on this front. The attitude cited in the name of a prominent administrator to the effect that Yeshiva was an institution and not a movement, is, in the long run, both spiritually and institutionally negative. It is reflected in the mindset of some *talmidim* who equate moving west of New Jersey with exile to the Antipodes. We need to regain ground lost in *hinnukh* and *rabbanut*, and to break fresh ground in addition.

There are, however, internal issues as well (although, in a sense, outreach, too, is an internal issue). Progress in the *beit midrash* has been purchased at a price — not, to my mind, inevitable, but real nonetheless. Concentration has been accompanied by constriction. On the one hand, it has manifested itself in insularity — the unwillingness or inability to imbibe from the reservoirs of Arnold's conception of culture, "the best that has been thought and said in the world," as constituting the *hokhmah* which can be found *ba-goyim*, and obtuseness to many of the concerns, pragmatic and spiritual, which beset the Jewish and general world on the other. In this connection, I am afraid we are witness to an erosion in religious Zionist fervor — admittedly, characteristic of American Orthodoxy as a whole, but especially disturbing at a Torah center. In a very different vein, constriction is, concomitantly, occasionally reflected in intolerance bordering on demonization with regard to spiritual opposition. And, contrary to the Rav's legacy, it is manifested in the benign neglect with which many regard the learning of *Tanakh* and *mahshavah*. In part, constriction finds expression in superficial and simplistic personality, in the inability to recognize the complexity of thought and experience, and even in the difficulty of some to cope with life and to make meaningful decisions. And there are some who find the Yeshiva's atmosphere to be disheartening — not quite depressing, but also not conducive to *ivdu et Hashem be-simhah.*

These are serious concerns — not just superficially functional, but genuinely spiritual — and they require serious attention. I freely acknowledge, moreover, that, to an extent, they may have been engendered or encouraged by some of the very same factors which have served to vivify the *beit midrash*. With regard to my own sentiments, however, let there be no question. If forced to choose between the *yeshiva* and the college of my student generation and the present vintage, I need not hesitate for a moment. *Ashreikhem*, current students, *she-zekhitem le-khakh.*

Love Hurts:
My Family and Yeshiva

By Yehudah Mirsky

My immediate family's involvement with Yeshiva began in the 1920s and ended in the 1980s. It is a story of idealism, achievement, love, and heartbreak. I share it with the Yeshiva community for the sake of memory, telling the truth, and healing. This essay is dedicated to all the people, remembered and forgotten, who fully devoted their lives for the idea that Yeshiva, however imperfectly, represents.

Our story begins in 1927 with the arrival of my grandfather, R. Shmuel Kalman Mirsky, to Yeshiva. An *illui*, he grew up in Jerusalem and received *semikhah* at age thirteen. After the First World War, he embraced religious Zionism, acquired a secular education and a law degree, and became a disciple of R. Avraham Yitzhak Kook, chief rabbi of Palestine. When family circumstances made him relocate to the United States, Dr. Bernard Revel, who had warm correspondence with R. Kook and followed the activities of his circle, recruited my grandfather for the faculty of the newly-founded Yeshiva College.

My grandfather taught at Yeshiva for some forty years, mainly at TI and at BRGS. During that time he also served as rabbi of the Young Israel of Boro Park, where, among other things, he taught the first *daf yomi*

Rabbi Yehudah Mirsky, MTA '78, YC '82, is a Research Fellow at the Van Leer Institute in Jerusalem and a Fellow in Religion at Harvard University, where he is writing a dissertation on the ethical teachings of Rav Kook. Ordained by Rabbi Zalman Nehemiah Goldberg of Jerusalem, Rabbi Mirsky is a graduate of Yale Law School and served as Special Advisor in the U.S. State Department's Human Rights Bureau.

class ever on American shores. Those were the days when, unbelievable as it sounds, Boro Park was a bastion of cultural Hebraism and Mizrachi-style Zionism, part of the Hebraist culture that once thrived here. My grandfather served, as my father did later, as president of the Histadruth Ivrith of America, and was involved in a host of communal activities. Prolific author and scholar, he founded and edited several periodicals, most notably *Talpiot* and *Sura*, authored some dozen books, collections and critical editions and literally hundreds of articles. My grandfather passed away in 1967; he finished his decades-long work on the *Sheiltot de-Rav Ahai Gaon*, a project he initiated in the 1920s at the suggestion of R. Kook and which took him to the Vatican and other great libraries in search of manuscripts, literally on his deathbed.

His son, my father, David, entered MTA in the fall of 1934; among his classmates was Gershon Cohen, later to become chancellor of the Jewish Theological Seminary of America, and his lifelong friend Sidney Furst, who became a leading figure in postwar psychoanalysis. They, like my father, were products of the very rich Hebraist culture that once thrived in America and is now a distant memory.

After MTA, my father went on to YC and graduated in 1942, along with his future brother-in-law, my uncle Joseph Sokolow, who is an active alumnus; my uncle's son Moshe has enjoyed a distinguished scholarly and teaching career of his own at Yeshiva and his grandson Shalom graduated MTA last Spring. My father had been preceded at Yeshiva by another future brother-in-law, my uncle Rabbi Dr. Gersion Appel, class of 1938 and one of Dr. Revel's last pupils, who went on to an exemplary career as both pulpit rabbi and scholar, becoming professor of philosophy at SCW. His children and grandchildren also attended Yeshiva University in their time. Another of my uncles, Meir Havazelet, would in his time also become a professor at Stern College.

But all that came later. The 1930s and 1940s found my father in Washington Heights, learning in the *beit midrash*, studying English and Hebrew literature, and, along with several friends, founding in 1938 the YC Drama Society, advised by longtime English professor Irving Lin. Chief among my father's theatrical collaborators was his lifelong friend Morris Epstein, whose sparkling wit hung lightly over great erudition, and who went on to become professor of English at SCW before dying all too young in 1973. YCDS productions in those days were reviewed by theater critics of major newspapers.

After graduation, my father stayed at Yeshiva to learn for *semikhah* at RIETS and drew continually closer to Dr. Samuel Belkin, who in those days was still giving a regular *shi'ur* and would eventually come to refer to my father in public as "my son David."

After finishing *semikhah*, my father studied English literature at Columbia and edited the *Jewish Horizon* magazine of the Mizrachi before returning to Yeshiva in 1948. His scholarly work chiefly focused on Milton, *haskalah* poetry and on the place of Jews and Judaism in modern English literature, and he was tenured as professor of English and Hebrew literature. He also began to work at Dr. Belkin's side during the years of Yeshiva's transformation from a liberal arts college and seminary to a full-fledged university.

Those were the heady postwar years, when the federal government poured money into higher education and traditional Judaism began to emerge from the shadows onto the American scene. Dr. Belkin and those who, like my father, shared his vision, seized the moment not only to build Yeshiva as such, but, in emphasizing the humanities and sciences, sought to make it a source of moral and intellectual leadership in society at large.

My father was one of those who worked with Dr. Belkin on the myriad details of building these institutions; for example, they worked together on the creation of AECOM at a time when Jewish professors were still stymied by discrimination and quotas. Over the years, Dr. Belkin had my father take on projects in virtually every niche of Yeshiva in order to, as he said, give him exposure to all its workings.

At the same time, Dr. Belkin called on my father to serve as a liaison to the outside world. My father regularly represented Yeshiva University in Washington, Albany, the Middle States Association, and at other bodies of higher education, general, Jewish, and Christian. He represented Yeshiva at UN and embassy functions, and my mother Sarah regularly served as hostess for official gatherings. My father was also responsible for the various lecture series that brought figures like Isaiah Berlin, Bernard Lewis, Jacob Talmon, Philip Roth, and Irving Howe to Yeshiva.

This reaching outward was complemented by working for the Orthodox world. Dr. Belkin encouraged his people to help *Haredi* institutions struggling to build themselves. My father negotiated for SATs on Sundays for *shomer Shabbat* students, accreditation for *yeshivot* and even, with Dr. Belkin's approval, gave free technical advice to the then-newborn Touro College out of the belief that the world needs as much Jewish education as possible.

In 1963, my father became University Dean of Admissions and, in 1968, Dean of SCW. It was during his years at SCW that the *beit midrash* for women first opened, and I will never forget his proud recounting of hearing young women talk in learning. In 1975, he was appointed University Vice-President for Academic Affairs.

My father's years in YCDS also left their mark when, in the 1960s, years before PBS, he developed several educational TV series on minorities in American literature under Yeshiva's auspices. Beyond Yeshiva, my father was chairman of American Professors for Peace in the Middle East, president of Histadruth Ivrith, secretary of the Council of Higher Education Institutions for New York State, and active in other Jewish and non-Jewish organizations.

My father was a rare mix of *talmid hakham*, literary humanist, ironist and, with his gentle mix of altruism, grace, and wisdom, a genuine *tzaddik*. He was human, of course, but we all should be so human. He also had a passion for building educational institutions, without caring who got the credit. In the expansive, broad-minded Yeshiva of those years he found his métier and calling.

All that abruptly changed in the mid-70s with ascendancy of R. Dr. Norman Lamm to Yeshiva's presidency. My father's closeness to Dr. Belkin, his support, as a member of the university's search committee, for the candidacy of R. Emanuel Rackman, along with his considered dissents to a number of Dr. Lamm's early administrative decisions, made him *persona non-grata* under the new administration. His responsibilities were progressively trimmed; more painfully, colleagues, including those whose own careers he had fostered, began to keep their distance, disinvite him from their *simchas* and more, amid a general climate of fear. His salary was reduced under the pretext that he was insufficiently credentialed. One Sunday morning, without any warning, he saw a want ad for his own position in the Sunday *New York Times*.

This was, to put it mildly, a terribly painful time. My father bore it with great dignity and never lost his gentle way. But it hurt. He returned to the classroom after some absence and discovered, he told me, that the academic level of the college had declined far more than he had known.

With time, my father recouped some of these losses; the University's reorganization came to the attention of the Middle States Association and Yeshiva's very accreditation was called into question and my father's services were sorely needed. The University turned to him for help, and he was able to rejoin the upper echelons of the university administration with the title of Special Assistant to the President. He kept teaching his classes, resumed long-neglected scholarly projects, and began to write in new directions. He spent some time at Oxford's Centre for Postgraduate Hebrew Studies. And then, in 1982, he suffered a heart attack and died.

I graduated YC several months after my father's death. I left Yeshiva deeply estranged and embittered by all that had happened to him. I watched from afar as Yeshiva seemed steadily to drift farther to the religious right and deeper into mediocrity. I saw my father's name steadily vanish from institutional memory and the university's commissioned histories. I kept my distance; I never visited, never answered mail from the Alumni Association, and left my BA off my resume. I went to Yale Law School and eventually to Washington to work in government. I tried to put as much distance as I could between myself and Yeshiva and to learn the ways of the powerful, so that what had happened to my father would never happen to me.

With time, a different realization took hold; a dozen years after graduation, working in the State Department by day and learning and teaching Torah by night, I came to see that the ideals of Yeshiva had indeed struck deep roots in me after all, the institution's best efforts at poisoning those commitments notwithstanding. A number of years down the road, before making *aliyah*, I taught at Yeshivat Chovevei Torah and there, in an electric *beit midrash* atmosphere generated by some twenty students and a handful of *rebbeim* in a converted basement, I felt I had finally come home to what Yeshiva University was supposed to have been. For noble ideals, I realized, it really never is too late.

Writing in the pages of *The Commentator* in 1981, after and despite his tribulations, my father said: "Torah...can meet whatever challenges history may throw up to it...the Jew need not fear to move out and meet the challenge of history." That faith is bigger than any institution or person, bigger than us all, and still a source of strength. Once, several years ago, I poured out my heart to an old friend about how it seemed that all that my father had worked for, the great humanist vision of Yeshiva University, was crumbling, and with it all he left behind. "No," my friend said, "what he left behind was you." And I thought: "not only me." I realized that the real legacy of my father and the great people he worked with over the years, the final measure of that devotion, is us, the students of Yeshiva past, present and future — who we are and what we do with our lives and the Torah we write in, and with, our lives.

Yeshiva From Birth (YFB)

By Joshua L. Muss

The imprint on my forehead at birth read "YC '62." There was no discussion, no suspense, and no doubt about it.

My grandfather left Russia, a married teenager, towards the end of the nineteenth century. He traveled to Shanghai and then to South Africa, finding employment as a contractor, and, with a growing family, reached America and settled in Brooklyn in 1906. He thrived as a builder. With little religious or secular schooling, he earned a graduate degree in religious education by literally building *yeshivot*. He was honored for that by Yeshiva University. My mother and family came to the Bronx in 1916 from the Polish town of Swislocz. Some thirteen years later they welcomed the arrival of a landsman and distant relative, R. Samuel Belkin.

My father — a rabbi, a lawyer, and a businessman — was a member of the first graduating class, YC '32, and was an alumni leader and a board member of RIETS. He was once quoted as saying that everything that he became he owed to Yeshiva. My mother was a founder of the Yeshiva University Women's Organization; many meetings took place in our apartment. My brother Stan and I were a first offering.

Our first neighborhoods were lonely outposts generically known to children of pulpit rabbis — Patchogue, Long Island and Flushing, Queens. Yeshiva day school, Ramaz, was a subway ride into Manhattan. The commute continued through high school — Forest Hills to MTA. The

Mr. Joshua L. Muss, MTA '58, TI '62, YC '62, HLS '65, is a long established New York City real estate developer. He was very active in student activities as an undergraduate and is currently active in many civic and Jewish organizations. He presently serves as Chairman, Board of Directors, Yeshiva College.

journey ended, happily, in a dorm room in Rubin Hall. I was fortunate to be assigned for four years to a room dedicated to my grandparents' memory, a room with a great view of Manhattan — unimpeded by the yet-to-be-built Belfer Hall — and which afforded me an unusual opportunity: I stayed put while upper and lower classmen passed through my floor, sharing with me a very diverse menu of maturity and wisdom.

Academic images, much faded, recall the affectionate garbled brilliance of R. Menahem Brayer, memory drills for the Reb Maurice Wohlgelernter's fearsome finals (forgotten by the day after), the lilting poetry of the great Bialik, delivered by the great Havazelet, German beer songs belted out by Rosenberg's rogues (the louder you sang, the higher the mark), and the inspiring historical perspectives and philosophical insights from the legendary classes of the youthful Rabbis Greenberg, Shmidman, and Lamm.

From a social point of view, allowing for the several years that have passed and changes in landmarks, technology and social mores, I'm absolutely certain that little has changed: deadlines at *The Commentator*; all night cram sessions rewarded by a late night trip to Schmulka Bernstein or sunrise at Ratners; stirring political oratory in the student council; social consciousness on issues beyond campus (civil rights was current, and it was the dawning of the Age of Aquarius); the *shlep* to late night tennis practice at a Harlem armory and a shlep to anywhere for matches; jam sessions, ad-hoc engagement parties, and, of course, the ongoing challenge of the cafeteria.

The facilities were lousy. At the time, there was hardly anything that was "good" and much that just "wasn't" — no labs, no gym, certainly no swimming pool, no on-campus pedestrian mall, and the main classroom building was shared with the high school; in fact, little had changed since my father's time. And, of course, we were uniformly mistreated by the administration. But we loved Yeshiva.

We were challenged by the brilliance of motivated classmates and by dedicated teachers who were inspired by their students. Tirelessly, we balanced those eighteen hour days that made everything that followed easy. We achieved what we set out to achieve. The pre-meds all made med school, good absorption into top law schools, graduate students evolved into tenured professors, and some terrific educators and brilliant rabbis emerged. Lasting relationships were forged because we all had so much in common: a kinship that networked us and followed us into our professions and communities where we kept up with each other's families, introduced our children to each other, and continued the bond that began generations ago and will endure, please God, for many more to come.

Sure, we wore blinders to the outside world, a world that we discovered soon enough in graduate school or as we set out to make a mark in life. And, for the most part, we were well up to the task. But that camaraderie, a sense of dependence on any one of hundreds of like-minded fellow students, inures to this day, and is unmatched in any alternative academic setting.

More than any graduates of any academic institution in the world, it is necessary to continue our fealty to YC. If the word love doesn't jump to mind, consider the words obligation or survival. There is a need to give back to the students, to ease their burden, and to make their experience more meaningful and more productive and somewhat more comfortable because we know just whom it is that they are. They are us.

From Out of Town

By Stanley Raskas

In September of 1961, I left St. Louis, Missouri for my freshman year at YC. I had just graduated from a public high school with over two-thousand students but less then a *minyan* of *shomer Shabbat* peers. The 1,000 mile, five hour DC-9 plane ride was short in comparison to the culture gap between University City High School and YC. I anxiously awaited the opportunity to be in a class of two-hundred students, where my friendships would not have to be defined by who understood my personal religious observances.

Over eighty percent of the students in my freshman class were from the tri-state area. Most of those students took in stride the Jewish amenities available in New York. For those of us from out of town, even establishments like Tov Me'od Cafeteria (aka The Greasy Spoon, across from the main building) and Chopsies Pizza were a luxury. I was in TI and I can still remember the twenty minute morning break, when all the local eateries were a zoo, with scores of students trying to catch an egg on a roll or some other late breakfast item.

At TI, I had some memorable professors. Sitting in my first *Gemara* shi'ur with R. Israel Wohlgelernter was an experience. His enthusiasm and ability to make a page of *Gemara* come alive was infectious. As the pace of a class progressed, his rapid fire delivery engaged us in the topic of the day. When he wrote on the black board, his Hebrew verses went up quicker than the news tape in Times Square. It was in this class that I

Mr. Stanley Raskas, YC '65, RIETS '69, is a partner in The Oxbridge Group, a boutique investment banking house. He presently serves as Secretary, Board of Directors, Yeshiva College, and is coordinating the College's seventy-fifth anniversary celebrations.

began on a track that led to a year in Israel after graduation and eventually on to RIETS. It is interesting to note that no one in my freshman class had spent a year in Israel as is common now.

Many of my teachers at TI had backgrounds which included life in Europe and during Holocaust. In *Humash*, Dr. Meir Hershkovics embodied an air of *deveikut* and *emunah* that permeated his classes. Dr. Moshe Carmilly often spoke to us about his European experiences during our *Navi* classes. I remember when we studied Amos, which talks about the sins of all the nations and that God will not forget; Dr. Carmilly described walking almost shoeless over mountains to flee from the Nazis. We also had tastes of *Eretz Yisrael*. Memories of TI and Yeshiva come to mind every time I visit Israel and pass Ahad Ha'am Street. The great Hebrew writer came alive for me in the classes of Dr. Meir Havazelet. Having only heard Hebrew in St. Louis that came with a heavy American accent, his lectures in beautiful Hebrew were a treat to my ears.

After a few weeks at Yeshiva, I received a letter from my grandfather, R. Tuvia Geffen, who was the rabbi in Atlanta, Georgia for close to sixty years. Born in Kovno, Lithuania he came to the United States after receiving *semikhah* in Kovno. In the letter, he informed me that R. Yitzhak Elchanan Spektor was his *sandik* in Lithuania. My grandfather went on to say how pleased he was that his grandchildren were attending the *yeshiva* named after the rabbi of his former community. On a personal level, this gave me a feeling of the continuity and unity of our people throughout the world.

Towards the end of the first semester, I realized that I was truly immersed in a Jewish world. The out-of-towners did most of their shopping on 181st Street. At that time, 181st still had a few nice stores, plus the local Carvel store, which stayed open late and was frequented by many students. On one December day, I made my way down to 181st Street to make some purchases, but all the stores were closed. It then dawned on me that it was December 25 and that, of course, nothing would be open. Despite having had a ten-day December vacation in public school, at Yeshiva it had totally slipped my mind that the secular world had a day off.

During my first three years at Yeshiva, I lived in the Rubin Dorm, then only a few years old. It is hard to imagine today, but at that point there was only one pay phone on every floor, that's one for over forty residents, and no private telephones in the dorm rooms. When a call came in, there was a scream down the hall and everyone listened to see if it was a call for them. Personal calls were constantly interrupted by people walking down the hall and kibbitzing with the person on the phone. There were still two World War II vintage small barrack style buildings on Amsterdam Avenue where the library now stands. English classes were held there before the construction of Furst Hall. In my junior year construction began on the Morgenstern Dorm. It was supposed to be available for our senior year. The construction schedule ran late, and at the start of our senior year there was a shortage of dorm rooms. I spent two months in Muss Hall with four people in a room until the "Morg" was open.

Those of us from out of New York developed our own Shabbat camaraderie. We did get invitations from classmates and we had Shabbatonim, which exposed us to the thriving communities of Far Rockaway, Flatbush, Eastern Parkway, the West Side, and other areas.

The social scene was also very different for YC students in the 60s than it is today. There were social events with Stern College for Women on a regular basis. The major social event of the year was the Dean's Reception, which featured various entertainment programs and which was held in such places as the George Washington High School Auditorium. Many students brought dates to this event, as the term "*shiddukh* date" was unheard of in those days.

The informal educational experiences at YC left as great a mark on me as the formal ones. I attended the 1962 literary presentation where author Philip Roth was challenged on his presentation of Jewish themes and characters. While all three authors in attendance were prominent writers, only at Yeshiva could the Roth challenge have taken place.

During this time, the Pope and the Catholic Church began a major ecumenical thrust, and everyone debated how we should respond. I recall the Rav announcing that he would deliver a lecture on the topic. Lamport Auditorium was packed that night as people from far and near came to get a sense of his direction.

On the international scene, the issue of Soviet Jewry had become an active cause for us. The question at that time was whether quiet diplomacy or active demonstration was the route to take. As an active participant in the student councils, a number of us visited different rabbis in Brooklyn who had extensive ties with the USSR. We were curious to hear their opinions. Subsequently, many of us participated in the first major rally on behalf of Soviet Jewry, which was held outside of the Russian Embassy in Manhattan.

Some of these informal educational experiences even took place during class. My most vivid recollection was during my freshmen chemistry class. We had the privilege of having the famous Dr. Samuel Soloveichik as our professor; we fondly called the Rav's brother "Solly" when we were not in class. Dr. Soloveichik was quite nervous, and I can still picture the chemistry room on the fourth floor of the original main building. On occasion, he ran experiments in the class, and all those in the first row had a tendency to move their desks towards the rear as he lifted the beaker of hydrochloric acid to pour into another substance. But the incident which always comes to my mind was not a laboratory mishap. It was the middle of the winter and our chemistry class took place between 5 and 6 pm. In the midst of one class, Dr. Soloveichik stopped and asked us to excuse him for a few minutes. He proceeded to a corner of the room, and we realized he was davening *Ma'ariv*. When he finished, he opened a thermos and poured himself a cup of coffee. He explained he had been observing *yahrzeit* that day, and, in the true Lithuanian custom, he had fasted. He did not want to miss the class, but he needed the drink to finish the lecture. To me this was the living embodiment of *Torah u-Madda*.

After my four years at YC, I went on to learn at Yeshivat Merkaz Harav Kook in Jerusalem and then returned to RIETS. After serving as the founding rabbi of the Young Israel of Scarsdale, I returned to my hometown of St. Louis, Missouri and the world of business for the past thirty years. The Yeshiva tradition has continued in our family, as our four married children and their spouses all graduated from Yeshiva and Stern. Our youngest son now attends Yeshiva. Our oldest son continued the out-of-town tradition at Yeshiva by starting a club called the "Rest-of-the-Country Club." This group even had T-shirts printed with a map of the USA with only forty-eight states — New York and New Jersey were missing.

I am amazed at the leadership positions in both the Jewish world and in the secular world occupied by people who attended Yeshiva with me. There is hardly a Jewish organization which has not benefited from both the lay and professional leadership of Yeshiva graduates. In the areas of medicine, law, accounting, and education, names of Yeshiva graduates pop up constantly. In the financial and business world, I find that I have an automatic rolodex just based on the people I met through Yeshiva. As I traveled for business, I knew that I could always find a friendly Yeshiva graduate to help me navigate the local scene.

If I have any reservations, it concerns our alumni. It appears to me that not enough of our alumni show *hakarat ha-tov* to our Alma Mater. While not everything was perfect about our Yeshiva experience, including facilities and course offering, we still received an educational foundation in *Torah u-Madda* to last a lifetime. We also gained friendships and experiences which were not available in many other places. My hope is that as we celebrate the seventy-fifth anniversary of YC, more alumni will join us in this celebration.

The Master Teacher

By Shlomo Riskin

It was June 24, 1963, the day I was to take the last of my qualifying examinations for rabbinical ordination at RIETS, one day after my wedding, and two days after I had been informed that the Talmud class I had been promised to teach in MTA had been cancelled due to a lower-than-expected enrollment. To say that I was panicked out-of-my-mind would be an understatement. Here I was with a new bride (an eighteen year old Religions major at Barnard), a three-year rental contract for an apartment at 100 Overlook Terrace, and no tangible means of support. The telephone rang: "This is Moshe Besdin speaking. (Could it be the R. Moshe Besdin, Director of the James Striar School for young men without Yeshiva background — many of whom I had taught at Yeshiva University Seminars — who had a legendary reputation as a master educator but whom I had never formally met?) I would like to offer you a full-time position, teaching Freshman Bible and Sophomore *Gemara*. May I depend on you?"

I was flabbergasted, frightened, and flattered all at the same time. I mumbled into the phone my appreciation of the offer, but that I had never taken a course in pedagogy and I was more than a bit daunted by the prospect of teaching students who would only be a few years my junior (I was then just twenty-three years old — and looked about sixteen). He waved away my protestations, telling me that he would observe my class-room manner and have a weekly lunch meeting with me, during which

Rabbi Dr. Shlomo Riskin, BTA '56, YC '60, RIETS '63, BRGS '73, is the founder and dean of Ohr Torah Stone Colleges and Graduate Programs. He is Chief Rabbi of Efrat.

time I would receive on-the-job training. "I'm a *beit midrash* watcher," he concluded, "and I've had my eye on you for a long time. I'm sure you'll do fine."

So began an association which was one of the most significant relationships of my life. From September 1963 until June 1977 — for as long as I taught at JSS — I ate lunch with R. Besdin Monday through Thursday, 1-3 pm, at the Tov Me'od restaurant (affectionately known as the Greasy Spoon). R. Besdin loved to monologue — and I became his most ardent listener. He was for me a *rebbe*, a mentor, a personal counselor, and a second father: every skill I acquired in educational methodology, every new initiative I established in the formative years of my rabbinate, every attitude I developed in my approach to Judaism and to life, were shaped and refined by this generous, genuine, wise, incisive, and consummately normal *talmid hakham*, who was both modest and decisive, inspiring and down-to-earth, and completely devoid of any modicum of self-importance or hypocrisy.

The James Striar School which he created — he was not only its first director, but he was the individual who shaped its contours, determined its curriculum and had the most abiding influence on four decades of its students — was probably the very first *yeshiva* for *ba'alei teshuvah* in Jewish history. The student body (two hundred to three hundred strong) was comprised of graduates of secular high schools from all over America and occasionally even from far-flung areas of the globe (I had a student from Barbados, West Indies), each of whom had been influenced by some religious inspiration: a Yeshiva University seminar, a synagogue rabbi or youth group, a religious relative or friend. Because R. Besdin believed that a school was formed in its admissions office, he himself interviewed every prospective student; he made sure the candidate was serious about his Judaism, willing to assume an observant life-style, and able to read, although not necessarily able to understand, a Hebrew text. Each interview lasted at least an hour; by the time it was over, he had weeded out anyone whose main interest was merely getting into a private college, and he had established an inextricable bond with anyone he had decided to admit to the program.

The JSS curriculum consisted of the study of traditional Jewish texts: the Bible and its classical commentaries (R. Besdin himself taught this class to every one of the incoming students), the *Mishnah* and the Talmud. R. Besdin would regale me with his philosophy of education during those unforgettable lunches. "Teach it, not about it," which meant that he was against a paperback, even Artscroll, form of Torah-in-translation or a Judaism-lite article about Biblical or Talmudic thought. His "it-illogical" theory of learning meant that a serious student would welcome the opportunity to take the necessary intellectual plunge and grapple with the text itself — learn to read it, translate it, understand it and internalize it, slowly but surely progressing from *Humash* to Rashi, to *Mishnah*, to Talmud. He actually called himself a "hederologist," after the *heder*, the Jewish school in the European *shtetl* that successfully taught hundreds of generations of Jews how to properly learn and understand a classical Hebrew text based on the single educational principle that if you can't properly read and translate the original verse or Talmudic passage, you will never truly understand it.

R. Besdin also had traditional notions of class-room management. He walked the halls before class was due to begin to make certain that each *rebbe* was on time, and he demanded thorough preparation and lucid explication from every member of his faculty. Because we were teaching not only divine texts but also supremely human subjects — flesh and blood students — we were paid for two extra periods a week, at which time we were expected to meet with our individual pupils for regular counseling sessions. In all of this he remained *primus inter pares*: the master teacher, thoroughly knowledgeable, in love with his subject matter as well as with his students, always accessible, and totally committed.

R. Besdin detested pretense and pretension. There was a tendency among freshmen *ba'alei teshuvah* to attempt to skip steps in the educational process and in their religious progression, to try to appear to know and to be more than what they actually knew and were. If he saw a beginning student expose his ritual fringes or wear a black hat, he would take him aside and warmly chastise him: "Remember, it is proper and even laudatory to attend a formal dinner with a tuxedo and top-hat. But if one wears a tuxedo and top-hat along with torn pants, he becomes a clown!" He understood that climbing up too quickly can result in crashing down just as quickly; true education must be a gradational, step-by-step process.

R. Besdin was an accomplished Torah scholar — he knew *Yoreh De'ah* virtually by heart, with all the comments of the *Peri Meggadim* — but I believe that his real love was the Ramban's commentary on the Bible. He had great respect for world literature — he especially enjoyed quoting long passages of Shakespeare — he played a mean game of tennis, he was immensely proud of his charming and beautiful wife, he deeply believed in romantic love, and he gloried in the various and varied successes of each of his children. Above all else, however, he was the consummate teacher, for whom teaching Torah was not only his profession but was truly the existential definition of his very being. And the Torah that he taught was constantly interspersed with the wise reflections of a renaissance man whose faith was profound without being fanatic and who genuinely believed that every individual was granted the God-given right to choose his/her life-style and life commitments. He saw the task of a teacher as the attempt to lovingly expose and wisely guide, never to forcefully coerce or underhandedly manipulate.

R. Besdin had a clearly formulated philosophy of Judaism, which stressed the Maimonidean Golden Mean and included a commitment to Torah together with *derekh eretz* (both in terms of respectful interpersonal relationships as well as professional pursuit). The source of his theological outlook was our classical Jewish texts, especially the Bible and its commentaries of Rashi and Ramban. The Divine Covenant with Israel was, for him, the very basis of the uniqueness of our nation, and so R. Besdin was fond of explaining (in his interpretation of a difficult passage of the Ramban) that whereas a contract depends on the fulfillment by both parties of its stipulations, our covenant has the Divine guarantee that there will always be a nation Israel through whom redemption will eventually come, no matter what. A contract can be revoked if one of the parties reneges; the covenant is eternal. He had great respect for our traditions, and the vital force of a Judaism which has been transmitted — parent to child, teacher to disciple — for the past four-thousand years. Indeed, he believed that Isaac's test in the *akeidah* was greater than was Abraham's; after all, Abraham heard the Divine Voice ask for the sacrifice of his son, whereas Isaac heard it only from his father. In this fashion, Isaac is the truest representative of the Jewish people, who have constantly been ready to lay down their lives for their faith not because they heard the command directly from God but because they heard it from their parents and teachers.

And, in addition to all of this, R. Moshe Besdin had a twinkle in his eye, a warm sensitivity, and sense of humor in his heart. Which one of his myriads of students wouldn't yearn to be lovingly called by him once again a "trumbenick," or doesn't think of Lavan as a "villain with style"? I remember that R. Besdin once suggested that we cut out the "knish" (generally kasha) with which we concluded our daily sandwich-and-salad each day; after all, calories and cholesterol were beginning to make a difference on both of us. But then, towards the end of our two-hour session, he looked at me seriously. "Reb Shloime," he said, "I've been noticing the woman who makes the knishes in the back. Do you know that in all the time we've been sitting here, no one has ordered a knish. She has had nothing to do. If she's fired, it would be on our conscience. You wouldn't want that to happen." I dutifully got us two knishes, as an act of *mesirat nefesh* on behalf of the knish-cook, of course.

So indebted did I feel towards R. Besdin that I asked him to be the *sandak* for my first son's circumcision; of course he acquiesced to my request. During the lunch that I asked him, however, he seemed quite agitated. His son-in-law, with a PhD in Jewish History, was having difficulty in finding a suitable teaching position. "Plumbers," he railed. "Jewish children have to study to be plumbers. It's easier for plumbers to make a living than it is for Jewish educators." He went on and on, quite disturbed by the situation.

The next morning, the morning of my son's circumcision, I called R. Besdin at 6:00 am. I apologized for the early telephone call, but I explained that I hadn't slept all night. "I'm concerned about your *kavannah* (internal intention) when you will be sandak," I explained. "I don't want you to intend my son to be a plumber. A plumber is fine, but I would still want that my son be a Torah teacher." R. Besdin laughed heartily, "You surely know I wasn't serious," he said. "There is no profession as exalted and or satisfying as being a teacher. Even our morning blessing refers to the Almighty God Himself as a *melamed*, a teacher. A good teacher can always look in the mirror at night and know that he/she spent the day in a significant way. An educator paves the way for the next generation of Torah, participates in eternity. I wouldn't trade my life with anyone in the world." Neither would I — thanks to the many life-lessons I was privileged to learn from the greatest teacher I have ever known, R. Moshe Besdin.

Samuel Belkin and the Legacy of the 50s

By Sheldon Rudoff

Within six months of the beginning of the 50s, the United States was once again at war. Having hardly recovered from World War II and its aftermath, the Korean War began in June, 1950 and the United States found itself embroiled in the conflict. Students in colleges around the country pursued their studies mindful of the fact that upon graduation they would face the prospect of military service, a consideration that strongly influenced their choice of college and career.

At Yeshiva, it was a time of increased enrollment and the continuation of the remarkable growth that had commenced just five years earlier when it achieved university status. Since 1945, several graduate schools were established, and in 1950 Yeshiva attained its crowning achievement — the granting of a charter for the establishment of a medical and dental school, which, in 1953, became the Albert Einstein School of Medicine.

The person most responsible for this growth and the dominant figure at Yeshiva in the 50s was R. Dr. Samuel Belkin. His was an infrequently seen but prevailing presence. The institution was small enough to be subject to his one-man rule, which he exercised quietly but decisively. It had been ten years since Dr. Belkin assumed the leadership of Yeshiva upon the sudden demise of Dr. Bernard Revel, and seven years after his assumption of the presidency, when at the age of thirty-two he became America's

Mr. Sheldon Rudoff, YUHS `50, YC `54, RIETS `57, was editor of The Commentator *in 1953-54 and is a Senior Partner at Labaton, Sucharow and Rudoff, LLP. Mr. Rudoff has served as President of the Orthodox Union and the Beth Din of America and has been active in many areas of Jewish communal life. He is a recipient of the Bernard Revel Memorial Award for Community Service (1989).*

youngest college president. Since 1935, he had been a RIETS *rosh yeshiva* and instructor in Greek at the College. At age twenty-four, he was the youngest *rosh yeshiva* in Yeshiva's history, admired and respected by his students and colleagues. His new responsibilities as president compelled him to leave the classroom and his role as a much-beloved *rebbe*. It was obvious to us that his contacts and relationships with students was a role he sorely missed. Accordingly, we took full advantage of his open door policy, which gave student representatives and student leaders access to him and his office, which was conveniently located alongside the building's entrance on the ground floor. When we brought our complaints about faculty and administration to him, he knowingly and sagaciously smiled and, more often than not, sided with the students.

Dr. Belkin served as a member of the *Va'ad ha-Semikhah*, together with R. Moshe Shatzkes and R. Joseph Ber Soloveitchik, until the oral *semikhah* examinations were discontinued in the late 50s. Anyone who experienced a *semikhah behinah* conducted by those three Torah giants came away with a greater appreciation of Dr. Belkin's *gadlut* in Torah. Often, R. Shatzkes and R. Soloveitchik would engage in their own discussion of the particular *sugya*, frequently leaving the candidate far behind. Then they would suddenly turn to the befuddled examinee and ask (in Yiddish): "And what do you have to say?" It was at this point that Dr. Belkin would intervene and repeat and explain the question in a way that not only clarified the issue but hinted at, if not gave away, the answer.

A significant but not much noted event took place in January of 1954, when at the behest of R. Nahman Bulman, then director of Residence Halls, Dr. Belkin agreed to meet with the dormitory students in an open forum. It turned out to be a challenging discussion with him. Practically every aspect of Yeshiva and Dr. Belkin's philosophy for the University was questioned — the establishment of the medical school, with its inherent halakhic problems, the sanctioning of sending out rabbis to officiate in non-*mehitzah* synagogues, the policy of Yeshiva with respect to *minyan* attendance, the nature of "synthesis," and the philosophical basis of an institution which seeks to combine *yeshiva* and secular studies under the same roof and in the same individual.

Some of Dr. Belkin's responses remain vivid in my mind and valid to this day. "*Minyan*," he declared, "is not a matter of policy but of *Shulhan Arukh*." Or "the trouble with Jewry in America is not mixed pews, but mixed minds." And "if not for the medical school, the doors of Yeshiva could not remain open today." Despite Yeshiva's rapid growth and his dedication to its continued expansion, "The Yeshiva must be in the center." Finally, "synthesis" does not mean "Chemistry *a là Gemara*," but is something that must be achieved within the personality of the individual rather than in the subject matter.

Most students left that evening believing that Yeshiva's president and *Rosh ha-Yeshiva* had acquitted himself very well. Dr. Belkin, however, confided that he felt he was under attack, and to my knowledge, never exposed himself to that type of forum again.

That Dr. Belkin focused his activities during this decade beyond the walls of the Yeshiva was undoubtedly due to his feeling that the Yeshiva was in good hands. His predecessor, Dr. Revel, valiantly tried to "import" outstanding European *roshei yeshiva* to Yeshiva. Thus, in 1922, the Maichater *Illui*, R. Shlomo Polachek, and in 1929, R. Moshe Soloveichik were brought to RIETS. Ironically, the Nazi persecution both before and during World War II brought to these shores and enabled Drs. Revel and Belkin to bring to Yeshiva outstanding European *rebbeim* such as R. Joseph Arnest, R. Avigdor Cyperstein, R. Henoch Fishman, R. Yerucham Gorelick, R. Dovid Lifshitz, R. Yaakov Moshe Lessin, R. Moshe Shatzkes, R. Shmuel Volk and R. Mendel Zaks (son-in-law of the Hafetz Hayim). They enhanced the existing distinguished faculty of which R. Joseph Soloveitchik was the acknowledged head. R. Soloveitchik was at the height of his intellectual and oratorical powers. By this time, his *Yahrzeit Shi'iur* in memory of his father, R. Moshe, was the singular annual event in the *yeshiva* world and Torah community. *Talmidim, rabbanim* and laymen literally filled Lamport Auditorium to the rafters to listen to four to five hours of impassioned explications of *halakhah* and *aggadah*. In these *shi'urim*, R. Soloveitchik revealed to his regular Talmud students yet another dimension of his unique persona; that of *darshan* extraordinaire, whose rhetorical depth and breadth was unequaled. To have studied with him was a privilege which we appreciated even more, both in and out of Yeshiva, as the years went by.

It was R. Soloveitchik, in his moving eulogy for Dr. Belkin on *Hol ha-Moed Pesah*, 1976, who delivered, in his inimitable manner, an insightful portrayal of the forces that drove this "wandering, restless *yeshiva bahur*." Samuel Belkin, the product of the European *yeshiva* world between the wars, knew very well of the limited opportunities that were open to *yeshiva-*

leit. They either remained in the *yeshiva*, entered the rabbinate or *hinukh* or married well, and occasionally engaged in the world of commerce. It was only in rare instances that professional opportunities were open to them. In America, Dr. Belkin discovered a land of opportunity. It was his goal that no door to any professional or graduate school be left closed to Yeshiva graduates. This commitment was also probably a reflection of his life experience; his father was murdered in a pogrom when he was a young child. His teenage years at Yeshivot Mir and Radin were marked by extreme poverty. Ordained by the Hafetz Hayim and by R. Shimon Shkop at age seventeen, he arrived in the United States in 1928 without funds, friends, family, or the ability to read or speak English. He never attended high school or college but was nonetheless admitted to Brown University in 1931, where he was elected to *Phi Beta Kappa* and received a PhD degree. He matriculated at Harvard in 1933-34 before returning to Yeshiva in 1935.

Thus, at Yeshiva he created a graduate school of education and social work, a science center, a medical school, and a law school. The establishment of these schools not only served Yeshiva College graduates but opened up to them admission to top-drawer universities. Enrollment at Harvard, Yale, and Columbia Law Schools was no longer aberrational. In the 50s, pre-med became a prominent major at Yeshiva. Medical schools around the country were accepting Yeshiva College graduates. The proliferation of Yeshiva graduates in medicine, law, accounting and every aspect of professional, commercial and communal life that exists today is surely a realization of Dr. Belkin's Great American Dream.

Dr. Belkin's vision included a role for the American Jewish community as well. On the occasion of that community's three-hundredth anniversary, he stated: "An ideal Jewish community in a non-Jewish world is one which endeavors to integrate itself in the larger community, which renders service to the community at large, enjoys all the privileges and bears all the responsibilities entailed, but at the same time is aware of its separateness and distinctiveness in the spiritual and intellectual fields." Fifty years later, that message remains cogent and meaningful.

The incoming college class of September 1950 was far different from what we experience at Yeshiva today. In the fifties, the feeder schools for Yeshiva College, besides Talmudical Academy, were Torah Vodaath, Chaim Berlin, Ner Yisrael, Rabbi Jacob Joseph School, and other *metivtas* from around the country. It was from these institutions that the likes of

Rabbis Julius Berman, Saul Berman, Benjamin Blech, Abba Bronspiegel, David Hartman, Aharon Lichtenstein, Aaron Rakeffet, and Sherman Siff came to Yeshiva College. Sadly, this is no longer the case, notwithstanding the fact that RIETS *rebbeim* rank among the finest *roshei yeshiva* in the country.

Perhaps it was recognition of the homogeneity of the student body in the early fifties that led Dr. Belkin to introduce what was then thought to be his most controversial undertaking — the establishment of the Jewish Studies Program. The program was designed to attract students with little or no background in Jewish studies, many from non-observant homes. After it was announced, the *beit midrash* was afire with fears of "dilution of the Yeshiva." Student and faculty protests were organized, ironically led by R. David Hartman, a recent *musmakh* of Yeshiva, and a promising young rabbinical student named Shlomo Riskin. Dr. Belkin, of course, prevailed and R. Moshe Besdin turned the source of all that concern into one of Yeshiva's proudest achievements.

A most significant accomplishment of the 50s was the establishment of SCW. Made possible by an initial gift by Max Stern and his family, SCW opened its doors in 1954. The announcement of the establishment of a college for women was greeted by YC students with a sense of bemusement, if not bewilderment. Stern was to be located far enough away not to be a threat but close enough to be of interest. A satirical article which appeared in *The Commentator* at that time considered the outrageous possibility of a shuttle service between the schools. In retrospect, the founding of SCW ranks among the most important sociological events in American Orthodoxy in the last half of the twentieth century. It brought young women from around the continent to the center of Jewish life and observance that could be found in New York City. Numerous Jewish families that exist today may never have come into being but for SCW. Intellectually, the founding of SCW surely stands as the century's seminal event in higher education for Jewish women.

In consonance with the calm of the Eisenhower years, campus life at Yeshiva in the 50s was relatively quiet, although not uneventful. McCarthyism caused hardly a ripple at Yeshiva, which was a bastion of Democratic liberalism. In a poll conducted during the Eisenhower-Stevenson election campaign, Yeshiva students preferred Stevenson 16-1. Student life was relatively serene. A national survey of drinking on campus found Yeshiva students to be teetotalers, except for the weekly imbibing of *kiddush* wine.

In 1953, Dr. Moses L. Isaacs, who had been a faculty member at the College since its inception, stepped down as dean after decades of service. Dr. Belkin replaced him with a complete outsider: Dr. Henry Guterman, a history professor at a small Pennsylvania teacher's college. Dr. Guterman had been forewarned about the "evils" of *The Commentator* editors, and his initial orientation to Yeshiva and its students was a wary experience for both. He reinvigorated the history department and raised the bar considerably for history and political science majors when he required outside readings and term papers. In 1959, Dr. Guterman's tenure as Dean ended and he was succeeded by Dr. Isaac Bacon, who remained at the post for nearly twenty years.

A quiet but significant change had taken place at *The Commentator* as well. For years, its senior editors were undergraduates who were not enrolled in the *yeshiva* program. Since the editors were selected by the outgoing board, this was a situation that was quite easy to perpetuate. A mistaken perception that freedom of the press was exercised too freely by *The Commentator* often placed it beyond the pale of acceptability in the eyes of certain members of the administration, faculty, and student body. Inexplicably, in 1952, and for many years thereafter, the senior leadership of *The Commentator* was taken up by *yeshiva* program students, who may have been no less irreverent or restrained than their predecessors. Dr. Belkin, however, sensed the shift and seized the opportunity to install R. Israel Miller, a distinguished alumnus, as advisor to the publication. We were informed that R. Miller would not serve as a censor. However, all material was required to be reviewed by him before publication. It became a ritual to slip under R. Miller's door at his nearby Bronx home, in the wee hours of the morning, articles which were simultaneously sent to the printer for publication. It was a great tribute to R. Miller's skills as the consummate diplomat and gentleman (attributes that were recognized in the ensuing years by the great esteem in which he was held by the American Jewish Community) that he exercised his role to suggest, cajole, and persuade. Rarely, if ever, did those of us at *The Commentator* clash with him over content or policy.

An overwhelming concern of Yeshiva students during this period was the fledgling State of Israel. Communication with and travel to and from Israel were not easily facilitated. A visit to campus from our Israeli counterparts or Mizrachi leaders was a significant event. These contacts ultimately led to the establishment of a program which was to have far-reaching effects on the institution, its students, and their families. It began in the 50s, with the offer of a six-month stay in Israel under the auspices of the Jewish Agency extended to a handful of TI students who were preparing for careers in Jewish education. It was inconceivable at that time that a year of study in Israel would eventually become *de rigueur* for almost every Yeshiva student.

By the end of the decade, the Korean War had evolved into the uneasy truce that exists to this very day. It was eclipsed by the Cold War, which heated up considerably in the turbulent 60s with the Cuban Missile Crisis. Vietnam was on the horizon. But I leave that story of another decade, for another time, by another alumnus.

My Teaching at Yeshiva

By Marvin Schick

I taught at Yeshiva College over forty years ago, for about a year and a half during the 1961-62 semesters. At the time, I was completing my doctorate in political science at NYU and an opening arose at Yeshiva when a veteran professor had passed away suddenly. There was no expectation that I would become a regular member of the faculty and, in fact, by the fall 1962 semester, I was teaching full-time at Hunter College.

The classes were held at a building that was called Muss Hall, which, although newly opened, was nothing to write home about; it was a functional structure with few of the accoutrements that I found later at various campuses. I shared an office with a number of other faculty, some adjuncts, as I essentially was, and some full-timers, including Charles Liebman, who was preparing a seminal study on American Orthodoxy that appeared shortly thereafter in the American Jewish Year Book. After making *aliyah*, Liebman emerged as perhaps the foremost scholar in the sociology of Judaism. When he passed away in September 2003, we lost a person of much integrity and insight.

The students were mostly bright and motivated, but I can't say that they earnestly dug into the material or generated what can be called much intellectual excitement. This may have been because they were mostly political science majors and more than a few were headed toward law school. When I meet a student from that period, invariably he has become a lawyer and, invariably, a rather successful one. A more important factor in this lack of enthusiasm was, and probably still is, the nature of

Dr. Marvin Schick is President of the Rabbi Jacob Joseph School and a writer on contemporary Jewish life.

the Yeshiva College experience, primarily the dual educational program. While few of the students seemed particularly interested in mastering Talmud or Judaics, they all went through the motions — and generally seriously. Since they also wanted to have time for athletics and other diversions, there was scant interest in excelling in subject matter beyond what was required to get a good grade. The time limitations inevitably limited out-of-class contact with students, an experience which is a vital part of campus life in most places.

There was even less contact with other faculty members, except for the few with whom I shared an office. Perhaps this was due to my temporary status, but I am certain that it arose as well from the way YC was organized and administered. I had ongoing contact with Dean Isaac Bacon because of my own work and because of paperwork requirements with other school administrators. What struck me then was the paternalistic nature of Yeshiva, the way faculty members, including those who were senior, were treated as employees who had a very limited role in curriculum matters and no role in faculty hiring and promotion. This was so unlike what I encountered everywhere else in my subsequent academic career.

Admittedly, there could have been faculty meetings that I did not know of, but I am certain that the departmental dynamics that are par for the course at most universities was absent at that time at Yeshiva. There was no such thing as salary scales or faculty participation in tenure decisions or in a host of matters that are familiar fare elsewhere. When, in 1980, the U.S. Supreme Court ruled in a faculty dispute arising at Yeshiva that faculty members were not employees covered by the National Labor Relations Act because they essentially were managers who participated in all kinds of key decisions, my reaction was that Yeshiva had pulled one over the justices. This is a prime example of a bad case resulting in bad law.

As a part-time college teacher, I had little directly to do with what might be termed the religious life on campus. I had no contact to speak of with Judaic faculty, nor did I participate in any events of a religious nature. At the time, the religious faculty was dominated by R. Joseph B. Soloveitchik and other notable figures who had already been around for quite a while and who continued to be dominant through the 1970s and into the 1980s. There were few, if any, young American-born and educated Torah scholars on faculty of the sort who are now predominant and who have clearly contributed enormously to the prestige of RIETS.

As I recollect, the religious atmosphere at Yeshiva at the time was *pareve*. There were students who studied in the *beit midrash* with intensity but they were relatively few in number. At the other end of the spectrum, there were students who had no use for religious study, and I was told that more than a few deviated substantially from religious norms; there were even radios playing in the dormitories on Shabbat. But overwhelmingly the student body at the time appeared to be solidly Orthodox, with few interested in pursuing careers in the rabbinate, religious teaching, or Jewish communal life.

I have been told that there are still some students whose behavior is deviant in a religious sense. It is impossible to avoid this in an institution of the size and diversity of Yeshiva. What is more striking is the abundant evidence of how many of those who have gone through YC and continued in RIETS are intensely committed to Torah study and to careers that enrich the Jewish people. Forty years ago, few would have thought that the Yeshiva University of the twenty-first century would have so strong a religious character. I certainly did not believe that this would be the case. Happily, I was wrong, and happily the Jewish people worldwide have benefited as a consequence.

Potpourri of Memories

By Alvin Schiff

Some of the best years of my life were the eight semesters I spent at YC. As a Bostonian, I was destined to go to YC. My religious-Zionist home background and growing up with the Rav virtually guaranteed that I would be a student at RIETS. Moreover, my mother worked hard to raise funds for Yeshiva as secretary of the Women's Association of New England.

I also received support regarding my decision to attend YC from an unexpected source. My mother was a first cousin of R. Avraham Karelitz — the Hazon Ish — the Talmudic luminary of the first half of the twentieth century and my parents' *shadkhan*. During the last fifteen years of his life, the Hazon Ish lived in the modest home of my uncle, R. Gershon Schreibman, who would come each summer to the United States *"tzu kempfen par shabbos"* — to do battle for Sabbath observance. When I completed my sophomore year in high school, my uncle suggested that it would be a good idea to seek guidance from the Hazon Ish regarding the choice of a *yeshiva* in New York to attend after the completion of high school. My father, known as the Brezer *Illui* in Lithuania, skeptically agreed. There were four possibilities for me: Mesivta Torah Vodaath, Yeshivat Chaim Berlin, Mesivta Tifereth Jerusalem, where R. Shmuel

Dr. Alvin I. Schiff, YC '47, founded Yeshiva's Department of Graduate Jewish Education (now known as the Azrieli Graduate School of Education and Administration) in 1959, which he directed for 11 years, and is currently it's Irving I. Stone Distinguished Professor of Jewish Education. Dr. Schiff is executive vice-president (emeritus) of the Board of Jewish Education of Greater New York and recently received the President's Prize in Jewish Education in Jerusalem by Israel's President Moshe Katsav.

Greineman, cousin of both the Hazon Ish and my mother, was the *menahel*, and RIETS.

The following summer, my uncle returned with a Yiddish note penned on a brown paper bag. Translated, the message said: "Avremeleh [my Yiddish name], I think that it is a good idea for you to study in Revel's *yeshiva*. There you can excel in learning if you so desire. Moreover, you could study for a trade or profession in the secular department. But, remember, in the cold weather you should wear a warm coat." This latter reference refers to the environment in which I would be exposed to secular studies. In order not to be unduly influenced, I would need Judaic reinforcement.

As a poor boy, I was fortunate to receive a four year movie industry scholarship to attend YC. And, I will be indebted forever to Yeshiva for the generous stipends I received for food and dormitory.

In a real sense, my four years at Yeshiva were worry free. I enjoyed both the Jewish and general studies and life in the dormitory. I vividly remember my first *havrutah* with R. Zevulun Charlop, who is now the dean of RIETS, and R. Mayer Fulda, a longtime faculty member at YC. They were considerably younger than the college-age students in my *Gemara shi'ur*; yet, they were clearly the best *talmidim* in R. Ephraim Steinberg's *shi'ur*. I felt very comfortable with the *shi'urim* in Yiddish and enjoyed R. Steinberg's ebullient personality. Later on in the Yeshiva, I was most impressed with R. Noah Borenstein's brilliance, R. Moshe Aharon Poleyeff's gentle scholarship and the towering charismatic personality and vast knowledge of R. Joseph B. Soloveitchik, in whose Shabbat and Yom 'Tov shi'urim I participated regularly during my High School years in Boston.

YC was an academic experience I really loved, especially the lively class discussions of Dr. Abraham Luchins, a brilliant psychologist. (I think that I may have been the first student to major in psychology at YC.) I was very proud of my article in *Masmid* on "Social Influence on the Perception of Complex Objects," based upon the research of Dr. Luchins. I liked the organized approach of Dr. Sidney David Braun, a dedicated French linguist, who, in a way, treated us like High School students, and the gentle genius of our mathematics professor, Dr. Jekuthiel Ginsburg. Of course, I cannot forget the comments of Dr. Alexander Litman, our philosophy professor, on "sub-gartelian" (below the *gartel*) logic, and the intense efforts of Dr. David Fleisher to make us love Shakespeare and

Chaucer. As poet laureate at the senior class dinner, I recall trying to capture Dr. Fleisher's personal approach to English poetry when I said: "To be sure, we'll never forget the musings of our Sweet David/ He can make love regained, whenever you so crave it." On the debit side, there was the absent-minded easy-going visiting professor of Sociology, Count Theodore Abel, whose classes were deadening. Several students never showed up for class and nevertheless passed the course.

There are some special memories I have about my stay at YC. In February of my sophomore year in 1945, the left oblique muscle of my left eye became paralyzed, causing me to see double. R. Joseph B. Soloveitchik and Dr. Samuel Belkin took special interest in my plight and arranged examinations at the New York Presbyterian Hospital and a weeklong stay at Beth Israel Hospital. The diagnosis of a possible brain tumor or multiple sclerosis greatly worried R. Soloveitchik and Dr. Belkin. The Rav suggested that I not go to his *shi'urim* until my paralysis disappeared. Actually, I missed *shi'urim* for two months. The neurologists and ophthalmologists who treated me were unable to determine the cause of the paralysis, which self healed in seven months.

Max Bear came from the Samson Raphael Hirsch School in Frankfurt am Main to be the director of the dormitory. Everything about him was unique — his heavy accent, his booming high-pitched voice, his overly sincere desire to make the dormitory livable, and his difficulty in understanding the nature of American Jewish youth, not all of whom were as serious about their studies as he thought they should be. Most dorm students did not like him, but I did.

Living with a roommate I knew from my days at *Ha-Shomer ha-Dati*, Asher (Arthur) Kahn, was an uplifting experience. I was exposed to his scholarship — never less than one hundred percent on every exam he took — his *menschlichkeit* — he would sneak out of the dormitory each weekday night at about 2 am and return at 6 am from the Jewish Memorial Hospital, about a half a mile from Yeshiva, where he volunteered to help patients because of the wartime nursing shortage in the hospital — and his orderliness and modesty. During his senior year, Asher was the head counselor in the dormitory. As a junior, I was assistant head counselor. I reveled waking up students each morning at 7 am with reveille on my bugle; this, I found, was easier than banging on doors to wake them.

From my junior year until the day he died, I had a very special relationship with Dr. Samuel Belkin, Yeshiva's president from 1943 to

1975, at which time he was then appointed chancellor of the University, a position that he held until his death in 1976. In my junior year (1945-46), I was the chairman of the SOY Jewish Affairs Committee. As such, I had many discussions with Dr. Belkin about the relationship of the student body to Jewish issues. The period of 1945-47 was the memorable time of the United Nations resolution regarding Israel statehood. I represented Yeshiva University — Yeshiva received university status in 1945 — on the Youth Zionist Actions Committee (YZAC) and encouraged my fellow students to participate actively in pro-Israel programs and activities. Prior to the United Nations vote, YZAC organized a rally in midtown Manhattan, and I rounded up students to participate in it. The dean of YC, Dr. Moses L. Isaacs, who was a member of the Agudath Israel, did not take kindly to my involvement in and encouragement of the student participation in the rally. In fact, he brought the matter up at a faculty meeting, noting that I was disrupting the school schedule. But I was not censured. Interestingly, it was Dr. Belkin who came to my support.

In addition to my SOY involvement, I took advantage of extracurricular opportunities at YC. In my freshman year, I starred in the dramatics society's show about a troubled basketball player who had difficulty combining sports with study.

The extracurricular activity in which I invested most of my time and energy was the *Hug Ivri*, which I founded during my sophomore year. By the time I graduated in 1947, *Hug Ivri* was, by far, the largest club in the college. About one quarter of the student body wore *Hug Ivri* pins indicating their interest in spreading the use of the Hebrew language. Needless to say, my intensive involvement with the *Hug Ivri* helped me decide to make Hebrew language instruction a pivotal part of my professional career.

I cannot close these comments without reference to some of our teachers and their personal teaching traits — the air of confidence and superiority of biology professor Shelley Safire, who gained international fame with his work on fruit flies at Columbia University; the careful, diligent teaching and laboratory guidance of biology instructor, Dr. Meyer Atlas; the antics of our diminutive chemistry professor, Dr. Eli Levine, who required the students in his class (all forty-seven of us) to sit in alphabetical order; the humorless sincerity of history professor Alexander Brody, whom I liked because of his integrity; the eloquence of our instruction in Jewish sociology by R. Joseph Lookstein; and above all, the ethical bearing of our Jewish philosophy professor, Dr. Leo Jung, with whom I maintained a close relationship until his death at age ninety-seven.

Not to be missed were the required Jewish studies courses as part of the academic program — Hebrew language with the dean of YC, Dr. Shmuel Sar, *Tanakh* with Dr. Shmuel K. Mirsky, and Jewish History with Dr. Sidney Hoenig. Since they were not credit bearing courses, these courses were not taken seriously by many students.

Like so many things in life, there is no logical ending to these comments — so, I'll end off here.

Math, Physics, and Mischief

By Larry Schulman

Though I've enjoyed reading the memories of my fellow alumni, I still come away with a feeling of unreality. Were we on the same campus? And then there's my usual puzzlement when reading autobiographical memoirs that includes distant, early years: how do these guys remember all that stuff?

So what follows is a different, if spotty, view of my time, 1959-1963, in the shadow of the Golden Domes over Amsterdam Avenue. Perhaps, to set the tone, I should mention that my greatest unfulfilled project was (together with co-conspirators) to repaint those domes to something more golden and less patina green. (Don't try this.)

Which is to say that we — Orthodox Jewry in general — were not as serious in those days. For whatever reason, we and (le-havdil) our historical offshoots have moved to the right in the last decades. Speaking about the others at least, I do not think it has been a boon to humanity. Of course in my class, for those not completely focused on religion, there were things we were serious about, in my case mathematics and physics, for others civil rights, and yes there was the occasional undergraduate not serious about anything. (Now that I'm on the other side of the dais, I find this not to be all that much of a rarity.)

But distraction from my beloved sciences was inevitable. I read with interest and appreciation the article of Yehudah Mirsky about his father David Mirsky, whom I now realize was important in the history of the

Dr. Larry Schulman, YC '63, did his graduate work at Princeton University and then to held faculty positions at Indiana University, the Haifa Technion (where his kids grew up), and now Clarkson University in northern New York.

institution. He was my English professor, and from the myopic perspective of an undergraduate all I knew is that he set a new standard of writing and expression for me. I hated — perhaps not *every* moment of — it, but it has certainly influenced the rest of my life. Somehow there was also time for a stint as a *Commentator* reporter under then Editor-in-Chief Murray Laulicht, another place to learn how to express yourself–succinctly. And finally, the major non-science experience of that freshman year was the *shi'ur* of Rabbi Yisrael Weiss. Coming from the boonies (Elizabeth/Newark, New Jersey) this was the majors. Looking for *peshat* turned out to be a lot tougher than understanding Rolle's Theorem.

But math and physics were the real centers of my life (which my wife complains is still the case) and there I had astounding luck. For a brief flicker of time Yeshiva became a serious player in this arena. The BGSS was born a bit before I entered, and phased out some years later. But during my four years I had a fantastic educational experience. I learned a lot more than in my subsequent graduate studies at Princeton. My baptism of fire (if you'll forgive the expression) was an innocent-sounding course in Algebra in my sophomore year. OK, it was a graduate course, but Algebra? How bad could it be? The instructor was D. J. Newman, with whom I later had contact in his capacity as coach for the Putnam mathematics competition (I was a varsity player in *something*). I am nostalgic for that kind of professor. I am nostalgic to be that sort of professor. Nowadays certain university officials insist that the aim is to make the student a satisfied customer. Not Donald Newman. He marched ahead, and after each two hour lecture I would spend many more hours parsing his words, algebra books before me, trying to master the subject. For the second semester of this experience he needed to sign something to again allow me, an undergraduate, to attend. True to form, he didn't recognize me — even though a priest from Fordham and I had gotten the only A's in the course.

Which is not to say that some of our instructors weren't both outstanding mathematicians and inspiring teachers: Bernard Epstein comes to mind. I took Complex Variables with him, but it was in a Real Variables course that his students were so amused by his constant request, "Give me an epsilon," that for the last lecture of the semester they prepared a large poster with the Greek letter beautifully calligraphed, and presented it to him — GAVE it to him — as a token of his wonderful instruction.

In physics, since this is now my field, I can attest that we had world-class scientists as our teachers. For freshman physics I had Joel Lebowitz, now a friend and colleague (and incidentally besides being a leader in the field of statistical mechanics a significant battler for human rights, including, for Jews in Soviet Russia). One of the most original minds in physics is David Finkelstein, with whom I was lucky enough to have my first quantum course. Again this is someone who has become a friend and colleague, but with some special features that befit original minds. At one point he was my guest at the Technion and we made a little party at my house in his honor. The guest of honor of course sat in a big comfortable chair. After the party he left but returned two minutes later. The keys to his car were missing. We turned over the big chair and shook it, but to no avail, and it was only masterful self-control that kept me from turning him over. (Ultimately I broke into the car with a coat hanger, but that did not yield keys lying in the floor, and my skills did not extend to hot wiring the engine.) Any of you who has studied quantum mechanics knows that it SHOULD make you worry, that reconciling it with the world you thought you knew is not easy (more of a strain than relativity), so that having Finkelstein to guide us into this intellectual challenge was as good as you could get. I won't try to make my list exhaustive, but it really does go on.

One of the big improvements in college education since my time is what is known as REU (Research Experience for Undergraduates). The real fun of science is the research, and it is easy to go through years and years of study without finding this out. Here too I was lucky. Harry Rauch, another of the math professors, had National Science Foundation money which he used to support an undergraduate over the summer. But along research lines, my best experience was again with Finkelstein. He gave a General Relativity course. As you (should) know, the first and most famous test of this theory was Eddington's measurement of the bending of light around the sun during a 1919 eclipse. (Besides its scientific import, this was hailed at the time as a triumph of science over nationalism; a British scientist confirmed the theories of a German, shortly after the end of World War I.) It occurred to me while taking this course that light from distant stars or galaxies could bend around other intervening masses, so I estimated the effect, estimated the likelihood of observing this, and did all the things a real scientist would do. This was my term paper, as it were, for Finkelstein, who guided me through it with exemplary comments —

and selective silence. This was my first "discovery." I later learned that I had been scooped by Einstein (hence my admiration of Finkelstein's silence), which detracted not at all from the fun. Two comments: today this phenomenon is the basis of Amicrolensing — an important tool for discovering and measuring dark matter. And Czech friends have uncovered correspondence from a Jewish engineer in Prague who wrote to Einstein (I think in 1922) proposing this idea.

Another feature about YC in those days, and I hope this has not changed, was having extremely talented fellow students. I had been accepted to some fancy-shmancy places where — except for those admitted for their parents' donations — the intellectual level was guaranteed to be high. But Yeshiva was a place people went to because they had other priorities; Yeshiva could still have outstanding classmates. One is now a professor of mathematics at the Hebrew University with our last near-contact being that we did our *miluim* in the same communications-oriented structure near Tel Aviv. Others were of a similar caliber, although the vagaries of life and the proliferation of scientific specialties have kept their progress from me. And finally not everything does revolve about science, so that some college friendships have lasted a lifetime, although here too geography is destiny, and living away from the centers has weakened my connections.

Before I entered Yeshiva, a recent graduate, my late cousin Allen, told me he had done all his studying after 3 am. Of course I discounted this, although Allen was not one to try to make a big impression on his little cousin. It turned out that for me it was 5 am. Why? Three to five am was the time that we — my roommate(s) and the guys down the hall — solved the big philosophical problems of the day. I hope that's still happening today.

Finding an Unlikely Home

By Abraham D. Sofaer

I spent three years at YC, from 1959 to 1962, before I graduated and went on to law school. They were tough years. I commuted from my parents' apartment in Queens (three trains each way), worked part-time in the library, and took the usual double load of courses as a student in the Jewish Studies Program. Nonetheless, I am grateful for the opportunities Yeshiva provided me to learn and to grow, and for the abiding connections it helped me to make with the Jewish people.

In retrospect, it is amazing that I became a Yeshiva student and how much I learned and benefited from the experience. As a Bombay-born Jew of Iraqi origin, I was raised in a relatively observant home. We Iraqi Jews had kosher kitchens, we were taught to read Hebrew, we attended synagogue regularly, observed the Holy Days, and boys were taught what they needed to know to be *bar mitzvah*. During the 1940s and early 1950s, Zionist organizations were active in our community; I was in the local Ha-Bonim group, and the Maccabim arranged for sports activities for Jewish kids.

This solid ethnic background did not carry with it scholarship or real comprehension. I did not understand or speak Hebrew, and I could not read or understand any of the other religious literature, including *Mishnah* and *Gemara*.

I moved from India to the U.S. when I was fourteen years old, in

Hon. Abraham D. Sofaer, YC '64, was a U.S. district judge in the Southern District of New York (1979-85), served as Legal Adviser to the Department of State (1985-1990), and is currently the George P. Shultz Distinguished Scholar and Senior Fellow at the Hoover Institution at Stanford University.

1952. I graduated from a Jewish high school in Connecticut, but I had more exposure during my early years to Christian-run schools, such as the Cathedral Schools in Bombay and Poona, than to Jewish education. I was not ready to go to college in 1956, so I enlisted in the U.S. Air Force. This experience reinforced my secular orientation. Interestingly, though, the pressures of military life and a growing need to understand life led me to begin to study religion. I read widely, if not deeply, into Christianity, Buddhism, Taoism, Zoroastrianism, and aspects of Hinduism. After a couple of years of this, it occurred to me that I knew even less about my own religion than about the others. So, I began reading about Judaism, and especially the Torah, which I grew to love and enjoy. When I began to read rabbinic sources, I quickly ran into a dead end. The available translations of virtually all sources at the time were very poor, superficial, and more confusing than illuminating. I went to the local Orthodox rabbi in Alexandria, Louisiana, where I was stationed in 1958, and asked if he would help me to learn enough to access the Hebrew and Aramaic sources. He said he was too busy, but that I should go to YC, where I could get a secular degree and at the same time learn more about Judaism. I sent for information and applied for admission (and for scholarships and loans, since I could not afford even the tuition).

A considerable time passed, and I called the Admissions Office to find out the status of my application. They told me that my application was pending, and that they could not say when it would be decided. By then, it was early 1956, and I needed to know soon whether I would be in college that fall. I asked the office if I could come to New York for an interview. They did not say yes, but they did not say no. I got the sense that they did not know what to make of my application, but were reluctant to deny it outright. I decided to take my chances and I told the office that I was soon going to be in New York and would report for an interview. They told me I could come, but insisted that they could not promise that anyone would be able to meet me.

I don't remember the date on which I arrived at the Admissions Office, but I do remember getting there at around 11 am. The secretary in charge told me that no one was available to see me. I asked if I could sit and wait. She said "OK, if you want to." I sat there for two hours, went to lunch, and returned. At around 4 pm, the secretary came over to me and asked me if I intended to stay. I said I would stay as long as they let me. She went away and came back a little later with a plain, black yarmulke.

"Do you mind wearing this?" she asked. "Not at all," I said, putting in on and going back to my book. Something was going to happen, I felt, and I hoped the fact that it had not occurred to me to wear a yarmulke would not hurt my chances. Sure enough, the secretary soon returned and said "Rabbis Besdin and Mirsky will see you now."

R. Moshe Besdin, of blessed memory, was the founder of the JSP program. He was a learned man, but his great strength was his warmth and generosity of spirit. He wanted to bring boys to Yeshiva who had very little background and teach them to become educated and observant Jews. He was well aware that the boys who came into JSP would rarely become fully observant; his aim was to bring every boy closer to the ideal than would have been possible without the program. He succeeded beyond any reasonable expectation, and in the process earned the respect and devotion of the entire Yeshiva community. He was a small man, with a big, warm smile, and an even bigger heart.

R. David Mirsky, of blessed memory, was a professor of English, in addition to being a *talmid hakham*. He had the classic look of a European Jewish scholar: fine features, pale complexion, delicate hands, intelligent, penetrating eyes, and a sweet smile. The students loved him and flocked to his courses. He was wise, compassionate, and clear minded. No doubt, R. Besdin had him in the room to share the burden of dealing with my application.

The two rabbis welcomed me, but with an air of unease. Why was I interested in Yeshiva? Did I know it was an Orthodox institution? Was I observant? Specifically, did I keep Shabbat, wear *tefillin* every day, and eat kosher? I did not lie, but I stressed the positive. I was not Orthodox, but I did observe many commandments. I always fasted on Yom Kippur. And, above all, I wanted to learn.

They appreciated my honesty, but they were dubious. The boys at Yeshiva came from Orthodox homes. They were young and impressionable. I had no religious background to speak of, and I had been exposed to a completely secular lifestyle. What had brought me here anyway?

That simple question, it turned out, gave me the chance to tell the story of my search through the world's religions, of my decision to study my own religion, and of the frustration I felt in not being able to understand the original sources. "What sources?" R. Mirsky asked. For example, I answered, something as basic as The Sayings of the Fathers. "What about *Pirkei Avot*?" he pressed. "I read it in English," I replied, "and many of the statements made no sense in translation." "Which ones?" I told them one of the sayings that had surprised me. It said, I recounted, that a person who walks on the road studying Torah and who stops his study to note the beauty of a tree or field will lose his soul. How could that be, I asked? I understood that Torah study was important, but such a punishment for appreciating nature seemed inexplicably harsh.

Suddenly, R. Besdin and R. Mirsky relaxed and got involved with me as a person. They both agreed this was a difficult passage and said, as I had suspected, that the translation did not do justice to the saying. R. Besdin went to a bookshelf and found the passage. "The saying is *mishnah* nine, by R. Yaakov, and the words in Hebrew do not at all suggest a punishment." The Hebrew words, it became clear to me from their comments, meant "it is as if [the person] bears the guilt for his soul." One should not interrupt Torah study, even to admire God's work; but the consequence was not a punishment but only the prediction that such conduct would put the person's spiritual life in jeopardy because of the relative importance of Torah, or simply because even two such wonderful things should not be enjoyed at the same time. This made much more sense to me, and the process through which they explained the words and the possible meanings led them to realize that I sincerely appreciated the discussion.

R. Besdin looked at me intently and asked that I leave the room. A few minutes later I was invited back, and both the rabbis seemed serious but relieved. "We are going to admit you to Yeshiva," R. Besdin said. "Thank you," I replied. "We insist on only two things," R. Besdin continued. "First, you must act here as a member of the community. Wear a yarmulke at all times and participate fully in JSP. Second, you are older and more experienced than most of our students. You must give me your word that you will not attempt to influence anyone to turn away from Torah." "Of course," I said, "I give you my word." Not lacking *chutzpah*, I added: "Rabbi, I hope you will also make it financially possible for me to come, as I have no money and my parents cannot afford to help." They both nodded. "You will be able to come," R. Besdin said.

My experience at Yeshiva over the next three years (I had completed a year of college while I was in the Air Force) was even richer than I had hoped. JSP consisted of sixteen hours of classroom work each week, four hours per day from Monday to Thursday. We learned Hebrew, Torah, *dinim*, and some *Mishnah* and *Gemara*. Among the teachers we had was the awesome and inspiring R. David Hartman, who now runs a world-famous institute in Israel. He made the Jewish Holy Days and the very idea of blessings come alive. To this day, I think of him as I bless the bread I eat and every time I drink a beer. A blessing, we learned, is an affirmation of life through a specific act reflecting a particular element of a wonderful world. Each blessing heightens the consciousness and thereby the meaning of the act involved. It was fabulous stuff.

The College also had great teachers, and we all realized they were inadequately paid. Dr. Louis Feldman taught the classics, Latin, Greek, and Ancient History, and his classes were filled with the best students. I recall that Dr. Feldman once debated on the issue whether one can be an observant Jew without a conventional belief in God. He noted the Midrash: "Would that they [the Jews] abandoned Me, but observed My commandments"; he described Judaism as a way of life, not just a set of beliefs. I am sure he made clear that he personally believed in God as Creator. But he clearly had the better of the argument as far as I was concerned.

The professor that meant the most to me was my brilliant and inspirational friend, R. Yitz Greenberg. In 1959, Yitz was a young man just back from Harvard with a PhD in American History. I majored in Yitz, taking a total of twenty-seven credits of his classes (nine courses) in a three-year period. What a privilege. He used his graduate history reading lists, demanded in-depth knowledge, and at the same time continually challenged us with the ethical issues involved in everything we studied. Often accused of being a "liberal" thinker, Yitz in fact has always been skeptical of man's ability to be moral and decent, and for this reason firmly convinced us of the need for existential commitments to fundamental norms and principles. To him, a "self evident" norm (as Jefferson used it) meant a principle that is "obviously necessary" based on humanity's history of inequality, intolerance, and barbarism. He inspired devotion in ideas, but even more in ideals, because, as he taught, the mind can so easily mislead due to its unavoidable attachment to body, with all its irrational power. These lessons resonated with what I was learning about Jewish law, which is derived from mandates based on our experiences as a people. Yitz became my mentor; he presided at my wedding and at virtually every ceremony associated with the birth of my children.

Yeshiva also provided me with fellow students who were outstanding (some ninety-six percent of my class went on to graduate school) and good friends. The Debate Team was my favorite extra-curricular activity, and it didn't hurt to have colleagues there like Gerry Neugeboren, Shlomo Riskin, Murray Laulicht, Abe Gafni, Stuart Berman, Jerry Hornblass, and others, who have all gone on to be important community leaders. The best student during my years at Yeshiva was Henry Krakauer; he not only had a perfect grade-point average, I remember seeing a bulletin from the College Board stating that he had broken the curve on three separate GRE exams (he had answered every question correctly, requiring that the tests be rewritten). Henry went on to contribute greatly to the rational evaluation of medical procedures and their costs, at the National Institutes for Health. My classmate Richard Barnett did amazingly well in all his courses, while holding down a full-time job to support his mother. Dan Krasner and I stayed in touch and studied for the New York bar together. Charles Persky and Herb Bloom were so interesting and creative that I learned as much from listening to their conversations as from my classes. Other friends, like Charlie Maurer, Josh Muss, and Jack Weinberg were superb people who went on to great success as lawyers, doctors, businessmen, and rabbis, among other things.

Finally, YC gave my fellow students and me the opportunity to go on to the very best graduate schools. I was able to win scholarships in history and law, ending up at NYU Law School on a scholarship that paid my tuition, room, and board. This enabled me to compete with my classmates on an equal basis. In fact, Yeshiva gave its students a substantial advantage: the heavy load we carried made the regular law-school curriculum seem relatively easy. Nothing I have done since Yeshiva has compared to the size of the workload I carried for those three years.

In my final year at Yeshiva, an interesting thing happened that took me back to that first interview with R. Besdin and R. Mirsky. Dean Bacon called me in one day and asked me to go on the road as the student representative of the College to speak to Jewish community groups. I never became as observant a Jew as R. Besdin had hoped, but I lived up to my commitments.

My relationship with Yeshiva did not end there. In 1980, President Norman Lamm of Yeshiva University conferred an honorary Doctors of Law degree upon me, and it is clear to me that Yeshiva is very fortunate to have had his leadership. While I have not had many opportunities to go back to the school, I have been a faithful supporter. Most recently, my wife Marian and I were happy to help the College support a young Jew from Burma, Sammy Samuels, who is planning to go back to Rangoon (where my father was born and spent his youth) to keep that small Jewish community alive. I will always be grateful that Yeshiva found a place for me and that it continues that tradition of inclusion and sustenance by finding room for Jews from anywhere who are prepared to learn.

Tribute to My Teachers

By Charles Sheer

The ideological debate that dominated YC when I entered in 1960 set the intellectual parameters of my life, both personally and professionally. "Synthesis" was the buzzword of the campus. Although there were various takes on the nature of each element and their respective places in our lives, synthesis of Torah and modernity was the presumptive Yeshiva *hashkafah*. Our concern was how to do it, not whether the religious life could/should/ must entail a serious engagement with Western Civilization.

The text that encapsulates the challenge (or torment) of that undertaking is the Rambam's responsum to the Provencal scholars of Lunel. This group, led by Rabbeinu Yonatan ha-Kohen, had written in essence a book review of *Mishneh Torah*. Rambam's rejoinder to this group of scholars opens with a magnificent cover-letter in which he declares his passionate life-long devotion to Torah study, the beloved bride of his youth. However, he admits, there have been others who compete for his affection. Various co-wives were brought into the home, initially — he insists — to serve her as assistant cooks, bakers, etc. In the end, the amount of time that remained for "conjugal bliss" with his beloved wife was diminished, "for my heart was divided into many compartments because of various sorts of *hokhmah*."

Rambam's remarkable candor and his willingness to express in public this profound tension gave license to the debate about synthesis. His self-revelatory and startling metaphor rang true even in the 60s. Many of us

Rabbi Charles Sheer, YC '65, BRGS '67, RIETS '67, is the Jewish Chaplain and Director Emeritus of the Hillel at Columbia University and Barnard College, where he served for thirty-four years.

who had been seduced by the worthy charms of the "foreign women" we encountered in Modernity and — to the dismay of some — even in the halls of Yeshiva, found solace in his words. The Rambam does not apologize for his dalliance; these women are "co-wives" who have a place in "her" home. They are not "Women of the Night." But, as in all cases of competing loves, there are only two options; somebody wins/loses or the lover of many remains in constant tension due to multiple competing lovers.

I came to YC from a *yeshiva* in Los Angeles and was assigned to a *shi'ur* taught by R. Dr. Moshe D. Tendler. For the first time in my life, I heard Torah taught by someone who was gifted with profound and encompassing mastery of Talmud and *halakhah* together with similar expertise in the world of science. Here, already in my first year, was a living example of one whose life entailed both Torah and *madda* — literally — and had managed to bridge the gap between these worlds. I wondered what kind of daily conflict he must endure as he elected to close the volume of *Shas* he was studying in order to undertake his scientific research or deliver a biology lecture. As I undertook my struggle between competing worlds, I wondered whether my *rebbe* had worked out some formula to divide his day (and heart) between medical research and Talmud study. The example of R. Tendler — like the Rambam centuries ago — demonstrated to me that is was possible to embrace both worlds and live in both.

In YC, my English professor — Dr. Maurice Wohlgelernter, a RIETS *musmakh* affectionately called "the Reb" — offered another model of successful integration. He was passionate about his teaching and had the reputation for a number of hallmarks. First, he gave failing grades to every freshman for his first few compositions. Second, he would lecture about poets and authors while encircling the classroom desk in some kind of daily *hakafah*. Third, when a student wished to make a point in an exam about a given author, he had to cite a verse or passage from the author. No proof, no points given.

But his contribution to my life was that he taught us how to read a text by examining the language fully and exactingly. When he analyzed a poem, he uncovered the meaning of every metaphor and considered all possible nuances. He emphasized that we needed to interpret the text fully, appreciating and enjoying its artistry. He was enthusiastic about his material and he communicated his love of literature to the class.

Rabbi Dr. Maurice Wohlgelernter was an English professor who taught us to approach literature the way one analyzes a page of Talmud. The result: we learned how to read a text — any text — whether it be secular or holy. Torah and *madda* were both enriched for me because of the Reb's teaching.

The proof of his impact on my life is easily demonstrated. The two volumes of English Lit that I studied with him are a mere arm's-length from the computer at which I write. Next to them is a volume of poetry I used for one of his courses. It is now tattered and torn from use: I used to give poetry readings from this volume in a camp for many years, passing down the *mesorah* from the Reb. And it is probably no accident that the course I am teaching in the university is entitled "The Bible as Literature."

My last two influences were both faculty who were new to Yeshiva in the early 60s. Both were rabbis who had recently finished a PhD at Harvard: R. Aharon Lichtenstein and Dr. Irving "Yitz" Greenberg.

Simply put, I majored in "Yitz" Greenberg, professor of history, at YC. I took every course he gave, especially in American and European intellectual history (one year he created a new course on the Mussar movement which offered a fascinating historical and ideological appreciation). He initiated me to an intellectual journey that has continued life-long by exposing me to thinkers — Jewish and non-Jewish — such as R. Yisrael Salanter, R. Samson Raphael Hirsch, R. Eliezer Berkovits, as well as St. Augustine, Luther, Schleiermacher, Jonathan Edwards, Horace Bushnell, Erich Fromm, and others. Many of these have become part of my interior life. The issues they examined and their varied approaches to living and thinking continue as guides to this day.

I believe I ultimately became a campus rabbi because the university environment was the ideal context to think and work in the world that Yitz Greenberg introduced to me decades ago.

One of the most valuable lessons I learned from R. Yitz was that the conflict between values and ultimate commitments was simply part of the natural course of living as a committed Jew in any age. The challenge of synthesis may be wider and deeper than it was in the world of Maimonides. But, in either case, a vibrant and dynamic Judaism will not only survive, it can thrive and inspire and guide. It can come out quite well, even when compared to whatever is in first place in contemporary society.

My final model — R. Aharon Lichtenstein — inspired my generation at Yeshiva as he has done for countless numbers these past three decades from Israel. I recall the first time I heard him speak in Rubin Lounge at an *oneg Shabbat*. Shabbat on campus was the central socio-religious moment of Yeshiva life in those years. Each Shabbat hundreds of students attended meals, davening, and the various programs that were held. R. Lichtenstein's profundity was apparent, but it was his use of Matthew Arnold and Shakespeare, in conjunction with rabbinic and Talmudic texts, that was unique to my experience. I had never heard a rabbi who was fully conversant in English literature and who used these resources seamlessly in conjunction with traditional Jewish sources.

A student asked R. Lichtenstein a question about his remarks. In his response, R. Lichtenstein asked the student whether he had in mind a particular concept as expressed by author X, or maybe he had in mind the point of view of Y. Now, the eighteen year old student who asked the question had probably never heard of or read these two individuals. But what impressed me was that R. Lichtenstein was genuine in his expectation of his audience. He thought it appropriate to presume that we could have read these texts or that we should see them as part of our world. They belonged in a conversation on Shabbat dealing with a "Jewish" topic because such texts enhance life, and wisdom is wisdom is wisdom. That these thinkers were gentile, possibly distant from religion in general and Judaism in particular, was not an issue so long as their ideas mattered. And that was what was important. That Shabbat talk was over forty years ago, but the impact is still fresh.

Of course, R. Lichtenstein's greatest contribution to my growth was during the three years when I had the privilege of being a member of the *kollel*. I recall the great clarity and order of his *shi'urim*. He demonstrated how to present a page of Talmud or a Rambam from a developmental perspective, focusing on the basic concepts first, and weeding out texts or issues that should be set aside for later treatment. I often recall how, in my preparation for a *haburah*, I had been seduced into focusing on an obvious or interesting aspect of the *sugya*, only to find that he set it aside in his presentation since it was not the central issue to be tackled. When I organize a lecture, I use him as a model.

R. Lichtenstein also served to educate some of us in the methodology of the Rav. Like many in Yeshiva, I strove to gain admission to the Rav's *shi'ur* and, by my senior year, had succeeded. I realized, after two years, that this move was premature, and that what was most appropriate for my growth in learning was basic exposure to more pages of Talmud — straight and unadorned, without the sophisticated conceptual analysis, the grand sweep of Brisker *derekh*. Also, the Rav was a demanding *rebbe* in those years, and I found the atmosphere in the *shi'ur* to be tense. Although I cherish those years in the Rav's world, I found that I did not really get the method of Brisk until exposed to the more structured introduction via R. Lichtenstein. His skills as a pedagogue enabled me to click with this approach during my *semikhah* years in ways that have endured.

R. Lichtenstein was, for me, a crowning presentation of Torah and *madda*. His formative role in my learning during my *kollel* years, together with his love for and utilization of literature to enhance religious thinking and observance, are treasures that have remained with me.

From the start of my college career at Yeshiva through my *semikhah* years, I had the remarkable opportunity to witness Torah and *madda* being incorporated in the lives of outstanding models. These four teachers provided me with interests, commitments and values that shaped my life as a Jew and, ultimately, as a *"rav be-Yisrael."* I remain in their debt as my teachers and models, as I am indebted to Yeshiva University, which provided the context for me to be exposed to such unique personalities.

The *Torah u-Refuah* Continuum

By Robert N. Taub

It has been forty-seven years since I completed my senior year at Yeshiva College, yet until asked to do so, I never thought to review that experience or analyze its contribution to my current career and life attitudes. Yeshiva was my starting point for a lifetime of formal medical and scientific training and teaching, encompassing two doctorates, four subspecialty certifications, four tenured and endowed professorships, and numerous fellowships and investigatorships; yet I know that I never really left, never really completed my Yeshiva education. Thankfully, the anxieties, merciless self-criticism, feelings of inferiority, and justified and unjustified rebellion and anger toward one's teachers are most intense during adolescence and college. These emotions have slowly receded into the shadow of the past, and my *alma mater* now reemerges into daylight, awaiting scrutiny and validation.

It is easiest to assemble my memories of Yeshiva as a scrapbook of visual scenes and sound bites: aging buildings housing an uneven assortment of towering, intense intellectual virtuosos, impresarios, and quieter, scholarly types; cliques of *talmidim* of differing attitudes and degrees of commitment to Torah study; secular teacher-student aggregates of various sizes which continually formed and dissolved, sometimes interacted but rarely synergized. When I dwell upon my sensations as a

Robert N. Taub, MD PhD, YUHS '53, YC '57, is Milstein Family Professor of Clinical Medicine and Director of the Mesothelioma Center at the Columbia University College of Physicians and Surgeons, and Attending Oncologist at the New York Presbyterian Hospital. He is a recipient of an honorary American Cancer Society Professorship of Clinical Oncology, and has received awards from The Israel Cancer Research Fund, The Leukemia Society of America, the Mount Sinai Hospital, and the U.S. Public Health Service.

college student, I automatically recall specific rabbis and professors and how a new insight suddenly flashed during their classes or discussions. It is tempting to substitute these sharply remembered experiences for a more considered reflection upon the general atmosphere of the university and how it came to shape my later years. I do have vivid memories of R. Yeruham Gorelik, whose incisiveness and biting iconoclastic wit could not hide his profound love and respect for all serious intellectual strivings, and whose personal encouragement of my medical training was enormously helpful. Professor Herman Wouk stood out for his lengthy handwritten-in-red-ink critiques of my weekly sermon writing exercises, which convinced me forever of the power of precise language and the need for multiple drafts of manuscripts and thoughts.

Yet this kind of deconstruction, studying the most colorful fish in the aquarium, tells little about the ocean that spawns them. Yeshiva is a miraculous paradox compounded of many essences: the Italianate golden-domed Washington Heights edifice that masks the *mesirat nefesh* that went into its maintenance, the complex collective consciousness of the students and graduates that currently inhabit it, the forceful initiative of those who have gone forth into the world with its message, the cold wind of the secular world that creeps in through every crack. The Yeshiva campus was and still very much is the site of the intellectual "big bang" of Modern Orthodoxy. Yeshiva's ideas have expanded exponentially to fill the Jewish universe with energetic religious constructs and ethical life forces.

My interest since the age of twelve had been focused on the natural sciences, and I squeezed as many as I could from Yeshiva's curriculum; premedical studies were a forgone conclusion. In my time, YC was strong in mathematics, but had only begun to focus on biology. The advent of AECOM had galvanized many Yeshiva students towards medicine, so that even without a full array of laboratory facilities or science courses, we were strongly motivated to acquire the necessary knowledge and technical skills for admission to medical school. Despite the drawbacks, Yeshiva provided an ideal scholarly environment for me. Its atmosphere was permeated with a deep commitment to all serious inquiry. It permitted and encouraged an omnivorous intellectual curiosity that simultaneously and routinely digested advanced Torah study and advanced organic chemistry. The discourses in different classes would jump from Rambam to Rameau, from *tzitzit* flying in the wind to tsetse flies in the African summer, from chemical bonds between two atoms of carbon to calendar adjustments based on testimony of two Jews gazing at the moon. The term "synthesis," attributed to R. Dr. Bernard Revel, was often used at that time to describe Yeshiva's program and its goals, but had never been precisely defined. It had come to be defined ostensibly by showcasing graduates versed in both Torah and worldly data. Needless to say, they had acquired each in a different classroom and had not necessarily mixed or used them together.

Though several of my rabbis were inclined toward a parochial view of *Torah u-Madda* — namely that secular wisdom was significant only in so far as it enhanced the ability to learn Torah — I envisioned a broader role for such synthesis. And while I was admonished in morning *Gemara* class, admittedly in jest, not to strive for higher than a passing grade of seventy on any of the secular tests given during the afternoon, I knew, groaningly, that grades a lot higher than a mediocre seventy would be needed to become a physician. But I felt impelled to become a physician. Throughout college I remained deeply drawn to all things biological and all things scientific. Anti-Semitic quotas had just begun to fade, replaced by a grudging but significant acceptance of Jews to careers at the best American medical schools. I was the first to be accepted directly from YC to the Yale University School of Medicine; a classmate was the first to enter Harvard Medical School.

I felt no inconsistency between my religious beliefs and what I was learning in college classes. I am not sure whether at that time I was actually able to keep the rules and postulates of both in my brain simultaneously without conflict, or whether I sensed that there might be a conflict but refused to act on it. For whatever reason, I was able to allow both Torah and *madda* to coexist in a single mindset, much like an English infant brought up in China that learns to speak both languages fluently. I unquestionably owe this to the time spent living and thinking as a student in YC and learning daily to embrace complexity and paradox. As R. Norman Lamm put it, "...we consider that it is the will of God that there be a world in which Torah be effective; that all wisdom issues ultimately from the Creator, and therefore it is the Almighty who legitimizes all knowledge."

I have come to appreciate the enormous present value of the catalytic milieu provided so long ago by Yeshiva within which my ideas could mix and coexist. There are several practicing medical oncologists among Yeshiva's graduates, and the training at Yeshiva allowed us later in our careers to develop concepts of medical patient management, practical patient care, and medical ethics within a framework of modern Jewish Orthodoxy. Problems regarding end-of-life management, resuscitation and intubation, definition of death, and subjecting the patient to experimental treatment arise continually in my practice as a senior medical oncologist at Columbia University Medical Center. All of the halakhic aspects of these issues are predicated upon accurate medical information regarding prognosis, extent of suffering and the natural history, etiology, and pathogenesis of individual diseases. Conversely, what is not as well understood is that oncologic care is best rendered when its provider comprehends the relevant halakhic principles.

A great contemporary *posek* permitted a young man who had just been diagnosed with Hodgkin's disease to donate his sperm to a sperm bank in advance of receiving powerful intravenous chemotherapy for his disease. Although such donations ordinarily are halakhically forbidden, the *posek* was provided with the medical opinion that if prevented from doing so, the patient might erroneously conclude that his doctors were anticipating that he would not survive to have children. This, in turn, could cause that person to approach his treatment with a less than fully enthusiastic and positive mental attitude. This ruling is an example of how current analytical tools can be brought to bear on a difficult medical/ halakhic problem and allow satisfactory resolution to be reached.

The skill level of the physician can be no less determined by his medical knowledge as by his Torah erudition. In the *Torah u-Madda* universe, the spheres of medicine and *halakhah* do not and cannot exist as separate planets. Each is an infinite dimension that helps define the measure of the other, and the effectiveness of the Modern Orthodox physician depends upon his ability to function within such a continuum.

In his last letter, Maimonides, who continued to study Torah and heal the sick until the last days of his life, wrote in the year 1200:

> There is one thing, however, I should like to share with you, Rabbi Jonathan and all your colleagues who read my works. Although from my childhood the study and dissemination of Torah and Talmud have been my major preoccupation to which, as it were, I was betrothed as the "wife" of my youth in whose love I found constant delight, "strange women" from Moab, Ammon, Edom, Sidon, and Heth whom I first took into my house to serve as my wife's handmaid have become nevertheless her rivals and take up much of my time. While the beauty and charm of my "wife"

continued to enchant my heart, I was at the same time distracted
by a variety of disciplines and sciences.

My undergraduate experience at YC allowed and encouraged me to
develop many types of Judaic and scientific rational thought. This has led
to lifetime enjoyment of the gifts afforded by both.

Reb David — Ha-Rav David Lifshitz:
An Intimate Portrait

By Chaim I. Waxman

This is anything but an objective portrait. R. David Lifshitz was, after all, my *rebbe* and my father-in-law with whom I was very, very close. And yet, I hope that what follows is not too far from the mark and will offer some insight into the significant role he played at Yeshiva University for almost fifty years. I begin with a brief biographical sketch.

R. David Lifshitz was born in Minsk, Russia, in 1906. In 1919, his family moved to Grodno, where he was a student of the famed R. Shimon Shkop at his *yeshiva*, Sha'arei Torah. He later studied in the Mirrer Yeshiva, where he received *semikhah* and stayed until 1932. In 1933, he married Cipora Joselovitz, the daughter of the renowned rabbi of Suwalk (a provincial capital in northwest Poland/Russia), R. Joseph Joselovitz. Upon the untimely death of his father-in-law in 1935, R. Lifshitz became chief rabbi of the city and its twenty-seven congregations, and he developed the reputation of being a warm, involved spiritual leader, concerned with not only his own congregants but with all Jews; until his death he served as president of Suwalki Benevolent Society in the United States.

In the autumn of 1939, when war broke out and Jews were being rounded up by the Germans, R. Lifshitz chose to stay with his community even though he had several opportunities to leave. After the death of his infant child, however, the city's Jews compelled him to escape. He, his wife, and surviving daughter ultimately secured a U.S. visa, traveling

Dr. Chaim I. Waxman, YC' 63, BRGS '65, RIETS '66, is Professor of Sociology and Jewish Studies at Rutgers University.

through the Soviet Union to Honolulu and then to the U.S. mainland.

From 1941 to 1942, he and his family lived in New York; they then moved to Chicago, where he was a *rosh yeshiva* at the Hebrew Theological College until 1944. During World War II, he was active in Va'ad Hatzalah, the official Jewish rescue organization.

Dr. Belkin actively sought to have R. Lifshitz join the RIETS faculty and, in 1944, he came to RIETS as a *rosh yeshiva*, occupying a position that his mentor, R. Shimon Shkop, had filled twelve years earlier as a visiting *rosh yeshiva*. He taught upper-level *shi'urim*, primarily in *masekhtot Kiddushin, Gittin, Ketuvot, Shabbat,* and *Hulin.*

In many respects, Reb David, as he was affectionately known, helped preserve the old Eastern European *yeshiva* tradition at RIETS. He had a full beard, dressed in the traditional garb, spoke in Yiddish, and his *shi'urim* consisted of detailed examinations of the *Gemara* as well as the opinions of the major *rishonim* and *aharonim* on the topic discussed. He also had a distinct stature to his presence. He was always meticulously dressed and he walked in a princely manner.

Reb David was a constant presence at Yeshiva. He lived nearby and, from the time he moved in, the *beit midrash* was also where he davened. He was at his regular seat in the corner alongside the *aron kodesh* every morning and evening. Indeed, he was typically among the first to arrive before *shaharit* and among the last leave after *ma'ariv.*

He manifested a unique combination of Lithuanian *yeshiva* intellect and spirituality. In addition to his *beki'ut,* encyclopedic knowledge of Talmud and Halakhic literature, he was a very spiritual person. This manifested itself most clearly in his highly inspiring *tefilot* in the *beit midrash,* especially during the *Yamim Nora'*im. His awe-inspiring rendition of *Avinu Malkenu* on Yom Kippur is unforgettable. The same holds true for the way his entire body shook as he shook the *lulav* and *etrog* during the *Sukkot tefilot.*

Reb David is probably best-remembered as an incredibly warm individual who was genuinely concerned with the well-being of every *talmid* in the *yeshiva.* I recall numerous occasions when he would stop students on the street and tell them that they shouldn't go out without a jacket in the cold of the winter.

His home was always open to his students, and he concerned himself not only with their performance in his class but with every aspect of their lives. Many would consult with him about every conceivable personal question, and he genuinely shared in their all of their achievements and losses.

On the evenings of *Hanukah* and *Purim*, *hagigot* for students, present and past — once you were his *talmid*, you were always his *talmid* — were held in his home. The tables were filled with refreshments prepared by my mother-in-law, and the students would talk and sing together for hours. Reb David would have each student there sing a line from one of the songs he selected, and then he gave an inspiring *sihah*, a talk which usually lasted for close to an hour.

Though he had his own *hagigot*, he was always present at those held in the *beit midrash* for the entire student body of the *yeshiva*, and he would always lead the singing and dancing there.

Every year, on *Rosh Hodesh Adar*, he would have signs posted in the hall near the *beit midrash* announcing the annual *Hatmadah* Drive, his personal campaign to encourage the *talmidim* in the *yeshiva* to learn more. His primary focus was always on sacred learning.

Throughout his years at RIETS, he also played a leadership role in communal affairs, especially in Agudath HaRabbanim, Union of Orthodox Rabbis, and Ezrat Torah. These activities added further to the presence of the old *yeshivishe* world and RIETS.

At the same time, Reb David was quite progressive, especially for someone with his background. When, in the 1960s, he realized that most of his students did not understand Yiddish, he stopped giving his *shi'urim* in that language. However, in contrast to other *rebbeim* in RIETS, he gave them in Hebrew. Many were very surprised to learn that he was fluent in *Ivrit*; many are unaware that at the age of twelve, he co-authored a commentary on *Mishlei* and *Daniel*, together with his childhood friend, Avraham Rosenshtein, who later Hebraicized his name as Even-Shoshan and authored the most important Hebrew dictionary of the twentieth century.

Few are aware that Reb David was fluent in Hebrew literature and poetry, and that he was able to engage in conversation with students at TI on material they studied in their classes. I vividly recall one day in the summer of the early 1980s, when I drove him from Jerusalem, that he burst out in praise of the view by reciting a poem on the subject by none other than Hayim Nahman Bialik.

After the establishment of the State of Israel, Reb David was active in guiding the relationship of American Orthodoxy to Israel. In the early

1950s, he helped create the movement in Israel for a coalition of all religious elements, both Zionist and non-Zionist. The high esteem which he enjoyed in all religious circles enabled him to help establish the *Hazit Datit* (United Religious Front), which ran on a single slate for the Israeli parliamentary elections.

Eretz Yisrael and *Medinat Yisrael* were among his greatest loves throughout his adult life. His first visit there was in 1952 and, in later years, he spent almost every summer and more there, and he frequently began his first *shi'ur* of the academic year with reminiscences of his latest stay in Israel and with a song of love for the country.

Reb David was the unique embodiment of that very special elite type of leader who combined or synthesized, if you will, the role of *rosh yeshiva* and the role of *rav*. Even as *rosh yeshiva*, he was known as the Suvalker Rav. He never relinquished that title. Nor did he ever relinquish his dedication to the rabbinate and his total dedication in carrying out the duties of a *rav*.

Although Reb David encouraged students to continue learning and, ideally, to become either *rebbeim* in *yeshivot* or shul rabbis, he understood that not everyone was cut out for those positions. When he sensed that a student was not going to enter those sacred positions, he encouraged him to do well in his general studies, to go to graduate school, and to be become the best professional he could while, of course, not forsaking regular sacred learning.

Finally, he was a model of beautiful behavior in his interactions with his neighbors, Jewish and not. Anyone who saw him in his many daily walks from his house to the *yeshiva* could not but be impressed with his warm greeting of everyone he met along the way, in his building, on the street, and in the *yeshiva* buildings. His very presence and demeanor were a true *kiddush Hashem* and a rare model.

How fortunate were we to have known him. To know him was to love him and to be loved by him.

Man Thinks; God Laughs

By Howard Wettstein

I wish I could say that I applied to YC in 1960 because of a desire to learn Torah. The truth is that it was a good school, better than my record deserved, and my father urged me to consider Yeshiva rather than the other places to which I had been accepted. Given my spotty record in high school, he probably didn't trust my going away to school and, as he said, it would not hurt to learn something about my religion. I met R. Moshe Besdin for an interview and agreed (without great enthusiasm) that I would observe what was required were I to be admitted to the Jewish Studies Program. Not a promising beginning.

And then the strangest thing happened. I came to campus and found, from the first day, something completely unexpected. It began with R. Besdin's *Humash* class. A serious, devout man, he was altogether warm and wonderful, a person who loved his students, loved the text beyond words, and whose mission it was to make a *shiddukh* between the two. The other thing he loved were good, tough questions, the tougher the better, as long — and this was really important — as they were serious and sincere. And I discovered, with his help, my mind and my spirit.

I had lived as a suburban American secular Jew, entirely bored by high school, neither an athlete nor a scholar, and hardly a player in the social world of my school. The contrast was almost unbelievable. In JSP, I found something I loved thinking about, Judaism, the Bible, the tradition. The proverbial treasure was all along right under my bed.

Over the next six months, I found myself enthusiastically adopting

Dr. Howard Wettstein, YC '65, RIETS '65, is Professor of Philosophy and Director of the University Honors Program, University of California, Riverside.

traditional observance. I remember sheepishly asking R. Besdin whether I should wear *tzitzit*. Trying now to reconstruct the question, I think I was asking whether I was getting ahead of myself. Mine was a slow, steady movement under R. Besdin's wise influence towards more and more rigorous practice. He looked at me quizzically and said "Of course." Perhaps I was a bit late on that one.

One of Yeshiva's great gifts to me was the sense that I had found a home, a community. It is a gift for which I will always be grateful, and R. Besdin was the first of many benefactors. That year we began to study *Mishnah* with a man who could have passed for Clark Gable, R. Moshe Chait. I don't remember very well *Mishnah* with R. Chait — the memory merges with the later study of *Gemara* with him, a wondrous thing. *Gemara*, I've often thought, is perfect training for analytic philosophy, and it was especially so with R. Chait, a stunningly clear thinker and expositor. I can still hear him responding to our conjectures about what did and did not make sense: "I'm not so sure about that." He taught us what to ask and how to ask, and his love for learning was contagious.

R. Chait's way in learning had much to do with his background at the highly analytical Hafetz Hayim Yeshiva. I've met people critical of that approach; it's sometimes said to be plodding. But the clarity about such difficult and subtle matters seemed worth everything. Yeshiva guys have all heard *mussar* about how one "does not die from a question." But I learned to appreciate good questions in a new way, to take pleasure just from seeing a new problem, or an old one, in a new way. Although I could not have put it this way at that time, I was learning to ask *Tosafot's* questions, quite a worthy ambition.

So far I've spoken only about JSP, about my mornings at Yeshiva. I can't say that I felt any great enthusiasm for my early college courses. Success meant medical school, and I was doing adequately, but only adequately. Evenings on the other hand, like mornings, were something special. To explain this, I need to say more about my religious development. While I was very much taken with learning and observance, I remained deeply troubled by belief. Granted that the religious life was sweet and so much more, was I doing the right thing? I sometimes think of this as a bad case of epistemic conscience. Granted that the beliefs worked for my life, were they true? Was there evidence that verified them? And if not, was I no better than the guy across town at say, Fordham, who had quite different beliefs?

Sydney Goldenberg was a visiting student from Toronto, an Orthodox Jew who came to spend a year at YC. Syd was a philosophy major — a brilliant guy and a charismatic person. We must have spent hundreds of hours talking in Rubin Dorm. It was almost as amazing as what I was getting in the mornings at JSP, in this case an introduction to philosophy, a new world of thought, one in which rigor and discipline could really make a difference. How could I have lived on this earth and not known of these things?

Over the next couple of years, I became a philosophy major, taking all the courses of another benefactor, Alexander Litman. Dr. Litman was an original. He was a gadfly, not a religious Jew but one who had clearly studied Talmud, at least enough to construct wonderful jokes, poking fun at the tradition in a way that, to me, was never offensive. Litman had a unique way of teaching philosophy. We learned less philosophy than we might have, but we learned to love and revere the subject. Equally important, Dr. Litman engendered a feel for the serious questions and an orientation in philosophy, one that still seems to me sound.

Back to the mornings: In my sophomore year I moved up from the "B" class, for beginners (where I deservedly started), to the "A" class. I started learning *Gemara* with R. Chait. I also began to seek out experienced RIETS students with whom to learn. With some, I was able to help with the analytical aspect, while they were linguistically, of course, much stronger. With others (one I remember with great fondness was R. Michael Hecht), I was not able to give them anything except the presence of a young man who loved the learning and was very grateful for the help.

After my sophomore year, I decided to spend the summer learning. I was to work part-time, and I lined up a *havrutah* in my community. My late father, Hy Wettstein — who passed away at ninety-two years of age last year — was the MTA basketball coach for some thirty years. He founded the NYC Jewish High School Basketball league and taught Physical Education courses at YC during that period. My father respected my desire to study, but he was a great believer in balance, in what he would have called well-roundedness. It seemed to him a bit too much to spend the summer indoors rather than work at a camp where I could get away from the constrictions of the rigorous Yeshiva program. The resolution was that my father was to speak with R. Besdin, whom my father greatly respected (and I think this held the other way around as well). The problem was that R. Besdin was also a practical man, a person of considerable balance. My father (unbelievably) convinced my teacher that I should go to camp. I played my trump card. If my father would agree to talk to one more of my teachers, R. Chait, I would agree to do whatever the consensus was. I learned that summer with my father's blessing. And I love the story.

After three years in JSP, R. Besdin and R. Chait thought I was ready to move into RIETS. It was with great anticipation and a sense of great privilege that I joined the *shi'ur* of R. Aharon Lichtenstein. I vividly remember the first day, preparing carefully and hearing the first question R. Lichtenstein asked about the text. I heard his question and thought — it's as if I'm there right now — "I need to stay here for awhile and I'll learn to think." As is well-known, my *rebbe* was blessed with a terrific mind (including, but not limited to, encyclopedic knowledge), with substantial pedagogical gifts, and a human character easily as impressive. What a model for one who aspired to teach! I mentioned that I can still hear R. Chait's characteristic "I'm not so sure about that." Equally vivid is a remark characteristic of R. Lichtenstein: "Good. You are right and I am wrong." To say this with pleasure seemed to me the mark of a real teacher.

During the two years with R. Lichtenstein, I had a sense of substantial growth in learning and even more of how little I knew and how much there was to learn. But this was fine; I was setting out on a course that was to take a lifetime. I also developed something of a feel for the Brisker *derekh* in learning. Some of the brilliant distinctions provided still another level of clarity and of learning.

There were times that I understood the halakhic consequences of the Brisker distinctions better than I understood the distinctions themselves. For example, the basic distinction between *issur heftza* and *issur gavra*. There is no question that many halakhic consequences flow from the distinction. But I couldn't quite get clear about the distinction itself. Was it metaphysical, an actual difference in the (spiritual?) constitution of the object or of the person? Or was it something more legal?

This sort of theoretical worry, so pressing to me, made sense to some who knew much more than me, and to others it made no sense at all. And I predict that some readers will have one reaction and some the other. There is a similar sort of issue in philosophy, a basic methodological distinction between the ways of Plato and Aristotle. Plato makes distinctions that prove their worth, some maintain, by the intellectual work they do; for example, he distinguishes between the Form (or Idea) and the items in the world that exemplify the Form. Even though Plato explains a great deal with his apparatus, other philosophers find the whole thing quite baffling, as I do. What is Plato talking about? What exactly are Forms? The Aristotelian way is to resist such distinctions, such posits, until one is clear about what one is positing. Some philosophers just don't get Plato's distinctions; some just don't get Aristotle's questions.

I used to go to various people for help with such things, to my *rebbe*, to a wonderful, learned young rabbi in Brooklyn, Dennis J. Weiss who later, I think, became a *rosh yeshiva* at Touro, to R. Parnes at RIETS, and to R. Chait. But whatever my worries about these things, my *rebbe* and his introduction to the Brisker way made for growth in learning that was more than I could have dreamed of just a few years before.

After my fifth and final year at Yeshiva, I was to enter the *semikhah* program and the *Kollel*. I spent the intervening summer at Camp Morasha, in the *Kollel*, teaching *Gemara*, playing inept basketball, and obsessively thinking about theological fundamentals. Various circumstances had enlivened the theological issues that were with me since my beginnings at YC. They had never been entirely resolved, but they had gone dormant as my learning and involvement developed.

I have a colleague who says that obsessiveness, the ability to go over and over an argument or line of thought way beyond what would seem natural to most people, is a virtue in philosophy. About my theological concerns I was obsessively obsessive. When it began to appear hopeless that I would find a positive resolution, I became more obsessive, thinking, as it were, that I had to convince God of my doubts. When I say hopeless, I don't mean that the process was somehow depressing. It was an exciting time of life, having achieved something in my learning and feeling strong enough to question what I felt that I had to question.

In the end, I could not resolve my doubts. I had talks with R. Lichtenstein and R. Chait and R. Besdin. And I deeply appreciated their *hessed*; they obviously cared. Were I to leave, this would cause pain to my teachers — there was no question about that. But I never had the sense from them that that was the issue; they cared about me and never doubted that my process was an honest one. On the one hand, no one could help resolve my concerns, but on the other, the process made the tradition, the community and its values even more impressive. The last thing R. Besdin said to me — I will never forget it — was that I should come back to talk with him, "if not about religion, about philosophy."

Looking back I think that leaving was not as hard for me as it might have been for others, especially those who were, so to speak, born to the tradition. I had only five years or so of immersion, and powerful as it was, I was returning to a world I knew well, and returning from a position of strength and achievement.

But the moment I entered that world it took on a new coloration. The world of academic philosophy was, with important exceptions, a relatively cold and competitive world, a world of *mahloket* that was often not *le-shem shamayim*. I loved the work and the ideas, and I found friends who were serious about philosophy and supportive, but the environment was not my natural habitat.

My career in philosophy has been, by many measures, quite successful. I am a professor in a fine department, one that I helped build. I've edited books and published my own work, just last year a book with Oxford University Press. I've been privileged to work on ideas and issues that are intellectually fundamental, as philosophy promised to be. And teaching is all that I hoped it would be; there are days that I'm incredulous that they pay us money to do what is so pleasurable. At the same time, the world of academic philosophy is a relatively cold one, hardly the world of the *beit midrash*.

Some ten or twelve years ago, in my mid-late forties, something began to change. I began to read poetry, something that my strong analytic bent seemed to preclude earlier. I felt a renewed longing for intellectual and spiritual community. My mother died, a cataclysmic event, and *kaddish* brought consolation. For reasons quite extraneous, I made my first trip to Israel, for a philosophy conference in honor of a UCLA professor to whom I felt quite indebted.

On this trip, I made contact with the formative influences on my life, R. Lichtenstein and R. Chait. I had not seen R. Lichtenstein since my wedding to Barbara Lipner in 1969 at which he was the *mesader kiddushin*, a recollection that always leaves me breathless; in 1969, I was long gone from Yeshiva and no longer observant. Seeing him again was, as always, a sort of awe-inspiring thing. His personal qualities were very striking in light of my experiences in academia. He invited my family to come over very early one Sunday morning before he went off to the Gush, and we all sat and talked. For my children to meet my *rebbe* was another gift, the power of which is beyond any words I can muster.

Since that time, I have had something of the sense I had all those years ago in JSP. I started to return to observance, something that was made much easier by the fact that Barbara had remained observant throughout. As at Yeshiva, my involvement picked up steam as I began to reconnect with learning. This latter process was difficult; finding the right *havrutah*, for one who had learned seriously but had forgotten so much, turned out to be much more difficult in the "real world" than it was at Yeshiva. But R. Chait, hearing of the difficulty from my friend R. Yitzhak Frank, made a *shiddukh* with a young *rebbe*, a RIETS graduate, R. Menachem Diamond, at the Hafetz Hayim Yeshiva in Jerusalem, and we have been learning every summer for some years now. The learning, with various people here and there and anywhere I can find them, adds immeasurably to my life, now as it did in the early 60s; it's probably the most difficult and most satisfying thing I have ever done. A friend of mine, observing my strange path, recalled the Yiddish line that translates roughly as "Man thinks, God laughs."

From Olyphant, PA to Washington Heights, NY

By Leon Wildes

My college studies were scheduled to begin at St. Thomas Aquinas University, the University of Scranton, on the following Monday. On Thursday night, my father received a telephone call from his brother-in-law during which my dad mentioned my recent graduation from Olyphant High School — the only Jew in the graduating class of one hundred in the small mining town in Pennsylvania where I was raised.

"Are you really going to send him to study with priests in Scranton, like his older brother? You know that as a Jewish father you have an obligation to give your son a Jewish education." My dad protested that his sons were really not *yeshiva* boys, but the trusted brother-in-law, who had assisted my dad in coming to the United States thirty years earlier, explained that his sons also went to a college and continued their religious study at the same time under one roof at YC. That was the first time that we had ever heard of Yeshiva.

My father instructed me to collect my report card and proof of the honors I had received at graduation while he visited his teacher and mentor, R. Henry Guterman of Scranton, to collect a reference letter. Next thing I knew, we boarded a passenger train from Scranton at 3:00 pm. In New York, we were met by my cousin Joseph Sokolow, whose father made the fateful telephone call. He drove us to his alma mater in Washington Heights, where we proceeded to have some unscheduled

Mr. Leon Wildes, YC '54, is the founder of Wildes & Weinberg, P.C. in New York and is an adjunct Professor of Law at the Benjamin N. Cardozo School of Law in New York, where he teaches immigration law.

meetings with Morris Silverman, Registrar of the College, and Dr. Pinkhos Churgin, dean of the TI.

Mr. Silverman tried to be helpful, but he felt that he would have to investigate the quality of my high school education when I told him that Pennsylvania schools did not have Regents exams. Dr. Churgin addressed me in Hebrew for at least five minutes as I sat at his desk. When he stopped, awaiting my response, I told him that I had not understood a word that he said, but that I would certainly love to learn Hebrew and all the other subjects taught in the Institute. I had been duly impressed with the entire institution; I watched Dr. Churgin excuse himself from his Hebrew monologue with me to rise and greet my father as he entered the room, and I was similarly impressed with the man's character.

What resulted, back in 1950, was a kind of experiment in which I and nine other students were provisionally accepted to the college upon the hopeful condition that we would qualify for admittance to either TI, where classes were conducted entirely in Hebrew, or to RIETS for a more concentrated pre-rabbinic study of Talmud.

I returned home that Sunday night with my father and called my friend, who was to have started school with me the next day. I told him that I had changed my mind and would not be attending the University of Scranton. He eventually dropped out of school and took a job selling jewelry, which brought him to New York. On his visits to New York, he would generally stay in my dorm room and he, too, learned to appreciate what went on at YC.

All ten of us were accepted as full students at either RIETS or TI. I had chosen TI and began my studies with high school students much younger than I, but I advanced a full year each semester until I had mastered the Hebrew language and was with students my own age. During that fateful initial semester, we spent our mornings under the tutelage of R. David Mirsky, a brilliant and kind teacher, and Joe Sokolow's brother-in-law, who was a professor both at the college and the Jewish studies department. At the end of the semester, all of us were accepted into our respective departments and stayed on to graduate from YC. The group included students who were to become doctors, dentists, Conservative and Orthodox rabbis, as well as myself, a lawyer. One of us ultimately became a rabbi who teaches Talmud at Yeshiva to this day. In essence, we were the experimental forerunners of the JSP, and I shall be ever grateful for the influence which Yeshiva has had in my life.

The college dorm was a drab and dreary place. Rooms had cold concrete floors and no one ever thought to carpet them. One could catch pneumonia trying to take a shower in the fourth floor communal shower/bathroom. Those of us, the losers, who were not invited out for Shabbat and had to spend our weekends in the dorms, generally bought food to make our own meals. The fact that we did so comments loudly upon the unfortunate state of the food served in the dining hall on Shabbat. There was never a Shabbat program, a visiting faculty member, or any other significant activity other than the *minyan* we ran on our own; it was not an encouraging thought to anticipate spending Shabbat in the dormitory at Yeshiva. Despite all this, I loved the joint program at YC, had an opportunity to get close to both my professors in the college and TI, and gained immeasurably from the whole experience.

I no longer have any personal relationship with anyone from Olyphant. My parents have passed on and the little Jewish community seems to have also disappeared. I stayed on in New York to attend law school, marry, and establish a home and a professional life, largely with the friends I made at YC. My college experience thus became the foundation of my new life. It was no surprise that at the recent fiftieth anniversary party of the YC class of 1954, practically every face was still a familiar one.

I found it only natural to continue my interest at YC after my graduation. Although I took two degrees in law at NYU, it was Cardozo School of Law where I chose to apply for a teaching position, and I have continued that association as an Adjunct Professor for twenty-five years now. Before the college even had a board of directors, I joined its Undergraduate Advisory Council and became active in working with YC students. Because of my own experience, my interest was clearly in the area of student life, and I now chair the Student Life Committee of the Board of Directors of YC. This provides me with one of my main sources of gratification; it permits me to visit the campus occasionally, to meet with student leaders, and to be involved in the active Shabbat program that now exists.

When I attended the college, the list of graduate areas of study that YC offered was quite short. We had no school psychologist to counsel us, no placement center to help us find jobs, no athletic center, and none of the other programs and facilities which are now an integral part of the school's offerings. What we did have, however, was the abundant support and camaraderie of a small but warm student body and an accessible, supportive faculty and administration. Notwithstanding its expanded size, those ingredients are all still present today.

"Mr. Yeshiva" Almost Always Kept His Hat On

By Efraim Zuroff

It would be hard to imagine a more dramatic departure. Standing in front of the *aron kodesh*, facing a packed *beit midrash* as the presiding officer at the 1962/5722 *Hag ha-Semikhah* marking the ordination of thirty new RIETS *musmakhim*, Dean Samuel L. Sar introduced Yeshiva President Samuel Belkin and promptly dropped dead of a heart attack.

This type of drama was hardly the sort which Dean Sar would have chosen had he been able to orchestrate a proper farewell from the institution to which he devoted practically his entire adult life. A no-nonsense Litvak who eschewed theatrics and empty gestures, he never would have even imagined such a scenario, let alone arranged the star role for himself. On the other hand, his dramatic exit seemed to fulfill his own prophecy. Asked once by Dr. Belkin when he planned to retire from his positions as YC Dean of Men and Professor of Bible, having reached the age of sixty-seven and having already suffered a severe heart attack, Sar replied, according to one version, that he would not leave voluntarily and "would have to be taken out on a stretcher."

The inner contradictions of the multi-faceted life of Shmuel Leib (Samuel) Sar were obvious to those who played leading roles in creating Yeshiva University and shared his vision for Yeshiva and modern Orthodoxy in America. He combined Eastern European Torah scholarship with a

Dr. Efraim Zuroff, YUHS '66, YC '70, is the director of the Israel Office of the Simon Wiesenthal Center and the Center's chief Nazi-hunter. His pioneer study of the Vaad ha-Hatzala, The Response of Orthodox Jewry in the United States to the Holocaust: The Activities of the Vaad ha-Hatzala Rescue Committee 1939-1945 *was awarded Yeshiva University's Samuel Belkin Literary Award in 2000. Dr. Zuroff is Dean Sar's eldest grandson.*

love of *Tanakh* and the Hebrew language, a penchant for academia with a life-long career in administration, an appreciation for the advantages of America with a passionate commitment to religious Zionism and the welfare of the State of Israel, and a concern for his own family with an overriding sense of obligation and responsibility for the greater good of *Klal Yisrael* that forced him to travel overseas for lengthy periods to Jewish communities all over the world.

This was, for example, the main theme of the impassioned eulogy which R. Joseph B. Soloveitchik delivered at Dean Sar's funeral, held in Lamport auditorium the day after his demise. The Rav spoke about the dichotomy between the *keri* and the *ketiv* of a *Sefer Torah*, representing a person's exterior, his visual public image (*keri*) and his emotions, thoughts, and internal essence (*ketiv*). In the case of Dean Sar, there was a chasm between his image and his true interior; this marked his greatness, but it also had a tragic dimension. The Rav likened Dean Sar to the story of the Book of Ruth, which is full of contradictions since it lacks any halakhic directives but was included nonetheless in the *Tanakh* because of its preoccupation, from beginning to end, with *hessed*, deeds of human kindness. So, too, Dean Sar presented a detached, somewhat cynical exterior, but was in fact a person who was imbued with a deep love for the students, someone who had literally helped thousands of students and enabled them to continue and complete their educations — and did so in secret. But besides that, Dean Sar was also a creative and imaginative innovator who applied his numerous talents and natural charisma for the good of the Jewish people rather than for his own personal gain, a person who was always striving to improve and to achieve, a person who, as the Rav phrased it, "had the strength not to be smug or self-satisfied." And it was those wonderful characteristics of his complicated personality that the Rav said he would miss so much.

Shmuel Leib Sar was born on *Shushan Purim* 1893 in Ligmiany, which at the time was part of the Czarist empire, but which straddled the Polish-Lithuanian border after World War I and became famous as the place where Jews from Poland and Lithuania (which for many years did not maintain diplomatic relations or permit border crossings) were allowed to meet one day a year — on *Tisha be-Av*. Shmuel Leib was the oldest of six boys, who subsequently scattered all over the world; the exception was his youngest brother Efraim, a well-known *illui* who learned with the Hafetz Hayim in Radin and ultimately became a *rosh yeshiva* at one of the *yeshivot* of the Novardok network in eastern Poland. Efraim, his wife Beyla, and two sons, Hirsch and Eliyahu, were murdered in Vilna, where they had fled to together with his *yeshiva* shortly after the invasion of Poland. Dean Sar was able to help obtain entry permits to Shanghai for the family in mid-May 1941, but they were never utilized due to the Nazi invasion of Lithuania on June 22, 1941.

As a young child, Shmuel Leib was sent to learn in the nearby *yeshiva* at Vidz, from which he moved on to Ponevezh and later to a branch of Telz at Shaduva. In Shaduva, he learned for more than five years with R. Yosef Bloch, son-in-law of the noted R. Eliezer Gordon. Sar received *semikhah* and then set out on the unique journey that ultimately led him to his life's work. During the decade prior to World War I, R. Mayer Tzvi Jung sought to prepare Lithuanian-trained *yeshiva* students to serve as rabbis for communities in the Austro-Hungarian Empire. Shmuel Sar was one of the students whom R. Jung sent to Vienna to pursue a rigorous program combining a morning of learning *Yoreh De'ah* with an afternoon devoted to secular studies. Shmuel later followed Jung to London when the latter was appointed Chief Rabbi, but ultimately chose to immigrate to the United States, arriving in Baltimore in 1914. Shmuel Sar's first job was as superintendent of a network of *Talmud Torahs*; despite strong opposition, he introduced Talmud as part of the curriculum. Simultaneously, he undertook undergraduate studies at Johns Hopkins University and Mount Vernon Collegiate Institute and began law school at the University of Maryland, where he studied with Prof. Albert Ritchie, who later was elected governor of the state.

In 1919, Sar was invited by Dr. Revel to join the staff of Yeshiva as secretary of the administration and Talmud instructor. In reality, however, Sar became a central figure in the institution shortly after his arrival due, in part, to the fact that at this point Dr. Revel was forced to spend most of the year in Tulsa attending to family business. Sar became Dr. Revel's main advisor and confidant, and was Dr. Revel's eyes and ears at Yeshiva in his absence. In effect, he stepped into the void and within a short time assumed the multiple tasks of officer manager, director of fundraising, and head of public relations, besides being in charge of the placement of rabbis and Hebrew teachers.

Shmuel Sar brought considerable wit, diplomacy, and negotiating skills to these daunting tasks, which he fulfilled with a great sense of commitment and devotion. These were hard times for Yeshiva, which faced serious financial difficulties, compounded by the establishment of YC in 1928, the Depression, and the growing needs of an expanding student body. Time and again, Sar had to marshal all his numerous talents to provide imaginative solutions for a plethora of complicated problems facing the institution and its students. In that respect, he became Yeshiva's ultimate problem solver; as he was described in Gilbert Klaperman's *The Story of Yeshiva University*: "With a calm and deliberate manner, Mr. Sar was always in charge of the situation. In his mind, he carried thousands of names and addresses of people he had never met but who had made a contribution to the Yeshiva; he never forgot a name, a face, an occupation, or a joke. He was a diplomat, a tactician, and a skilled negotiator."

Following Dr. Revel's untimely demise and the ascension of Dr. Belkin to the presidency, Sar was appointed Dean of Men, a position which reflected his multiple tasks on behalf of the student body, which officially included placement of chaplains and distributing weekly stipends. In practice he was the address for any problem and considered it his responsibility to take as good care of the students as possible, from *shiddukhim* to job placement to educating them about the importance of Torah, Am Yisrael, and Eretz Yisrael. In addition, he continued teaching his beloved *Mishlei* to generation after generation of Yeshiva students. It was thus only natural that Dr. Belkin, in his eulogy for Dean Sar, gave him the ultimate compliment by referring to him as "Mr. Yeshiva."

Besides his devotion to Torah learning and Jewish education, Dean Sar believed the highest level of *Avodat Hashem* could only be reached by active service on behalf of his fellow Jews. He was active in communal organizations such as the Joint Distribution Committee, the United Jewish Appeal, and the *Mizrachi*. Probably the most important initiatives in this regard were his three lengthy overseas trips, the first two to Europe to assist the remnants of European Jewry — first in 1945 to visit the Displaced Persons camps in Germany and again in 1948 as director of the Central Orthodox Committee of the Joint Distribution Committee to provide kosher food, religious articles, religious education and qualified personnel for the numerous Orthodox survivors — and the third to Latin America to help stimulate a renewal of Jewish education and communal life.

A lifelong religious Zionist, Dean Sar was one of the leaders of the *Mizrachi* both in the United States and in world Jewish bodies. He served as Acting President, Chairman of the *Vaad Hapoel* of American *Mizrachi* and represented the movement in the *Merkaz Olami* (world center). He also played an important role in the creation of Bar-Ilan University in Israel together with his good friend Dr. Pinkhos Churgin. Dean Sar visited *Eretz Yisrael* seven times and in 1950 was offered the post as director-general of the Ministry of Religious Affairs by the Minister Rabbi Yehuda Leib Maimon. Dean Sar turned down the offer for a combination of technical and family reasons, as well as his refusal to leave Yeshiva."

Perhaps the best indication of Dean Sar's devotion to Yeshiva was the fact that his children continued in his footsteps and worked at Yeshiva for their entire lives. His son Dr. Eli Sar was Director of Medical Services at YC and SCW for close to fifty years, his daughter Esther Zuroff was Director of Student Services at SCW for three decades, and his son-in-law Rabbi Dr. Abraham Zuroff was the supervisor of all four Yeshiva high schools and the principal of YUHS for Boys for thirty years and later served for an additional thirteen years as adjunct assistant professor of Jewish Studies and academic advisor to all incoming students at YC. In all, the Sar-Zuroff family has collectively served Yeshiva for more than one hundred and sixty years, a tradition which continues with great-grandson Aaron Koller, who currently teaches Bible at YC.

It was known that Dean Sar very rarely removed his hat; he was always on the go, constantly on his way from solving yesterday's problem to averting tomorrow's crisis. Possessing a cynical, humorous, penetrating, and refreshingly candid personality, he would often note that his name, spelled in Hebrew as *zayin reish*, had a number of possible variations. Did it mean stranger or foreigner, or perhaps a wreath of glory or victory, or did it refer to the tyrannical Czar? Such musings were typical of Dean Sar, a person full of ostensible contradictions, and in that regard a quintessential modern Orthodox Jew, whose vision, talent, devotion, and charisma helped create Yeshiva University.

PART III

THE LAMM YEARS

Searching for *Torah u-Madda*

By Shalom Z. Berger

The most significant personality at Yeshiva College when I first arrived in the late 1970s most probably was Joe DiMaggio. In all honesty, the name that carried the most weight was Joe DiMaggio. It was not his years of guarding the outfield fences across the Harlem River at Yankee Stadium in the 40s that gave him this aura of authority at Yeshiva — DiMaggio was enshrined in the Hall of Fame years before and the Yankees of the 1970s had a different look, following their purchase by George Steinbrenner — rather it was his position as "pitchman" for the Bowery Savings Bank. The word on 185ᵗʰ Street was that Yeshiva's financial situation was such that the Bowery was going to foreclose on the uptown real estate properties of the university, spelling the end of almost one-hundred years of the *Torah u-Madda* experiment in Manhattan. "Say it ain't so, Joe!" was the cry of me and my classmates.

But where was the *Torah u-Madda* that had been one of the drawing cards that attracted me to YC? Having completed two years of study in Yeshivat Har Etzion, I knew the ins and outs of the *beit midrash* and happily spent my mornings within its four cubits. Yeshiva's original building gave off a whiff of intrigue, with forbidden floors above the dormitories in RIETS (now Muss) Hall, back entrances into Lamport Auditorium where the Rav still gave his annual *Yahrtzeit shi'urim*, and a coal chute off of 186ᵗʰ Street that old-timers still reminisced about. The *rebbeim* were a generation of *talmidei hakhamim* who had arrived at Yeshiva as refugees

---

Rabbi Dr. Shalom Z. Berger, YC '81, RIETS '84, AZG '87, '97, directs the e-communities of the Lookstein Center for Jewish Education in the Diaspora at Bar-Ilan University. He lives with his family in Alon Shvut, Israel.

from the Holocaust, and their accents and appearance gave off an aura of the guardians of Torah and traditional Jewish values.

My schedule of classes at YC was also impressive, as were the extra-curricular activities offered on-campus. I grappled with the questions of the ancients in my philosophy courses, rode with Hrothgar and Beowulf in English literature, and made it my business to attend all of the performances put on by the dramatics society. (I will admit it publicly here: I never attended a single YC intercollegiate sports event. Nevertheless, my close reading of the back pages of *The Commentator* kept me abreast of the goings-on in that realm.)

One building that offered the pretense of combining the best that the Jewish and academic worlds had to offer was the library. In the age before you had access to everything anyone could possibly want to know on the internet, knowing that between the Pollack and Gottesman libraries you could find virtually any book or *Sefer* on a topic of academic or religious interest — if not on the shelf then by interlibrary loan — was powerful stuff, indeed. It also offered the opportunity to discuss pressing questions of library trivia, such as: Were the numbers above the counter on the fifth floor really meant as a *Sefirat ha-Omer* reminder, or was there an expectation that there would be such a demand — and backlog — for closed-shelf books? Or: Was the library really built backwards (this question was more meaningful in the days that students entered the library directly onto the second floor from an entrance off of the parking lot across from Furst Hall)? Even here, though, there was no synthesis. The fifth and second floors were two separate worlds that serviced separate realms of the "holy" and the "profane."

In the courses offered by the college, there was little, if any, attempt to combine the two. Case in point: My freshman philosophy course was given by R. Dr. Sol Roth, who at the time was rabbi of the Fifth Avenue Synagogue and President of the Rabbinical Council of America. He so successfully hid his knowledge and erudition of things Jewish while playing the role of professor that a classmate who wanted to explain a concept by using an analogy from the realm of *halakhah* first asked Prof. Roth whether he was familiar with the idea of Shabbat (Professor Roth indicated that he was, in fact, familiar with the concept). The closest my Talmud *shi'urim* got to synthesis was my trying to imagine the Rav and R. Yeruham Gorelik as the protagonists of the Hayim Potok novels.

So, as the popular expression went, I loved my Torah and I loved my *madda*. But where would the two combine into the synthesis that Yeshiva was all about? Surprising to me, it was not nearly as far off as I had thought. My major was mathematics, which took me on a regular basis to Belfer Hall, where Yeshiva had only recently closed their graduate school for mathematics. Several of the tenured professors — among the world leaders in their field of interest — ended up teaching undergraduate courses; this is how I met Professor Leon Ehrenpreis.

Dr. Ehrenpreis entered the classroom with the distinctive gait of an absent-minded professor. He informed the class that although the course was scheduled for Tuesday and Thursday, he couldn't make it on Thursdays. Actually, Tuesdays weren't so good either. Would Sunday afternoons work? And so, we studied differential equations, complex analysis, number theory, and other fascinating topics on Sunday afternoons.

It soon became clear that Dr. Ehrenpreis had interests beyond mathematics. As a doting father, he occasionally would bring his children to class with him (apparently their schools were not open on Sunday afternoon). They would sit in the back and draw on the extra blackboard and occasionally ask the questions that we were too embarrassed to ask. For example:

Child: Abba, isn't this supposed to be a math class?

Dr. E.: Well, yes it is.

Child: Then why are there only letters on the board? Why don't you use numbers?

Then there was the time that the good professor informed us that he would be running in the New York City Marathon that coming Sunday, so he might be a little late for class. True to his word, he completed the race, took a taxi uptown, showered in his nephew's dorm room, and came to lecture.

None of this prepared us, however, for his revelations about how he got *semikhah* from R. Moshe Feinstein (he claimed not to have answered too many of the questions right, but was impressive in his presentation of some of his own Torah ideas), or his unified theory of the *mahlokot* between Rava and Abaye in *Shas* (he believed that they had different basic understandings of how *halakhah* perceived the passage of time), which he somehow wove into the fabric of the math course he was teaching. Later he offered a course in astronomy and *halakhah*, but due to limited registration, he gave only a few Club Hour lectures on the subject.

As we all know, it is the unconventional teachers who stand out in memory. In Dr. Ehrenpreis I had the good fortune to meet up with someone who embodied the values of *Torah u-Madda*. Totally unassuming, his contributions to his field of mathematics were unique, yet his message to his students at YC was that his family was primary and that *limmud Torah* was central to who he was.

Almost everyone has moved on since the lean years of the 1970s. Joltin' Joe has left and gone away. Following years of the successful stewardship of President Norman Lamm, the economic concerns that plagued Yeshiva in the past are barely remembered today. Having made *aliyah*, my own connection with my alma mater is limited to occasional visits to the Yeshiva and *The Commentator* websites, and less frequent visits to the campus while in the United States. And, on occasion, I wonder. Where the elusive *Torah u-Madda* is on today's campus?

Two Outstanding Educators

By Yitzchak Blau

My three years at YC were a period of tremendous personal growth. I found the dual curriculum exhilarating, rather than frustrating, as productive thinking in a variety of disciplines went on all day. Each day included a high quality *Gemara shi'ur* given by R. Michael Rosensweig, excellent morning and evening *havrutot*, afternoons studying the humanities with Dr. Will Lee, R. Shalom Carmy, and BRGS courses with Dr. David Berger. Additionally, I had the pleasure of watching my father, *Mashgi'ah Ruhani* R. Yosef Blau, and his unique ability to get along with everyone in the Yeshiva University world, irrespective of outlook and personality, while maintaining his fine integrity.

R. Rosensweig's *shi'ur* followed up nicely on the *shi'urim* I had heard in Israel from R. Aharon Lichtenstein, whose *shi'ur* employs Brisker conceptual analysis on the page being learned and the central *rishonim*. R. Rosensweig utilizes the same analysis but widens the scope considerably. This extended reach included such difficult tasks as mining the *Shakh* for relevant lines as well as placing each *sugya* within a broader network of *sugyot* in an attempt to conceptualize the totality of *Shas*. Thus, we often began the year with an introduction to the topic that lasted anywhere from one month to two and only then began to learn pages consecutively. As I feel that R. Lichtenstein's more narrow focus provides an easier route to learning the method, I was happy to have had that experience first

Rabbi Yitzchak Blau, YC '90, BRGS '93, RIETS '94, is currently a rebbe at Yeshivat Hamivtar and previously taught at the Yeshivah of Flatbush High School. He frequently contributes articles to periodicals such as the Torah u-Madda Journal *and* TRADITION. *He lives in Alon Shvut, Israel with his wife and four children.*

before proceeding on to R. Rosensweig's *tour de force*.

I very much enjoyed both writing for and being on the staff of *Hamevaser*. This publication provided a forum for students interested in thinking intensively about a broad range of Torah issues to discuss these ideas with others similarly inclined and to learn how to express them in writing. Of course, we made some youthful errors, but that too became part of the learning process. Occasionally, students and *rebbeim* objected to something written and this also, at times, enhanced our education. Indeed, one of the best aspects of Yeshiva is the variety of ideologies present under one roof. Although the challenges of keeping the debate respectful and maintaining a feeling of common institutional identity were not always met successfully, the general ability of different groups to function together in one *beit midrash* was quite impressive.

R. Carmy and Dr. Lee transcend the most common shortcomings of academic culture. Academic culture prizes research and writing far more than teaching. "Publish or perish" goes the academic mantra, not "teach more effectively or perish." No professor has been overheard in recent memory saying "I am up for tenure and need to improve my classroom management." Unfortunately, this sometimes, though certainly not always, leads to a situation in which professors teach poorly, pay little attention to the educational needs of the students, and fail to give students the time of day outside of the classroom.

Dr. Lee exemplifies the opposite model. Committed to teaching much more than publishing, he dedicates countless hours to grading student papers, commenting on how to improve almost every sentence on both the first and second drafts of papers, even in literature courses and not only in writing courses. I failed to truly appreciate his dedication until I took another English professor for a course on Milton and received as feedback for a hard-worked paper the grand total of a solitary check on the opening page. When I actually became a teacher and struggled to motivate myself to grade student papers, my appreciation grew even stronger.

His pedagogic excellence was manifest in the classroom as well. Employing the Socratic Method, he encouraged much student input in the analysis, and managed to do it without the class discussion losing direction and purpose. The norm was for us to read the poems, but he occasionally graced us with a reading of his own. In particular, I recall a Dr. Lee rendition of W. B. Yeats' "The Lake Isle of Innisfree" that left me longing for the quiet of a rustic cabin by the lake.

My initial approach to English literature focused exclusively on content with an indifference to style. Dr. Lee taught me, and it took a while for the message to seep through, that the means of expression also mattered, both on its own terms and a reflection of content. As R. Hayim Brisker realized, clarity of expression and clarity of thought bear a reciprocal relationship. Internalizing this message enabled me to read poems more deeply and to attempt to improve the poor quality of my own writing.

During my second year of *semikhah*, Dov Fogel, Benjie Samuels and I asked Dr. Lee if he would still meet with us to discuss literature. He agreed to meet with us once a month on early Friday morning, and he even brought muffins and coffee to the first meeting. In this forum, he introduced us to Garcia Marquez and Borges, and I am particularly in his debt for the latter. Few professors would agree to such an arrangement.

R. Carmy's dedication to students mirrors that of Dr. Lee. The endless hours he spends talking to students on the fifth floor of the library and in the cafeteria (he somehow only needs a doughnut and hot water to stay energetic) testify eloquently to that effect. Students often begin these conversations wondering if they can add a point of value unrealized by their erudite and brilliant teacher. R. Carmy takes each student's ideas seriously and the students discover that they truly can contribute to the ongoing search for edification.

This last phrase brings me to a second fault found in academic culture. Professors tend to approach their fields of knowledge from the objective standpoint of the spectator, conveying no sense that these subjects should truly impact on how we live our lives. William Barrett noted that the Greeks philosophized to discover how to live the good life while contemporary professors of philosophy discuss Hegel and Schopenhauer without a clear sense of whether it matters. In R. Carmy's class, it was clear that we searched the gamut of Jewish and Western thought as part of a quest for the true and the good. On this topic, he likes to cite the Kierkegaardian maxim: "The truth that matters is the truth that edifies."

Beginning from this standpoint generates a study that avoids the overly sharp bifurcation between disciplines often found in academia. A student taking R. Carmy for Bible would discover that Auden could help illuminate a chapter of *Tanakh*, notwithstanding the complaints of more technically minded scholars. Any work that grants insight into the human condition can ultimately make us better at understanding Torah. Additionally, the student of R. Carmy discovers that asking theological questions about *Tanakh* not only does not distract from the business of learning, but is an indispensable component of the endeavor. While not every chapter of *Tanakh* should be reduced to a *mussar schmeuss*, these prophetic texts do attempt to convey religious meaning.

This seriousness of purpose did not mean a dearth of light moments in class. From R. Carmy's beginning to teach while removing his sweater on the way in to his penchant for odd bits of medical knowledge to his references to the Police Philosopher — the class did incorporate its share of smiles. These were not the smiles of coarseness or frivolity but the joy that accompanies integrity and accomplishment. In a related vein, G. K. Chesterton points out that saints, contrary to popular imagination, often radiate a particular joy.

When I compare my college experiences to that of peers at secular universities, I often find that these two individuals provided me with a better education. To this day, YC includes the opportunities for a glorious learning dynamic if one selects the best courses. It is a shame that this great opportunity finds itself under siege from a three-pronged attack. The move to the right of some at Yeshiva leads to an unnecessary narrowing of vision regarding which aspects of human endeavor have Jewish value. The growing utilitarian pragmatism of America has students interested solely in GPA and the most lucrative jobs. Finally, the bugbears of relativism, historicism, and deconstructionism promote an environment in which nihilism and power politics replace the search for "the best that has been thought and said in the world." Reducing all ideas to responses to the socio-economic reality of their time and thinking that texts mean whatever we want them to do not inspire the thought that great books and ideas matter.

When I encounter students who fail to take advantage of the best courses available at YC, I am reminded of the well-known legend about a person who ignores his allotted time to pick up and acquire diamonds in the mistaken belief that such gems are worthless. The afternoons at YC offer the chance to collect precious materials. Pick up the gems.

Truth-Seeking as the Mission

By Michael J. Broyde

I came to MTA as a freshman in 1978 at the age of fourteen and left RIETS in 1992 at the age of twenty-seven, having happily spent nearly all of my adult life until that point as a student at Yeshiva. I left for a job as a professor at Emory University, where I still work. But I reflect on my Yeshiva years all the time, and those who have gotten to know me or hear me speak at the Young Israel of Atlanta know that I speak frequently about them.

Although I was at Yeshiva for some landmark events (I was at R. Norman Lamm's speech at the height of the financial difficulties, when closing the doors of Yeshiva was in the air, and I was in the Rav's last formal *shi'ur*), no single event left me shaped as a person. Rather, when I look back at my time at Yeshiva, I see that a number of different people at a number of different times reinforced in me a sense of its complex mission. That complex mission was to seek truth, and not to be content with half-truths or incomplete truths, never mind to be repulsed by falsehood.

No single person sold me on that mission — but many shared it with me. I still remember speaking to R. Michael Hecht (an unsung hero of Yeshiva, if there ever was one) when I was in eleventh grade about a complex topic that I was troubled by. He turned to me and said, "Truth seeking is complex, and a lot of hard work. Think about this topic some more and then we can speak again." It was then that I began to understand that the goal of Yeshiva was not to point me to a specific

Rabbi Michael J. Broyde, MTA '82, YC '85, RIETS—Yoreh Yoreh '88, RIETS—Yadin Yadin '92, is professor of Law at Emory University. He is the rabbi at the Young Israel in Atlanta, and a haver in the Beth Din of America.

result, but rather to force me to develop a set of truth-seeking skills that allow me to discern the difference between truth and falsehood. Dr. Barry Potvin similarly shared with me a sense that scientific research was really a search for truth — and not just a tool to get into medical school. Dr. Moshe Bernstein shared the same vision in the context of Bible study, and that was surely the vision of Talmud study in R. Mordechai Willig's *shi'ur*, where I was privileged to sit and learn for a number of years — exposed to the hard analytical learning of *Gemara* and *halakhah* on a daily basis, with truth being the currency of the realm.

No one of these people alone formed me, but I see now a common goal that united the many different people who taught me; it was a recognition that the ultimate value of an education is to seek truth.

Even as a student, I sensed that this search for truth was somewhat disquieting to many. Many students simply wanted to go on their merry way, not plagued by any doubts, examination of the world around them, or digression from their professional goals, and this created some social tension within the community. Other students had already searched for truth and had found it; they spent their time at Yeshiva not searching for truth but proselytizing for the truth that they had found and needed to share. Both of these results, I now realize, are inevitable in a healthy environment that seeks truth.

So too, as I look back — and read some of the somewhat bitter accounts of my fellow alumni — I realize that truth-seeking sometimes leaves people somewhat disappointed in Yeshiva as an institution. Many express their frustration at having to have looked so hard on their own or have related that they were disappointed with Yeshiva because they found truth elsewhere. Such was not my experience. I found the search for truth to be itself a mission of a great deal of value, and learning how to look for truth made my days at Yeshiva ever so valuable. This mission is important, I think, even when, perchance, the truth that one finds is not at Yeshiva, as it was there that many of us were given the skill set to find this truth.

I remember as a Yeshiva College student discussing the Jewish calendar with a friend, and he remark that it would have been much simpler if the Jewish calendar was just a solar or just a lunar calendar (as almost other faiths are). I realized then that the mission of Yeshiva University was somewhat like the Jewish calendar. The Jewish calendar seeks to reconcile two somewhat incompatible truths: the solar year and the lunar months, which do not ideally match up in one year (or even a few years), but yet they are both astronomical truths that can not be ignored. While some might like to build their calendar around only one of these truths and simple ignore the other for the sake of simplicity, the Jewish tradition did not adopt that view, but instead adopted a complex mathematically driven calendar of nineteen year and two-hundred and thirty-five lunar months that produces balance and ultimate truth seeking, but is not for the simple-minded. Yeshiva University balances two complex truths (Torah and secular studies) that are certainly not always fully compatible at least in the short run, and it is only in a complex universe committed to truth seeking that such really works.

The Talmud in *Shabbat* teaches us that "the seal of our Creator is truth," and Yeshiva trained me to search for that seal in every aspect of my life — and I am grateful for that lesson.

When Revel Almost Died

By Michael Eisenberg

I am now thirteen years removed from the events of the academic year of 1991-1992, but I remember it like yesterday. When I broke the news of the impending closure of the Bernard Revel Graduate School of Jewish Studies, the entire editorial board of *The Commentator* felt like we were covering an event that was important and exciting. It was the only story that I worked on that year and one of a few which *The Commentator* covered that reverberated outside the cozy walls of the University.

In my wildest imagination, I did not think that it would kick off the frenzy of student activity that ensued. Prospectively, I did not understand how deeply the graduate school cut to the core of the University's faculty and administration. Even retrospectively, I scratch my head as to how BRGS got to be such a political hot potato.

Like all great stories, this one started serendipitously. I was on line at a Bar Mitzvah buffet behind two Yeshiva board members and overheard the conversation about the decision to close BRGS. Through persistent questioning, we managed to get the story confirmed by other board members and then we printed *The Commentator* issue one day early in an attempt to beat the administration to the announcement. We caught the faculty, students, and administration by surprise. Again, to our amazement, it mattered.

Students began organizing and my phone was ringing off the hook

Mr. Michael Eisenberg, YC '93, lives with his wife and 6 children in Jerusalem, where he is a General Partner at Israel Benchmark Capital, a California and Israeli-based venture capital firm.

328

from concerned faculty members. To make sure we kept up with the fast-changing events, we printed a special four-page edition of *The Commentator* after only one week instead of the normal two weeks. The newspaper included a long petition signed by students and faculty members and an analysis into some accounting considerations that went into convincing the board to close the school.

Protests ensued almost immediately, including the first student demonstration I had seen at Yeshiva, which blocked the entrance to Furst Hall with a sit-in for hours. The protest then marched with a beating drum up to President Norman Lamm's office. I still remember the look on R. Lamm's secretary's face as the students entered the office. Frankly, the protests were a mix of angry students who had labored for degrees and thought the carpet was being pulled out from under them and high-minded Jewish academics for whom closing Revel violated their core beliefs about what a Jewish university should be.

I was just the reporter, pushing a good story that could make a difference, although the administration took much of its aim at me and some of the student protest leaders. The Dean of Students leaned on us frequently to stop publishing articles, sometimes harshly. There was a clear gag imposed on the professors. As is well documented and became a refrain at *The Commentator*, R. Lamm would not talk to us at all on this topic.

The story made it to the outside press and student pressure did not abate. Pressure mounted on the University to change course. We all know how this saga ended. R. Lamm constituted a special committee and, with some positive intervention from one of the Revel Board members, the basic framework of Revel was preserved.

While we were aggressive in looking for news, *The Commentator* pursued a very careful line of accurate reporting and community service. We asked questions of rabbis all along the way, to make sure we were staying away from scandalous libel. In the heat of it all, we saw this all as a student-led holy war. Students were forcefully acting for an important cause for our great institution. Even thirteen years removed, I still believe the students saved a very important component of our Jewish university.

That said, part of me wishes it had not grown to such proportions. In the professional environment I operate in today, people would have viewed the reporting through a lens of professionalism and we would have viewed the administration as an object to be reported. In a normal university, that air of distance may have prevailed as well. However, in our close knit Jewish community and university, it became intensely personal. Administration members felt under personal attack and responded in kind. There was a sense of embarrassment to Yeshiva, which was a shame and which I think was a negative reflection on all involved, myself included. Although I am not sure we could have or should have done anything differently, on a human level, I regret that today some of the protagonists are still scarred. While wheels of change were set in motion, personal relationships, cultivated over years, were irreparably harmed. That is unfortunate. I hope we have all learned life lessons from the experience; I certainly have.

In 1991, this seemed like an obvious case of using creative financial interpretations to support someone's ideological goal. To this day, I am not certain who initiated the idea. Today, I view this, somewhat retrospectively and without complete certainty, as a case of internal corporate, university politics that spiraled out of control. What is clear to me is that without the watchdog of a student press, BRGS would have closed. I also believe that the episode ushered in a new era of student activism, that, when carried out in a Jewish behavioral framework, is very powerful and desirable.

We all live a more liberal and feisty existence in university than we do when we move on in life — and that is healthy. As Winston Churchill said, "If you're not a liberal at the age of twenty you have no heart; if you're not a conservative at the age of forty, you have no brain." I am somewhere in between those ages now. While I have no regrets about those 1991-1993 years as News Editor and Editor-in-Chief, nor do I regret *The Commentator* scooping the BRGS story, I certainly would have preferred a more collaborative approach to engendering change in the University. It would have built better long-term relationships between students and the University and, perhaps, maintained some of those now ruptured personal relationships that the brouhaha brought about.

The More That Things Change...
The More They Stay The Same?

By Leonard Hammer

It is somewhat gratifying for me as an alumnus of YC currently residing in Israel to reflect on a particular unfortunate incident that occurred when I was a student at Yeshiva. I say gratifying since the incident had a longer term affect on me personally, while the desired immediate impression on the student body at the time sadly seems to have been largely lost.

I attended Yeshiva from 1983-1985 and majored in Political Science. I was active in the Political Science Society and — thankfully — established a rather strong relationship with my professor, Dr. Ruth Bevan, who not only supported me back then, but has continued to patiently answer my occasional questions and queries to this day. In fact, Dr. Bevan is probably the reason for my veering towards academia. Her fantastic course in "Contemporary Political Ideologies" was a wake-up call to philosophical applications and analysis of political systems. From then on, I perceived political events in a different light and began to grasp the power of ideas.

Among the other staff members was Dr. Blanche Blank, whose expertise was American Politics. I still remember engaging in what seemed like repetitive debates about the American political psyche that were, upon reflection, introspective exercises into understanding one's own political views and allowing for their expression. I remember that Dr. Blank's claim to fame was that her husband was some type of business entrepreneur. While I do not know if that was the case, she certainly was

Dr. Leonard Hammer, YC '85, is a Senior Lecturer, Safed College and at the Rothberg School of Overseas Studies at Hebrew University. He lives in Hashmonaim, a small yishuv near Modi'in.

a classy lady in the traditional American sense. I recall that the third member of the department was Dr. Bernard J. Firestone. His forte was international relations. He was quite rigorous and a bit intimidating — I think that was intentional — but he was also quite sharp, and while the classes were small, they were enlightening. Dr. Firestone has since moved over to Hofstra University, where he is now the dean of Hofstra College of Liberal Arts and Sciences. Finally, there was Dr. Michael Hecht, who taught the constitutional law course. You could sense his excitement and enjoyment of teaching the course, and he provided true insight into legal analysis and the manner in which to engage American case law.

In my senior year, I was president of the Joseph Dunner Political Science Society, named in memory of Dr. Bevan's husband, Dr. Joseph Dunner, a longtime YC faculty member. I remember it was an election year, and we thus published an election pamphlet offering viewpoints and analysis about the upcoming elections. I cannot recall the name of the publication, but it was glossy in the style of the National Review or New Republic (well, at least in style, if not in substance). We also ran a "Meet the Congressman" evening, where we met with now-Senator Charles Schumer, then a congressman from Queens. We also participated in the obligatory Harvard Model UN and ran a fun dinner downtown at the end of the year for all members. I seem to recall that Dr. Bevan was the only one who knew how to properly use chopsticks.

In my position as president of the Joseph Dunner Political Science Society, I desired to offer stimulating and interesting lectures and presentations. Thus, I attempted to initiate a speaker series of representatives from Israel, Egypt, and the Arab League, with the intention of offering a forum for dialogue between the students and the speakers. I invited a number of speakers from the United Nations to participate, including Clovis Maksoud from the Arab League, currently a professor at American University in Washington, DC. I went through the proper channels, including all administrative hurdles and approvals, and proceeded to advertise the event.

The protests that followed and the ire that was raised at my invitation of an Arab League member, an organization that did not recognize Israel, created an unfortunate maelstrom of events, leading to the regrettable dismissal of some first-rate, solid, individuals who had recently started their employ at Yeshiva in the newly created position of Student Affairs Coordinators.

Needless to say, I felt terrible; I was merely trying to engage the students in dialogue and debate with individuals in the real world, some of whom maintained a pro-Palestinian stance. Indeed, part of my desire was to provide tools to students to enable them to engage individuals outside of the Yeshiva in proper debate, should the need arise, and open the eyes of the student body to the claims and demands of the different factions involved in the Middle East conflict.

The experiment failed miserably not only because of the ensuing terminations, but also as evidenced by the students' actions surrounding the speakers that followed.

The Egyptian representative came to campus a few weeks later. The Camp David Peace Accords with Egypt were still fresh, and in fact, Egypt and Israel were encountering teething difficulties at the time. Funny enough, although some of these problems remain to this day and Israel-Egypt relations continue to have their ups and downs, peace has, on the whole, remained effective and lasting. Instead of engaging in dialogue and attempting to understand the position of the Egyptian representative, students entered the room and began chanting and shouting anti-Arab slogans. The Egyptian guest was dismayed but not surprised and attempted to handle the situation in a calm and open manner.

I felt quite disappointed in myself, as the underlying goal of the speaker series was to enhance dialogue and communication, and in the end the dialogue either did not ensue or was in the context of shouting canned slogans that tended to reflect poorly on what could be understood as Yeshiva's close-minded student body.

Ironically, when the Israeli speaker visited a few weeks later, almost no one showed up.

Especially today, in this world of information explosion and trite sound bites, it is important to not only be able to engage individuals with whom you argue, but to also maintain an intimate understanding of their perspective and approach. I find that living in Israel many times tends to harden the stance of the American *oleh*; many express the rather dubious claim that they used to be open-minded to all sides of the Israeli-Palestinian conflict, but that has changed now that they live in Israel. I never fully grasped that claim, and I think it reflects a lack of understanding concerning the individuals involved in the conflict and the issues that remain to be resolved. Listening to others is just as important a form of expression as engaging one's voice. This, I think, is one lesson I learned from my time at Yeshiva.

Looking Back One Score and Some More

By Nathaniel Helfgot

I had the privilege and good fortune to attend YC in the early and mid 1980s, with a two and half year hiatus of learning in Israel. It was a time of great excitement and enthusiasm. New buildings were constructed or projected for construction. The Harry Fischel Main Beit Midrash, showing its age and wear and tear, was totally refurbished and rededicated in honor of the towering philanthropist and good friend of the Rav, Mr. Joseph Gruss. In the mid 1980s, work began on the Max Stern Athletic Center and other physical improvements and amenities, such as Morg Mart, a refurbished Morg Lounge, and the college book store. We also had a small *sefarim* store on campus called Shaller's on Amsterdam and 186th Street. In addition, programs like the Gruss *Kollel Elyon*, quickly dubbed the "Super-*Kollel*" by students, with its $15,000 stipend, were just getting off the ground. Many of today's prominent younger *roshei yeshiva* at RIETS and other institutions of Torah learning were in those first classes of the *Kollel Elyon*. Dr. Norman Lamm initiated the *Torah u-Madda* project in the early 1980s with an exciting range of lectures, publications, and programs that reinvigorated the discussion and thinking about the core values of Yeshiva University.

The SOY Seforim Sale had not yet grown to its current gargantuan proportions, but it was slowly bursting out of its humble beginnings in Klein Hall, now known as the Muss Hall beit midrash, into the basement

Rabbi Nathaniel Helfgot, YUHS '81, YC' 85, RIETS '89, AZG '89, is Chair of the Tanakh and Jewish Thought Department, and a maggid shi'ur at Yeshivat Chovevei Torah Rabbinical School. He currently serves on the steering committee of the Orthodox Forum, the plenum of the Orthodox Caucus, and the American board of Yeshivat Har Etzion.

of Furst Hall near the Biology Labs. The restaurant of choice was the Kosher Chinese Deli, Schmulke Bernstein's of blessed memory, on the Lower East Side, while the most popular food event on campus was usually some form of "Hoagie Night." Sushi had not entered the culinary lexicon of the Orthodox Jewish community. Engagement parties in Morg Lounge were the new rage, and in fact, the Rav himself sponsored one in 1981 when one of his premier older students, Hayim Ilsen, became engaged. Parenthetically, in those years the fare was simple, a bit of *nosh* and some cake, a one-piece band, a *devar Torah*, usually given by R. Blau, and dancing — separate, of course, but with no *mehitzah*.

With all the excitement and good times, there was, as the decade moved on, also a sadness that pervaded the campus as we witnessed the slow but steady decay of our master and teacher, the Rav. First, the large public *Yahrtzeit* and *teshuvah shi'urim* that had made such an impression on me as a young teenage boy in MTA in the late 1970s came to an end. As the 1980s wore on, Parkinson's disease and its medical treatment continued to wreak havoc on the Rav's health. His daily *shi'ur* schedule became more erratic and his public activity became more curtailed. By 1984, the Rav was no longer able to walk across the block from his apartment in the Morg Lobby to Furst Hall, and the *shi'ur* was relocated to the room next door to his apartment. By 1986, a few short months after I graduated, the Rav's weekly treks to New York, along with his public career, came to a halt, never to resume again. This decline and the confusion and disappointment that accompanied it had a profound effect on the atmosphere at Yeshiva at the time. Many learning options and rabbinic personalities, now familiar to all YC students, had not yet come on the scene to fill the growing vacuum that was emerging in the minds of many students and the public at large.

The YC I remember from twenty odd years ago was a less polarized campus religiously, with a student body that would have defined itself by and large as passionately committed to both the ideology and social and cultural mores of Modern Orthodoxy and religious Zionism. Most students in the Yeshiva program and the *beit midrash* had all gone through pretty homogenous Israel *yeshiva* experiences. At the time, most students who studied in Israel attended one of three *yeshivot hesder* — Gush, Sha'alavim and KBY — or the one American-style institution that existed, BMT, which was intensely Zionistic in orientation as well. The *yeshivot hesder*, with all their minor differences and nuances, were all solidly Zionist and supportive of Yeshiva University. The *shi'urim* were all in Hebrew and students often roomed with Israelis. The phenomenon of a totally American *shi'ur* in English in a *hesder yeshiva* was inconceivable. The plethora of small American *yeshivot* in Israel where hardly a word of *Ivrit* is spoken and a religious Zionist/Modern Orthodox *hashkafat olam* is hardly advocated was still a decade away. Thus, the tone in the *beit midrash* at the time was one of intense learning coupled with the spirit, attitudes, and cultural mores that had been imbibed in the Israel programs of the time. Hats and jackets amongst YC students in the *beit midrash* were a rare sight, while white shirts and blue pants on Shabbat and special events was a common mode of dress.

Finally, I fondly recall an intense and passionate activism that dominated the campus culture, especially in relation to Russian Jewry — glasnost was still a half decade away and Anatoly Sharansky was still languishing in prison — as well as intense engagement with Israel and its struggle. HASC was virtually unknown to the student body and the most popular summer job YC students competed for — besides positions at Camp Morasha — were either as an advisor on the Counterpoint seminars in Australia or serving as an unpaid *Techiya* volunteer running day camps and programs for *sefardi* children and Russian elderly in underprivileged neighborhoods in Israel. *Techiya* was a wonderful *hessed* organization that had been founded in the early 1970s by RIETS *Rosh Yeshiva*, R. Hershel Reichman, a humble and gentle giant of *hessed*.

At the same time, it must be said that those years were also ones in which we all painfully experienced the loss of innocence. The picture of an Israel that only went to war as a last resort took a beating with the quagmire that unfortunately became the Lebanon War. And as the years passed the picture of the valiant religious settlers of *Gush Emunim* that so captured the hearts of Yeshiva students in the 1970s was tarnished by the revelations of the *Mahteret*, the Jewish underground and its plans to blow up Arab school buses and the Mosque on *Har ha-Bayit*. Support for Israel, of course, remained firm, but the campus, in line with much of American Jewry, began to reflect, if only faintly, the real world of the growing disagreements and tensions that permeated Israeli society and the general Jewish world in the wake of the Lebanon War, the pullout from Yamit, the underground, and other crises that came to the fore. One particularly significant event that stands out in my mind was the controversy that erupted on campus when the late Meir Kahane was invited to speak in 1985 by a student group on the topic of expelling the civilian Arab populace from *Yesha*. The invitation and his presentation resulted in a large protest by YC and RIETS students, who challenged his selective use of traditional sources to advocate his militant vision for the Jewish State.

Twenty years have passed but these and many other crucial moments of learning, living, laughing, crying, schmoozing, and just thinking come back in floods and waves. Those formative years in my life are irreplaceable and I will always be indebted to YC for the education and atmosphere it provided me. The friends, faculty, and *rebbeim* whom I was fortunate to meet and make part of my life, including mentors such as R. Yosef Blau, R. Shalom Carmy, and Dr. Will Lee — his rookie year was 1983 — are forever inscribed in my heart.

Yeshiva by Choice

By Robert Kantowitz

As my fellow seniors at MTA assembled in the fall of 1972, few of us had begun to think seriously about college. Like legions before and after us, we had taken the SATs and achievement tests the previous spring, but mid-fall was traditionally the time to begin the process of college applications. To our surprise, we discovered that some of our classmates were missing; several had stealthily managed to decamp to college after three years of high school, apparently without the benefit of transcripts or recommendations. Yeshiva College was concerned that it could lose many of its target students to the city colleges that had early admissions programs. By the same token, YC was keen to attract students who might otherwise go to Ivy League universities. In those times, there were far fewer feeder high schools to YC. MTA and the old Brooklyn Talmudical Academy were the main ones; Frisch had yet to graduate a class, and those of us who would later establish DRS-HALB High School were yet students ourselves. Moreover, even for observant high school students who were interested in continuing their Torah studies, if one had high enough grades and scores, the YU in New Haven was considered as attractive an option as the YU in Washington Heights.

In an amazingly short time, YC announced that it would entertain applications for early admission in January from current high school seniors. I viewed this as a no-lose proposition; I could try out college and

Mr. Robert Kantowitz, YC '76, received his MA in physics from Yeshiva's Belfer Graduate School of Science that same year. He received his JD from Harvard Law School and now is a banker with Societe Generale in New York. He is vice-chairman of the Yeshiva College Board of Directors and chairman of its Academic Affairs Committee.

still decide whether or not to continue at YC or — as I fully expected — go to MIT or Columbia in the fall. I matriculated in January with about thirty others.

To fulfill the entrance requirements for other colleges, I still needed to complete another semester of physics. Pre-computer registration procedures being what they were in those days — mostly a combination of chance and "connections" — the only physics course that fit into my schedule was a section labeled "physics for physics majors." Today, we would say that it was on steroids, requiring five class hours a week rather than the usual three. But it was all that fit into my program; out of necessity, I officially became a physics major.

Among other things that happened that semester, some wonderful professors in the Belfer Graduate School of Science brought the subject to life. Indeed, because this was not supposed to be the regular watered-down course for pre-med students, the professors taught it as aggressively (some would say ruthlessly) as they would teach an advanced course at an elite science-oriented institution. They demanded that we master material far beyond our backgrounds and mathematical training, and somehow we rose to the challenge. I remember late nights working out the equations and theorems line by line with a friend, much as we would puzzle over a difficult section of *Gemara*, and we learned as much math in these physics courses as we did in our math courses. The BGSS professors also encouraged a few of us to enroll in the new "BA-MA" program — another gimmick — in which we could theoretically get both degrees in four years. The precise details had not even been fully worked out, yet no one did anything to dispel my utterly outrageous presumption that I could complete the entire program in a half year less than that.

The principal initial attraction of YC to me was, perhaps paradoxically, the secular studies, especially physics. The undergraduate department was tiny, with but one full-time professor, the wonderful Peretz Posen, a European-born gentleman who embodied *Torah u-Madda*; he was learned in Torah and delivered his physics lectures without notes. BGSS was populated with relatively few students, but they included some from places like Korea and Argentina, not exactly what one normally saw at Yeshiva. (I recently glanced at the Yeshiva University alumni directory and chuckled to discover that I attended school with, and remember, two of the four Yeshiva graduates in India and the single Yeshiva graduate in Nigeria.) The BGSS professors fervently believed in their mission, and they gave us a top-notch, if somewhat narrow and traditional, grounding in the subject. With about ninety of my credits in physics and associated subjects, there was little room for anything else; the fourteen credits of Hebrew on my transcript may have set a record for the lowest total ever.

Lest I give the wrong impression, *limmudei kodesh* were not unimportant to me. As I suggested above, I just believed, as did many of my contemporaries, that we could find learning wherever we went to college. A modest number of students in those days chose to spend a year in an Israeli *yeshiva* before college, but it was not considered an almost automatic rite the way it is now, and a second year was practically unheard of. In the same vein, in terms of college choices, Yeshiva was viewed as a reasonably decent option but one that required serious compromises in academic quality. In my case, though, because I was going into a small department with serious instructors, I believed that I was going to get a great secular education, and I was not disappointed. It was still a difficult decision, but after a merry-go-round of changing my mind from one day to the next, I opted to stay at Yeshiva; in the end, it was the desire to have the best access to *limmudei kodesh* that made the difference.

Once at Yeshiva, and increasingly over the years since, I have realized that there is a world of difference between the *limmudei kodesh* and the atmosphere at Yeshiva and what was, or even today is, available elsewhere. At Yeshiva, there are no scheduling conflicts between college and *limmudei kodesh*, other than the self-imposed problem of not having enough hours in the day or week to pursue as much of both as one would like. In another setting, I might have easily remained observant and perhaps matured as a person and in my commitment to Torah Judaism, but I would not have experienced the kind of growth in learning that I had at Yeshiva.

Learning in IBC with R. Israel Wohlgelernter and R. Aron Kreiser, and then in MYP in the *shi'urim* of R. Hershel Schachter and R. David Lifshitz, provided me, more than I could know at the time, with a love of learning and the tools to make it a lifelong part of what I am.

There were other things about Yeshiva that made the years pass quickly. Classes were almost always small — in advanced physics, one could find himself and a classmate alone in the room with the professor — so that we were by necessity active participants, whether prepared or not, rather than spectators in large lecture halls. Almost all the students were packed into just two dormitories, so we got to know each other well.

As important as the absence of scheduling conflicts between *limmudei kodesh* and secular classes, the extra-curricular activities involved no compromise of Shabbat or *kashrut*, an oft-overlooked problem on other campuses. Because the class days were so long, we worked on things like *The Commentator* and the Yeshiva College Senate well into the night.

The Vietnam War was still going on, and one was always cognizant of other students' draft issues and their frequent interactions in this connection with the registrar's office. I myself barely missed the draft; although I had number sixteen in the lottery for my year, the Army closed the draft boards just in time. And through a series of maneuvers — an oddly scheduled summer section in thermodynamics, a custom-designed lab course not in the catalogue, a couple of stare-downs with the chairman of the chemistry department to get credits and to get into courses, a midnight rendezvous with a sympathetic assistant registrar to check precedents in the files to support a negotiated deal on workload maximums — I had the last laugh and I got both my BA and my MA in physics in only three-and-a-half years on a warm, sunny, late spring day in 1976.

And by dint of good grades and scores, and through the good offices of Dr. Michael Hecht, I got in to as fine a law school as I would have had I gone elsewhere to college. Ah, yes, law school; I was one of a growing number of science majors who, worried about the slim employment prospects, tried out law school. After all, what else could one do with all those science and math credits? For me it was a great choice; I loved it and never returned to the labs. I practiced law for a few years and then went into banking. I still read physics and math articles and books occasionally, both because I remain interested in the subjects and because I need to stay a step or two ahead of my own children, who are now approaching college themselves.

Obviously, some things have changed. The YC education has improved to the point that it's far less of a sacrifice than it once was to opt to go to YC over other top schools. Indeed, we attract a large pool of talented students whose focus on *limmudei kodesh* impels them to come to YC. The Yeshiva degree has always impressed graduate and professional schools as an indicator of students' perseverance and ability to tackle incredibly large amounts of material (and in the turbulent post-Vietnam years, not to be too belligerent); now it also bespeaks a high quality secular education as well. But we also need to remember that college is about learning and not about rushing through as I did, and we need to remember that the things that unite us far outweigh differences, for example among the Jewish studies programs, each of which, in its own way, is a *le-khathila* and not a *b'diavad*. In short, YC is not perfect, but it is better than ever, and we who care deeply about our school hope that it is continuing to improve all the time.

Academic Journalism at Yeshiva

By Aryeh (Robert) Klapper

Toward the end of my freshman year at YC, I was tapped for *Hamevaser*, then a journal that appeared about five times a year, not counting Purim. Alan Stadtmauer came over to me at dinner in the cafeteria and asked me to join, probably at the suggestion of R. Shalom Carmy. I stayed on *Hamevaser* for the next five years, making many lifelong friends, and I consider that association one of the best and most important experiences of my life.

We had no office and no computer when I started, and floppy disks had not been invented. Every article had to be typed from manuscript into the computer at the neighborhood newspaper's office on 181st Street off Fort Washington Avenue, then printed and physically cut and pasted onto layout boards. We were only given access to that computer late at night, so every issue involved multiple all-nighters, complete with trips to the next-door bar to consult with the publisher when we had technical issues. I recall one time, just before *Pesah*, when we realized after midnight that our otherwise complete next issue had a half page of blank space. After several hours of frantic brainstorming, one staffer found a photo of a recent wedding on the publisher's desk. We cropped out the church and the top of the groom's head, and printed a *mazal tov* to two friends who had recently married — that left only a quarter page. But we were out of ideas. Around 5 am, I was leafing desperately through a book called "How

---

Rabbi Aryeh (Robert) Klapper, YC '89, BRGS '89, RIETS '94, is Rosh Beit Midrash of the Summer Beit Midrash (www.summerbeitmidrash.org). He has served as Orthodox Rabbinic Adviser and Associate Director for Education at Harvard Hillel, and as Talmud Curriculum Chair at Maimonides High School (Brookline, MA). He currently teaches at Gann Academy and is developing the Center for Modern Torah Leadership.

to Draw in Pencil" and found a page of pyramids. We printed "*Hag kasher v'samei'ah*" over it and put the issue to bed.

By my junior year I was Literary Editor, and able to indulge my then-deep biases against commas and in favor of semicolons. One of our co-Editors-in-Chief, however, had equally deep biases against semicolons and in favor of commas. Editing sessions thus became grammatical horse-trading sessions, with the result, I fear, that many sentences went on and on with no punctuation whatsoever. I became Editor-in-Chief in the middle of my senior year and kept the position for a year and a half, during which I inserted a diatribe against "amalekommas" into a Purim edition article.

So *Hamevaser* was fun, and the camaraderie was amazing. But *Hamevaser* also played a very important role in my own and my friends' religious development. We provided a space in which students could think seriously and publicly about the crisis of religious Zionism, the relationship between ethics and *halakhah*, historicism, feminism, chosenness, and a host of other critical issues that were largely ignored or off-limits in MYP. Twenty years later, I still find myself writing and giving *shi'urim* that are expansions of my own and my friends' *Hamevaser* articles, and I read my friends' current publications and recognize them.

Hamevaser was also a strong positive influence on Yeshiva as a whole. Our investigative journalism and editorials stimulated numerous reforms in MYP; for example, the eventual development of the assistant *mashgi'ah* positions, and we prevented, mitigated, or exposed significant abuses of rabbinic power within Yeshiva.

Hamevaser developed us as leaders by allowing us to take responsibility for our religious environment and showing us that we could make a difference. Many of my *Hamevaser* colleagues have founded or been instrumental in the development or invigoration of creative Jewish institutions, such as Yeshivat Har Etzion's Virtual Beit Midrash, the Avi Chai Foundation, Ma'ayan Torah Studies for Women, the Beth Din of America, and the Summer Beit Midrash; at least four are or have been high school principals, and many more are *roshei kollel* or *ramim*. Almost all are ongoing contributors to the development of a Torah community that sees itself as obligated to engage all forms of knowledge with integrity and treat all human beings as created *be-tzelem Elokim*.

Among the life-lessons I take with me from my time on *Hamevaser* are the necessity of a free press for a moral society and the importance of telling authors that you've read and appreciated their work.

Diversity at Yeshiva

By Joseph Lipner

During our freshman year in 1981, a friend and I explored every rooftop at Yeshiva College. How different each roof was from one another! Furst Hall offered nothing but a blank rectangular space covered with loose stones and open to the sky. The high school's roof invited you right up to those Moorish turrets and green-plated domes and to mysterious rusting structures that controlled the building's heat. A visit to the top of Belfer exposed you to dizzying views of the Bronx and Manhattan and dangerous winds that whipped off the Hudson and East Rivers. We also visited the medieval looking tower that rises improbably from a grassy field bordered by Amsterdam Avenue and the ramp exiting the George Washington Bridge. At the top of its rickety spiral staircase, we found a squatter's apartment equipped with cot, clothes-pile, and furniture built from cartons. Who would have guessed that three city blocks could be filled with spaces that held so much variety?

So it was with my Yeshiva College classmates. They were the most diverse group of people I have ever met. More diverse than my friends' classes at Columbia and Harvard colleges; more diverse than my class at Harvard Law School; more diverse than the teeming population of Cambridge, Massachusetts and Los Angeles, California, where I later lived, or the businessmen, criminals, jurists, scientists, and scholars I have met during the course of my law practice across the United States.

Yes, my classmates were all male, all Jews, almost all white, and, with vanishingly few exceptions, religiously observant and Orthodox-

Mr. Joseph Lipner, YC '85, is a partner at the Los Angeles law firm of Irell & Manella LLP. His practice focuses on intellectual property litigation and appellate law.

345

identified. But these men were diverse in their spirit and their ideas. They lived out their college lives against the backdrop of Yeshiva's peculiar philosophy of loyalty to Torah and immersion in secular learning, and each one's reaction to that philosophy — as proponent, opponent, or someone who did not give a hoot — threw his personality into sharp relief. I went to school with scholars who labored in Torah day and night and thirsted for better understanding of the coded Aramaic secrets of the Talmud; with profane young men who thought Judaism was nonsense and were biding their time to leave both college and religion; with guys who displayed such deep kindness and spiritual goodness that I would not be surprised if they were among the hidden thirty-six hidden saints on whom the world depends; with intellectuals, both true and pseudo, who reveled in conversation and a sharp exchange of ideas; with idealists who felt sure they would transform the world as soon as they left Washington Heights; with fiery Zionists who argued that we should be building a Hebrew society instead of wasting our time with Calculus; with grinds seeking a fast track to law, medicine, or accounting; with would-be lovers who searched for women at SCW and other points across the five boroughs; with men who took pleasure in rock and roll music and midnight drives down the Harlem River Parkway to Shmulka Bernstein's for spare-ribs and egg-rolls; with jokers who kept us laughing; with depressives who kept to themselves; with dreamers, regular guys, and holy men. The differences between the Christian right and the radical left pales in comparison.

Take my time in the Yeshiva College Dramatic Society as an example. Since roughly Elizabethan times, the theater has not been a matter of moral controversy — except at Yeshiva. Some *rebbeim*, and those classmates who lived strictly for Talmud study, considered my participation in dramatics as, at best, *bitul Torah*, and at worst something that smacked of the forbidden. I understood this reaction; even if not quite in opposition to *halakhah* and Jewish values, the theater does seem challengingly separate from them, and YCDS was the theater in microcosm, with all its silliness, intrigues, adrenaline, and magic. Acting — the height of my career came with the title role in the YCDS production of "Pinocchio" — was a very different experience than learning a *blatt* of *Gemara*. In directing the dramatic society, Dr. Anthony Beukas, who spoke respectfully of Yeshiva's rabbis and our own religious obligations, also exhibited a real commitment to creating magic on stage. The conversation between these two worlds was exciting and meaningful because it had to do — please excuse the slightly non-Jewish turn of phrase here — with the future of our immortal souls.

My fellow actors were examples of the range of students who attended Yeshiva in the 1980s. One of the guys with whom I acted became a respected and important religious Jewish educator. Another lives now as an openly gay man. From the same genetic and religious pool came enormously different lives.

Students' reactions to afternoon classes — Bible studies, which fell somewhere on the border of Torah and college studies, and liberal arts — differed dramatically. My most intense academic and religious learning experience came in the Bible classes taught by R. Dr. Moshe Bernstein, perhaps the most talented teacher and scholar I have ever met. In other schools, Biblical scholarship would have come with a generous dose of hostility to traditional religion, but Dr. Bernstein combined intellectual rigor with commitment to Jewish thought and religion. Different students had sharply different reactions, however, to applying modern scholarship to the sacred texts; for example, we studied the similarities and differences between our holiest books and ancient Ugaritic epic poems. Some reacted with hostility. For others, using modern intellectual tools to examine the Bible demeaned their religious life. In a less direct way, the reactions of students to such talented teachers as Dr. Joan Haahr and Dr. William Lee in the English department and Dr. Louis Feldman in Classics, who taught their classes with fierce independent value and rigor, ran the gamut from enthusiasm to muted hostility.

Politics at Yeshiva also implicated issues of spiritual truth, not to mention matters of life and death. While I was in college, Rabbi Meir Kahane, founder of the JDL and tireless promoter of the expulsion of Arabs from Israel, spoke on campus. I stood with the demonstrators against R. Kahane and held a protest sign that said, "*derakheha darkhei noam*" — the Torah's ways are ways of pleasantness. Sometime during the talk, R. Kahane stopped what he was saying, noted my sign, and said: "Am ha-aretz — ignoramus — let me show you the 'ways of pleasantness' of the Torah," and proceeded to expound on the Biblical directive calling for the destruction or expulsion of the seven nations. In contrast to the demonstrators, a classmate of mine with whom I had been in *shi'ur* since high school supported R. Kahane at this talk, quite literally, proceeding with him arm-in-arm up to the podium. This same classmate later settled on the West Bank near Nablus. Palestinians murdered him while at Joseph's Tomb at the start of the recent Palestinian intifada.

The fact that the moral, spiritual, and religious stakes were so high at Yeshiva, that any disagreement implicated the next world in addition to the current one, brought out the personalities of all these white, male Jewish college students with an almost mystical clarity. Many of these friends and colleagues of mine were also — and I say this in the most affectionate and admiring way — crazy. There was an air of whimsy and experimentation at Yeshiva that I have not encountered since. Students did odd and adventurous things — like deciding to visit every rooftop at YC, for example — with humor and excitement. It could have been the time of life, of course, because we were young and had so much energy. But I like to think that the electric charge of energy came not only from our youth but from the differences between YC and the mundane workaday world. From our involvement in a project that was holy.

A Fish in Water

By Elazar Muskin

It was September 1975 when I arrived as a new student at YC. I had just finished three years of learning at Yeshivat Kerem B'Yavneh in Israel and didn't know what to expect as I started this new chapter in my life. Actually, I was reluctant to enroll at YC. From my earliest memories as a child in Cleveland, I recalled how my teachers at the Hebrew Academy told me that no serious Torah student would go to Yeshiva University. From their more insular perspective, the combination of a *yeshiva* with college simply wasn't acceptable. At best, Yeshiva University was a compromise; at worst it was a *"makom tumah,"* a place where one would be inspired to reject the Torah values that my teachers had instilled in their students. Even the presence of R. Joseph B. Soloveitchik was not a mediating factor. My elementary and high school rabbis had no respect for the Rav. They couldn't understand how a Torah scholar could have a PhD in philosophy and endorse secular studies.

My parents, however, knew that the Rav was the leading Torah scholar of our generation and that Yeshiva was a great Torah center where one could learn Torah while pursuing a serious secular education. With their encouragement, and the realization that many of my friends from Kerem B'Yavneh were going to YC, I enrolled with ambivalent feelings, worried that I would be greatly disappointed in the Torah environment on campus.

Right before leaving for my first semester in New York, I met a family

Rabbi Elazar Muskin, YC '78, BRGS '80, RIETS '80, is rabbi of Young Israel of Century City in Los Angeles.

friend and neighbor, Mike Senders, who had attended Yeshiva many years before. When he heard that I had decided to enroll at Yeshiva, he sensed my concerns and coached me for what to expect. He told me that I would find every type of student, just as in any Jewish community, including the entire spectrum from the seriously religious to the non-observant. It was up to me, he instructed, to choose my friends, knowing that this would define what kind of experience I would have at Yeshiva.

With all of these conflicting ideas running through my mind, I arrived in Washington Heights for the first time in my life. That summer I had taken a few courses at John Carroll University in Cleveland, where the campus is located in a gorgeous suburban setting with stately buildings and beautifully manicured grounds. That, I thought, was what typical college campuses looked like. Imagine my shock when I saw garbage littered all over the streets leading up to the Yeshiva campus. "Oh No!" I thought, "Is this where I am going to spend the next six years of my life?!"

But my negative feelings quickly disappeared as I entered the *beit midrash* in the main building for my first *havrutah*. I couldn't believe my eyes. Standing in front of me were some of the greatest Torah scholars in the world. As each *rosh yeshiva* appeared, I thought to myself that nowhere else could one find so many outstanding Torah personalities in one location. I recall seeing on my first day in the Yeshiva not only my *rebbe*, R. Yehuda Parnes, but also R. David Lifshitz, R. Yeruham Gorelik, R. Mikhel Bornstein, R. Yosef Arnest, R. J. David Bleich, R. Hershel Schachter, R. Moshe David Tendler, R. Abba Bronspiegel, and R. Hershel Reichman.

After *shi'ur*, as I was heading back to my dorm room in Rubin Hall, I saw a large group of students walking from Furst Hall towards Morgenstern Dormitory. They were surrounding someone, and it appeared that everyone was straining to hear what the man in the middle was saying. I inquired after what was going on and was told, "Don't you know? That is the Rav, and you will see this every Tuesday, Wednesday, and Thursday. Those are the days the Rav gives *shi'ur*." And then the fellow added, "If you think that is a large crowd, just wait to see what happens when the Rav delivers a public address. Thousands of people come to hear him and it is a sight you will never forget."

The most amazing sight of all, however, occurred at night. I couldn't believe my eyes when I entered the *beit midrash*. There were hundreds of fellows learning until late at night. This was after a full day of both *shi'urim* and college courses. When, I wondered, would the students find time to complete their college assignments? Invariably, the answer was, "very late nights." Indeed, that was the typical experience. R. Zevulun Charlop, dean of RIETS, once remarked that he thought there were more students learning at night at Yeshiva University than in any other *beit midrash*. I don't know if his observation was scientifically correct, but R. Charlop was rightfully proud of the dedication and devotion that so many of Yeshiva's students had for Torah study.

After seeing all of this, all of my concerns about Yeshiva dissipated and I embarked on six years that I loved. At Yeshiva, I received an outstanding Torah education as well as a first rate secular education. I met friends that I still have to this very day and I am grateful for all that Yeshiva University offered me. My horizons were expanded and I found a home away from home.

The Ongoing Conundrum of Yeshiva College

By Gil Student

The college years are a time of personal growth and development, introspection and self-definition. The college student is, in the course of his studies, exposed to a wide variety of world views and, at this crucial stage in personal development, expected to find his own seat among the many tables. For an Orthodox Jew, committed to Torah and tradition, what setting offers more intellectual options within the framework of Orthodox Judaism than YC? It can, indeed, be plausibly suggested that the Orthodox student's ideal college experience is only at Yeshiva. Yet, it remains quite ironic — and this is only the first of many ironies we will encounter in this short essay — that YC itself has, from its inception until today, engaged in its own struggle with self-definition. What is Yeshiva College? Is it a college for *yeshiva* students? A *yeshiva* for college students? A *yeshiva*-college hybrid and, if so, which of a variety of types? This is no small matter, and the resolution of this issue would dramatically impact the direction of the school.

Perhaps Dr. Revel was clear about what he intended for YC when he wrote, "the chief purpose of the college department of the Yeshiva is, and should always be, to afford those students of the Torah who are continuing their studies in an atmosphere of love and loyalty to the Torah and Jewish ideals, an opportunity to acquire the learning and culture of the modern world, in addition to the learning of the culture of Israel." Yet over fifty years after Dr. Bernard Revel articulated his vision for YC, the debate continues. In the winter of the academic year 1993-4, following

---

Rabbi Gil Student, YC '94, is the founder of Yashar Books, a new publisher of Orthodox books.

the confiscation by college administrators (with the approval of the student council president) of a student publication deemed obscene, Dr. Will Lee, one of the journal's academic advisors, penned a lengthy essay on the subject, which was published in the December 8, 1993 issue of *The Commentator*. In this essay, titled "Yeshiva, Yes, University, Yes," Dr. Lee eloquently argued that Yeshiva College must embrace both the traditions of a *yeshiva* and the traditions of a university. When these traditions come into conflict, as they inevitably will, we must struggle to resolve the clash in the fairest and most sensitive way possible. "Is there any such thing as Yeshiva University? Yes, but not without controversy and contradiction... At its best, Yeshiva University aspires to be both infinitely *yeshivish* and 100 percent a university... Torah and Madda, yeshiva and university, inevitably clash at times..."

In response to this articulate argument for *Torah u-Madda* by a highly respected but non-Jewish faculty member, R. Aharon Kahn, *rosh yeshiva* and at the time also a *rosh kollel* at RIETS, wrote a highly sophisticated, multi-lingual (English, Hebrew, Aramaic, Latin, and French) rebuttal. R. Kahn, in a writing style worthy of his two masters degrees, argued that *Torah u-Madda* is ultimately untenable and must be rejected by the halakhic Jew. The traditions of the university cannot be upheld by a traditional Jew. A true college education, R. Kahn concluded, is not for a Jew dedicated to Torah.

> We Jews were never given the charge of keeping the torch of the university ideal. We were charged with the keeping of the Torah... Yeshiva University was a *yeshiva* first and, after the advent of the college, continues to be a *yeshiva* foremost. Rav Dr. [Norman] Lamm insists that the *yeshiva* is the heart of Yeshiva University. Then he is the keeper of the heartbeat. Yeshiva University is a *yeshiva* at which there is a college.

The irony of the non-Jewish professor with no advanced Torah education arguing passionately and effectively for *Torah u-Madda* against the equally convincing *rosh yeshiva* who exemplified these values was lost on no one, certainly not the astute Dr. Lee. In the final missive on this topic, Dr. Lee noted this oddity and concluded that *Torah u-Madda* is, indeed, possible and readily achievable if one is only ready to struggle with conflict.

[Rabbi Kahn's vision] may be the best choice for him and for some *talmidim*, particularly in RIETS, but it is by no means the only valid choice within the boundaries of Torah Judaism for each and every one of our undergraduates, who must make their own decisions... While keeping the Torah at the forefront of students' hearts and minds, Yeshiva University reaches out unafraid to knowledge in general, to a broad range of kinds of knowledge, and to a vast multitude of choices in life. Hence the tensions; hence the messiness; hence the room for disagreement and individualism; hence the creativity.

As a YC student at the time, I did not notice much undo concern over this public debate. It did not trigger any new introspection on the part of students or administrators. This was not, however, due to apathy but, quite the opposite, due to a strong interest. We students were constantly thinking about and debating these issues. The public back-and-forth by the respected faculty members was only symbolic of our entire YC experience: self-awareness and the struggle for self-definition. In this respect, Yeshiva College provided the ideal college experience.

AFTERWORD

By Jonathan D. Sarna

"One of the most puzzling features of American academic life today," observes George M Marsden, a leading scholar of American evangelicalism and himself a practicing evangelical Protestant, "is that even in these times of evangelical resurgence there is still not a full-fledged evangelical university in America." "Why," he asks, "was the severance of evangelicalism from the main currents of American academic life so total?"

One might have expected, given Heinrich Heine's well-known proverb "*Wie es sich christelt, so judelt es sich*" ("As Christianity goes, so goes Judaism"), that the same question might be asked of Orthodox Judaism. But that emphatically is not the case. Although the number of American Orthodox Jews is tiny in comparison to the number of American evangelical Christians, a full-fledged Orthodox college — Yeshiva — has existed in America for seventy-five years. As contributors to this volume amply demonstrate, Yeshiva College is anything but severed from the main currents of American academic life.

The challenge of reconciling religion and the academy — or what is known at Yeshiva as *Torah u-Madda* — has been central to Yeshiva from its earliest days. "It will be the aim of the Yeshivah College to spread knowledge of Judaism in its wider sense, together with general culture," Rabbi Bernard Revel wrote in 1928. He justified the goal by comparing it to "the harmony between Shem and Japhet spoken of by our sages." Revel,

Dr. Jonathan D. Sarna is the Joseph H. & Belle R. Braun Professor of American Jewish History and Director of the Hornstein Program for Jewish Communal Service at Brandeis University. His many books include American Judaism: A History *(Yale University Press).*

an ordained European-trained rabbi with an American PhD, personally embodied the ideals that he preached, and so did many of the faculty that he hired. To this day, as many of those who write in this volume attest, the men (*only* men at Yeshiva College) whom Yeshiva graduates look back and remember are those who modeled *Torah u-Madda*: the Rav most of all, but also the university's long-serving presidents following Revel, Drs. Samuel Belkin and Norman Lamm, as well as its world-famous Orthodox scholars, the one most-often mentioned here being Professor Louis Feldman.

At the same time, Yeshiva graduates have also very-much modeled the worshipful devotion of *talmidim* to a *rebbe* more commonly found in a *yeshiva* than a university. The loving portraits here of such rabbinic luminaries as R. Shimon Romm, R. Moshe Shatzkes, R. Shlomo Polachek, R. Shlomo Drillman, R. Moshe Aharon Poleyeff, and others — written, in some cases, by admiring family members — bespeak the reverence for *roshei yeshiva* which in some ways distinguishes Yeshiva from more secular academies, and even from contemporary rabbinical seminaries. A comparison of this volume with *Telling Tales Out of School: Seminary Memories of The Hebrew Union College — Jewish Institute of Religion* (1965) reveals a great deal about the chasm separating these two quite different Jewish institutional cultures.

In other ways, however, readers familiar with academic life will find these memories of Yeshiva's past remarkably familiar. The probing admissions officer who took a chance with an iffy candidate, and saw it pay off; the favorite professor who enlarged the minds of his students, teaching them to think in new ways and see the world with fresh eyes; the loyal faculty-member who served with distinction under one university president only to become *persona non grata* under his successor; the activist who rallied to organize the faculty against the administration, and paid the price; and, of course, the perennial financial crises–these stories, *mutatis mutandis*, could be told about practically every American university; they are not distinctive to Yeshiva at all.

Yeshiva was also not distinctive in welcoming European scholars to its faculty. American universities long played a vital role in the transfer of knowledge from Europe, and a wide range of campuses were enriched, beginning in the 1930s, by the intellectual migration set off by the Nazis. Jewish institutions of higher learning in America, without exception, boasted overwhelmingly European-trained faculty well into the postwar era; few Jewish scholars, prior to World War II, were trained in the

United States. Nevertheless, both in terms of whom it hired and why it hired them, Yeshiva set itself apart from these others; in that respect its mission *was* distinct. The goal, articulated by Bernard Revel as early as 1915, following the merger of the Eitz Chaim *yeshiva* and the Rabbi Isaac Elchanan Theological Seminary, was to create "a bridge over which the Torah could be brought from Europe to America and without compromise be made meaningful in contemporary American life." As a result, where others brought scholars steeped in *Wissenschaft des Judentums* to America's shores, Yeshiva brought over distinguished rabbis and Torah scholars. The recollections preserved in this volume demonstrate how successful that strategy proved to be. Thanks in part to these Old World sages, the great traditions of the European *yeshivot* survived the Nazi inferno. Yeshiva College students, without ever having setting foot in the Old World, experienced and later perpetuated the different East European traditions of Jewish learning to which they were exposed. Consequently, and contrary to most expectations, traditional Jewish learning not only survived in America, it thrived.

To be sure, Revel's quest not just to perpetuate Torah, but also to make it "meaningful in contemporary American life" proved a perennial source of controversy. Careful readers will discern these tensions between the lines of some of the recollections provided here, and particularly in the appendix. These debates echo ones that have recurred throughout Yeshiva College's history, and parallel debates over modernism that once rocked so many institutions of higher education affiliated with Protestant denominations in the United States. But where Protestant colleges and universities resolved the problem either by abandoning their religious commitments (as most of the great universities did), or by abandoning their academic integrity (as the bulk of evangelical colleges did), Yeshiva has not. Instead, it relies upon Judaism's longstanding tradition of *makhloket*, giving voice, in volumes such as this one, to a wide spectrum of views.

Perhaps there is a lesson here for those, like George Marsden, who wonder whether a full-fledged faith-based university can be reconciled with the main currents of American academic life. The answer, as this volume and seventy-five years of Yeshiva College history suggest, is yes. Given a fierce love for tradition, a strong commitment to freedom of thought, and a healthy respect for disputation, both religious faith and academic integrity (*Torah u-Madda*) can vigorously be sustained.

APPENDIX

Nostalgia Isn't What it Used to Be:
Reflections on YC and Modern Orthodoxy

By Chaim I. Waxman

There have been a number of articles articles in this volume reflecting on YC during the 1960s and, either explicitly or implicitly, bemoaning the contemporary absence of general intellectual excitement and specific *Torah u-Madda* approach. The writers are colleagues and good friends whom I respect and with whom I am frequently, though certainly not always, in agreement. I, too, am aware of the dramatic changes in American Orthodoxy during the second half of the twentieth century and I, too, yearn for the intellectual excitement of the 1960s. Nevertheless, as I contemplated their specific reflections on YC at the time, I was reminded of the many notable quips of the late Professor Nathan Goldberg, who challenged and inspired me to think sociologically. "Gentlemen," he would remind the class, "the good old days weren't so good."

I have no doubt that the authors of the aforementioned articles actually experienced the intellectual excitement to which they referred. However, their experiences were not necessarily reflective of YC in general. They may have just as well have been atypical. I know for a fact that not every YC student during the 1960s experienced what they did.

I begin with my own experience. My previous educational background did not lead me to begin to appreciate or even seek the intellectual opportunities available at YC. My first two years of high school were at Telshe Yeshiva in Cleveland, where I internalized the notion that secular

Dr. Chaim I. Waxman, YC' 63, BRGS '65, RIETS '66, is Professor of Sociology and Jewish Studies at Rutgers University.

studies were *treif*, taboo, almost on a par with the three cardinal prohibitions of committing idolatry, murder, and adultery. My second two years of high school were spent at Mesivta Chaim Berlin in Brooklyn, where there was a more pragmatic approach to college — it was acceptable for the purposes of learning a profession, but certainly not for what the sociologist Thorstein Veblen called "idle curiosity," by which he meant intellectual curiosity and which he viewed as the true "mission" of a university. (The notion might be called, *le-havdil*, "curiosity *li-shmah*").

After high school, as a result of circumstances which are not pertinent here, I went to Israel to learn at Yeshivat Kerem B'Yavneh, the then new and only *yeshivat hesder*. It was for me a year of tremendous growth in Jewish learning and knowledge, as well as in Zionism and a sense of intimate connection to the entire Jewish people. However, I cannot say that it inspired me to general intellectual curiosity. In some ways, it did just the opposite, because the overall focus was still somewhat parochial. Be that as it may, I "fell in love" with Israel and did not want to leave. My parents, however, felt very differently and insisted that I return and get a college degree.

I had no idea what I wanted to be "when I grew up," but in my senior year of high school I developed an interest in crime and criminal law. My heroes were Clarence Darrow and Perry Mason, and my high school yearbook lists my future profession as a criminal lawyer. When thinking about which college to attend, I had heard, incorrectly, that CCNY had a pre-law program which required only three years of undergraduate study. I enrolled in the *metivtah* of the Rabbi Jacob Joseph School on the lower East Side, and at CCNY at night. To make a long story short, I did not gain much from that year at CCNY and, the following year, I enrolled at YC and RIETS. I was placed in the *shi'ur* of R. David Lifshitz, who later became my father-in-law, and did well in that part of my Yeshiva experience. As for the YC aspect, I made it through, and that was all I was interested in at the time. Although I did appreciate Prof. Goldberg's sociology courses, I was not really "into" sociology until my senior year, by which time I was already married. I did not begin to become intellectually curious until that year, and that part of my development actually took place in graduate schools, at the New School for Social Research and at BRGS. At YC, I was a *yeshiva bahur* in an institution that enabled him to learn intensively and get the college education that his parents insisted he get.

Nor was I unique. I recently had occasion to look through my YC
Year Book and, though I didn't study it systematically, my sense is that
there were quite a few such "*yeshiva bahurim*" in the class, as well as many
who came to YC for professional reasons. The intellectually curious were,
even then, a relatively small group, even as I now view them as the elite.
In other words, YC was a heterogeneous institution back in the 1960s,
and I suspect it is such now as well.

Though I have no empirical evidence for the current constituency
of YC, I do have some data about the institution in the late 1980s because
I then conducted a survey of students from YC and SCW, the primary
objective of which was to determine their understanding of the concept
of "*Torah u-Madda.*"*

After meeting with focus groups from both YC and SCW and also
discussing the objectives with the deans and program directors at those
colleges, it was decided that the most expeditious and productive way of
arriving at such a determination would be to question the students on a
variety of issues that are likely to be viewed as problematic. The major
issues were: secular education, social contact with non-Jews, relations
with non-Orthodox Jews, the roles of Jewish women, the Holocaust,
Israel, and cheating in school and in business. Accordingly, I designed an
instrument with questions pertaining to those areas.

Unquestionably, there were a number of methodological limitations
to the survey. Ideally, all of the undergraduates would have completed the
questionnaire. This was unfeasible for a number of reasons which need
not concern us here. Nevertheless, a significant sample, consisting of
about a third of both YC and SCW students, was achieved. Also, at YC,
the response rate of the MYP students was much greater than their actual
percentage of all YC students. Be that as it may, this is not the place for a
full report on that study. However, several of the findings are pertinent.

In contrast to the image of the students being removed from the
affairs of the country and the world except as they directly pertain to
Jews, the majority of the respondents viewed such involvement as an

---

* *In its May 16, 2005 edition (Vol. 69:12), The Commentator, in conjunction with the*
undergraduate student councils of Yeshiva University, published an updated survey called "Religion
Index 2005: Surveying the Social, Political, and Religious Ideology of the Male Undergraduate
at Yeshiva University." The study, jointly authored by Commentator editors Eli Hamburger, Zev
Nagel, and Dovid Wildman, featured a revised question bank, based largely on Dr. Waxman's
1980s questionnaire. The findings are also available in the Pollack Collection at the Mendel
Gottesman Library of Yeshiva University, call number LD6371.Y43 H36 2005.

imperative. For example, more than two-thirds agreed with the statement, "Jews have an obligation to become involved in the affairs of the country and the world and, therefore, should be involved in all political issues." That percentage appears to be considerably higher than that typical of the American population as a whole, at least as indicated by the prevalent voting rates in both national and local elections.

A number of the questions explicitly asked about commitment to *Torah u-Madda* and the responses indicate that such commitment was rather high. For example, more than 80 percent disagreed with the statement: "Ideally, a Jew should study Torah only, without any secular study." More than 75 percent disagreed with the statement: "Secular study is permissible only insofar as it is important for one's livelihood." More than 80 percent agreed with the statement: "It is a Jewish value to learn as much as one can, including secular study." Eighty-five percent disagreed with the statement: "Some types of secular study, such as the natural sciences, are important for the observant Jew, but not such fields as literature, history, philosophy, and fine arts." And 80 percent agreed with the statement: "All spheres of knowledge are intrinsically important for the observant Jew."

When asked why they came to Yeshiva, quite a few students reported that they wanted to be able to continue learning their Talmudic and halakhic studies in a certain style while gaining a secular college education. As one YC student expressed it in a focus group session, "I wanted to combine the college education and to be able to continue learning in a *yeshiva* setting. I had experienced a special kind of learning in an Israeli *yeshiva*, and I wanted to continue that kind of learning while getting a broad-based liberal arts education." When asked if that kind of combination was not basically the same as that of those who learn in other *yeshivot*, such as Chaim Berlin, Mir, and Ner Israel, since they, too, manage to learn in *yeshiva* and get a college degree, one YC student responded, "I'm familiar with that. I was at XYZ Yeshiva for two years, where people do that. Precisely because I saw the kind of college education they were getting, I chose not to do that. I found that they were getting a very narrow summary of what college was. They only took courses that were specifically for their career goals, and they never really went to college; they attended classes." Responses such as those do not support the notion of an undergraduate body for whom *Torah u-Madda* is irrelevant.

There may now be some young *roshei yeshiva* who define Modern

Orthodoxy as a necessary accommodation in order to earn a living, but I doubt there are now at Yeshiva any European *roshei yeshiva* who imply or assert that their European background renders them more authoritative and who assert that Modern Orthodoxy is *treif*, a prohibited hybrid, a form of *sha'atnez*. There may now be some American-born *roshei yeshiva* who tell their students that they went to college and therefore knew that it is of little value beyond the pragmatic, but there aren't any European *roshei yeshiva* at Yeshiva University telling them that they should be in a "real" *yeshiva*.

True, the late Charles Liebman and Irving "Yitz" Greenberg are no longer at YC. Significant as they may have been, they were only two individuals, one in political science and the other in history, neither of which discipline drew the majority of YC students even at that time.

Moreover, Dr. Samuel Belkin was a *musmakh* and a talmudic genius, an *illui*, but with all due love and respect, in his capacity as president of Yeshiva University he rarely manifested that side of himself. Indeed, although President Richard M. Joel does not have rabbinic ordination, he appears to manifest as much of, if not more, of an overt commitment to *Torah u-Madda* as did his predecessors.

Has YC changed from what it was in the 1960s? Most certainly. So has American Orthodoxy; indeed, despite the notion of Orthodox unchangeability, so has Orthodox Judaism in general. My children's Orthodoxy is different from mine, as mine was different from that of my parents. American Judaism has changed and so has American culture. More often than not, it is not the changes that are problematic; it is the inability of some individuals to reconcile themselves to change. A truly Modern Orthodox individual should not feel alienated because of change; they should persist in the twin objectives of mastering the world — *ve-kivshuha* — and perfecting the world — *tikkun olam be-malkhut shadai* — which can only be accomplished if one is truly connected with the world.

Nor can we forget that American culture as a whole has changed dramatically from what it was in the 1960s. American society, at least until 9/11/01, became much more individualistic. The overwhelming majority of students on college and university campuses are there not for "idle curiosity" but as an avenue toward getting a job. Indeed, it would be very surprising if YC did not reflect similar, if not identical, changes.

On the other hand, I cannot refrain from pointing out the growth of centers of intensive Jewish life on university campuses around the country where Orthodox students attend. Whereas in the 1960s R. Irving Greenberg appropriately pointed the college campus as an arena in which Jewish students are most vulnerable to the threat of mixed dating and then mixed marriage, some of those same campuses are today arenas where the Orthodox students can intensify their Jewish as well as general knowledge and activity. There are today viable alternatives to Yeshiva which were not as available in the 1960s, and one cannot generalize about Modern Orthodoxy on the basis of Yeshiva.

Finally, the stereotype of the so-called *haredim* is increasingly inappropriate for the United States. As I and others have discussed elsewhere, there has been a dramatic shift in their stance toward not only non-*haredim* but to non-Orthodox Jews, in general, and even to the larger American society. By the end of the century, the *haredim* were heavily engaged in religious outreach and in national and international social and political activities. Does all of that mean that American Orthodoxy has not moved "to the right?" No; it most certainly has. However, as a colleague and I hope to demonstrate, much of that is a function of significantly higher levels of Jewish education and knowledge, and such a move has historical precedents. Be that as it may, the move to the right is very mixed, and both Modern Orthodoxy and YC are alive and kicking.

Letters

While the YUdaica series ran, The Commentator *received numerous letters and responses from readers. Reproduced here is only a selection of those letters.*

New Haven Yeshiva

Dear Sir:

I greatly enjoyed the interesting article by Rav Nathan Kamenetsky about the first prominent European *Rosh Yeshiva* to serve at RIETS ("Rabbi Shlomo Polachek: The Unassuming *Illui* of Maichat"). Your paper is to be commended for publishing studies of this caliber.

I must take exception to Rabbi Kamenetsky drawing a sharp distinction between RIETS and Yeshiva College on one hand and the Rabbinical Seminary of New Haven founded by the Communal *rav* of New Haven, Rav Judah Heshel Levenberg, on the other hand.

There is very little published material concerning the *yeshiva* in New Haven. However, Rabbi Levenberg's son-in-law, Rabbi Isaac H. Ever, authored a comprehensive Yiddish biography of his father-in-law (available in the Mendel Gottesman Library and at www.hebrewbooks. org) which includes much useful information about the *yeshiva* in New Haven and later in Cleveland, Ohio, as well as much information about Rabbi Levenberg's tragic life in the U.S.

On page sixty-nine of this volume we read that among the *yeshiva's* stated goals was the opportunity for its students to complete their secular education. Hardly a goal that the Alter of Slabodka could get excited about. But a goal that Rabbi Dr. Revel could well appreciate.

On pages 112-113 of the same volume we read about the formation of a sort of *Mekhinah* attached to the *yeshiva* which was to obtain a "permit" from the Superintendent of schools. In addition the school had elected to place itself under the supervision of the New Haven Board of Education for at least two grades. Thus this *yeshiva* was hardly the Torah-only school that Rabbi Kamenetsky portrays it as.

Of course, the final word as to what the *yeshiva* was really like goes to those few *talmidim* who are still alive. But apparently the stated objectives of the school did not neglect secular studies and thus the *yeshiva* seemingly was not far from the Yeshiva College philosophy in that regard. Clearly this school was willing to take steps to accommodate itself to the New World, too.

The school did differ from RIETS in that it was a Mussar *yeshiva* permeated by the spirit of the Slabodka school of Mussar, with a full time *mashgi'ah ruhani*, Rabbi Sheftel Kramer (father-in-law of the late Rabbi Y.Y. Ruderman of Baltimore's Ner Israel Rabbinical College), and in that its goal was not to produce professional rabbis, which seemingly was a goal of RIETS.

I must also note that the founders of a supposedly more "right wing" school in New York, Yeshiva Torah Vodaath in Brooklyn, called the school the same name by which the yeshiva in Lida was known as — Torah ve-Da'as. This clearly indicated the proposed *hashkafah* of this institution. Only later with the appointment of Mr. (*gadol merabban shemo*) Shraga Feivel Mendlowitz as *menahel*, did the school reflect the philosophy of its new educational director. Even so, under his leadership Torah Vodaath had a full high school program.

As far as the first American school reflecting the European values of "Torah only," I believe the honors go to the followers of Rabbi Chaim Abraham Dov Ber Levine of the Bronx in the mid 1930s. Known as "The *Malakh*," this old line Habad Hassid instilled a deep feeling for the "real thing" in his young followers (known as the *Malakhim*) from Torah Vodaath, and after being expelled from that *yeshiva* he started a *yeshiva* completely free of secular studies led by Rabbi Yankel Schorr, the brother of Rabbi Gedaliah Schorr.

Sincerely,
Zalman Alpert
Reference Librarian, Gottesman Library
Yeshiva University

Response to "New Haven Yeshiva"

Dear Sir:

Thank you for remitting for my response to Librarian Zalman Alpert's letter about my article on the Maichater *Illui*. As he states, I indeed drew a "sharp distinction" between the Yeshiva of New Haven and RIETS, but I defined their basic difference amorphously in terms of their "philosophies," not in whether secular studies were offered within them, as Mr. Alpert understood and amplified upon.

While both schools had a secular studies program within their curriculums, as Mr. Alpert points out convincingly, its philosophic underpinnings varied in each. I can best define the distinction by referring to a debate several years ago on the pages of the Israeli quarterly *Hama'ayan* regarding R. Samshon Raphael Hirsch's position on *"Torah im Derekh Eretz."* Some, like R. Shlomo Wolbe, understood it to mean that the German rabbi approved partaking of the undesirable *"Derekh Eretz"* for the sake of advancing "Torah" — a *heter* to study in German universities: while others, like the late Dr. Zev Low, proved that the *tzaddik* R. Hirsch considered *"Derekh Eretz"* in the service of Torah in post-emancipation Germany an inherently positive value. Similarly, New Haven needed to provide some undesirable secular studies in order to attract American students (and in order to obtain a State of Connecticut permit to operate a school): they were a necessary evil. RIETS, however, saw secular studies as the key to integrating its graduates into American Jewish society and enabling them to take on leadership positions within it. New Haven considered the American boys who took up their bundles and crossed the ocean to study in European *yeshivot* as the ideal; it was simply trying to save the boys the expense and the trouble of having to wander far from home to become European yeshiva *bahurim* by providing them with a piece of Europe just north of New York City. In essence, it was enabling them to become Europeans-in-the-New World, an American anomaly.

RIETS considered these boys misguided dreamers wanting to recapture a lost past: its philosophy was that building Torah in its new home, America, required secular studies. (In my *Making of a Godol*, I write about someone who told my father proudly that he will not be providing his son with a secular education. Thereupon my father objected, "But he'll grow up and not even be able to read the street signs." When the other replied, "R. Hayim Soloveichik also could not read Russian," my father retorted, "But R. Hayim's *shamosh* was able to read Russian. Do you expect your son to have a *shamosh*, too?!" In this anecdote, my father also did not see secular studies as intrinsically more worthy than a necessary evil: in the person of my father's interlocutor, it demonstrates to what extreme this approach to secular studies can be taken.)

The difference between the two *yeshivot* pertaining to the study of Mussar, which Mr. Alpert portrays, may well be based on how they viewed themselves. While the "European *yeshiva*" of New Haven maintained the decades-old educational program of the European *yeshivot*, the function of which included the building of character by means of Mussar, RIETS, seeing its purpose as building a new type of *yeshiva* (fit for the new Torah center of America), believed that, together with the mainstay study of Talmud, more important than Mussar was the study of the basic philosophy of Judaism within a new society. The difference between the two institutions insofar as goals, to which Mr. Alpert refers, was a manifestation of the philosophic distinction between them. RIETS saw itself as part of America — as Dr. Revel wrote in 1915, "I see no conflict, no inconsistency between Americanism and Judaism" — and naturally felt that it could and should provide rabbinical leadership for it; New Haven saw itself as part of Europe, incongruous with Americanism, and had to let its graduates decide as individuals on their own whether they wanted to submit themselves to "America" (by becoming *rabbanim* therein) or remain private citizens, "European" yeshiva *bahurim* on the foreign soil of America.

If, as my article posits, the advent of the fulfillment of R. Hayim Volozhiner's prediction that the center of Torah would cross the Atlantic to America was realized with the arrival of the Maichater in RIETS, it should be added that America remained the world's Torah center for only a short while, say, for two decades following WWII. Afterwards, Israel, where Torah study was on a much higher level, took over that crown. (Although the Old *Yishuv* counted among its members world class Torah scholars, *talmidei hakhamim* of the highest caliber, I would not consider it the world's Torah center in its time. If R. Hayim Volozhiner's prediction was correct, he didn't either — because the physical support for the Old *Yishuv*'s survival had to be brought in from abroad constantly. In my article, I attribute to R. Polachek the position that no locus can be considered a Torah center if it is not self-sufficient in "*kemah*." The reason why I postpone Israel's attainment of the Torah center status until circa 1965 is because Israel was not self-sufficient economically until that time.) But Israel, too, remained the Torah center for just numbered decades. Now, with globalization, I daresay that the term "Torah center" has taken on another meaning than in the time of R. Hayim of Volozhin, and the words of the Tanna R. Yossi ben Kisma in *Pirkei Avot* concerning the invaluable merit of "residing in a *makom* Torah" have become, by and large, anachronistic. With a computer in hand, the limiting power of geography has been vanquished: one "resides" no longer where his body is, but anywhere his mind takes him. Thus, the "Torah Center" is now determined only by the "Centrality of Torah" within one's heart.

Nathan Kamenetsky
Jerusalem, Israel

"The 60s"

Dear Sir:

I have just read R. Dr. Irving Greenberg's "Yeshiva in the 60s" and, much as forensic altercation runs counter to my grain and instincts, I am constrained, almost in sheer self-defense, to respond. I shall not comment in depth upon the wide range of issues relating to Dr. Greenberg's "spiritual odyssey" and his current haven. I shall focus, instead, upon factual errors, some trivial, others significant, which permeate the piece, with particular attention to the numerous inaccuracies and gross misrepresentations concerning myself.

Dr. Greenberg identifies me as part of a clique of "newcomers" who sought to "improve the yeshiva, not just the College." I, indeed, had this aim in mind. However, I was by no means a "newcomer," having been affiliated with Yeshiva University since 1949 — first, as a *talmid*, later, as an assistant to the Rav, and, from 1961, as head of the resuscitated *kollel*, and, finally, from 1963, as a *maggid shi'ur*. Secondly, I was not brought to the college to teach English literature specifically (as I had done at SCW); and, most important, the improvement I sought was hardly in the direction and by many of the means enumerated. I never acted to have all the *shi'urim* switched from Yiddish to English; the notion that "relevance" should be a prime condition in the selection of a *masekhta*, I regarded, then as now, as antithetical to the ideal of Torah *li-shmah*; and the implication that I joined in advocating "less *pilpul*, more *bekiyut*" is pure fantasy. So is the assertion that meetings to thrash out such an agenda "were held mostly in the apartments of the Liebmans and the Lichtensteins at 17 Fort

George Hill" — and this, not only because neither family resided at that address, or because, while we were genuinely friendly with the Liebmans, our social relations with the Greenbergs were relatively marginal, but inasmuch as our involvement in the process under consideration was far from what has been suggestively implied. We certainly were involved in serious discussion, but were hardly privy to the semi-revolutionary ferment conjured up by Dr. Greenberg's recollections.

With respect to the conclaves organized by David Hartman in the Laurentians, they were indeed often heady and stimulating, but not as focused upon the *Shoah* as implied; and the notion that Emil Fackenheim needed to be "ignited" on the subject by Dr. Greenberg's "burning interest" is simply preposterous. Most egregious, however, is the account of the *gerut* cited. *Ma'aseh she-hayah kakh hayah.* The Conservative member of the *beit din*, far from being a *shomer mitzvot*, wavererd, by his own account, between atheism, agnosticism, and faith, and certainly did not maintain a halakhic commitment. When some of the Orthodox rabbis among us realized what was transpiring, we consulted briefly and decided to have three of us engage the *ger* in an impromptu discussion of *halakhah*, in the hope of eliciting a *kabbalat ol mizvot*, which in the opinion of those *rishonim* who held that only this phase required a *beit din*, could salvage the process. I recall the incident vividly, including being drawn into the dancing, with great ambivalence, in order not to embarrass the *ger*. I also recall that, as I realized in which direction the wind was blowing, the event — and not a presumed "drift to the right" — drove me into disaffection for the whole enterprise. (Incidentally, the protagonist subsequently underwent a fully Orthodox conversion in Israel.)

My sharpest revulsion, however, is reserved for Dr. Greenberg's account regarding the contretemps over his interview and my response to it. I shall not challenge his claim that my "tolerances for exploration" are too constricted, as they do, indeed, fall far short of his. I readily concede a major concern with "preserving Judaism" and admit to the conviction that if we are to strive, as we should, for "affirming it and its sovereignty in modern culture," we must be certain that what is being affirmed is what has, in its integrity, been authentically preserved. What riles me is the account of "the furor," and, particularly, the remarks concerning the Rav. Dr. Greenberg habitually asserts that the Rav — or, for that matter, small fry fish like myself — fundamentally agreed with many of his cherished views regarding modernity et al but lacked the courage to assert them, to walk through the doors the Rav had himself opened. This ploy is doubly effective. At one fell swoop, it abducts a giant from a rival camp to one's own; secondly, it enables one to bask in the contemplated glory of his own integrity and strength, while attributing a "failure of nerve" to others. It is, however, unabashedly, a blatant example of what Steven Schwarzschild called "imperialism of the soul." The thought that refusal to ride the crest of the *zeitgeist* may be wholly principled rather than a reflection of temerity often refuses to penetrate.

In this case, there is also icing on the cake: a self-image which includes not only being a "profile in courage" but suffering the status of a persecuted *nirdaf* as well. Dr. Greenberg depicts a scenario which includes a political cabal in opposition to him, which proceeded to enlist me to "refute" him. This is, to the best of my recollection, patently erroneous. I wrote in response to provocative statements and not under pressure. As to the contention that I had largely agreed with his positions but had only regretted the tone of the interview, this is an unkind and ungrateful cut. In the desire to be generous, I suggested that perhaps the interview did not quite reflect Dr. Greenberg's truly more traditional views, which had somehow become skewed in a wide-ranging but imprecise discourse. At the time, Dr. Greenberg, in turn, assented that there was some truth to this conjecture. Now, however, he informs us that this concession was made "disingenuously" — confirming, that from the ideological standpoint of his opponents, the original criticism was indeed warranted. I suggest that anyone who has the patience and the interest read the original exchange and judge the tone and the substance of my remarks for himself.

One could comment upon the article further. I, for one, find the total omission of any reference to Israel in a survey of the 60s, startling. I also take issue with the implication that, as regards the *Shoah*, "Orthodoxy did not have all the answers," but supposed that it did, while Dr. Greenberg did indeed. The Rav's Orthodoxy preached that, with respect to such issues, a Jew needed to strive to sustain his covenantal commitment in the face of the questions, rather than pretend to have answers. These salient points are not to my present purpose, however. Much water has passed under the bridge since those heady 60s. Dr. Greenberg has gone on to carve out a prominent career in the field of Jewish public service, even as he has adopted and advanced views regarding such crucial issues as the covenant and Christianity which the traditional Torah world has categorically rejected. The mutual disaffection which has regrettably ensued may, in the eyes of some, render much of this discussion irrelevant. Nevertheless, even as a matter of historical interest, it is important to keep the record straight.

Respectfully,
Aharon Lichtenstein
Jerusalem, Israel

Response to "The 60s"

Dear Sir:

Rav Aharon Lichtenstein's critical reaction to my account of "Yeshiva in the 60s" warrants a response because it illuminates what happened at Yeshiva in the interim. His tone expresses his feelings that I sought to attack or embarrass him and to co-opt him to my religious-educational positions. I did not want to do that. Then and now, I consider him a leader and an avatar of Modern Orthodoxy at its best — although I differ with certain of his policy judgments, which, I think, have resulted in Modern Orthodoxy losing some ground. There also were and are substantial ideological differences between us. Still, I always felt that this was a matter of *elu ve-elu*. Certainly, I acknowledge that he was no member of any clique of "newcomers," let alone "semi-revolutionaries." Nor did I intend to claim that we were close social friends. I actually wrote: "...we (husbands and wives) got together for 'salons' to develop our thoughts on modern Orthodox issues" (no semi-revolutions there). To the extent that I failed to distinguish clearly to the reader between what were my views of improving the Yeshiva and his differing views, I apologize. Obviously, he was offended by my unintended lumping of the two of us together, but I did not want to "homogenize" our views. Personally, I am committed to and uphold these differences.

I believe that a primary reason that Yeshiva College had a spiritually exciting and intellectually stimulating atmosphere in the 60s was that the members of the Yeshiva community did have a variety of opinions and they freely spoke, argued, and debated them. There were outstanding and respectful debates between the right, left, and center of Modern Orthodoxy, and the atmosphere was one of *kin'at sofrim tarbeh hokhmah*. The students benefited the most from the interchange, but the outside community also was stimulated.

Nothing has so enervated the capacity of Yeshiva during the past two decades to instruct and nurture the general Jewish and Modern Orthodox communities as the shutting down of this *mahloket le-shem shamayim.* I believe that spiritual stagnation and deadening of inquiry is the result of denying or delegitimating differences rather than clarifying and growing from them. In this atmosphere, even R. Lamm had to struggle to uphold his views in the Yeshiva. This delegitimation is truly the violation the *Gemara* describes as the cause of the plague that decimated Rabbi Akiva's students, *mipnei she-lo nahagu kavod zeh la-zeh.*

In my recent *Commentator* article, I described how in the atmosphere of the 60s a number of us — including Rav Aharon — joined and learned with Conservative and Reform rabbis over a number of years, to our mutual benefit. Although we differed substantially in our views and our tactics, we even celebrated a *Klal Yisrael gerut* together. R. Aharon's recent reaction reveals that he was much more uncomfortable and ambivalent then (more than I realized then) and that he was more distanced from that group. I missed this because I was personally transformed by my encounter with the group, as were so many of the other participants. I continue to believe that there is nothing to be ashamed of in that collective behavior in that time of greater *ahdut* in *Klal Yisrael* — even if the moment passed. Therefore, in my recent *Commentator* article, I did not think to veil the fact that once some of us from Yeshiva and other Orthodox institutions experimented or worked with non-Orthodox rabbis or tried to engage in *tikkun olam.*

Just as I was shaped by that *Klal Yisrael* encounter in the 1960s and on, so was I transformed by confrontation with the Holocaust, from then until now. The *Gemara* states that Jeremiah and Daniel refused to repeat the words of Moshe Rabbeynu, *ha-kel, ha-gadol, ha-gibbor ve-ha-nora,* with meaning unchanged, because after the *Hurban* repeating the same old words and meaning would be a "lie." *Ha-Kadosh Barukh Hu amiti hu, ve-lo kizvu bo.* Not until the *Anshei Kenesset ha-Gedolah* reinterpreted these words by reinterpreting the scope and nature of *Hashem*'s intervention in the world did they restore *Hashem*'s crown and make these words central to our central prayer, the *Amidah.* The desire to praise and speak truthfully to *Hashem* in the light of the new and greater *Hurban* of our time is the nub of my attempt at a theology after the *Shoah.* R. Aharon disagrees with my theological interpretations. Unfortunately, at Yeshiva, because of the more right-wing influence of the past two decades, my views are dealt with by exclusion and suppression rather than by reasoned debate — to the detriment, I believe, of both sides. But here is not the place to expound my views on the Holocaust and *halakhah* further.

This brings me to the current interchange between us. Summarizing our exchange in the 1966 *Commentator*, I wrote that I was disappointed that R. Aharon ignored my argument for Orthodoxy's self-criticism and self-questioning as well as my calls for its need to be more forthcoming to *Klal Yisrael's* views in its response to the *Shoah* and Israel reborn. I regretted that he was silent in the face of my delegitimation and dismissed as "a nice nineteenth century notion" the argument that intellectual/spiritual space — even for errors — was needed for exploration of the challenges of modernity. I should add that I never believed that R. Aharon was recruited or joined in any cabal when he differed with me in 1966. I do not believe there was any cabal in the 1960s and truly regret using the phrase "The opposition found the only other person at Yeshiva who had the credibility to 'refute' my views." I meant to say that R. Aharon's article served the purposes of those who opposed my views because he was credible as being both fully modern and Orthodox.

In his recent response, R. Aharon argues that low tolerances for religious exploration preserve Orthodoxy. I believe that when the limits are too tight, in the resultant climate of opinion, fresh new thinkers in Modern Orthodoxy are constrained and are not free to articulate approaches that effectively deal with new issues, such as in theology or historical-critical studies or feminism, because they risk being delegitimized. When a variety of responses are not developed and Orthodoxy appears not to be listening or incapable of responding, we lose credibility and we lose people.

R. Aharon has every right to remain true to his own principles, but he has not yet drawn the lessons of these two decades. The failure to defend the philosophical need to explore the full range of issues and approaches has had a chilling effect on religious seeking and honest conversation about problems in the community. This has encouraged a turn toward following authority and learning without asking questions. One outcome is a generation of *lomdim* and *talmidim* who master halakhic details but are not trained to grasp religious principles. Often, they are hobbled in wrestling with the large and serious religious questions of our time. Unlike *Hashem*, they are often uncomfortable or unwilling to live in the midst of *Benei Yisrael*, even *betokh tumatam*. Unable to deal fully with spiritual challenges, the community has moved toward protecting its religious judgments by valorizing conformity and censorship. It has grown more insular. The balance of *bein adam la-makom* and *bein adam la-haveiro* has been lost — yet people fear to speak out. As a result, Modern Orthodoxy has lost out in the open society; people slip into secularism or assimilation on the left or shift towards haredism on the right. Rav Aharon does not want these outcomes, but I think that he might have put them in check by defending the need for a wider range of religious thinking and debate.

This brings me to my personal experience of delegitimation. R. Aharon describes the account of my encounter with the Rav during the 1960s controversy as a "ploy... [designed to] abduct a giant" to my side. The point of that story was not about me but what it showed about the Rav and his feelings about the atmosphere growing at Yeshiva being generated by some of his *talmidim*. The Rav was unhappy with the trend toward what Heschel called pan-halachism, learning and observance not suffused with *ruah* and ethics. Whatever the Rav's differences with my views, he refused to denounce them in public because he respected them and did not want them to be delegitimated.

R. Aharon feels that I presented myself tendentiously as a "profile in courage" and "as suffering the status of a persecuted *nirdaf.*" I never felt that way about my place at Yeshiva in the 60s. I related that the original interview was published without my advance knowledge in order to impart the ambiguity of the incident, although I take full responsibility for these words now, I actually stumbled into that controversy, and, far from acting nobly, reacted with confusion and uncertainty. As I wrote "I disingenuously tried to soften and minimize the implications of my words." Since that time, with my work on the *Shoah* and pluralism, the situation has become more polarized. I will only say that as I came to grasp more firmly the enormity of the *Shoah* and the amazing blessing and challenge of freedom, I have managed to continue to explore without yielding or giving in to my fears of exclusion.

In general, the approach of exclusion is a mistake. Given the lessons of Jewish history in which breakthroughs (such as Hasidism, Maimonidean approaches, *Mussar* and Zionism, etc.) were hounded by delegitimation, plus the experience of modern culture, which has shown that deeper and more powerful ideas emerge out of a freer exchange, Modern Orthodoxy should not have gone this route.

Since anger and caricature are not R. Aharon's usual style, obviously my words must have hurt him. I regret this. I also regret having to enter into this exchange because, to my mind, Rav Aharon remains one of our best leaders. However, on his watch at Yeshiva, the cause of *Torah u-Madda* went into exile in its own home. The Jewish people, which needs Torah teachings that speak credibly inside Jewry's real life situation, is the poorer for it. Now, along with many others, I have real hopes for a renaissance of Modern Orthodoxy at Yeshiva. Rav Aharon, as a leader in Modern Orthodoxy and as *talmid muvhak* and continuer of the Rav's teachings, should take the lead in undoing the recent constriction of *weltanschauung* and in turning with outstretched hand and spirit to all of *Klal Yisrael*.

Sincerely,
Irving Greenberg
Riverdale, New York

POSTSCRIPT: Rav Aharon writes that my reference to igniting Emil Fackenheim was "simply preposterous." Again, the true point of this reference was that open, respectful spiritual interaction between Orthodox and non-Orthodox was constructive for both. For Fackenheim, encounter with the *Shoah* was seminal; for me, it was the Reform theologians' emphasis on covenant that brought me to focus fruitfully on this central aspect of halakhic thinking.

But since I must defend the record: until 1965, Emil Fackenheim was a leading religious existentialist thinker who believed that religion was unaffected by history or historical events. After two years in the Canadian group, he was transformed in his thinking. In his first book on Holocaust theology, he wrote of the "incalculable inspiration" he received from the group.

In his opening major work in Holocaust theology, entitled *God's Presence in History*, he acknowledged this sea change and articulated his new view that Judaism was shaped by epoch making events. The paper that I read in the group's first year was entitled "God's Acts in History;" it deals with the *Shoah* and reborn Israel as orienting events shaping our religious understanding, much as the Exodus and the *Hurban* did in earlier eras of Jewish tradition. In the preface to *God's Presence*, Fackenheim wrote: "...I owe a fundamental debt to Irving Greenberg's concept of 'orienting experience:' his stubbornly historical thinking has liberated me from some false philosophical abstractions" (ibid. p. v).

Index